Object-Oriented Interface Design
IBM Common User Access Guidelines

> **Note**
>
> Before using this document, read the general information under "Notices" on page xv.

Library of Congress Catalog Number: 92-85439

ISBN: 1-56529-170-0

Published by Que Corporation
11711 N. College Avenue
Carmel, IN 46032

First Edition (December 1992)

This edition replaces and makes obsolete the previous editions, *Systems Application Architecture Common User Access Guide to User Interface Design,* SC34-4289-00 and *Systems Application Architecture Common User Access Advanced Interface Design Reference,* SC34-4290-00.

Order publications through your IBM representative or the IBM branch office serving your locality. Publications are not stocked at the address below.

A form for comments appears at the back of this publication. If the form has been removed, address your comments to:

IBM Corporation
Department T45
P.O. Box 60000
Cary, North Carolina 27512-9968
U.S.A.

You can fax comments to (919) 469-7718. Comments can also be sent electronically to IBM by using the following methods:

Internet address   cua_reader_comments@vnet.ibm.com

Bitnet address   cua_rdrc at vnet

IBM MAIL Exchange   usib4hf5 at ibmmail

When you send information to IBM, you grant IBM a non-exclusive right to use and distribute the information in any way it believes appropriate without incurring any obligation to you.

Contents

Summary of Changes

This manual contains the following changes:

Part 1. CUA Guide: minor editorial changes were made.

Part 2. CUA Reference: the following additions and changes were made.

- Chapter 8, "Common User Access Interface Components":

Action Window	The first guideline was moved to the **When to Use** section.
Help Menu	The fifth guideline was changed from recommended to fundamental.
Keyboard	The functions and descriptions of the Shift+F8 and F8 keys were modified.
Notebook (Control)	The graphic was modified.
Pointer	The first **When to Use** was changed from fundamental to recommended.
View Menu	The graphic was modified.
Windows Menu	A fundamental guideline was added.
Workplace	The second guideline recommended.

- Value set control was added to Appendix C, "Comparison of 1989 and 1991 Rules and Recommendations" on page 529.

- Information was moved and headings were changed in several of the bidirectional language usage sections of Appendix D, "Common User Access and National Language Support" on page 541.

Notices

The following paragraph does not apply to the United Kingdom or any country where such provisions are inconsistent with local law: INTERNATIONAL BUSINESS MACHINES CORPORATION PROVIDES THE PUBLICATION "AS IS" WITHOUT IMPLIED WARRANTY OF ANY KIND, EITHER EXPRESS OR IMPLIED, INCLUDING, BUT NOT LIMITED TO, THE IMPLIED WARRANTIES OF MERCHANTABILITY OR FITNESS FOR A PARTICULAR PURPOSE. Some states do not allow disclaimers of express or implied warranties in certain transactions, therefore, this statement may not apply to you.

This publication could include technical inaccuracies or typographical errors. Changes are periodically made to the information herein; these changes will be incorporated in new editions of the publication. IBM may make improvements and/or changes in the product(s) and/or the program(s) described in the publication at any time.

It is possible that this publication may contain reference to, or information about, IBM products (machines and programs), programming, or services that are not announced in your country. Such reference or information must not be construed to mean that IBM intends to announce such IBM products, programming, or services in your country.

Requests for technical information about IBM products should be made to your IBM Authorized Dealer or your IBM Marketing Representative.

IBM and others may have patents or pending patent applications or other intellectual property rights covering subject matter described herein. This document neither grants nor implies any license or immunity under any IBM or third party patents, patent applications or other intellectual property rights other than the Copyright License described herein.

IBM assumes no responsibility for any infringement of third-party rights that may result from the use of the Specifications disclosed in this publication or from the manufacture, use, lease, or sale of the programs created using or containing the Specifications.

With respect to any IBM patents, you can send license inquiries, in writing, to the IBM Director of Commercial Relations, IBM Corporation, Purchase, NY 10577.

Trademarks

The following terms, denoted by an asterisk (*) on their first occurrences in this publication, are trademarks of the IBM Corporation in the United States or other countries:

Common User Access
CUA
IBM
Operating System/2
OS/2

Acknowledgments

We wish to thank all the people at IBM who helped make the Common User Access* (CUA*) guidelines for object-oriented user interfaces possible. In addition, we include all those at IBM who made the publishing of this book possible.

John Bennett	Jenny Kotora-Lynch
Karen Bernard	Marcos Lam
Richard (Dick) Berry	Lee Laske
Greg Bonadies	Theo Mandel
Fred Brown	Dean Marsh
Juanita Couch	Shirley Martin
Joe Coulombe	Skip McGaughey
Wendy Geene Coulombe	Dick Oakley
Dean Duff	Rebecca Oliver
Lorraine Elder	Rosalind Radcliffe
Jim Farver	Sarah Redpath
Katie Frye	Cliff Reeves
Dana Gillihan	Justin Richards
Al Groelle	Tom Richards
William Gunn	Dave Roberts
Anthony Hall	Cindy Roosken
Tom Hanson	Chuck Schafer
Lee Harold	David Schwartz
Haydon Harrison	Bob Shi
Sue Henshaw	Rodney Smith
Greg Hill	Don Spencer
Dave Hock	Deborah Swain
Tommy Horne	Karl von Gunten
Kay Jolly	Rick Zevin

Not included in the list, but also important contributors are all the Architecture Review Board participants. Thank you all.

Foreword

The IBM Common User Access* guidelines are intended to help product designers and developers create an interface that the user will find easy to learn and use. They are based on sound principles of interface design and on object-oriented relationships. Moreover, the guidelines reflect recent advances in personal computing technology and the growing demand by users that computers match their way of thinking.

The object-oriented workplace shell of IBM's new OS/2* 2.0 operating system is based on these guidelines. OS/2 2.0 users can interact intuitively and easily with objects because each object clearly represents a real workplace task. Thus a user can transfer knowledge about an object from the real world to the computer environment. The user can also transfer knowledge from one product to another, as well as predict how something new will work, thanks to consistent interface design.

As a result, end users of CUA products should experience higher productivity and satisfaction, while producing fewer errors.

This official guide, which combines two books originally published in the fall of 1991, is divided into two sections. The first—the "CUA Design Guide"—describes principles, components and techniques of user interface design and describes the process of designing a product with a CUA interface. The "CUA Reference" section identifies the CUA interface features, or components, and provides guidelines for using them.

We in IBM are especially proud of the *Object-Oriented Interface Design.* It is the work of a team of talented people at IBM. Their effort was recognized recently when they received the Thomas J. Watson, Jr., Design Excellence Award. As the award noted, "The CUA Design is revolutionary, in that it places a user's data first and foremost."

I hope these guidelines contribute to your excellence by helping you make the users of your applications more productive in their personal computing.

Earl F. Wheeler
IBM Senior Vice President
  and General Manager
Programming Systems
Somers, NY

About This Book

This book describes the guidelines that define the Common User Access* (CUA*) user interface. The Common User Access (CUA) user interface is an object-oriented graphical user interface that provides a consistent look and feel for products that adopt the CUA interface as their standard.

How This Book is Organized

This book has two parts plus appendixes and a glossary.

- **Part 1, "CUA Design Guide" on page 1** describes principles, components, and techniques of user interface design in general, as applied to a variety of software products for a variety of operating environments. Although it describes the process of designing a product with a CUA interface in particular, Part 1, "CUA Design Guide" is not a "cookbook" for producing a product with a CUA interface; instead, it is more like a textbook, intended to expose designers to the concepts that they should consider when designing any kind of user interface.

- **Part 2, "CUA Reference" on page 165** identifies the CUA interface components and lists all of the fundamental and recommended guidelines for designing and developing a product with a CUA interface for a programmable workstation. It provides an alphabetically arranged list of the interface components that are defined in the CUA interface. The graphical representations shown are examples only and are not intended to define how a component should appear in the interface for a particular product.

  Note that neither **Part 1** nor **Part 2** tells a designer how to create a specific product or part of a product. That is, the CUA guidelines do not tell a designer how to design an accounting product or a balance sheet, for example.

- The **Appendixes** contain the following information:
  - Design considerations for multimedia and touch input
  - Design considerations for the use of color
  - CUA interface National Language Support
  - Help for documenting the CUA interface in product publications and online information.

Who Should Read This Book

- **Part 1, "CUA Design Guide"** is primarily intended for software designers and user-interface designers, although programmers will want to read it to gain a general knowledge of the Common User Access user interface and the design process. You should be familiar with icons, windows, menus, and other components of graphical user interfaces, as well as with interaction techniques involving a pointing device, such as a mouse.

- **Part 2, "CUA Reference"** is primarily intended for application programmers planning to incorporate CUA interface design into new or existing applications. Use this book together with interface-building tools to produce applications that follow the CUA guidelines. You should have a thorough understanding of one or more programming languages, concepts, and techniques.

Conventions Used in This Book

The following conventions are used in this book.

- If a term is defined in the glossary (see "Glossary" on page 655), the term appears in *italic* type the first time or the most prominent time it is mentioned in the text.

- If a term represents a term that is found in a user interface—for example, in a window, in a menu, as a label for an icon, and so on—the term appears in **bold** type each time it is mentioned in the text.

Related Publications

The following manuals can be ordered through your IBM representative or your local IBM branch office.

- *Systems Application Architecture Common User Access Basic Interface Design Guide* (SC26-4583)

  Published in December 1989 by the IBM Corporation, this book addresses the design of software products for nonprogrammable terminals.

- *Systems Application Architecture Common User Access Basic Interface Design Guide 1991 Addenda* (GG22-9508)

  Published in September 1992 by the IBM Corporation, this book supplements SC26-4583.

- *Systems Application Architecture Common User Access Guide to User Interface Design*, (SC34-4289) and the *Systems Application Architecture Common User Access Advanced Interface Design Reference* (SC34-4290)

  Published by the IBM Corporation in October 1991, these books were combined into this book in an effort to make the current CUA information available in a more accessible form for a broader audience.

- *The CUA Vision: Bringing the Future into Focus* (G242-0215)

  Published by the IBM Corporation in October 1991, this package contains a DOS-compatible demonstration program and brochure of a CUA interface.

- *The CUA Vision: Bringing the Future into Focus* (GV26-1003)

  Published by the IBM Corporation in October 1991, this VHS videotape (GV26-1004 is in PAL format and GV26-1005 is in SECAM format) illustrates IBM's vision of how its customers will use computers in the future.

- *CUA Guide to Multimedia User Interface Design* (S41G-2922)

  Published by the IBM Corporation in June 1992, this book addresses the design of multimedia products for the programmable workstation environment.

Please Tell Us What You Think!

We hope you find this book useful and informative. If you like what we have done, please let us know; if not, please tell us why. We will use your comments to make the book better.

Please use one of the methods listed below to send your comments to IBM. Whichever method you choose, make sure you send your name, address, and telephone number if you would like a reply.

When you send comments to IBM, you grant IBM a nonexclusive right to use or distribute your comments in any way it believes appropriate without incurring any obligation to you.

To send comments by mail or FAX, use the form titled "What Do You Think?" at the back of this book.

If you are mailing from a country other than the United States, you can give the form to the local IBM branch office or IBM representative for postage-paid handling.

To FAX the form, use this number: (919) 469-7718.

To send comments electronically, use one of the following network IDs:

- IBM Mail Exchange: **usib4hf5 at ibmmail**
- IBM Bitnet: **cua_rdrc at vnet**
- Internet: **cua_reader_comments@vnet.ibm.com**

Thank you! Your comments help us make our information more useful for you.

Part 1. CUA Design Guide

Chapter 1. User Interfaces and Object Orientation

A *user interface* is the set of techniques and mechanisms that a person uses to interact with an object. Any kind of object has a user interface, and an object's interface is developed according to a user's needs and reasons for using the object. A user interface can be a set of buttons, like those on a telephone or video recorder. In the case of a computer, a user interface can include a keyboard, a pointing device, and the items that appear on a display screen. The user interface is the means by which a user communicates with a computer and vice versa. Many types of user interfaces are available for computers, including:

- Command-line user interfaces, in which a user remembers commands and types them

- Menu-driven user interfaces, in which a user is provided with a hierarchically organized set of choices

- Graphical user interfaces, in which a user points to and interacts with visible elements of the interface by using a pointing device.

What Is the Common User Access User Interface?

The Common User Access user interface is a graphical user interface that incorporates elements of *object orientation,* an orientation in which a user's focus is on objects and in which the concept of applications is hidden. Objects and object orientation are discussed in more detail in "Object Orientation in the CUA User Interface" on page 4. The CUA user interface is based on principles of user-interface design, on object-oriented relationships, and on field experience and user testing.

The CUA guidelines provide information about how the model on which a product is based should be conveyed to a user. The CUA guidelines also include specific details about designing and developing computer software and user interfaces. Products that adhere to the CUA guidelines and undergo usability testing should be comparatively easy to learn and use. As a result, users of products with a CUA user interface should find the products satisfying to use, efficient, and appropriate for the tasks that the users want to accomplish.

Who Will Use the CUA User Interface?

Although this book is intended for product designers, the CUA user interface itself is intended for a group of end users known as "knowledge workers." This group includes the many people around the world who make their living by working with information, which provides the basis for the decisions they make. These people might work in offices or in airplanes or anywhere they can have access to a computer.

However, the CUA user interface is not necessarily appropriate for every possible user of computers. For example, the CUA user interface might not be the most efficient interface for someone who performs a single, highly specialized task, such as the tasks in manufacturing process control or in retail sales. The CUA interface is most appropriate for users who perform a variety of information-related tasks.

Object Orientation in the CUA User Interface

Graphical user interfaces, including the CUA interface, are becoming more object-oriented. Object-oriented user interfaces allow for the development of a cohesive working environment in which each element, called an *object,* can interact with every other element. The objects that users require to perform their tasks and the objects used by the operating environment can work cooperatively in one seamless interface. That is, the boundaries that distinguish applications from operating systems are no longer apparent to users.

The most readily apparent feature of an object-oriented user interface is the pervasive focus on objects, as well as the principles applied to those objects, such as *object classes, object hierarchies,* and *inheritance.* These are discussed in the following sections.

Objects

In the real world, an object is an item that a person requires to perform work. For example, an accountant's objects might include a ledger and a calculator. An architect's objects might include blueprints, a T square, and a sharp pencil. In the CUA environment, an object is any visual component of a user interface that a user can work with as a unit, independent of other items, to perform a task. A spreadsheet, one cell in a spreadsheet, a bar chart, one bar in a bar chart, a report, a paragraph in a report, a database, one record in a database, and a printer are all objects. Each object can be represented by one or more graphic images, called icons, that a user can interact with, much as a user can interact with objects in the real world.

However, an object need not always be represented by an *icon,* and not all interaction is accomplished by way of icons. A user can interact with an object by opening a *window* that displays more information about the object and contains a variety of mechanisms for interacting with the object. A user can also manipulate an object within a window. Icons, windows, and interaction with objects are discussed in more detail in "Icons" on page 38, "Windows" on page 43, and "Interaction with Objects" on page 54.

Object Classes

The CUA environment includes three types, or classes, of objects:

- Container objects
- Data objects
- Device objects.

Each class of objects has a primary purpose that distinguishes it from the other classes, and all three types of objects can contain other objects.

Container Objects

A *container object* holds other objects. Its primary purpose is to provide a way for a user to group related objects for easy access and retrieval. An operating system typically provides a general-purpose container—for example, a *folder*—that can hold any type of object, including other containers.

Products often provide product-specific containers that have special features to serve the needs of the product's users. For example, a graphics product might provide a portfolio container in which a user could store and sort artwork according to subject matter or technique.

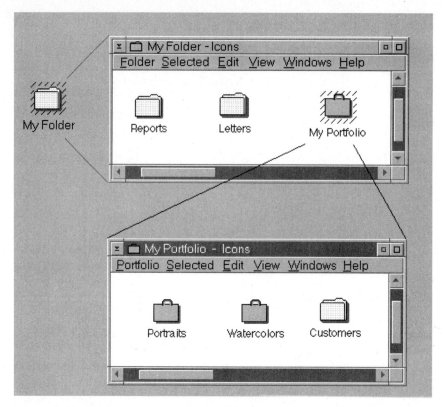

Figure 1. Container Objects. A folder object and a portfolio object are examples of container objects. Each provides a way for a user to group related objects for easy access and retrieval. The window to the right of the folder object labeled **My Folder** *displays the folder's contents, including a portfolio object. The window below the folder's window displays the contents of the portfolio object labeled* **My Portfolio.** *In this example, folder objects can contain portfolio objects, and portfolio objects can contain folder objects.*

Data Objects

The primary purpose of a *data object* is to convey information, such as text or graphics, or audio or video information. An example of a data object might be a newsletter object, which could contain text objects and graphic objects. Because the primary purpose of each object (text, illustration, and newsletter as a whole) is to convey information of interest to readers, each is considered a data object. Figure 2 on page 7 shows an example of a data object.

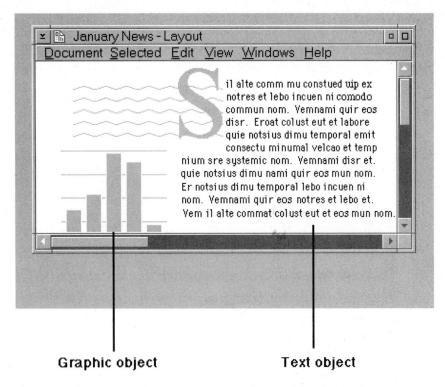

Graphic object   **Text object**

Figure 2. Data Object. A newsletter object is an example of a data object. It conveys information to a reader. It can also contain text objects and graphic objects, which are data objects as well.

Device Objects

A *device object* often represents a physical object in the real world. For example, a mouse object can represent a user's pointing device, and a modem object can represent a user's modem. Some device objects represent a logical object in a user's computer system rather than a physical object. For example, a wastebasket object can represent a logical object that disposes of a user's other objects, and an electronic mail out-basket can represent a logical object that delivers electronic mail to an intended recipient. The primary purpose of a device object is to provide a means of communication between a computer and another physical or logical object.

Some device objects can contain other objects. For example, a printer object can contain a queue of objects to be printed, and an electronic mail out-basket object can contain objects to be sent to the user of another computer system. Other device objects simply have settings that a user can configure. Device objects that contain other objects typically act on the contained objects. For example, a printer object will print the objects it contains, and an out-basket object will deliver objects to the intended recipient. Figure 3 shows two device objects.

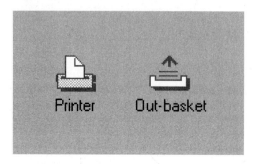

Figure 3. Device Objects. A printer object represents a physical device, and an electronic mail out-basket represents a logical device.

Object Hierarchies and Inheritance

Objects can be grouped according to similarities in appearance and behavior. These groups can then be arranged into *object hierarchies.* One relationship that can be illustrated in a hierarchy is *inheritance.* An object that appears below another object in the hierarchy has all of the characteristics of the object or objects above it. The object is said to "inherit" those characteristics.

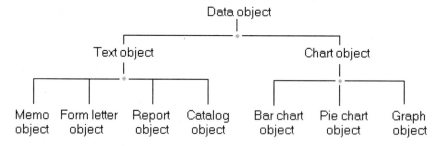

Figure 4. An Object Hierarchy Illustrating Inheritance. Each object that appears below another object in the hierarchy inherits all of the characteristics of the object or objects above it and can add new characteristics of its own.

In the hierarchy shown in Figure 4 on page 8, a bar chart inherits all of the characteristics of a chart object, but none of the characteristics unique to a memo. However, a bar chart object and a memo object will have in common those characteristics that each inherited from a data object.

Other types of hierarchies are possible. For example, objects can be arranged in a *containment* hierarchy that illustrates which objects can contain which other objects. Figure 5 illustrates a possible containment hierarchy.

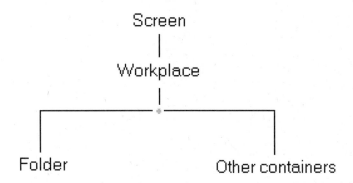

Figure 5. An Object Hierarchy Illustrating Containment. Each object that appears below another object in the hierarchy can be contained by the object or objects above it.

The Distinctions between Object-Oriented User Interfaces and Object-Oriented Programming

Object-oriented user interfaces share some concepts with object-oriented programming. However, the concepts are manifested differently. In an object-oriented user interface, the objects that a user works with do not necessarily correspond to the objects, or modules of code, that a programmer used to create the product. Inheritance and hierarchy in an object-oriented user interface are more subtle than in object-oriented programming. They are based on similarity in appearance and behavior, rather than on superclasses and subclasses of objects. Finally, an object-oriented interface incorporates the concept of containment, which has no parallel concept in object-oriented programming.

An important point for a designer to remember is that while object-oriented programming can facilitate the development of an object-oriented user interface, it is not a prerequisite. An object-oriented user interface can be developed with more traditional programming languages and tools.

Benefits of an Object-Oriented User Interface

Users sometimes are intimidated by the technical aspects of an operating system. An object-oriented user interface shields users by allowing them to interact with objects rather than with a distinct operating system and with separate applications that are often incompatible with one another. A user can focus more closely on the task at hand without having to be so conscious of the tools involved. Object orientation reflects the way a person works in the real world. For example, someone writing a memo can concentrate on the message without paying much attention to the tools being used to accomplish the task—pencil and paper in the real world, a memo object in an object-oriented user interface. When working in an object-oriented environment, users can be completely unaware that they are using an editor application to do their writing.

Furthermore, a fully object-oriented user interface provides a seamless environment in which a user's interaction with objects is the same across tasks. For example, a user can copy, move, delete, and open all objects the same way, no matter what the user's current task is or which objects are involved. A user could copy a graphic and move it into a cell in a spreadsheet, then place the spreadsheet into a document. Then the user could send the entire resulting object to someone else by placing it into an electronic mail out-basket. Each object is completely compatible with every other object, and objects can be combined and separated freely.

Most commercially available graphical user interfaces do not provide fully object-oriented user environments. They still rely on applications—that is, separate programs—many of which are not compatible and thus pose barriers to certain types of user interaction. The CUA user interface encourages full object orientation in user interfaces.

Chapter 2. Models of a User Interface

The term *model* is used in this book to refer to a descriptive representation of a person's conceptual and operational understanding of something. Some models are explicit and are consciously designed. These models typically can be represented by a diagram or a textual description. Other models, called mental models, are developed unconsciously. People create a mental model by putting together sets of perceived rules and patterns in a way that explains a situation. A typical person cannot draw or describe his or her mental model. In many situations, a person is not aware that the mental model exists.

A mental model does not necessarily reflect a situation and its components accurately. Still, a mental model helps people predict what will happen next in a given situation, and it serves as a framework for analysis, understanding, and decision-making.

With respect to user interfaces, three models come into play:

- A user's conceptual model
- A programmer's model
- A designer's model.

A user's conceptual model is a mental model. A programmer's model and a designer's model are explicit, consciously designed models. Each model represents a different audience's perspective of a user interface. Figure 6 on page 12 illustrates the three audiences and the factors that influence their perspectives.

Figure 6. Factors That Influence the Three Models of a User Interface. A user's conceptual model, a programmer's model, and a designer's model represent the perspectives of three different audiences for a software product. A user's conceptual model is influenced by the user's experiences in the real world, including experience with other computer systems. A programmer's model is influenced by the operating platform, the operating system, the shell, the tools, and the guidelines that are used to develop a product. A designer's model is influenced by the user's conceptual model, the programmer's model, and user interface design principles and guidelines.

The models for each audience are discussed in the following sections.

A User's Conceptual Model

A *user's conceptual model* is a mental model consisting of the set of relationships that a person perceives to exist among elements of any situation. A person develops a conceptual model through experience and then develops expectations based on the relationships in the model.

When confronted with a new situation, a person tries to interpret it by comparing it, often unconsciously, to some existing model. For example, if a computer user sees an object on a computer screen, and the object resembles a familiar object, say a telephone, the user transfers concepts from his or her existing model of telephones and makes guesses about how the computer's telephone object might work. Although this might seem to be a hit-or-miss approach to new situations, it is more efficient than building a new model from scratch, and people are satisfied when a new situation fits into their existing models.

However, if an existing model does not explain a new situation, and if people are unable to develop a new model, they become uncertain; they proceed hesitantly, and they can become frustrated, perhaps abandoning the new situation entirely because it is too unfamiliar. A user's conceptual model is somewhat resistant to change, but it can change over time as a user collects new evidence that helps a user refine or redefine the model.

To understand a user's conceptual model, a designer must understand a user's experiences (such as educational background and job training, as well as previous interaction with machines) and working environment (such as the type of hardware and system software in use). Also, a designer must understand what kinds of information a user needs and what functions a computer system should offer to help a user perform a task.

Unfortunately, a designer cannot simply ask all potential users of a product to describe or draw pictures of their conceptual models; most users are unaware that they have a conceptual model. Even users who are aware that they have expectations about a situation typically cannot provide the analytical insight that a designer needs. So a designer must gather information through techniques such as:

- Analysis of a users' tasks
- Surveys and interviews of actual or potential users
- Visits to users' work sites
- Feedback from users
- Usability testing.

Because each user's conceptual model is influenced by different experiences, no two users' conceptual models are exactly alike. Still, these techniques can help a designer compile a fairly complete picture of the conceptual models of a cross-section of users. A designer can then use this information, along with good design judgment and the CUA design principles and guidelines, to make decisions about how to design a product's user interface.

A Programmer's Model

A *programmer's model* represents a product or a computer system from the perspective of the person who writes the code that makes the product or system work. A programmer's model is often very different from both a user's model and a designer's model (described in the next section) because it necessarily includes a more thorough understanding of the computer hardware and supporting software that make a product or system run.

A programmer typically could draw a picture of a programmer's model because a programmer's model is more explicit than a user's conceptual model and is consciously created. The programmer's model concentrates primarily on the objects and relationships that the programmer uses to implement a product. For example, a programmer's model might include an object consisting of typed data fields in records in an indexed file. In a user's conceptual model, the same object would simply be an address book. In a designer's model, the concepts would be represented as a group of logically related objects (people's names, addresses, and telephone numbers) that make up an address book object. A programmer requires a level of understanding different from the level required by users. Therefore, although the elements of a programmer's model are vital to the development of a product, a designer should take care to mask the technical details, hiding them from a user without impairing a product's function.

A Designer's Model

A user-interface designer is like an architect. Just as an architect must understand the perspective of the person who is going to live in a house, as well as the perspective of the person who is going to build the house, a user-interface designer must understand the perspectives of the end user and the programmer.

A designer's model influences and is influenced by both the user's conceptual model and the programmer's model. There is no direct relationship between the user's conceptual model and the programmer's model. Figure 7 shows how the three models are related.

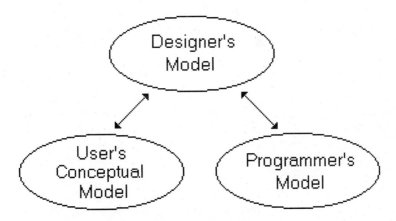

Figure 7. The Relationship among the Models of User Interfaces. A designer's model influences and is influenced by both the user's conceptual model and the programmer's model. No direct relationship exists between the user's conceptual model and the programmer's model.

The three primary elements of a designer's model are:

- Object relationships (the objects in the interface and their behaviors)
- Visual representations (the "look" of the interface)
- Interaction techniques and mechanisms (the "feel" of the interface).

Figure 8 on page 16 illustrates the parts of a designer's model and shows the relationships among the parts.

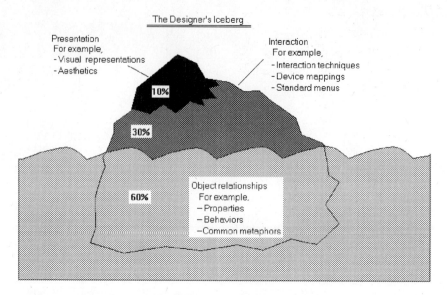

The Designer's Iceberg

Presentation
For example,
- Visual representations
- Aesthetics

Interaction
For example,
- Interaction techniques
- Device mappings
- Standard menus

10%

30%

60%

Object relationships
For example,
− Properties
− Behaviors
−Common metaphors

Figure 8. The Designer's Model Represented as an Iceberg. A designer's model includes object relationships, visual representations, and interaction techniques and mechanisms. Although the visual representations and interaction techniques are the most visible part of a user interface, the object relationships, which are based on a user's conceptual model, form the bulk of the interface.

Although the visual representations and interaction techniques and mechanisms are the most obvious elements of a user interface, the object representations make the most significant contribution to a product's usability.

Object Relationships

Object relationships are the most important part of a designer's model, and a designer should spend a considerable amount of effort defining them. At this stage of product development, a designer determines what objects a user requires, what the relationships are among the objects, and what properties and behaviors the objects should have. For example, if a designer is developing a model of a product for a car dealership, the designer might determine that a user—in this case a car salesperson—needs a car object and a customer object. The user might also need a worksheet object, in which information from both the car object and customer object can be combined. Finally, the user might need one or more container objects to contain the other objects.

When a designer chooses the objects and their properties, behaviors, and relationships carefully, and accurately matches them to the relationships in a user's existing conceptual model, the visual representations and interaction techniques follow naturally.

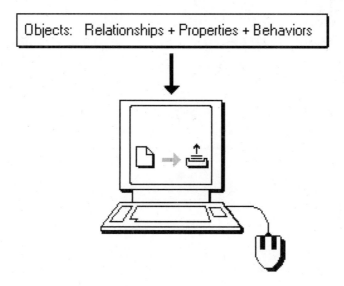

Figure 9. Object Relationships. A designer must decide what objects a user requires, what the relationships are among the objects, and what properties and behaviors the objects should possess.

Visual Representations

A designer's model also addresses the appearance of objects so that a product's objects are visually consistent with one another as well as with other objects in the operating environment. The two aspects to each visual representation in a user interface are the functional aspect and the aesthetic aspect. In designing the functional aspect of a visual representation, a designer is concerned with usability and with how well the visual representation conveys the purpose of the object being represented. In designing the aesthetic aspect of a visual representation, a designer is concerned with whether the representation is visually pleasing. A designer considers factors such as the shape, size, and color of the visual representation.

Typically, a designer's model provides a framework for both aspects of the visual representations. The framework includes ways to visually indicate to a user what the purpose or state of an object is, as well as ways to indicate similarity among objects. For a car dealership product, a designer might decide that all cars with prospective buyers should be identified by a similar symbol.

Visual specifications assist a designer in maintaining visual consistency, and they provide a foundation on which the designer can build. They also allow a designer leeway in determining which representations are most appropriate for a particular product.

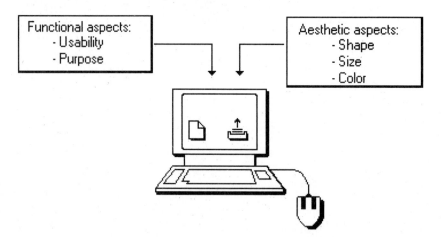

Figure 10. Visual Representations. A designer must develop specifications for the visual elements of an interface to ensure consistency. The specifications should address the functional aspects of visual representations, such as usability and purpose, as well as the aesthetic aspects, such as shape, size, and color.

Interaction Techniques and Mechanisms

Finally, a designer's model addresses a user's techniques for interaction with objects. A typical model includes more than one technique and more than one mechanism for interaction so that users can choose the technique and mechanism that best suits their tasks, their level of skill, and their preferred style of interaction.

A designer's model specifies a pattern of interaction in which users interact with similar objects in similar ways and in ways that seem natural to users. Again, consistency should be a designer's goal when developing this part of the designer's model. Toward that end, the CUA interface provides substantial guidance for interaction techniques and mechanisms. When developing a product with a CUA user interface, a designer does not need to develop a complete model of interaction. Instead, a designer's task is to choose from the CUA designer's model (see Chapter 5, "The CUA Designer's Model—A Summary" on page 93) those interaction techniques that are most appropriate for a particular product.

In a car dealership product, for example, a designer might determine that a salesperson should be able to place information into a worksheet object in any of several ways. The salesperson could place a car object on top of the worksheet object, thereby transferring information about the car to the worksheet. Or the salesperson could type information directly into the worksheet object. Finally, the salesperson could select portions of information from the car object and copy it to the worksheet object.

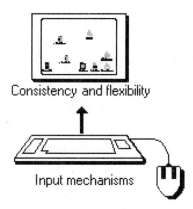

Consistency and flexibility

Input mechanisms

Figure 11. Interaction Techniques and Mechanisms. A designer must specify which techniques yield which results and must ensure that similar interactions yield similar results.

Accommodating the Differences between a User's Conceptual Model and a Designer's Model

Ideally, a designer's model is equivalent to a user's conceptual model, and a product works the way each user expects it to work. However, various factors can lead to a disparity between a user's conceptual model and a designer's model. For example:

- Not all users have the same conceptual models.

- Implementation constraints can restrict the function of a product to something less than a user expects.

- A computer product can provide useful features that do not have corresponding components in the real world or in a user's area of expertise, and therefore do not already exist in a user's conceptual model.

When a designer's model does not exactly match a user's conceptual model, the user often feels as if he or she is viewing a product through a haze, not quite seeing or understanding the product. Some components of the product look and behave as the user expects, while others seem somewhat different or even foreign. To dispel the haze, a designer should expose a user to the features of a product in a way that helps shape the user's conceptual model to incorporate the actual designer's model. Then the two become equivalent.

Consistency and the use of metaphors are helpful techniques for shaping a user's conceptual model. When a new feature is consistent with a product's other features, a user can predict at least some of the results of using the new feature and can accept the new feature more readily. Likewise, when a new feature is developed around a metaphor for something that exists in a user's conceptual model, a user can make guesses about the new feature by drawing analogies from the familiar concept. The user can then extend the existing conceptual model to incorporate the new feature. Electronic mail provides an example.

Although most people understand how to mail a letter by using a postal or courier service, few immediately understand how to send information by pressing a key on a keyboard or by placing a computer object on top of another computer object (for example, placing a document object on top of an out-basket object). By designing this type of information transfer around a mail metaphor, a designer encourages a user to draw on an existing conceptual model that describes and explains methods for getting information from one place to another.

Furthermore, if a designer has specified an interaction technique that is consistent with other interaction techniques that a user is familiar with, a user will be able to extend a conceptual model of mail to include electronic mail. For example, if a user knows how to mail a real-world document by placing it into the office out-basket, the user can easily learn to mail a document object by placing it into an out-basket object on a computer.

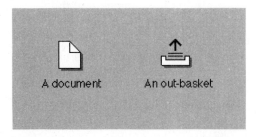

Figure 12. Metaphor. Electronic mail relies on a mail metaphor to help users understand the underlying concept of electronic transfer of information. To mail document objects, users place them into an out-basket object, just as users place real-world documents into real-world out-baskets.

A designer's model must also be flexible enough to accommodate growing sophistication in users. As users become more proficient in using a product, they might find that they do not like certain aspects of the interface, or they might realize that they want or need functions that they had not thought of before. A successful designer anticipates a user's progress and provides mechanisms that are robust enough to stretch as novice users become expert users. For example, when working with a printer object, a typical user wants information about which objects are in the printer's queue, as well as the orientation and number of copies the printer will produce. This information should be readily available. However, a more sophisticated user might want information about the printer's connections, baud rate, and communication protocol. This information should also be available, but it should not get in the way of the information needed by a typical user.

By layering information, a designer can keep a product's interface free of clutter and can avoid intimidating novice users while still meeting the needs of expert users. Chapters 3 and 4 provide information about the design principles and interface components that enable designers to create products that serve users' needs.

Accommodating the Programmer's Model in the Designer's Model

Ideally, a designer should create a model appropriate for users, and a programmer should write programming code that supports the designer's entire model. However, a designer must sometimes make concessions to the restrictions of a programming environment. For example, in a product that offers an electronic mail feature, a designer might specify that a user should receive some kind of immediate notification when mail reaches its intended recipient. But if the network that the mail travels on is subject to unpredictable delays, the designer might have to settle for a notification that arrives as soon as the network allows, rather than an immediate notification. The designer might also have to add a feature that lets a user know where a piece of mail is while in route.

When accommodating a programmer's model in a designer's model, a designer should be certain to shield users from complex details of a product's implementation. As shown in Figure 7 on page 15, there should be no direct relationship between a programmer's model and a user's conceptual model. Any aspect of a programmer's model that must be exposed to a user must first be filtered through the designer's model. For example, a typical user expects that the information displayed in a window is up to date. The user's expectation should be reflected in the designer's model. However, a programmer cannot always ensure that displayed information is up to date; perhaps a network delay interferes. To bridge the gap between a user's expectations and what a programmer can deliver, a designer's model can include a way for a user to manually refresh the display of information.

Just as an architect must know the strengths and weaknesses of building materials and the skills of the builders contracted to construct a house, a designer must be aware of the capabilities and limitations of the programming environment, and the skills of the programmers who will implement the design.

Chapter 3. Goals and Design Principles of the CUA User Interface

The primary goal of the CUA user interface is to help a user to transfer knowledge across products. If a user learns to use one product that has a CUA interface, the user can quickly learn to use any other product that has a CUA interface. Additional goals of the CUA user interface are to:

- Increase a user's productivity
- Increase a user's satisfaction with a product
- Reduce a user's error rate.

The CUA user interface achieves these goals by adhering to the design principles discussed in this chapter. The design principles are based on principles of human behavior, field experience, and results of usability testing.

Occasionally a designer must choose between two design principles if both pertain to a particular aspect of the user interface. Sometimes factors outside a designer's control can lead a designer to favor one principle at the expense of another. For example, cost, performance, and usability concerns sometimes conflict. A designer must balance them according to their effect on a user and a user's tasks. Above all, a designer must keep a user in mind when creating a user interface.

The design principles are grouped according to these categories:

- Placing a user in control of the user interface
- Reducing a user's memory load
- Making the user interface consistent.

If a designer conscientiously combines these design principles with knowledge of a product's intended users and with usability testing, the resulting product should be easy to learn and easy to use.

Design Principles That Place a User in Control

A user should always be able to communicate with a computer and should never feel that the computer is in control. Whenever possible, a designer should avoid program-driven sequences that prompt a user through fixed steps and directive messages. Program-driven interaction is like riding a train: a user must go where the program goes, according to its schedule. A designer should aim for user-driven interaction, which is like driving a car: a user goes where the user wants, according to the user's schedule. A product should allow a user alternative courses of action and should not limit a user's capabilities by imposing a designer's or programmer's preconceived notions of the "correct" sequence for accomplishing a task.

In general, a designer should approach product design with a "no user errors" philosophy. That is, a product should never make users feel that they are in the wrong—rather, users should feel that any shortcomings are in the product, not in themselves.

Using Modes Judiciously

A *mode* is a state of a product in which only certain actions are available to a user. That is, modes restrict a user's options. However, modes can be useful in some situations. For example, they can extend the capabilities of input devices by allowing several actions to be accomplished with the same technique, key, button, and so forth. Modes can also help an expert user perform a series of actions very quickly.

A mode limits a product's response to a user's actions. For example, if a user were typing a report using a product that has a typing mode and a line-drawing mode, the user would have to leave the typing mode to draw lines around a paragraph. Because typing would be an action unavailable in the line-drawing mode, the user would have to switch modes again to continue typing the report.

Modes can be useful in directing a user's interaction with a product. However, designers have historically overused modes without regard for how modes affect users. Users can feel powerless when a mode restricts their actions.

One drawback of modes is that the same action can produce a different result, or no result, in a different mode. For example, in a typical typing mode, a letter appears when a user presses a character key. In a line-drawing mode, perhaps only the cursor-movement keys have any effect; pressing a character key might produce no result.

Another drawback to modes is that users tend to forget which mode they are in unless a product clearly indicates the current mode. A user can be puzzled when an action leads to an unintended result. For example, pressing the right arrow key in a typing mode typically moves the cursor to the right. In a line-drawing mode, perhaps the right arrow key extends a horizontal line by some increment. If a user presses the right arrow key intending to edit some text, and instead draws a longer line, the user can be surprised, confused, or even exasperated.

To alleviate some of the problems associated with modes, a designer should try to use only those modes that require an ongoing user action, such as pressing a mouse button or a keyboard key, to maintain the mode. Also, a designer should specify some kind of mode indicator. For example, a pointer or cursor could have one visual representation when the user is in a text-editing mode and another when the user is in a line-drawing mode. Figure 13 shows examples of pointers used as mode indicators.

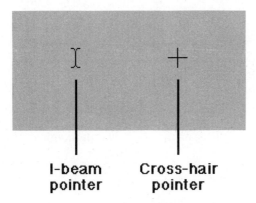

I-beam   Cross-hair
pointer   pointer

Figure 13. Mode Indicators. When a user is in text editing mode, for example, the pointer can change to an I-beam pointer to indicate the mode. When the user changes to line-drawing mode, the pointer can change to a cross-hair pointer.

If a designer finds it necessary to use a mode for a particular part of a product, the designer should keep the scope of the mode narrow and should allow a user to continue to interact with other parts of the product while the mode is in effect. For example, if a product requires more information from a user and displays a message window to elicit the information, the user should still be able to scroll the underlying window and interact with other parts of the window not affected by the lack of information. The user should also be able to interact with other objects.

In general, a designer should use modes with caution and should make them obvious and easy to get out of.

Displaying Descriptive and Helpful Messages

Chances are that at some point a user will interact with a product in a way that the product's designer did not anticipate. When that happens, the product should indicate to the user that it cannot interpret the user's action. Typically a product would display some kind of message, although in some situations an audible cue or a graphical cue would suffice.

Because a situation in which a message is displayed is often a situation in which a user needs the most support, messages should be clear and concise and should provide mechanisms for user interaction. A message should describe the situation objectively, without placing blame, and should help a user correct the situation. For example, if a user inserts a diskette that has not been formatted, and the user tries to save an object to that diskette, the product should display a message that tells the user that the diskette has not been formatted. The message should include mechanisms that allow the user to format the diskette and save the object without having to leave the message window. The message should also include mechanisms that allow the user to take other courses of action. Figure 14 on page 27 shows an example of an appropriate message.

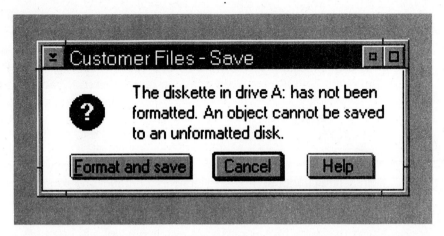

Figure 14. Descriptive Message. The message describes the situation without placing blame on the user, and the message provides a way for the user to change the situation without leaving the message window.

For additional information about messages, see "Messages" on page 84.

Providing Immediate Actions, Feedback, and Reversible Actions

The results of a user's actions should be obvious immediately. Immediate feedback allows a user to assess whether the results were as expected. If the results are not as expected, the user can choose an alternative action right away. For example, when a user selects a choice to change the font of some selected text, the appearance of the selected text should change immediately. The user can then decide if the resulting effect is desirable and can select another choice if it is not.

If the results of a user's actions cannot be made obvious immediately—for example, if a network delay interferes—a product should still provide some kind of feedback. For example, the product should indicate to the user that the action is being processed. However, a designer should make sure that a product's feedback does not interrupt a user's work.

The results of a user's actions should also be reversible. By providing reversible actions, a designer allows a user to learn by exploring, to try an action to see the result, and to undo the action if the result is not what was expected or desired. For example, if a user types a word and then decides a different word would be better, the user can press the Backspace key to undo the original typing. Likewise, a user should be able to redo any action that has been undone. A user feels more comfortable with an interface in which an action does not cause irreversible consequences.

If an action cannot be made reversible, a product should inform a user and should give the user an opportunity to select some other action. A product might display a message that tells what the outcome of a user's action will be and that indicates alternative actions for the user to select from. For example, if a user attempts to erase a diskette, the product should display a message that tells the user that if the action continues, the user will no longer be able to retrieve the information on the diskette. The message should also indicate alternative actions that the user can take, such as stopping the action or replacing the diskette in question with another diskette.

A designer is responsible for determining which actions can be undone and which cannot, but the designer should always keep users' needs in mind and should err on the side of more reversible actions rather than fewer reversible actions. A designer also determines how many actions in a series of actions can be undone.

Accommodating Users with Different Levels of Skill

Much of user interface design is focused on novice or casual users. However, many products offer features for more expert users as well. When designing a user interface, a designer should provide a way for a user to proceed at a comfortable pace, learning as much as necessary to accomplish the task at hand. A designer should also provide a way for a user to go beyond the basic level of knowledge required for frequently used features. A product should encourage exploration so that, as a user's expertise increases, the user is able to discover and use the product's more advanced features.

For example, a product might initially display simplified menus containing only those choices that a novice or casual user would use. However, the product could also contain a mechanism that allows experienced or expert users to display complete menus of all of the product's choices.

A novice or casual user requires different kinds of support than those required by a frequent or expert user. To accommodate a novice or casual user, a designer should rely heavily on visual cues and should avoid making a user type extensively or remember details. Another technique is to provide abbreviated menus and simplified windows. To accommodate a frequent or expert user, a designer can provide hidden mechanisms, such as shortcut keys, and condensed sequences of steps. A designer can also provide a way to remove some visual cues. For example, an expert user should be able to turn off the display of certain kinds of information that he or she does not require.

Users at any level of knowledge and experience can benefit from help information that describes a product's objects, choices, and interaction techniques, and offers a user assistance in completing a task. A novice or casual user might require extensive help information about each component of a product's interface, while a frequent or expert user might require only a brief description.

In general, an interface should be flexible enough to accommodate a full range of users, but a designer should make sure that the interface serves the needs of the primary users.

Making the User Interface Transparent

A user interface provides tools that help a user accomplish a task; therefore, an interface should focus a user's attention on the task or end product. Just as a chef is only incidentally interested in the tools of the cooking trade—pots, pans, and ovens—and prefers to concentrate on the finished meal, a user is only incidentally interested in the tools provided by a user interface—menus, pointers, keyboards, icons, and windows. A user prefers to concentrate on conveying ideas, calculating a return on investment, or replenishing an inventory, for example, and a designer should make sure that the tools provided by a user interface do not get in the user's way. A good user interface requires little conscious thought on a user's part.

Allowing a User to Customize the User Interface

Because they have varying backgrounds, interests, motivations, and experiences, no two users are exactly alike. To accommodate individual differences, a designer should create a flexible interface that each user can customize according to personal preference. A user should be able to customize the volume and duration of sounds, the intensity and hue of colors, the arrangement of choices in menus, the sequence of steps in a process, and any other aspect of the user interface. A designer should never underestimate a user's creativity or desire for imprinting personal style on a computer.

A designer should also recognize that different users have different physical characteristics and work in diverse environments. One user might want to increase the volume of audible cues on a system to compensate for hearing loss or for a noisy work environment. Another user might want to enlarge the visual representations of the interface's components to compensate for impaired vision or inadequate lighting. Allowing a user to completely customize a user interface can lead to higher productivity and higher user satisfaction. However, a designer should provide defaults that are satisfactory to most users and that a user can revert to.

Design Principles That Reduce a User's Memory Load

A user should never have to rely on memory for something a product can "remember." Because people are better at recognition than at recall, a product should present alternatives and let a user choose from among them. For example, a product could provide lists of items, such as choices in a menu. A user can recognize choices in a menu without having to recall commands or their syntax.

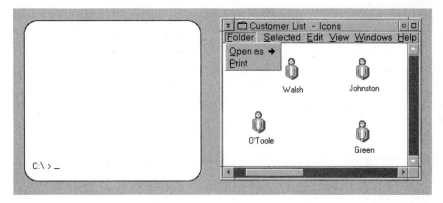

Figure 15. Recall versus Recognition. The window on the left offers few cues to a user, who must remember a set of commands and syntax. The window on the right presents a user with a menu, a list of items that a user can recognize and point to.

A product should also provide reminders to help a user keep track of the task at hand. For example, a product could provide visual cues, such as highlighting or progress indicators, or textual cues, such as status messages. Highlighting can remind a user that an object is selected, and a progress indicator can remind a user that a process is under way.

Another way to avoid overloading a user's memory is to provide default settings and to save previously selected settings. The window in which the settings are saved can also remind a user about which settings are in effect. For example, a user might want to change the colors that appear on a screen. After experimenting with various colors, the user might settle on a particular combination and save those settings. At a later date, however, the user might decide to revert to the original colors. By providing a default setting for screen colors, the product relieves the user of the responsibility for remembering the original colors.

Defining Meaningful and Concise Object Classes

In both the real world and in an object-oriented user interface, certain objects are better suited to certain tasks. For example, a telephone serves a person's needs for oral communication better than a typewriter does, while a person would be hard pressed to write a report with a telephone. When designing objects for an object-oriented user interface, a designer should consider the tasks a user will want to accomplish and then should ensure that the characteristics of the objects support the user's tasks.

A designer should clearly define the properties of each object and should establish a hierarchy of object classes based on these properties. The objects should be designed so that a user can easily recognize members of a class and can understand what distinguishes one class of objects from another. The distinctions among classes should be meaningful to a user and should not be based on underlying programming distinctions or requirements. For example, a product might contain a chart object and a parts catalog object. When a user works with a chart object, the user develops a body of knowledge about that object and comes to expect that other chart objects share certain characteristics and behave similarly. Likewise, a user develops a different set of expectations about a parts catalog object because it behaves differently from a chart object. From a user's perspective, these two objects have different purposes—that is, they belong to different object classes—even though they share some behaviors, such as opening and closing. A user does not care, and does not need to know, that to a programmer or a designer both objects are members of the data object class.

An object hierarchy should be concise. So should the visual representations of the objects in the hierarchy. Typically, each object in a class of objects is represented by the same type of icon. The individual objects are distinguished by different icon labels, which indicate the name of each object. If a user interface is cluttered with too many types of objects or too many types of icons, a user can become overwhelmed. To keep a user focused on the right objects, a designer should keep the number of object classes to a minimum while still allowing a user to accomplish a task without undue effort. If a product seems to require a new object class, a designer should first consider modifying an existing class. Likewise, a designer should consider modifying existing icons to represent new object classes. However, a designer should be sure that the visual distinctions among icons are obvious enough for a user to discern them readily. Reuse of an existing class allows a user to draw on previous knowledge of the class and decreases learning time.

Making Objects Concrete and Recognizable

When a computer object resembles a real-world object in appearance or behavior, or both, a user can transfer knowledge about the real-world object to the computer environment. By including familiar objects in a product, a designer can help users learn to use the product more quickly.

The visible representation of computer objects should be easily recognizable, and a computer object should resemble its real-world counterpart when possible. For example, in a car dealership product, an object that represents the general information about a car should resemble the general information found on the car's window sticker. Figure 16 shows an example of a recognizable object.

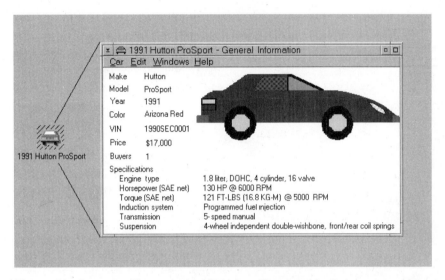

Figure 16. Concrete, Recognizable Objects. The car object's icon resembles a real car, and the information in the window resembles the information found on the sticker on a car window.

When an object represents a more abstract notion that does not have a real-world counterpart, the representation of the object should still help a user visualize and remember relationships.

Design Principles That Contribute to Consistency

Consistency helps a user transfer knowledge from one product to another and helps a user predict how something new will work. To create a consistent user interface, a designer should develop paradigms that provide for identical implementation of common functions throughout a product. For example, the CUA guidelines specify that a user should be able to use the same technique for editing text, regardless of where the text appears.

For any single design decision, a designer must consider whether being consistent with respect to one component of an interface can affect the consistency of other components. Some components of a user interface might be consistent in shape, location, or color. Others might be consistent in interaction techniques. A designer should make sure that components are consistent in the ways that a user would expect.

A designer must also remember that consistency is a means to an end—ease of learning and reduction of errors—rather than an end itself. Sometimes it is impractical or impossible to be completely consistent. In that case, a designer must make consistency compromises based on knowledge of a user's conceptual model and should be consistent in whichever way seems more natural to a user.

Sustaining the Context of a User's Task

Users can become confused if everything in front of them changes continuously, without apparent cause, while they work. To reassure a user and give a user a sense of continuity, a product should provide cues that help a user relate an effect to its cause.

A product should also maintain useful points of reference while a user works on a task. For example, when a user adds objects to a folder, the appearance of the folder's window should remain the same while the appearance of the window's contents changes.

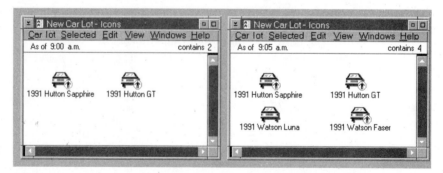

Figure 17. Sustaining the Context of a User's Task. The window on the left shows that the container contains two objects. When a user adds more objects to the container, the appearance of the window remains the same while the appearance of the window's contents changes.

Additionally, a user should be able to complete a step or a series of related steps without having to alternate between input devices. For example, a user should not have to use a pointing device to scroll text while editing that text from the keyboard. The text should scroll automatically when the cursor reaches the boundary of the area the user is working in, and the keyboard should have its own scrolling mechanisms, such as keys that move text up or down in the window, either a line at a time or a screenful at a time.

Finally, a user should be able to predict the result of an action. Two ways in which a designer can help a user predict a result are to provide consistent responses to actions and to provide actions appropriate to a user's tasks. A designer determines appropriate actions and responses by using task analysis and by relying on metaphors when suitable metaphors can be found. Also, by labeling actions with appropriate terms, a designer helps a user develop expectations about the outcome of those actions.

Maintaining Continuity within and among Products

A designer should not discount a user's experiences with other user interfaces, such as those provided in prior versions of a product, or those generally accepted as industry standards. Instead, a new product or a new version of an existing product should build on a user's knowledge. Therefore, a designer should be cautious in changing the behavior of an object from one version of a product to the next. A designer must test a new behavior to make sure that its benefits outweigh the drawbacks of forcing a user to relearn the object's behavior. One way to accommodate both new users and experienced users is to provide both the old and the new behavior for an object and let the users choose which to use.

Creating Aesthetic Appeal

The appearance of a product's interface can significantly affect a user's attitude toward the interface. Inconsistent design and haphazard placement of objects can confuse a user and can contribute to a user's dissatisfaction with a product.

When designing the appearance of a user interface, a designer should adhere to generally accepted practices for information presentation. By skillfully using white space, color, proximity, overlap, size and shape differences, and other components of visual communication, a designer can make an interface more efficient and effective and can increase a user's satisfaction with a product.

Using Visual Metaphors

To draw on a user's existing conceptual model, a designer should include elements that are familiar to a user. One way a designer can make an interface seem familiar is to use metaphors. For example, a designer could use a folder icon, which is a visual metaphor for a manila folder, an object familiar to a user. The folder is also a metaphor for the familiar concept of storage. In a computer environment, storage might be accomplished differently from what a user is accustomed to, but the metaphoric representations help a user draw on existing knowledge. Metaphors also help set the stage for expanding a user's conceptual model to accommodate the additional capabilities provided by the computer.

Figure 18. A Visual Metaphor for Storage. Because users have conceptual knowledge of folders, when they see a folder icon, they can understand that it represents storage.

Chapter 4. Key Components of the CUA User Interface

This chapter describes many of the key components of the CUA user interface. A designer can use these components when developing a product for a CUA environment. While many of these components appear in other kinds of user interfaces, the following descriptions refer specifically to the CUA implementation of these components.

Workplace

The *workplace* is the container that holds all objects in the CUA interface. It fills the entire screen and serves as a background for a user's work. Any object that appears directly on the background of the workplace is represented by an icon.

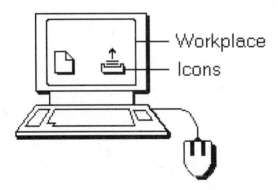

Figure 19. Workplace. The workplace is the container that holds all other objects. It fills the entire screen.

Folders and Work Areas

A *folder* is a general-purpose container in which a user can organize objects in whatever way the user sees fit. A *work area* is a more specialized type of container in which a user can organize objects according to the task or tasks the user wants to perform. Both types of containers can be provided by an operating system, and a product can provide product-specific containers based on these two types of containers. The visual representations of these containers can be tailored to fit the tasks for which a product will be used.

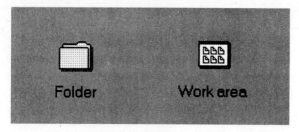

Figure 20. Folder and Work Area. A folder is a general-purpose container, and a work area is a container specialized for a user's tasks.

Icons

In the CUA interface, an *icon* is a small graphic image that represents an object. Strictly speaking, an icon is simply one view of an object (see "Views" on page 45); however, to be consistent with a user's conceptual model, a designer should design a product in a way that encourages a user to think of an icon as the object itself.

An icon should convey information about its corresponding object, and its appearance can change when something about its object changes. For example, the icon for a printer can change to indicate that the printer has run out of paper.

An icon doesn't have to be a static image. It can be an animated image or even a video image. Figure 21 shows examples of icons.

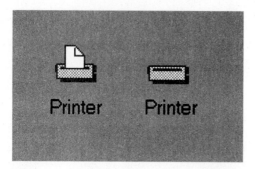

Figure 21. Icons. Icons are graphic images that represent objects. They can change to indicate a change in the objects they represent. The icon on the left represents a printer. The icon on the right indicates that the printer has run out of paper.

Pointers and Cursors

Pointers and *cursors* are visual cues that indicate where a user's next interaction with the user interface will take place. They provide a way for a user to select and interact with things that appear on the workplace.

The Pointer

Typically only one pointer appears on the workplace at a time, and it is associated with a user's pointing device, such as a mouse, trackball, or joystick. When a user moves the pointing device, the pointer moves correspondingly, and when a user presses a button on the pointing device, the object that the pointer is on is affected.

The pointing device used most often in a CUA environment is a two-button mouse. One of the two mouse buttons is called the *selection button* (see "Selection" on page 71). The other mouse button is called the *manipulation button,* and it is used for direct manipulation (see "Interaction with Objects" on page 54). A user can choose either the left or right mouse button for either function, selection or manipulation. If a three-button mouse is used, the third button is called the menu button.

The CUA pointer is usually shaped like an arrow. However, the shape of the pointer can change to indicate what kinds of actions are possible. For example, the pointer is shaped like an I-beam when it is over text that can be edited or over an area into which text can be placed. Products can provide product-specific pointers that serve the special needs of their audiences. For example, a graphics product might provide a special pointer to help a user draw lines accurately. However, before providing a new pointer, a designer should first consider modifying an existing pointer so that a user can transfer knowledge about the existing pointer rather than having to learn about a new one.

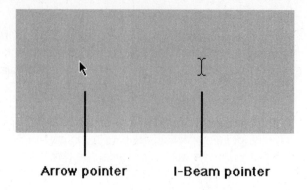

Arrow pointer   I-Beam pointer

Figure 22. Pointers. The pointer is usually shaped like an arrow, but it changes to an I-beam when it is on text that can be edited or on an area into which text can be placed. The pointer can change to other shapes as well, depending on the mode the user is in.

The Cursor

Typically only one cursor appears on the workplace at a time, and it is associated with a user's keyboard. When a user presses a key, information is transmitted to the operating system, and if appropriate, something appears or occurs at the cursor's position.

The CUA cursors are the *selection cursor* and the *text cursor.* The selection cursor is used to indicate which items a user can interact with from the keyboard. For example, a selection cursor can indicate which items can be selected or which items can display a pop-up menu (see "Pop-up Menus" on page 57). In some scopes of selection (see "Scope of Selection" on page 72) the selection cursor just indicates the cursor's position. In other scopes of selection, the selection cursor also automatically selects the item it is on.

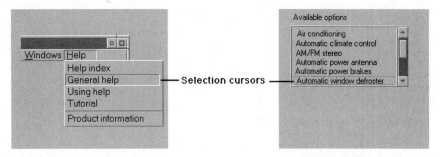

Figure 23. Selection Cursor. The selection cursor is typically a bar of color, a box with a dotted outline, or an area that appears to be pressed in relation to the surrounding window area.

The text cursor is used to type text. When a user is in insert mode—that is, when characters a user types are added to the existing characters—the text cursor appears as a vertical line. When a user is in replace mode—that is, when characters a user types replace existing characters—the text cursor can change in appearance. For example, the cursor can become a vertical bar of color surrounding the character that will be replaced.

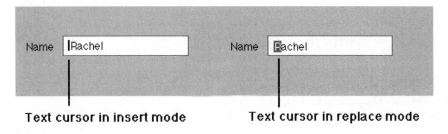

Figure 24. Text Cursors. The text cursor is a vertical line when a product is in insert mode. It is a vertical bar of color when a product is in replace mode.

Cursor Movement

A user can move the cursor by pressing a *cursor movement key.* Cursor movement keys include the arrow keys (labeled ←, →, ↑, and ↓) and the Home, End, Page Up, and Page Down keys. A user can also move the cursor by pressing and releasing a button on a mouse or other pointing device. When a user presses the selection button on a mouse, the cursor moves to the position that the pointer was on.

Mnemonics

A *mnemonic* is a readily recognized character that a user can type to move the cursor quickly from one place in a window to another. For example, if the cursor is on the first choice in a menu, a user can move the cursor directly to the last choice in the menu by typing the mnemonic for that choice. A mnemonic is typically indicated with an underline.

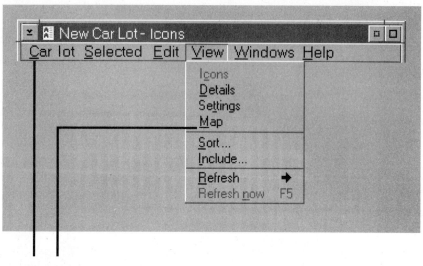

Mnemonics

Figure 25. Mnemonic. A mnemonic is a character that a user can type to quickly move the cursor to the choice containing the mnemonic. Each underlined character in the figure is a mnemonic.

Shortcut Keys

A *shortcut key* is a key or a combination of keys that a user can press to select a choice from a menu. The menu need not be displayed. Shortcut keys are provided for choices that a user will use frequently. Shortcut keys provide a quicker method of interaction, particularly for experienced users who are likely to prefer remembering the combinations to displaying and navigating through a menu for each desired choice.

A shortcut key is typically displayed next to the choice it pertains to so that a user can learn to associate the shortcut key with that choice. A designer might want to provide a mechanism that allows users to turn off the display of the shortcut keys. Figure 26 on page 43 illustrates some of the standard CUA shortcut keys.

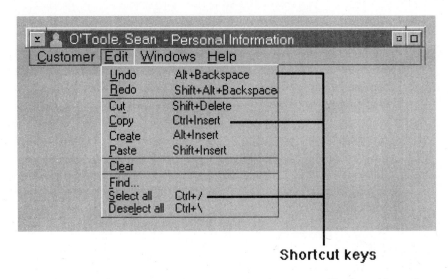

Shortcut keys

Figure 26. Shortcut Keys. A shortcut key is a key or combination of keys that a user can press to select a choice from a menu. A user can use a shortcut key even when the menu containing the corresponding choice is not displayed.

Windows

A *window* is a part of the CUA interface through which a user can view an object. A window is bounded by a window *border,* which separates the window from other windows on the workplace. Within the border are mechanisms that allow a user to manipulate the window and its contents.

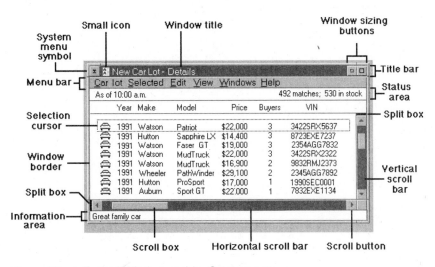

Figure 27. A Typical Window and Its Components

Figure 27 shows a typical window and its components. The system menu symbol, the window border, and the window sizing buttons allow a user to change the size and position of a window. The menu bar and scroll bars allow a user to work with the window's contents. The window title indicates the name of the object seen in the window, and it also indicates which kind of view (see "Views" on page 45) is displayed. The information area displays brief messages to a user about the object or choice that the cursor is on. Information about the normal completion of a process can also appear in the information area. For example, if a user copies several objects from one container to another, the information area in a container's window could display a brief message to tell the user when the copying has been completed.

A window and its content—that is, the information below the menu bar and above the horizontal scroll bar—are not permanently tied together. A user can completely change the content of a window without opening a new window. For example, a user can change the view (see "Views" on page 45) of the object displayed in the window. A user can also control how much of a window's content is visible by changing the size of the window or by splitting a window into separate portions called *panes*. Each pane can display different parts of the same object and can be scrolled independently.

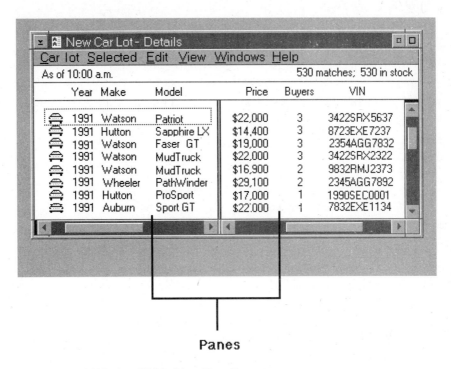

Panes

Figure 28. A Window Divided into Two Panes

The CUA interface provides two types of windows: *primary windows* and *secondary windows.* A primary window appears when a user opens an object, and it is where the main interaction between a user and an object takes place. A secondary window appears when a user needs, or needs to provide, information related to an object in a primary window. For example, a secondary window might contain a message (see "Messages" on page 84) or help information (see "Help" on page 91), or it might contain controls (see "Controls" on page 61) that help a user provide additional information.

Views

The content of a window is a *view.* A view is a way of looking at an object's information. Different views display information in different forms, which mimics the way information about an object is presented in the real world. Consider, for example, a user's manual for a personal computer system. A user's manual typically describes a computer system in several different ways. It provides:

- A picture of the entire system with each piece correctly set up
- A picture of each piece of the system

- A list of the pieces of the system, such as the display screen, keyboard, pointing device, and printer

- A list of the features of the system, such as the processing speed and memory capacity

- Step-by-step directions for setting up the system and for using each piece of the system.

Each of these ways of looking at or describing the computer system is a view of the system.

The CUA interface also provides different kinds of views for objects in the CUA environment. The appearance of a window's contents and the kinds of interaction possible in a window are determined, in part, by the type of view presented in the window. The four basic types of views are:

- Composed view
- Contents view
- Settings view
- Help view.

An object can have more than one view. In fact, most objects have several types of views.

To determine which types of views an object should have, a designer needs to consider which kinds of data an object contains. Some kinds of data have linear (or string-like) characteristics. For example, text can be thought of as a linear sequence of characters. An audio waveform is also linear, and so is a musical score. Other kinds of data have tabular (or array-like) characteristics. For example, a spreadsheet or text arranged in columns and rows is tabular. Still other kinds of data have neither linear nor tabular characteristics. Graphics and graphical components of an interface can be placed in various relative positions and still have meaning. They are said to have free-form characteristics.

A particular object can contain data that has one or more of these types of characteristics, but each characteristic might be displayed best in a different type of view. For each object, a designer should provide views that allow a user to display and work easily with each type of data contained in the object. When a user makes a change to the data displayed in one view of an object, the change should be reflected immediately in all other views of the same object (if the user has chosen to have the other views refreshed automatically).

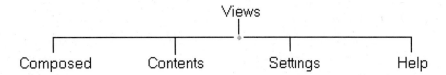

Figure 29. Views Available for Representing Objects in the CUA User Interface. The CUA interface provides four basic types of views plus two particular kinds of contents views. A product can have a composed view or contents view tailored for that product's users.

The four basic types of views are described in the following sections. Designers should keep in mind that these four types of views represent idealized views along a continuum of possible views. A designer can create product-specific views that fall somewhere between these categories. A designer should provide an appropriate name, based on the users' conceptual model, for each view in a product.

Composed Views

A *composed view* presents the components of an object in relative order and is appropriate when the relationships among the components contribute to the overall meaning of the object. Data objects in particular are likely to be displayed in a composed view. For example, a graph object or chart object would typically be displayed in a composed view because the arrangement of the components determines the meaning of the object as a whole. If the arrangement of the components changes, the meaning of the object changes. Figure 30 on page 48 shows an example of a composed view.

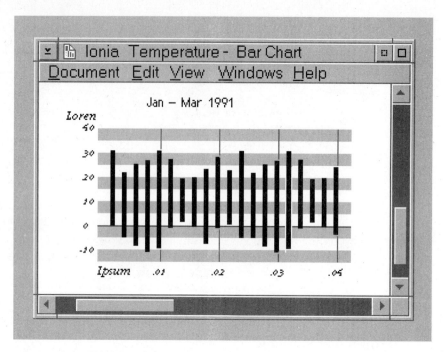

Figure 30. A Composed View. A composed view of a data object arranges the object's data in an order that conveys the data's meaning. If the data were arranged differently in a composed view, the object would have a different meaning.

Contents Views

A *contents view* lists the components of an object. The components can be ordered or unordered in the view; the order of the information displayed in a contents view does not affect the meaning of the object containing the information. For example, the data on which a graph object or chart object is based could be displayed as an alphabetic, numeric, or random list in a contents view. The data is still the same, no matter the order in which it is listed. Container objects in particular are likely to be displayed in a contents view, although data objects and device objects can also be displayed in a contents view. Figure 31 on page 49 illustrates a contents view.

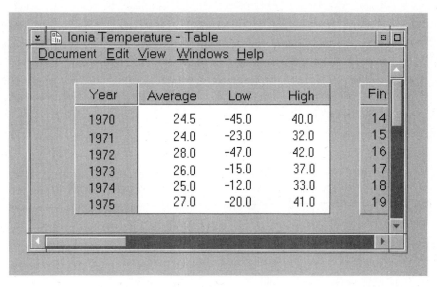

Figure 31. A Contents View. A contents view of a data object lists the data contained in the object. The order of the data does not affect the meaning of the object in a contents view.

The CUA interface provides for two standard kinds of contents views:

- Icons view
- Details view.

A designer can provide other product-specific kinds of contents views, depending on a user's needs. However, if a product includes objects that contain other objects, the product should provide at least the two standard kinds of contents views.

Icons View: An *icons view* displays each object as an icon and is appropriate when a designer wants to give a user an easy way to change the position of objects or to otherwise directly manipulate them (see "Interaction with Objects" on page 54). From a user's perspective, an icon is the object itself. From a designer's perspective, an icon is a composed view of an object. Note, however, that an icons view is a contents view. Figure 32 on page 50 shows an icons view of a folder object that contains several documents.

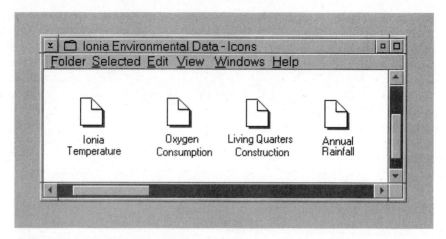

Figure 32. An Icons View of an Opened Folder. This view of the contents of a folder displays an icon for each contained object.

Reflections: An object usually is represented by only one icon. However, for some tasks, a user might find it convenient to represent an object with more than one icon. For example, a user might want a representation of a printer object in more than one place so that the user could have easy access to the printer from whichever folder or work area the user is working in. A user can create an additional icon, known as a *reflection*, to represent the same printer object.

Each reflection of a single object is related to the other reflections in such a way that when a user changes an object by way of one reflection, the change is reflected in all other reflections of the same object. However, if a user deletes a reflection, other reflections of the same object are not necessarily deleted. A user can choose to delete individual reflections or can delete all reflections of an object at once, at the user's discretion.

For related information, see "Icons" on page 38.

Details View: A *details view* combines small icons with text that provides additional information about objects. The type of information displayed depends on the type of object and the type of tasks a user wants to perform. The benefit of a details view is that the user doesn't have to open an object to gain quick access to some of the object's more frequently used information. Small icons are included in a details view to provide a way for a user to directly manipulate each object.

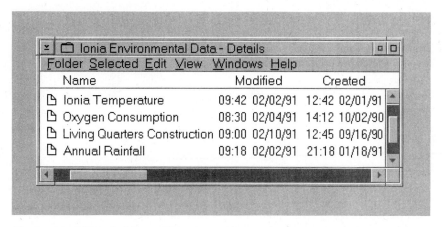

Figure 33. A Details View. *This view of the contents of a folder displays detailed information about each object in the folder. The details include the date the contained objects were created and the date they were last modified.*

Settings Views

A *settings view* displays information about the characteristics, attributes, or properties of an object, and it provides a way for a user to change the settings of some characteristics or properties. Not all settings can be changed, however. For example, a user cannot change an object's creation date even though the date might be displayed in a settings view of the object.

A settings view typically is provided for each type of object. In a settings view for a data object such as a document, a user could change the font, type size, color, or whatever other settings are appropriate for the document. In a settings view for a device object such as a printer, a user could change the number of copies, the page orientation, the output destination, or whatever other settings are appropriate for the printer.

Settings views can be applied more broadly as well. For example, certain kinds of information about an object can be thought of as settings. An address book object might contain objects representing the people that a user writes to, and the settings for each of these objects might consist of the person's name and address. Figure 34 on page 52 shows an example of a settings view.

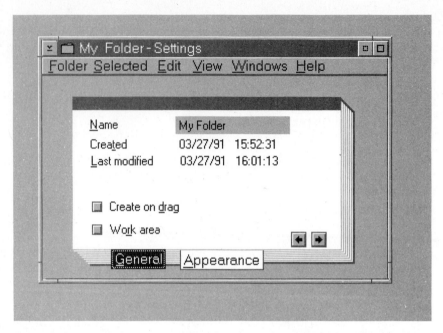

Figure 34. A Settings View. This settings view of a folder object displays the object's current settings and provides mechanisms that allow a user to change the settings.

Help Views

A *help view* provides information that can assist a user in working with an object. The type of information displayed in a help view depends on the type of help a user requests. For example, a user can request help for an entire window or for just part of one. Figure 35 on page 53 shows an example of help for the **Work area** choice in the My Folder - Settings window.

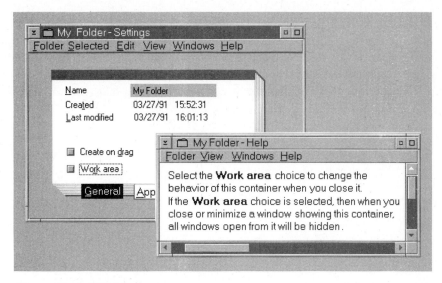

Figure 35. A Help View

For more details about the kind of help information that appears in a help view, see "Help" on page 91.

Distinguishing a Composed View from a Contents View

From a designer's perspective, the distinction between a composed view and a contents view can be somewhat blurred, depending on the object being viewed. For example, a product might provide a kind of view that lists the sections of a document, much as an outline does. Lists of an object's components are characteristic of a contents view. However, the product's view might list the sections of the document in a meaningful order, which is characteristic of a composed view.

Designers should not be overly concerned about which category a particular view falls into. Instead, designers should create views that convey information in a form that is meaningful to users, regardless of where the views fall in the continuum of view types. The names that designers choose for the views should describe the information displayed and should be easily understood by users. For example, a product could provide a "Formatted Text" view or a "Page Layout" view as the composed view of a document. The product could also provide an "Outline" view as either a composed view or a contents view of a document.

Interaction with Objects

Natural languages typically have many more nouns than verbs, and a graphical user interface typically contains more objects than actions. Just as the same verb can be applied to many nouns, the same action can be applied to many objects. The *object-action paradigm* is a pattern for interaction in which a user first selects an object, then selects an action. When a user selects an object first, the system can then present a list of actions that can be applied to that object; the user does not have to remember which actions are available. The object-action paradigm is really a continuum, with *direct manipulation* at one end and *indirect manipulation* at the other.

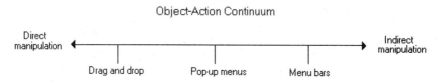

Figure 36. The Object-Action Continuum. At one end of the continuum is direct manipulation, in which an object and an action are closely bound. At the other end is indirect manipulation, in which a user selects an object, then selects an action. Between the two extremes are other manipulation techniques, such as drag and drop, pop-up menus, and menu bars.

Direct manipulation is interaction with an object by way of a pointing device. This interaction technique closely resembles the way a user interacts with objects in the real world. For example, using direct manipulation a user can "pick up" an object and put it into a folder. During direct manipulation, an object and an action are bound together closely.

Indirect manipulation is interaction with an object through choices and controls (see "Controls" on page 61). Indirect manipulation can be accomplished with either a pointing device or a keyboard. During indirect manipulation, an object and an action are separated. A user selects an object first, then the interface immediately tailors and presents a list of appropriate actions, which are displayed as choices that the user can apply to that object. The product, rather than the user, stores the information that tells a user which actions can be applied to the selected object. Users who interact with a computer by using a keyboard exclusively can use indirect manipulation to obtain results equivalent to those available through the use of direct manipulation.

Other manipulation techniques can fall between the two extremes. For example, using a *pop-up menu* (see "Pop-up Menus" on page 57) is more direct than using other kinds of menus, but it is less direct than dragging an object.

The following sections provide details about techniques and components used for interaction with objects.

Drag and Drop

Drag and drop is an interaction technique that falls at the direct manipulation end of the object-action continuum. It is called *drag and drop* because it involves moving an object from one place (dragging) and leaving it at another (dropping). For example, to change a value represented by a bar on a bar chart, a user could drag the end of a bar until the bar represented an appropriate new value. The user would then drop the end of the bar in the new location to complete the direct manipulation.

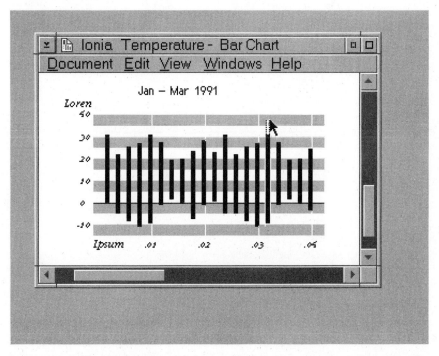

Figure 37. Direct Manipulation in a Bar Chart View of a Document Object. By dragging a bar, a user can change the value the bar represents.

Drag and drop often involves a *source object* and a *target object*. A source object is usually the object a user is working with, and a target object is usually an object that a user is transferring information to. For example, if a user drags a spreadsheet object to a printer object so that the spreadsheet will be printed, the spreadsheet is the source object and the printer is the target object.

The result of drag and drop can change depending on what the source object is and what the target object is. For example, if a user drags a spreadsheet object from one folder object and drops it onto another, the spreadsheet is moved to the target folder. However, if a user drops the same spreadsheet onto a printer object instead of a folder, the operating environment makes a copy of the spreadsheet and puts the copy into the printer's queue to be printed. The original spreadsheet is returned to its original location. Figure 38 illustrates printing a document by direct manipulation.

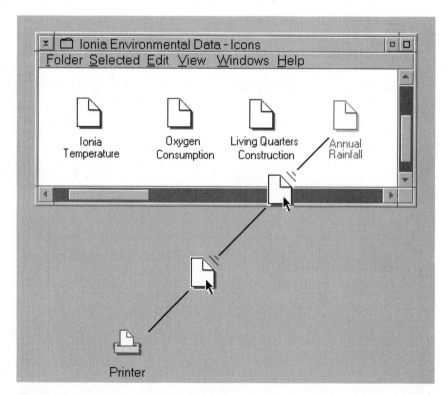

Figure 38. Printing by Direct Manipulation. A user can drag a document object to a printer object to print the document.

The CUA guidelines specify default results for drag and drop actions. The defaults are based on the types of objects (container, data, or device) being manipulated and on the following principles:

- When possible, the result of dragging and dropping an object should be the result that a user would expect, given the source object and target object being manipulated.

- The result of direct manipulation should be comparatively "safe"—that is, a user should not lose information unexpectedly.

- A user should be able to override a default result to obtain a different result.

Pop-up Menus

A second technique for interacting with objects involves the use of *pop-up menus,* which contain only those choices that pertain to an object at the time the menu is displayed. The menus are called pop-up menus because they appear to "pop up" next to an object when a user presses the appropriate key or mouse button. A pop-up menu is available for each object in an interface. Pop-up menus fall between drag and drop and menu bars in the object-action continuum. Access to an object's actions by way of a pop-up menu is more direct than access by way of other types of menus (see "Menus:" on page 61) because a user does not have to select a choice from a menu bar first. However, pop-up menus are less direct than drag and drop.

The content of a pop-up menu is based on an object's context, which includes the object's container, the object's contents, and the object's state. Variations in an object's context lead to variations in an object's pop-up menu.

When a user displays a pop-up menu for a group of objects, the menu contains only those choices that can be applied to all objects in the group.

Pop-up menus are particularly useful for objects that incorporate other objects of different types, each requiring a different set of menu choices. For example, in a page layout product that contains text objects, scanned-image objects, and chart objects, a user could see a different pop-up menu for each type of object.

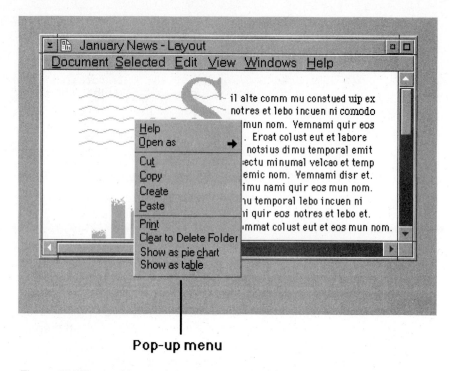

Pop-up menu

Figure 39. Pop-up Menu. A pop-up menu contains choices that can be applied to an object at the time that the menu is displayed. Different objects have different pop-up menus.

Choices and Controls

During indirect manipulation, a user interacts with an object by first selecting the object, then selecting a choice that performs the actual manipulation. The primary interface mechanisms for indirect manipulation are:

- Choices
- Controls.

Each of these interface components is discussed in more detail in the following sections.

Choices

A *choice* is text or a graphic that a user can select to modify or manipulate an object. Graphical user interfaces, including the CUA interface, are full of choices.

In the CUA environment there are three types of choices:

- Action choices
- Routing choices
- Settings choices.

Action Choices: An *action choice* immediately performs some task. For example, a choice labeled **Print** prints an object as soon as the user selects the choice.

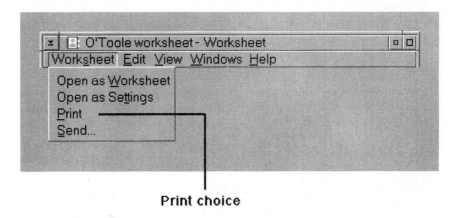

Print choice

*Figure 40. Action Choice.   The **Print** choice is an action choice. When a user selects the choice, an object is immediately printed on a user's printer.*

Routing Choices: A *routing choice* displays a menu or a window from which a user can select additional choices or specify additional information about the task the user is performing. Except when a routing choice appears on a menu bar (see "Menu Bars" on page 61), the name of a routing choice is followed by a rightward-pointing arrow or an ellipsis (...). The arrow indicates that the choice displays a menu, and the ellipsis indicates that the choice displays a window. For example, a choice labeled **Refresh** → displays a menu containing choices such as **On** and **Off**, which modify the **Refresh** → choice. A choice labeled **Sort...** displays a window from which a user can specify the order in which items should be sorted. Figure 41 on page 60 shows examples of routing choices.

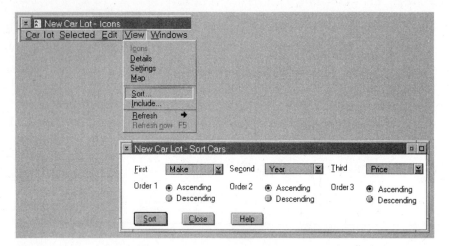

Figure 41. Routing Choices. When a user selects a routing choice, a window or another menu appears. The **View** *choice on the menu bar is a routing choice. When a user selects it, a pull-down menu appears. The* **Sort...** *choice in the* **View** *menu is also a routing choice. When a user selects it, the pull-down menu disappears and a secondary window appears.*

Settings Choices: A *settings choice* allows a user to display or change the characteristics or properties of an object. A settings choice can also be an action choice if the change in a setting occurs as soon as a user selects the settings choice. For example, a choice labeled **Blue** would allow a user to display or change the color of an object to blue. If the object's color changes as soon as a user selects the choice, the **Blue** choice is both a settings choice and an action choice.

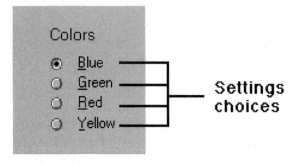

Figure 42. Settings Choice. A user selects a settings choice to display or change the characteristics of an object.

Controls

The CUA interface provides standard mechanisms for indirect manipulation. These mechanisms are called *controls,* and they are used to display or obtain certain kinds of information. Various controls can. be combined in a view to provide a user a way to modify an object.

Menus: A *menu* is a mechanism for presenting lists of choices to a user. Menus are a staple of most commercially available graphical user interfaces today. The CUA interface includes four types of menus:

- Menu bars
- Pull-down menus
- Cascaded menus
- Pop-up menus.

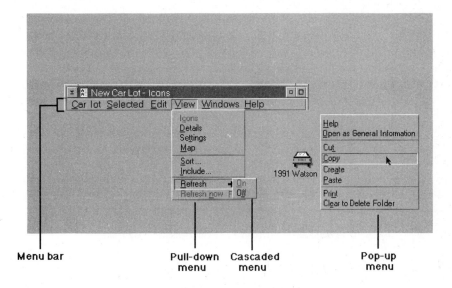

Menu bar   Pull-down   Cascaded   Pop-up
                   menu   menu   menu

Figure 43. Menus. The CUA interface includes menu bars, pull-down menus, cascaded menus, and pop-up menus.

Each type of menu is used for a certain purpose or in a certain kind of situation. Menu bars, pull-down menus, and cascaded menus are described in the following sections. However, because pop-up menus are used for direct manipulation rather than indirect manipulation, they are described at "Pop-up Menus" on page 57.

Menu Bars: A *menu bar* appears across the top of most windows, just below the window title. It is a horizontal list of routing choices. When a user selects a choice from a menu bar, an associated pull-down menu is displayed.

The name of each routing choice on a menu bar indicates what kinds of choices appear in the associated pull-down menu. By naming the routing choices descriptively, a designer encourages a user to learn by exploring.

Pull-Down Menus: A *pull-down menu* is displayed when a user selects a choice from a menu bar. Pull-down menus contain choices that are related to one another in some manner. For example, all choices in a pull-down menu could apply to:

- An entire object (the object displayed in a window)
- A selected object (within a window)
- Help information
- A view of an object.

Cascaded Menus: A *cascaded menu* is displayed beside a pull-down menu or a pop-up menu when a user selects a routing choice labeled with the → symbol. A cascaded menu contains choices that modify or are related to the routing choice. Cascaded menus provide a way for a designer to layer choices so that a user can have access to a wide range of function without being confused by lengthy lists of choices.

Entry Fields: An *entry field* is an area into which a user can type or place text. Its boundaries are usually indicated. An entry field is appropriate for situations in which the entire possible set of values cannot be predicted. For example, if a product required a user's identification number, a designer typically would specify an entry field as the mechanism for eliciting that information, because the designer has no way to predict the numbers of all possible users.

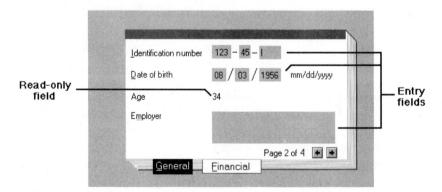

Figure 44. Entry Field. An entry field is an area into which a user can type information.

A variation of an entry field is a *read-only field.* A read-only field contains information that cannot be directly altered by a user. For example, a user cannot alter a read-only field by typing new information over the existing information in the field. However, if the value in a read-only field is calculated automatically according to the values in entry fields, a user could change the value in the read-only field by changing the values in the associated entry fields. For example, an **Age** field might be a read-only field containing a value calculated from an entry field that contains a birthdate. Although a user cannot change the value in the **Age** field by directly typing into the field, the user can change the value by changing the value in the **Date of Birth** entry field.

List Box: A *list box* usually consists of a read-only field and a scroll bar. It is used to display a fixed or variable list of objects or a fixed or variable list of settings choices. Because the display area can be scrolled, the list can contain more items than can be displayed at one time in the display area. The items in the list can be text or graphics, and a user typically can select an item from a list box.

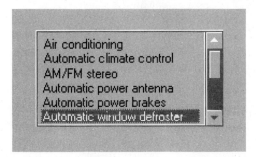

Figure 45. List Box. A list box displays text or graphics.

Combination Box: A *combination box* combines an entry field with a list box. A user can type information into the entry field or can fill the entry field by selecting one of the items from the list. A combination box is appropriate when a designer can predict possible values for the entry field and wants to serve the needs of both novice and experienced users. The list box portion of the control prompts novice users to select an appropriate value, while the entry field portion provides a quicker means of interaction for experienced users and allows users to type values not contained in the list.

Figure 46. Combination Box. A combination box combines an entry field with a list box.

Drop-Down List: If a situation calls for a list box, but a list box would crowd the window in which it is displayed, a designer can specify a *drop-down list* instead. A drop-down list is a variation of a list box in which only one item in the list is displayed until a user takes an action to display the rest of the list.

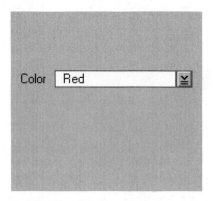
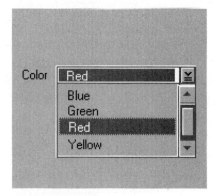

Figure 47. Drop-Down List. A drop-down list displays only one item in the list until a user takes an action to display the rest of the list.

Drop-Down Combination Box: If a situation calls for a combination box, but a combination box would crowd the window in which it is displayed, a designer can specify a *drop-down combination box* instead. A drop-down combination box is a variation of a combination box in which only the entry field portion is displayed until a user takes an action to display the list box portion of the control. When a user selects an item from the list, that item appears in the entry field.

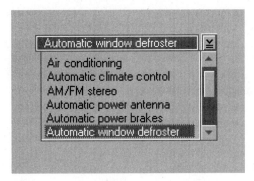

Figure 48. Drop-Down Combination Box. A drop-down combination box displays only an entry field until a user takes an action to display the list box portion of the control.

Spin Button: A *spin button* allows a user to choose a value from a finite set of related but mutually exclusive values that have a natural sequence. For example, a spin button would be appropriate for displaying the days of the week or the months of the year. A spin button is also appropriate for displaying choices that increase or decrease in constant units.

The values in a spin button are displayed as if they were arranged in a ring. When a user presses the up arrow (↑), the value displayed increases. When a user presses the down arrow (↓), the value displayed decreases.

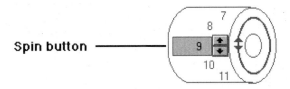

Figure 49. Spin Button. A spin button displays related but mutually exclusive choices that have a natural sequence or that increase or decrease in constant units. When a user presses the up arrow (↑), the value displayed increases. When a user presses the down arrow (↓), the value displayed decreases.

Push Button: A *push button* can be used to display an action choice or a routing choice. When a user selects a push button, the action or routing represented is carried out immediately. A push button is appropriate when a designer wants to give a user convenient access to a frequently used choice.

Figure 50. Push Button

A designer can replace the standard push button visual (shown in
Figure 50) with a product-specific visual if it clearly conveys the action
that the push button represents. For example, push buttons for a video
recorder object might resemble the buttons on a real video recorder.

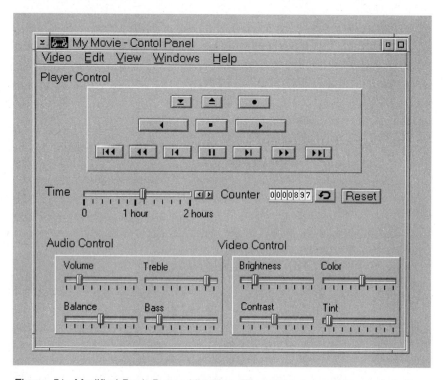

*Figure 51. Modified Push Button Visuals. The appearance of the push buttons
in this multimedia control panel has been modified so that the push buttons
resemble the buttons on a real control panel.*

The window sizing buttons that are part of a typical window are also
examples of push buttons with a modified appearance.

Radio Button: A *radio button* is so named because it operates like the buttons that used to be found on car radios: only one radio button can be selected at a time, and when a user selects a radio button, any previously selected radio button is inactivated.

Radio buttons are used to display mutually exclusive choices in situations in which a user must select a choice. Thus, a field of radio buttons always contains at least two radio buttons. Radio buttons prevent a user from selecting incompatible choices. For example, a product might contain the choices **On** and **Off** in a single context. Because it would not make sense for an object to be both on and off at the same time, a designer should specify radio buttons to display the mutually exclusive **On** and **Off** choices. Likewise, if a field of radio buttons pertained to a car's transmission, it would not make sense for a user to be able to select both an automatic transmission and a manual transmission for the same car. The radio buttons help prevent a user from making an error.

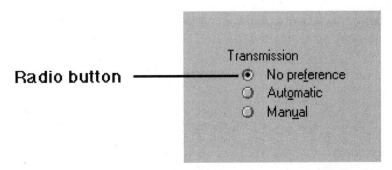

Figure 52. Radio Buttons. Radio buttons can be used to display mutually exclusive textual choices.

Value Set: Like radio buttons, a *value set* is used to present mutually exclusive choices. However, a value set is used primarily for graphical choices, and the choices are arranged in a matrix. Value sets are useful for creating palettes of tools.

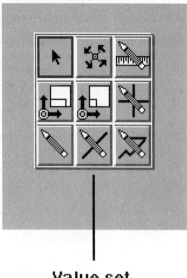

Value set

Figure 53. Value Set. A value set is a matrix of mutually exclusive choices. It is used primarily to display graphical choices.

Check Box: A *check box* is used to display a settings choice in a group of settings choices that are not mutually exclusive. Check boxes are appropriate for choices that have two clearly discernible states. For example, a check box would be appropriate for a choice that locked an object, because a user would easily understand that selecting the check box locks the object, and not selecting the check box leaves the object unlocked.

A field of check boxes can contain one or more choices, and a user can select one or more check boxes, or not select any.

Check box ———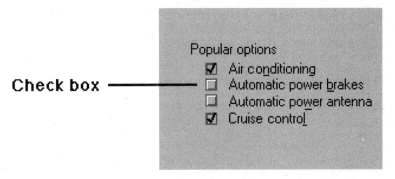

Figure 54. Check Boxes. Check boxes provide a way to display choices that are not mutually exclusive. For example, a car could have both air conditioning and power brakes. Each check box choice has two states, such as on or off. Users can easily understand that checking the air conditioning choice means that air conditioning is desired (on), while not checking automatic power antenna means that the antenna is not desired (off).

Slider: A *slider* is an analog representation of a value. When a slider is used to display a particular value amid a range of possible values, the slider typically shows a scale marked with equal units of value. For example, a designer might use a slider to indicate the volume level of an audio signal. The slider could indicate decibels.

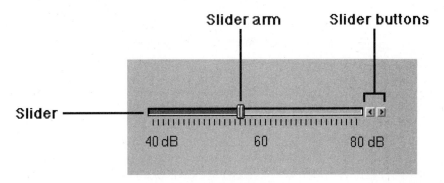

Figure 55. Slider. A slider can be used to display or manipulate specific values.

When a slider is used to display relative values with no corresponding quantitative value, the slider doesn't necessarily show a scale, but it does indicate what the relative extremes of the scale are. For example, a designer might use a slider to indicate an approximate temperature amid a range of acceptable temperatures. One end of the range could be labeled **Low** and the other end labeled **High.**

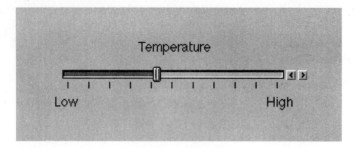

Figure 56. Slider. A slider can also be used to display or manipulate relative values.

Some sliders cannot be manipulated. For example, a read-only slider can be used as a progress indicator, but a user cannot alter the value represented by the slider.

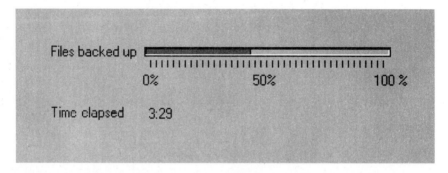

Figure 57. Read-Only Slider. A read-only slider can be used to display a value that a user cannot change directly. For example, a read-only slider can be used as a progress indicator.

Notebook: A *notebook* is used to display any kind of data that can be arranged in distinct groups that a user would find useful. Settings choices are typically displayed in a notebook because a notebook provides a convenient way for a user to change many settings at once. For example, a designer might place all of the settings for a document object into a notebook. Likewise, all of the settings for a printer object could be displayed in a notebook.

Objects and other kinds of choices can also be displayed in a notebook. For example, a product could provide a notebook to display a collection of graphic objects, such as clip art.

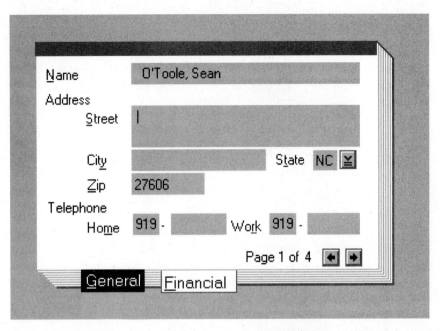

Figure 58. Notebook. A notebook is used to display objects or choices that can be arranged in logical groups that a user would find useful.

Selection

Through the process of *selection,* users indicate which items they want to work with. Users can select items by using a pointing device (typically a mouse) or keyboard. To select an item, a user moves the pointer or cursor to the item to be selected and then presses the appropriate mouse button or keyboard key. Most selection techniques that make use of a keyboard parallel those that make use of a mouse, although there are some exceptions.

During *explicit selection* users specifically indicate each item they want to work with. For example, users can move the pointer or selection cursor to each item. When a user explicitly selects an item, the item is highlighted with some kind of visible cue. When a user removes selection from an item, the visible cue is removed as well. The process of removing selection is called *deselection.* Because an item remains selected until a user deselects it, a user can apply more than one action to a selected item without having to select the item again before each action. A user can explicitly select more than one object at a time.

During *implicit selection* a user can gain access to an item's actions without explicitly selecting the item. For example, a user can display an object's pop-up menu by placing the pointer on the object and pressing the appropriate mouse button. The object is not selected, but its actions are available. Likewise, a user can move the cursor to an item and can get help information (see "Help" on page 91) about the item without explicitly selecting the item.

An implicitly selected item is not highlighted with a visible cue, and a user can implicitly select only one item at a time.

When a user selects an object, the object is not altered in any way, except that the object can become visibly highlighted to indicate that it is selected. A user can select and deselect an object any number of times without otherwise affecting the object. However, when a user selects an action, the action immediately affects whatever object or objects the user has selected. For example, if a user selects an action that updates an object's information, the information is changed immediately.

Scope of Selection

A *scope of selection* is an area within which a user can select items. For example, one scope of selection might consist of an individual control, such as a list box, while another might consist of a field of controls. Each window is also a separate scope of selection.

If a user selects something in a particular scope of selection, a previously selected item in that same scope can be affected, while items selected in other scopes of selection remain unaffected. For example, if a user selects an item in a secondary window, a previously selected item in that window can become deselected, while an item selected in a related primary window remains selected.

One-Based Selection and Zero-Based Selection

When a scope of selection requires that at least one item within the scope always be selected, that scope is said to have *one-based selection*. For example, if a list box contains the names of colors that can be applied to an interface component, a designer can make the list box a one-based scope of selection to ensure that a user selects a color.

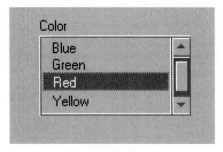

Figure 59. An Example of One-Based Selection. One-based selection means that at least one item must be selected. For example, in a list box containing colors that can be applied to an interface component, one color must be selected at all times.

When a scope of selection does not require that an item within the scope be selected, that scope is said to have *zero-based selection.* For example, a container object, such as a folder, can be zero-based if a user's task does not require that a contained object be selected at all times.

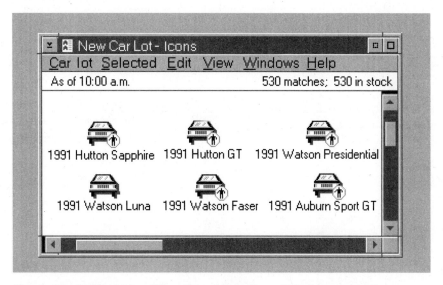

Figure 60. An Example of Zero-Based Selection. Zero-based selection means that an item does not necessarily have to be selected. For example, in this contents view of a container, no object is selected.

Types of Selection

CUA guidelines specify three types of selection:

- Single selection, which allows a user to select only one item at a time in a given scope of selection

- Multiple selection, which allows a user to select one or more items at a time in a given scope of selection

- Extended selection, which allows a user to select one item and then easily extend the selection to other items in the same scope of selection.

Each scope of selection uses one of the three types of selection. A designer decides which type to use by considering which result—only one item selected, more than one item selected, or usually one item but sometimes more than one item selected—a typical user will want during selection. The type of selection used is not affected by whether the scope of selection is zero-based or one-based.

Single Selection: *Single selection* is the process of selecting only one item at a time. When a user selects an item during single selection, any previously selected item in the same scope of selection becomes deselected. Single selection is appropriate for scopes of selection in which the Items displayed are mutually exclusive or in which a user typically wants to select only one item.

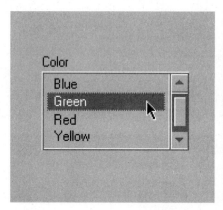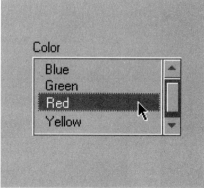

Figure 61. An Example of Single Selection. This list box has been defined as a single-selection scope of selection. When a user selects an item in the list box, any item that was previously selected becomes deselected.

Multiple Selection: *Multiple selection* is the process of selecting more than one item in a scope of selection. When a user selects an item during multiple selection, any previously selected items in the same scope of selection remain selected. Multiple selection is appropriate for scopes of selection in which items are not mutually exclusive in the context of a user's task.

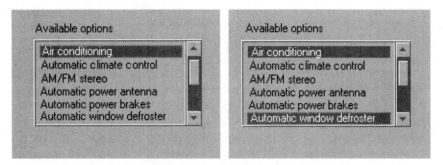

Figure 62. An Example of Multiple Selection. This list box has been defined as a multiple-selection scope of selection. When a user selects an item or items in the list box, any previously selected item or items remain selected.

Extended Selection: *Extended selection* is the process of selecting one item and then extending the selection to additional items. Extended selection is appropriate for scopes of selection in which a user typically wants to select only one item but occasionally wants to select more than one item.

To use extended selection in a scope in which single selection is the default, a user first selects one item. Then, to select additional items, the user explicitly indicates that the selection of the first item is to be extended to include the additional items. For example, a user might select an item then press a designated key on the keyboard, alone or in combination with a mouse button. When the user selects another item, the first item remains selected because the user has explicitly indicated (by pressing the designated key or button) that the initial selection is to be extended.

Extended selection accommodates the needs of inexperienced users, who tend to select only one item at a time, and it also accommodates the needs of experienced users, who tend to recognize that in some situations selecting more than one item is a more efficient way to work. Containers typically make use of extended selection. Figure 63 on page 76 illustrates extended selection.

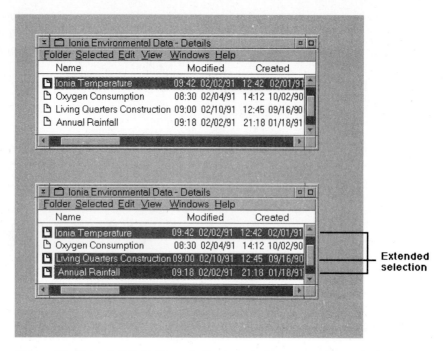

Figure 63. Extended Selection. In the top window, a user has selected one object. In the bottom window, the user has extended the selection of the first object to include additional objects.

Various scopes of selection use various types of selection. Figure 64 shows which types of selection can be used with windows and controls.

Figure 64. Types of Selection Used in Various Scopes of Selection

Scope of Selection	Type of Selection		
	Single Selection	Multiple Selection	Extended Selection
Window	•	•	•
Menu	•		
List Box	•	•	
Combination Box	•		
Drop-Down List	•		
Drop-Down Combination Box	•		
Spin Button	•		
Push Button	•		
Field of Radio Buttons	•		
Value Set	•		
Individual Check Box	•		
Field of Check Boxes		•	

Selection Techniques

In a CUA environment a user can select items in two ways. A user can:

- Select an individual item
- Select a beginning point and an endpoint, between which all items are selected.

The selection techniques for selecting an individual item are:

- Point selection
- Random-point selection.

The selection technique for selecting items between two points is called point-to-endpoint selection.

To determine which selection techniques are most useful to a user for a particular task, a designer should consider the type of data being selected and the form in which it is displayed.

Point Selection: During point selection, a user places the pointer or cursor on an individual item and selects it. Point selection can be used for single selection, multiple selection, or extended selection.

Automatic selection is a variation of point selection in which the steps of indicating an item and selecting the item are combined for keyboard users.

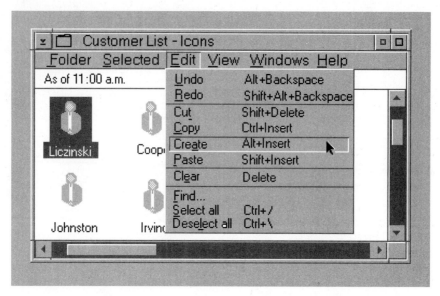

Figure 65. Automatic Selection. Automatic selection is a variation of point selection in which a keyboard user indicates and selects an item in one step.

Random-Point Selection: During random-point selection, a user places the pointer or cursor on an item and selects it. The user then moves the pointer or cursor to another item and selects it. The items do not have to be next to one another, and the user can select the items in any order. Each item becomes selected in succession. Random-point selection can be used for multiple or extended selection.

Point-to-Endpoint Selection: During point-to-endpoint selection, a user places the pointer or cursor at a beginning point, then moves the pointer or cursor to an endpoint. Each item between the beginning point and endpoint becomes selected. Point-to-endpoint selection can be used for multiple or extended selection.

Design Considerations for Selection

When deciding how selection should work in a product, a designer must make a series of decisions. The decisions are shown in Figure 66 on page 79.

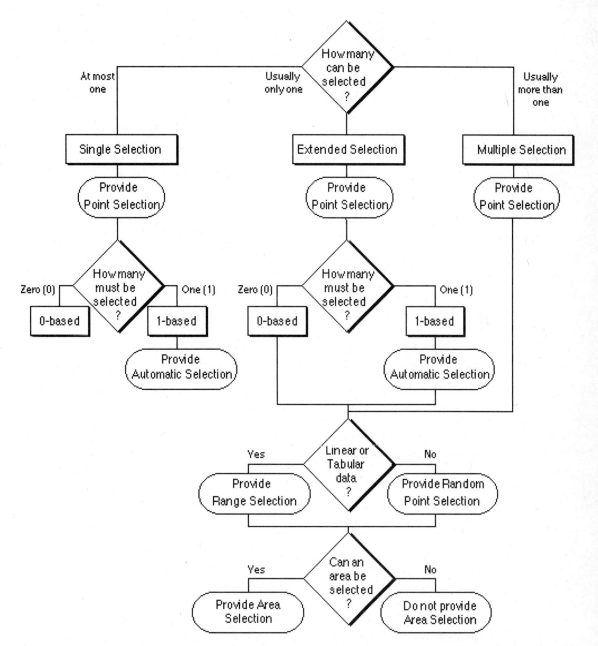

Figure 66. Decisions for Selection. A designer must first consider a user's objects and tasks to determine how many objects the user should be allowed to select at one time within a scope of selection. Next a designer must consider the minimum number of items that must be selected. Then, by evaluating the type of data being presented, the form in which it is presented, and the types of tasks the user will be trying to accomplish, the designer can determine which selection techniques to provide.

For each scope of selection, a designer must consider a user's objects and tasks to determine how many objects a user will want to select in that scope of selection. The designer also must consider whether a user *must* select at least one object in that scope. If so, the scope of selection is one-based. If not, the scope of selection is zero-based. If a user will want to select only one object at a time, then the designer provides single selection for that scope. If the user will want to select more than one object at a time, then the designer provides multiple selection for that scope. If the user will typically want to select only one object but might occasionally want to select more than one object, then the designer provides extended selection for that scope.

For single selection, a designer must provide point selection and should consider whether to provide automatic selection in addition to point selection. For multiple selection, a designer must provide point selection and either point-to-endpoint selection or random-point selection (or both).

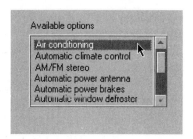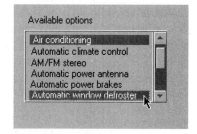

Figure 67. Random-point Selection. During random-point selection a user selects several items in any order. The items do not have to be contiguous.

For extended selection, a designer must provide point selection and can provide point-to-endpoint selection or random-point selection or both.

Areas and Ranges: When a user selects an item or items by using point-to-endpoint selection, the result is either a selected area or a selected range. An area is determined by the spatial arrangement of the selected items, while a range is determined by the meaning or sequence of the objects. For example, in a text document, an area of selection could be delimited by a rectangle defined by a user. A range of selection could be an irregular shape with a beginning point and an endpoint defined by a user, but with the intermediate points determined by the product. Figure 68 on page 81 shows the difference between an area of selection and a range of selection in text.

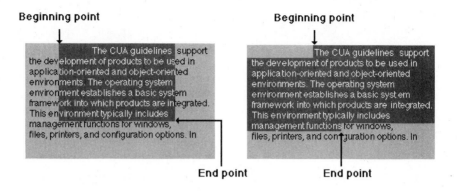

Beginning point

Beginning point

End point

End point

Area selection

Range selection

Figure 68. Area Selection and Range Selection in Text. In an area of selection, the boundary of the selected text is regular and is based on the spatial area indicated by a user. All items within the area (in this case, a rectangle defined by a beginning point and an endpoint) are selected. In a range of selection, the boundary of the selected text can be irregular. A user defines the beginning point and the endpoint, and the product determines which intermediate points are selected. For some kinds of tasks, a designer might want to provide both area selection and range selection.

To determine whether the result of point-to-endpoint selection should be an area or a range, a designer must consider the characteristics of the data displayed in the view of the object. A designer must also consider a user's tasks. If the data has linear or tabular characteristics (for example, text, audio waveforms, musical scores, forms, spreadsheets), a user will typically want a range of selection, but for some tasks a user might want an area of selection. For some kinds of data and tasks, a designer might want to provide both area selection and range selection.

Beginning point

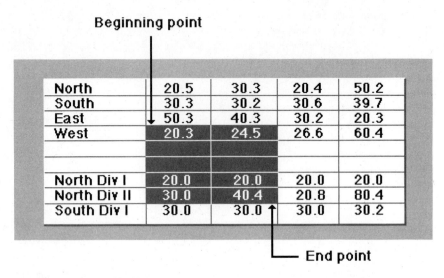

North	20.5	30.3	20.4	50.2
South	30.3	30.2	30.6	39.7
East	50.3	40.3	30.2	20.3
West	20.3	24.5	26.6	60.4
North Div I	20.0	20.0	20.0	20.0
North Div II	30.0	40.4	20.8	80.4
South Div I	30.0	30.0	30.0	30.2

End point

Figure 69. Range Selection in Tabular Data. For tabular data, a designer typically provides range selection. For example, in a spreadsheet, a user can define a beginning point anywhere in a cell, then can define an endpoint anywhere in another cell. The two cells, in their entirety, form opposite corners of the range of selection, and all other cells in the columns and rows between the corners are also selected.

Copying and Creating Objects

A user can copy or create objects from existing objects. When a user copies an object, the resulting new object is an exact duplicate of the original object. The new object can even have the same name as the original object, or the user can change the object's name. When a user creates an object, the resulting new object is similar but not identical to the original object, and it has a new name. The original object is, in effect, a template for the new object. A designer can provide designated objects that act as templates for creating new objects. The designated objects have special visual representations. Figure 70 on page 83 shows a template of a folder.

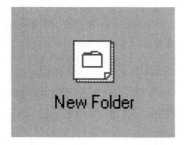

Figure 70. A Folder Template. A user can create a new folder by using direct or indirect manipulation on an existing object.

For example, if a user copies a text document, say an invoice, the new invoice will contain all of the text, settings, and other elements of the original invoice and will have the same invoice number. However, if a user creates a new invoice from an existing invoice, the new invoice will contain some—but not all—of the information in the original invoice. The newly created invoice might contain the same company name, mailing address, and entry fields as in the original invoice, but the invoice date and invoice number would be different, and the customer name and other entry fields would not contain the same information as the original.

A designer decides how much information is transferred from one object to another during object creation and bases the decision on the objects and tasks involved. In the invoice example above, a relatively small amount of information is transferred to the newly created invoice. For some objects and tasks, however, nearly all of the information might be transferred. For example, an attorney might work with a set of document objects containing boilerplate text. When the attorney creates a new object, all of the text, except for a client's name, date, and other particulars, is transferred to the new object.

A user can copy and create objects by both direct and indirect manipulation.

The Clipboard

When using indirect manipulation to copy or create objects, a user uses the *clipboard*. The clipboard is an area of storage provided by the operating system to hold data temporarily. A user can copy, create, and move objects to and from the clipboard. The objects are held on the clipboard until the user replaces them with other objects or until the user turns off the system.

The clipboard can hold entire objects or parts of objects, and it can hold any kind of object. For example, the clipboard can hold a single line of text or an entire document object, a single data record or an entire database, a single line segment or an entire graphic. Except when necessary to prevent the corruption of data, a designer should not restrict a user from placing any objects or parts of objects onto the clipboard.

Keeping a User Informed

For a user to be in control of his or her interaction with a product, the user must be aware of the state of objects, processes, or other elements of the interaction. The CUA user interface provides several ways for a product to communicate this kind of information to a user.

Messages

A *message* provides the most detailed kind of information to a user and is appropriate when the information is particularly important or urgent. Message windows often contain not only a description of a problem but also an explanation of how to correct the situation. They also contain push buttons that help a user decide how to continue working. Some message windows contain more elaborate groups of controls that allow a user to make more extensive corrections right in the message window.

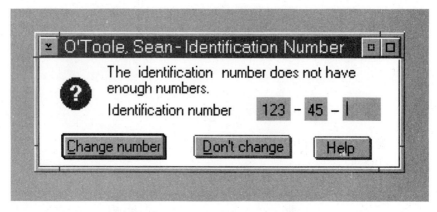

Figure 71. Message. A message describes a situation and can contain controls that help a user decide which action to take.

Progress Indicators

To provide feedback to a user during longer (typically five seconds or more) processes, a designer can use a *progress indicator.* A progress indicator is a visible cue that indicates progress toward the completion of a process, for example copying or sorting a group of objects. A progress indicator can indicate a specific amount of time. For example, a progress indicator could consist of a digital clock that displays the time remaining in a process. A progress indicator can also indicate a relative amount of time. For example, a progress indicator could consist of a slider that fills gradually as the process continues. When the process is complete, the slider is completely filled. A progress indicator can appear in its own window or in the window of the object that is undergoing the process.

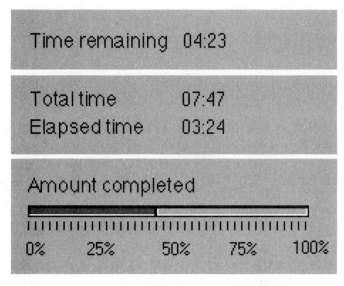

Figure 72. Progress Indicators. Progress indicators can take several forms. The top progress indicator indicates the time remaining in a process. The one in the center indicates both the total time a process will take and the time elapsed so far. The one on the bottom indicates the amount of the task completed in relation to the amount of the task yet to be completed.

Information Areas

An *information area* is a small area, usually at the bottom of a window, used to display a brief explanation or description of the state of an object. It can also be used to display brief help information or information about the completion of a process. Information areas are less disruptive than messages and are appropriate for information that is not urgent.

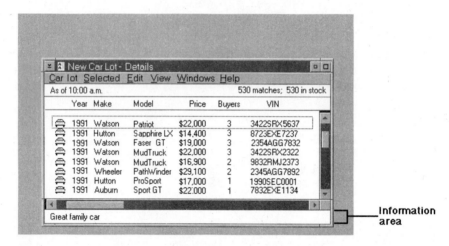

Figure 73. Information Area. An information area can be used to display a brief explanation or description of the state of an object.

Status Areas

A *status area* differs from an information area in that it displays information about the view of an object rather than about the object itself. For example, a status area could display a count of the number of objects in a container displayed in a view, or it could indicate whether the information displayed in the view has been sorted or filtered. A status area typically appears at the top of a window, below the menu bar.

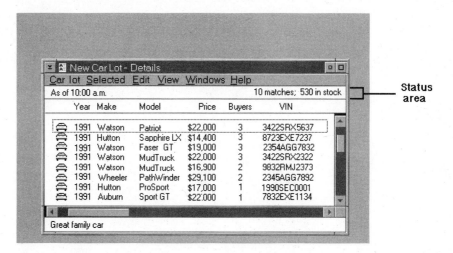

Figure 74. Status Area. A status area displays information about the view of an object. This status area indicates that this details view of a container object has been filtered according to some criteria specified by a user. Ten cars match the criteria.

Emphasis

Emphasis is a visible cue that distinguishes one object or group of objects from another and conveys information to a user. Emphasis is typically used to indicate that an object or group of objects is:

- Selected
- The source of a direct manipulation operation
- The target of a direct manipulation operation
- In use
- Unavailable.

Emphasis can be used to display other kinds of information appropriate for a specific product.

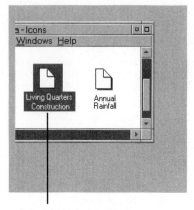
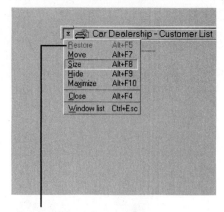

Selected-state emphasis   Unavailable-state emphasis

Figure 75. Emphasis. Emphasis is visible highlighting that conveys information to a user. The icon on the left has emphasis indicating that it has been selected. The emphasis on the first choice in the pull-down menu indicates that the choice is unavailable.

Exception Handling

An *exception* is any event or situation that prevents or has the potential to prevent a user's action from being completed in the manner the user expects. Exceptions occur when a product is unable to interpret a user's action.

Thoughtful application design can often prevent exceptions. For example, if a designer specifies a way to indicate to a user that a choice is unavailable, the user is less likely to try to select that choice. However, because a designer cannot predict every possible action a user might attempt, a product should include provisions for notifying users about exceptions and should provide ways to help users recover from them.

Users typically do not expect an exception to occur, although experienced users can learn to recognize situations that lead to an exception. For example, a user might habitually attempt to close an object without first saving any changes made to the object. Each time the user attempts to close an object, a typical product would notify the user that the object has been changed and that the changes are about to be discarded. Eventually the user would come to expect the exception.

When an exception occurs, a product needs to tell a user at least three things:

- How severe the situation is
- How soon the user must respond
- What actions the user can take to correct the situation.

Because most users do not expect most exceptions, a designer should take care to choose a notification method that will inform a user without alarming the user. There are many methods for conveying this information to a user. A designer should choose methods appropriate for the users' tasks and work environment, and a designer should apply the methods consistently throughout a product. In addition, the designer should make sure that the notification methods complement the help (see "Help" on page 91) provided by the product so that a user can completely understand the exception and how to respond to it.

Typical methods for notifying a user about an exception include:

- Audible cues
- Visible cues
- Textual cues.

Each is discussed in the following sections.

Audible Cues

An *audible cue* is a sound generated by a user's computer to draw a user's attention. A beep is an example of a simple audible cue. If a product will be used with computer hardware that has advanced audio capabilities, a designer can be imaginative in specifying more elaborate audible cues, such as speech synthesis, for example.

Visible Cues

A *visible cue* is a change in the appearance of a product's components. For example, if a user places an inappropriate type of information in an entry field, the color of the entry field could change to alert the user that the information falls outside the range of acceptable values for that entry field.

Figure 76. Visible Cue. A visible cue can be used to indicate to a user that different information is required.

If an object other than the object a user is working with requires some attention from the user before an exception can be resolved, the appearance of the object's icon could change. For example, if a printer has run out of paper, the icon that represents the printer could change.

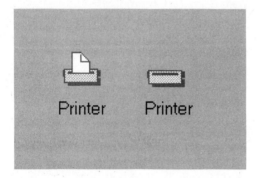

Figure 77. Visible Cue. A visible cue can be used to indicate to a user that an item in an interface needs attention from the user.

Textual Cues

When a user needs more information than can be conveyed with an audible cue or visual cue, a designer can use a textual cue. A textual cue consists of a word or words describing the exception. A textual cue can be displayed in a message window.

Examples of Exceptions and Their Corresponding Notifications

The following examples illustrate notification methods for alerting a user to a problem.

1. A user types an inappropriate value into an entry field.

   A product could do one or more of the following:

   • Generate an audible cue.

- Change the color of the background of the entry field containing the error.

- Display a message window that describes the error, explains how to correct the error, and provides controls that allow the user to correct the error from within the message window (for example, the message window could contain an entry field into which the user could type an appropriate value).

After the user supplies an appropriate value, the background color of the entry field would change back to its usual color, and the message window would close.

2. A printer runs out of paper, and the user has not opened a window for the printer object.

A product could do one or more of the following:

- Change the appearance of the printer's icon to indicate that the printer needs attention.

- Generate an audible cue.

- Display a message window as soon as the user opens a window for the printer object. The message window would describe the situation and would contain a push button that allows the user to close the message window.

After the user supplies the printer with paper, the printer's icon would change back to its normal appearance.

Help

A product should provide information to a user about how to use the product and how to recover from exceptions. Information about how to use a product is known as help information. Ideally, a product's help facilities should work together with its methods and mechanisms for exception handling to provide a user with all of the information needed to solve any problem the user might encounter.

Help information describes a product's choices, objects, and interaction techniques. Help information can help a user learn to use a product and can serve as a refresher when a user has not used a product regularly or recently.

Products designed for a CUA environment should provide several kinds of help:

- Information about the contents of a window and the tasks a user can perform in the window

- Information about any selected item, including the item's purpose and ways to interact with the item

- Information about the key assignments on the keyboard

- An index of all of the topics for which help is available

- Information about using the help facility.

Chapter 5. The CUA Designer's Model—A Summary

When combined, the classes of objects described in Chapter 1 (see "Object Classes" on page 5), the design principles described in Chapter 3, and the components of the CUA interface described in Chapter 4 form a designer's model of the CUA user interface. The following sections present a summary of how these parts are related in the CUA user interface.

The CUA designer's model contains all of the fundamental concepts, components, and relationships in a CUA environment. A designer can use the CUA designer's model as a foundation for developing products that are user-oriented. Elements of the CUA designer's model can be reused and extended to create a user interface appropriate for the intended users' tasks. Figure 78 on page 94 illustrates the CUA designer's model, including the interrelatedness of the components of the CUA user interface.

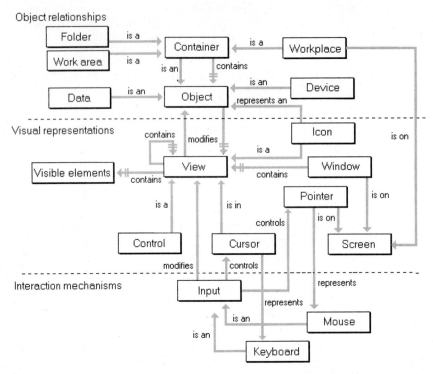

Figure 78. Designer's Model of the CUA Interface. Each arrow represents a relationship between two of the boxed items on the chart. Characteristics of the relationship are indicated by the direction of the arrow and by the text beside each arrow. For example, the arrow that points from Container to Object means that a container is an object. Double bars indicate a one-to-many relationship. For example, one container object can contain many other objects.

The three sections of the figure—object relationships, visual representations, and interaction mechanisms—correspond to the three layers of the iceberg model of interface design (see Figure 8 on page 16).

The figures in the following sections highlight and elaborate on some of the relationships in the CUA user interface.

CUA Class Hierarchy

In the CUA environment, container objects, data objects, and device objects inherit the attributes common to all objects. The workplace, folders, and product-specific containers inherit the attributes common to all containers.

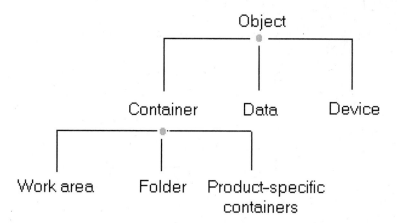

Figure 79. Class Hierarchy in the CUA User Interface. Each object that appears below another object in this hierarchy inherits characteristics of the objects above it.

CUA Containment

Most objects in the CUA user interface contain other objects. The workplace fills a user's display screen and contains all of the objects a user works with, including components of the CUA interface. Figure 80 on page 96 shows the basic containment relationships of components of the CUA interface.

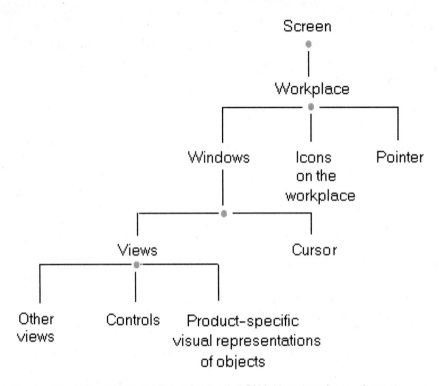

Figure 80. A Containment Hierarchy for the CUA User Interface. A user's screen contains the workplace, which contains windows, icons, and the pointer. Windows contain views and the cursor. Views contain other views, controls, and product-specific visual representations of objects.

CUA Visual Representations

The elements of a user's computer system are represented visually in the CUA interface. Figure 81 shows how the elements are represented.

Figure 81. Visual Representations in the CUA User Interface

This element...	Has this visual representation.
Screen	Workplace
Object	Icon and views
Mouse	Pointer
Keyboard	Cursor

CUA Views

The views available for representing objects are shown in Figure 82. For a more detailed discussion of views, see "Views" on page 45.

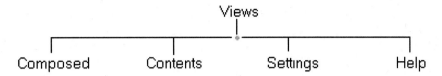

Figure 82. Views Available for Representing Objects in the CUA User Interface. The CUA interface provides four basic types of views.

CUA Interaction Mechanisms

Interaction in the CUA user interface consists of input and feedback. Figure 83 shows the elements of interaction in the CUA user interface.

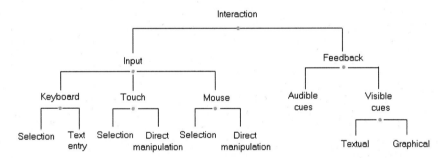

Figure 83. Interaction Mechanisms in the CUA User Interface. Interaction consists of input and feedback. Input can be by way of a mouse, keyboard, or touch. Feedback consists of audible cues and visible cues. Visible cues can be textual or graphical.

A user's input modifies a view, which can modify the object represented in the view.

Chapter 6. Designing a Product with a CUA User Interface

To illustrate one approach to the process of designing a product with a CUA user interface, we designed a sample product, and we documented our steps. This chapter describes those steps. Designers can follow these steps or can adapt this process to suit their needs.

We designed a product that could be used for selling new cars at a car dealership. Our design is a partial design only, intended to highlight the main design considerations and the processes a designer can follow when developing a user interface. A full-fledged product design would contain much more detail.

The product is an example only, and it is not intended to represent the practices of a particular car dealership, nor is it intended to represent the ideal product for all car dealerships. Likewise, our process is an example only. This process worked for us, but a different process might work equally well for a different group of designers.

Overview of the Development Process

The basic steps in our development process were:

- Researching and planning
- Designing
- Prototyping
- Testing.

Each of these steps entails one or more subprocesses of its own, and we went through each step for each part our product's interface. When we tested each part of our product, we compared the results with the objectives we set during the planning stage. If the results met our customer's requirements and our requirements, we proceeded to design the next part of the interface. If not, we changed the design and tested the product again. This process is known as an iterative development process. Figure 84 on page 100 illustrates the iterative development process.

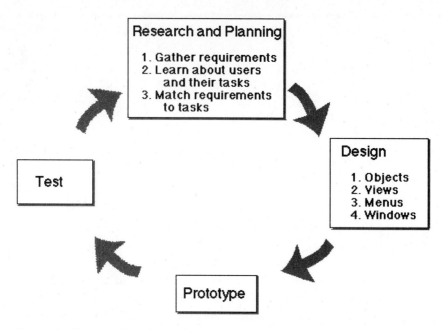

Figure 84. Iterative Development Process. For each part of our product's interface, we developed a prototype and tested the prototype. When the test results satisfied us, we moved on to the next part of the interface.

During each iteration of the development process, we kept in mind the design principles discussed in Chapter 3, "Goals and Design Principles of the CUA User Interface" on page 23. That is, we looked for ways to:

- Provide immediate feedback for each action
- Reduce the number of steps required to accomplish a task
- Provide full function with a small number of objects
- Increase a user's control over the product
- Reduce the potential for exceptions
- Reduce the effect of exceptions
- Allow a user to use either the keyboard or the mouse to accomplish a task
- Provide interaction techniques suited to the needs of novice users and expert users.

Finally we arrived at a satisfactory design.

The rest of this chapter describes the processes we used in researching, planning, and designing our product. Although prototyping and testing also have their own processes, a detailed discussion of prototyping and testing is beyond the scope of this book. However, we will say that we tested our product for consistent behavior and for compatibility with a user's expectations. We also sought feedback from test subjects about whether the product was pleasing to use.

Researching and Planning the Product

First we recognized that we were serving two distinct audiences: the people who buy a product (our customers) and the people who use a product (our users). Sometimes the two audiences overlap, but in this case, our customers were the upper management staff of a car dealership, while the users were primarily the sales staff and lower management staff.

To begin our iterative development process we had to:

- Gather requirements from upper management
- Learn about the users and their tasks
- Match management's requirements to the users' tasks.

Step 1. Gathering Requirements from Management

By interviewing the owner and general manager, we learned that they wanted to:

- Eliminate paperwork
- Reduce errors in locating cars and information about cars
- Increase the amount of time salespeople spend talking with customers by reducing the amount of time the salespeople spend tracking down information and getting approval of sales
- Sell more cars.

The information from management was result-oriented—that is, the managers did not tell us the details about how they sell cars, nor did they tell us how they expected us to design a product. Instead, they gave us high-level information about what they hoped to gain by using our product.

Step 2. Learning about Users and Their Tasks

To serve the needs of the users of our product, we had to gather information about the users. We interviewed a salesperson with extensive experience at car dealerships. He helped us compile a profile of car salespeople, the primary users of our product.

In particular, we were interested in salespeople's:

- Experience
  - How much experience do they have doing their job?
  - How much experience do they have using computers?

- How much experience do they have using similar user interfaces?
- Capabilities
  - With what styles do they approach their work?
  - How do they learn new systems?
- Motivations
  - How will the new product affect their work routine?
  - How will the new product affect their productivity?
- Desires
  - How would they like to use the product?
  - What kinds of features would they like to see in the product?

We found out that salespeople:

- Are not experienced in using computers
- Are not interested in programming computers
- Vary in their ability and interest in learning new procedures
- Use varied techniques to sell cars
- Are competitive
- Are knowledgeable about the products they sell
- Want to be able to communicate with their customers while they use the product.

After analyzing the characteristics of our product's intended users, we realized that our product's interface must:

- Be easy to learn

- Be flexible enough to serve users with different approaches to both learning and sales

- Contain elements resembling those already used in a salesperson's job

- Contain terms that are familiar to a salesperson

- Be sophisticated enough to withstand scrutiny of people who are knowledgeable about their field

- Be appropriate to be seen by a customer.

We also needed to learn about the tasks the users perform in their jobs. With the help of our expert salesperson, we drew an organization chart for a typical car dealership. The organization is shown in Figure 85 on page 103.

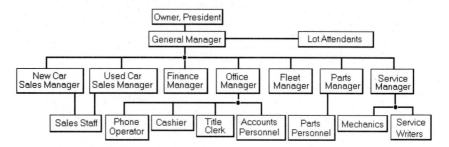

Figure 85. Typical Automobile Dealership Organization

We compiled a list of the dealership's personnel and of the main tasks that each person performs. Figure 86 shows the list of tasks.

Figure 86 (Page 1 of 2). Users and Tasks in a Car Dealership	
Users and Tasks	**Users and Tasks**
Owner, President • Meets with manufacturer's representatives • Manages dealership personnel • Studies market trends and forecasts • Examines accounting reports.	General Manager • Hires dealership personnel • Sets guidelines for profit margins • Determines pack fees (fees added to dealer invoice) • Sets labor costs for service.
New Car Sales Manager • Orders new cars and trucks • Reviews statistics of vehicles sold • Hires and manages salespeople • Approves sales.	Used Car Sales Manager • Reviews the National Automobile Dealers Association (NADA) values for comparable cars • Sets prices for used cars • Determines condition and value of trade-ins.
Salesperson • Sells cars and trucks • Maintains preferred customer lists • Reads used car sheets ("cards") • Writes follow-up letters.	Finance Manager • Prints sales contracts • Finds financing for customers • Manages manufacturer's financing programs • Sells extended warranties, debt insurance, and roadside services.

Figure 86 (Page 2 of 2). Users and Tasks in a Car Dealership

Users and Tasks	Users and Tasks
Office Manager • Manages office personnel • Handles titles and transfers, registration, loan payoffs with banks • Submits paperwork required by law • Works with the dealership's lawyer.	Fleet Manager • Orders fleets of cars and trucks for customers • Negotiates with purchasing agents at customers' businesses • Keeps track of customers' business inventories (quantity, age) • Estimates life span of customers' fleets.
Parts Manager • Orders parts and sets prices for parts • Manages parts counter • Updates parts inventory • Compares parts to service order.	Parts Personnel • Selects parts from shelves • Unpacks boxes of new parts and stocks shelves • Updates parts inventory • Compares parts to service order.
Service Manager • Sells service • Runs service specials • Trains mechanics • Handles service orders • Gives cost estimates for parts and labor.	Service Writer • Sells service • Writes a service order • Determines warranty work.
Mechanic • Fixes cars • Records time and parts used • Reads service bulletins and service manuals.	Lot Attendant • Matches manufacturer's invoice to dealer's invoice and adds dealer's invoice to window • Installs after-market options (stereos, pinstriping) • Prepares new and used cars (washes cars, removes plastic, installs hubcaps, checks tire pressure).

Because our sample product will be used during the process of selling cars, we looked at a salesperson's tasks in more detail.

In a typical sales transaction, a customer enters a showroom and inquires about a car or several cars. The salesperson in turn asks the customer what features and price range the customer is looking for. Using the information the customer provides, the salesperson gathers information about the dealership's cars that match the customer's requirements. The salesperson then presents the information to the customer.

If a car appeals to the customer, the customer takes the car for a test drive. If the customer still is interested in the car after the test drive, the salesperson and customer negotiate about the financial arrangements. They use a worksheet to record the details of the proposed purchase. Once they come to an agreement, the salesperson takes the worksheet with the agreed-to figures to the sales manager for approval. If the sales manager approves the sale, the salesperson passes the worksheet along to the finance manager. Figure 87 lists the tasks of the salesperson, the sales manager, and the finance manager.

Figure 87. Tasks Involved in Selling a Car	
Users	**Tasks**
Salesperson	• Finds out what the customer wants, needs, and can afford
	• Finds out what products the car dealership can provide that most closely match the customer's wants, needs, and budget.
	• Fills out a worksheet that lists the:

	− Make and model of car
	    − Price of the car
	    − Trade-in value of the customer's old car (if applicable)
	    − Down payment amount (if applicable).

	• Gets the sales manager's approval.
	• Gives the worksheet information to the finance manager.
Sales Manager	• Reviews worksheet and authorizes sales after considering:

	− Agreed-to price
	    − Trade-in value
	    − Options.

Finance Manager	• Arranges financing for customer • Completes the sale.

Step 3. Matching Management's Requirements to the Users' Tasks

After gathering requirements from management and analyzing the users' tasks, we had to match the requirements and the tasks. We realized that our product's interface had to provide:

• A way to record information about a customer (thus meeting the requirement to eliminate paperwork)

• Quick access to information about the dealership's stock of cars (thus meeting the requirements to reduce errors and to reduce time spent tracking down information)

- A way to combine customer information with dealership information (thus meeting the requirement to eliminate paperwork)

- A way to quickly transfer information among users—salespeople, sales manager, finance manager—without leaving the customer unattended (thus meeting the requirements to reduce paperwork and increase contact time).

Designing the Product

After we completed our research and planning, we began designing the product. First we designed our intended users' model; that is, we took the information we had learned about salespeople and used it to create a model that describes the way the salespeople would understand how the product works. Then we defined the objects, their relationships, and their behaviors, and we decided what kinds of views were needed to allow the salespeople to work with the objects. Then we designed the menus and choices for the objects, and finally, we designed the windows that contained the views and controls through which the salespeople could work with the objects.

Step 1. Defining the Objects

Our analysis of a salesperson's tasks gave us the base of information we needed to start defining objects for our product. At this stage of design, we were interested in what objects a user needs, how the objects are related, and how the objects behave.

Determining What Kinds of Objects Are Needed

To decide what objects a salesperson needed, we looked at the real-world objects a salesperson used to sell a car. We wrote a description of a salesperson's tasks and underlined all the nouns:

- Find out the customer's wants, needs, and budget.

- Find out what the car dealership has in stock that most closely matches the customer's wants, needs, and budget.

- Arrive at an agreement using a worksheet.

- Get approval from the sales manager.

- Give the worksheet information to the finance manager.

After underlining the nouns, we made a list of them:

- Salesperson
- Customer
- Wants
- Needs
- Budget
- Agreement
- Worksheet
- Car
- Dealership
- Stock
- Sales manager
- Finance manager.

To create our final list of objects, we edited the list of nouns to eliminate duplication and to combine those concepts that seemed to fit together. We ended up with this list of objects:

- Car
- Car lot (the entire collection of individual cars available for sale)
- Customer (including the customer's wants, needs, and budget)
- Customer list (the entire collection of individual customers)
- Worksheet (the commonly used term for the agreement)
- Worksheet list (the entire collection of individual worksheets)
- Salesperson
- Sales manager
- Finance manager.

These objects are described in the following sections.

Car Object: Each car object represents a real car for sale in the car lot. A car object contains descriptive information about the corresponding real car, such as its year, make, model, price, factory-installed options, color, and vehicle identification number (VIN). Because the primary purpose of a car object is to convey information, the car object is a data object.

Car Lot Object: The car lot object represents the physical lot where the dealership's cars are parked. Because the primary purpose of a car lot object is to hold car objects, the car lot object is a container object. A typical dealership sells new cars and used cars. The two kinds of cars are often parked in different lots. To make our product seem more familiar to users, we provided two car lot objects: a new car lot and a used car lot. Our sample product uses only the new car lot, but a fully developed product for a dealership would use both car lot objects.

Customer Object: Each customer object represents a real customer who has inquired about a car. A customer object contains descriptive information about the corresponding real customer, such as the customer's name, address, telephone number, and identification number. Because the primary purpose of a customer object is to convey information, the customer object is a data object.

Customer List Object: The customer list object contains all of the customer objects, much as the car lot object contains all of the car objects. It is a container object.

Worksheet Object: A worksheet object contains information about the customer and the car to be purchased, along with other information, such as the financial arrangements of the purchase. A worksheet object is a data object.

Worksheet List Object: A worksheet list object contains all of the worksheet objects, just as the customer list object contains all of the customer objects. It is a container object.

Salesperson Object: Each salesperson object represents one of the dealership's salespeople. A salesperson object contains descriptive information about the corresponding real salesperson, such as the salesperson's name, address, sales record, commissions, and bonuses. It is a data object. Because our sample transactions take place from the salesperson's perspective, we did not need to use the salesperson object. However, in a fully designed product for a real car dealership, a salesperson object might be used for payroll or personnel tasks.

Sales Manager Object and Finance Manager Object: At first we considered creating the sales manager and the finance manager objects so that they were like the customer and salesperson objects—that is, they would contain descriptive information about each person. However, to sell a car, a salesperson does not require descriptive information about either manager. From a salesperson's perspective, a sales manager and a finance manager receive and distribute information. Because the users of our sample product are salespeople, we decided to emphasize the passing of information by representing the finance manager and the sales manager as specially tailored out-baskets for electronic mail. They are device objects that automatically send their contents to the corresponding individual.

Figure 88 on page 110 shows our preliminary drawing of these objects.

Figure 88. Hand Drawing of Users' Objects. *The drawing indicates how the objects might appear on a salesperson's screen. We later realized that the sales manager object and the finance manager object could be represented differently, in a way that more accurately conveyed the nature of a salesperson's transactions with the real managers.*

Determining the Relationships and Behaviors of the Objects

Once we had determined which objects we needed, we had to determine how each object interacted with the other objects.

We drew a diagram to show the relationships among the objects.

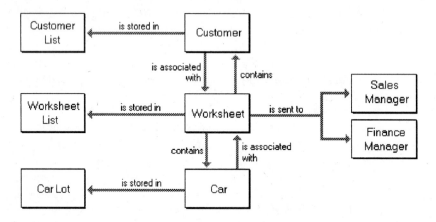

Figure 89. Relationships among the Car Dealership Objects

Then we considered the flow of information among the objects. To complete a worksheet, a salesperson combines information from a car object and a customer object. While we did not want to prevent a salesperson from typing or re-typing all of the information contained in those objects, we knew that typing is slow and can lead to errors. We knew we could provide a quicker and more accurate way to transfer the information by allowing a salesperson to manipulate the information directly—that is, by dragging the customer and car objects to the worksheet objects—or indirectly, by using action choices that allow the salesperson to copy information from one object and place it into another.

Once a worksheet is complete, a salesperson must get approval from the sales manager and then must send the worksheet to the finance manager to close the sale. One solution might have been to allow the salesperson to print a copy of the worksheet and carry it in person to the managers. However, one of the requirements we received from the dealership's upper management was to eliminate paperwork, so we decided that electronic mail offered the most efficient paperless solution. Also, by sending the worksheet electronically, the salesperson can stay in contact with the customer instead of leaving the customer alone while the salesperson locates the appropriate manager.

We had to decide what the results of direct manipulation would be for various combinations of source objects and target objects. In particular, we were interested in whether data should transfer from one object to another when a salesperson drags a source object to a target object. Based on the relationships we defined, we created the following table to illustrate the default results of direct manipulation of pairs of objects.

Figure 90 (Page 1 of 2). Default Results for Direct Manipulation. For certain pairs of objects, data is transferred from one object to the other when a salesperson drags it and drops it on the other.

Source Object	Target Object							
	Customer	Customer List	Car	Car Lot	Worksheet	Worksheet List	Finance Manager Out-Basket	Sales Manager Out-Basket
Customer	No data transfer	Customer is moved into customer list	No data transfer	No data transfer	Customer data is copied into worksheet	No data transfer	Customer data is copied and sent to finance manager	Customer data is copied and sent to sales manager
Customer List	No data transfer	No data transfer	No data transfer	No data transfer	No data transfer	No data transfer	No data transfer	No data transfer
Car	No data transfer	No data transfer	No data transfer	Car is moved into car lot	Car data is copied into worksheet	No data transfer	No data transfer	No data transfer
Car Lot	No data transfer	No data transfer	No data transfer	No data transfer	No data transfer	No data transfer	No data transfer	No data transfer

Source Object	Target Object							
	Customer	Customer List	Car	Car Lot	Worksheet	Worksheet List	Finance Manager Out-Basket	Sales Manager Out-Basket
Worksheet	No data transfer	No data transfer	No data transfer	No data transfer	No data transfer	Worksheet is moved into worksheet list	Worksheet data is copied and sent to finance manager	Worksheet data is copied and sent to sales manager
Worksheet List	No data transfer	No data transfer	No data transfer	No data transfer	No data transfer	No data transfer	No data transfer	No data transfer

Figure 90 (Page 2 of 2). Default Results for Direct Manipulation. For certain pairs of objects, data is transferred from one object to the other when a salesperson drags it and drops it on the other.

Step 2. Determining the Necessary Views

Once we had identified and defined the objects, we had to determine which kinds of views would give the salespeople the best access to the objects and the information they contain. In determining the views needed, we considered the ways in which a salesperson would interact with each object and its information. We also provided a help view for each object.

Views of the Car Object

Both a salesperson and a customer need to know general information about a car, and a salesperson needs a way to work with the information. We decided that the best way to present the information would be a combination of textual information and graphical information. The text would describe the make, model, and year of the car. The graphic would be a picture of the car. We drew a sketch of a proposed General Information view of a car.

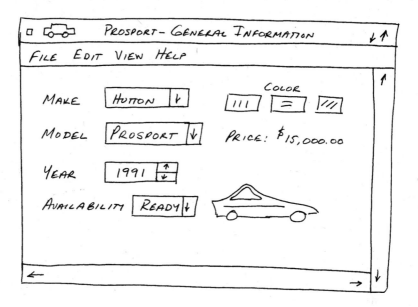

Figure 91. Hand-Drawn Version of General Information View of a Car Object

Views of the Car Lot Object

Because the car lot is a container, we knew we had to provide at least the two standard contents views: an icons view and a details view. For the icons view, we decided to group vehicles according to type, and we decided to represent each type of vehicle with a different icon.

Figure 92 on page 114 shows our initial sketch of an icons view of the car lot.

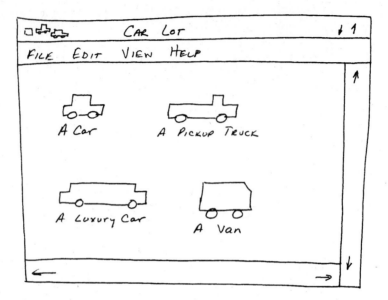

Figure 92. Hand-Drawn Version of an Icons View of the Car Lot

In a dealership that does not use computers in the process of selling cars, a salesperson typically searches manually through a file or listing of the cars available on the car lot. When a customer is ready for a test drive, a salesperson has to walk through the real car lot to locate the car. We decided that a more efficient approach would be to offer a salesperson several ways to look for particular cars available for sale, and we wanted to let the computer, rather than the salesperson, do the actual searching for available cars.

Because a customer is typically interested in only certain cars in the car lot, we decided to provide a way for a salesperson to specify criteria for which cars to include in either contents view of the car lot. We added a feature to the contents views to allow a salesperson to filter the view so that it displays only the cars that have the features the customer wants. (See "The Window for the Filtering Feature" on page 139 for more details.) By using this feature, a salesperson can filter the view of the cars according to:

- Year
- Make and model
- Color
- Price range
- Installed features.

We decided that once a salesperson has filtered the view so that only certain kinds of cars are displayed, the salesperson might also want to sort the displayed cars according to the same kinds of criteria. (See "The Window for the Sorting Feature" on page 142 for more details.)

Finally, we decided to provide a **Map** view that showed the positions of the real cars on the real car lot. The **Map** view is a composed view of the car lot. It saves the salesperson and customer time by pinpointing the location of the car that the customer wants to test drive.

The settings view for the car lot object provides a way for a user to change the appearance of some aspects of the car lot object. For example, a user can change the size of the icons that represent the car objects.

Views of the Customer Object

The general information associated with each customer includes the customer's

- Name
- Address (street, city, state, ZIP code)
- Phone numbers
- Identification number
- Driver's license number
- Date of birth.

Additional information associated with a customer might include detailed financial information, such as the customer's

- Assets
  - House
  - Car
  - Stocks
  - Savings
  - Income
- Debts
  - Rent or mortgage payments
  - Consumer loans
  - Credit card balance and credit limit.

This kind of information can be thought of as a customer's attributes or "settings," so we decided to provide a settings view. Settings views can be displayed well in a notebook. Figure 93 on page 116 shows our initial sketch of the notebook for the customer object.

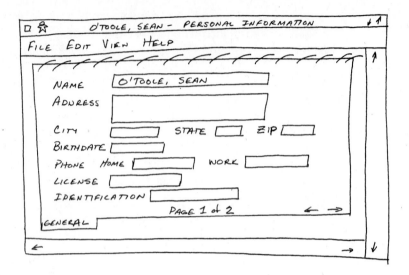

Figure 93. Hand-Drawn Version of the Customer Window

Views of the Customer List Object

The customer list is a container object; therefore it needed at least an icons view and a details view. We also decided to provide a mechanism called the **Include Customers** window that allows a salesperson to filter and sort the customer objects. Because the views of the customer list are similar to the contents and settings views of the car lot, we do not describe them further here.

Views of the Worksheet Object

Because the worksheet object is where customer information and car information is combined, we knew we had to design a view that displays the same kind of information that the car and customer objects contain. Figure 94 on page 117 shows our initial sketch of the worksheet object.

O'TOOLE – SPORTSCAR – WORKSHEET

FILE   EDIT   VIEW   HELP

ITEM	ORIGINAL	AGREEMENT
LIST PRICE	$10,000	$9,000
POWER SEATS	$1,000	$500
AM/FM STEREO	$200	$100
FLOORMATS	$50	NO CHARGE
TRADE-IN	—	($500)
TOTAL	$11,250	$8,100

Figure 94. Hand-Drawn Version of Worksheet

Views of the Worksheet List Object

The worksheet list, like the customer list and the car lot, is a container object. We provided the usual contents views: an icons view and a details view. We also decided to provide a mechanism called the **Include Worksheets** window that allows a salesperson, finance manager, or sales manager to filter and sort the worksheet objects. Because the views of the worksheet list are similar to the contents and settings views of the car lot and the customer list, we do not describe them further here.

Step 3. Designing the Menus

We consulted Part 2, "CUA Reference" for information about the standard CUA menus. To determine the product-specific choices we needed for our product, we considered how the object behaviors we had defined corresponded to the views we had decided upon. We also considered the relationships between various users and the objects. For example, a salesperson is not responsible for placing real cars into or removing real cars from the real car lot. To make our sample product seem more like the real world that the users are familiar with, we restricted the salesperson's access to the car lot object by providing a limited set of choices in the menus for the car lot object. A salesperson is allowed to view information about a car object in the car lot object but cannot add or remove car objects. In a fully designed product, some other person, perhaps a lot attendant or a sales manager, would have access to the car lot object to add or remove cars. However, because a salesperson is in the best position to know whether a customer is seriously interested in a car, the salesperson is allowed to create a new worksheet object and add it to or remove it from the worksheet list object.

The following sections discuss the menus for the objects.

The System Menu

When it is provided, the system menu is displayed from the system menu symbol at the upper left corner of a window. It contains choices that allow a user to work with a window itself. The following table describes the system menu choices.

Figure 95. Choices in the System Menu	
Choice	**Purpose**
Restore	Returns a window to its previous size
Move	Allows a user to move a window to a different location on the workplace
Size	Allows a user to change the size of a window
Minimize or **Hide**	Removes a window from the workplace. **Minimize** displays a graphic of a minimized window. **Hide** does not.
Maximize	Increases a window to its largest possible size
Close	Closes a window and all secondary windows associated with it
Window list	Displays a window containing a list of all windows open on the workplace
Split	Allows a user to split a window into two or more panes or to resize existing panes

Menus for the Car Object

From a salesperson's perspective, most of the information about a car object is fixed—that is, the information is based on a real-world object and cannot be changed unless something changes about the real-world object. For example, it would not make sense to allow a salesperson to change the color of a car object, because its color corresponds to the color of the real car that the car object represents. Because a salesperson can change little about a car object, the car object has only a few menus, and the menus contain relatively few choices. Figure 96 on page 119 shows the menus for the **General Information** view of the car object. For an illustration of the complete window, see Figure 108 on page 137.

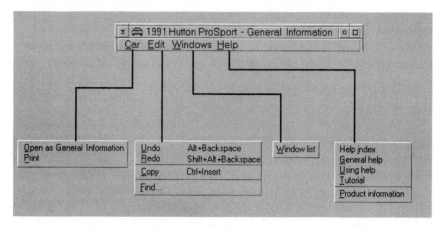

Figure 96. Menus for the General Information View of the Car Object

The table below describes the menu choices for the car object.

Figure 97 (Page 1 of 2). Menus for the Car Object		
Menu	**Choice**	**Purpose**
Car	**Open as General Information**	Allows a salesperson to open another window for the same car object. Because there is only one view for the car object, the name of the view (**General Information**) is part of the name of this choice.
	Print	Allows the salesperson to print the information about the car
Edit	**Undo**	Undoes the salesperson's last action
	Redo	Redoes the last action that the salesperson undid
	Copy	Stores a copy of the selected car object on the clipboard
	Find...	Displays a window that contains controls that allow a salesperson to search for specific car information

Menu	Choice	Purpose
		Figure 97 (Page 2 of 2). Menus for the Car Object
Windows	**Window list**	Displays a window containing a list of other windows that have been opened from this car object, from other objects associated with this car object, and from other windows associated with the car dealership product
Help	**Help index**	Displays a window containing an index of all of the help information available for the car object
	General help	Displays a window containing help information about the tasks a salesperson can accomplish in the window for the car object
	Using help	Displays a window containing an explanation of how to retrieve and use help information
	Tutorial	Displays a window containing help information about how to use the product
	Product information	Displays a window containing information such as the product's version number and copyright notice.

Menus for the Car Lot Object

Figure 98 on page 121 illustrates the menus and choices we decided upon for the **Icons** view of the car lot object. The menu bar choices are the same for the **Details, Settings,** and **Map** views, so those views are not shown here. These menus and choices allow a salesperson to interact with the information displayed in the views. Because a salesperson cannot change the contents of the car lot except by selling a car, the menus contain no choices that allow a salesperson to add cars to or remove cars from the car lot. For an illustration of the complete window, see Figure 109 on page 138.

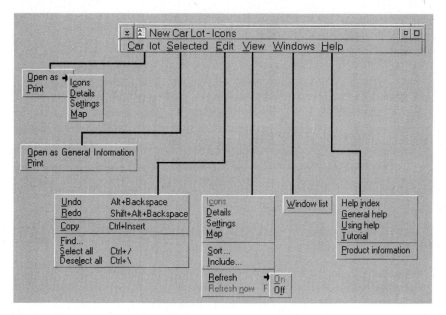

Figure 98. Menus for the Icons View of the Car Lot Object

The following table describes the menu choices for the car lot object.

Figure 99 (Page 1 of 3). Menus for the Car Lot Object		
Menu	**Choice**	**Purpose**
Car Lot	**Open as** →	Allows a salesperson to open a new window containing a different view of the same object. The **Open as** → choice leads to a cascaded menu that contains the names of the views available.
	Print	Allows a salesperson to print a list of cars in the car lot
Selected	**Open as General Information**	Opens a new window containing the general information view of the selected car. Because this is the only view available, it does not appear in a cascaded menu.
	Print	Allows the salesperson to print the general information for the selected car

Figure 99 (Page 2 of 3). Menus for the Car Lot Object

Menu	Choice	Purpose
Edit	**Undo**	Undoes the salesperson's last action
	Redo	Redoes the last action that the salesperson undid
	Copy	Stores a copy of the selected object on the clipboard
	Find...	Displays a window that contains controls that allow a salesperson to search for a specific type of car
	Select all	Selects all of the car objects in the car lot at once
	Deselect all	Deselects all of the car objects that were previously selected in the car lot
View	**Icons**	Displays the contents of the car lot object as icons
	Details	Displays the contents of the car lot object as rows and columns of related information
	Settings	Displays the settings for the car lot object
	Map	Displays the contents of the car lot object as a map of the car lot, with each car icon in a location that corresponds to the place where the real car is parked
	Sort...	Displays a window that allows a salesperson to specify the criteria that determine the order in which the cars are displayed
	Include...	Displays a window that allows a salesperson to specify the criteria that determine which cars are displayed
	Refresh→	Displays a cascaded menu containing the choices **On** and **Off,** which allow the salesperson to choose whether to continually update the view of the car lot
	Refresh now	Causes the view of the car lot to be updated immediately to reflect any changes in the car inventory since the last time the view was refreshed

Figure 99 (Page 3 of 3). Menus for the Car Lot Object		
Menu	**Choice**	**Purpose**
Windows	**Window list**	Displays a window containing a list of other windows that have been opened from this car lot object, from other objects associated with this car lot object, and from other windows associated with the car dealership product
Help	**Help index**	Displays a window containing an index of all of the help information available for the car lot object
	General help	Displays a window containing help information about the tasks a salesperson can accomplish in the window for the car lot object
	Using help	Displays a window containing an explanation of how to retrieve and use help information
	Tutorial	Displays a window containing help information about how to use the product
	Product information	Displays a window containing information such as the product's version number and copyright notice.

Menus for the Customer Object

Figure 100 on page 124 illustrates the menus and choices for the **Personal Information** view of the customer object. The choices are described in the following table. For an illustration of the complete window, see Figure 117 on page 146.

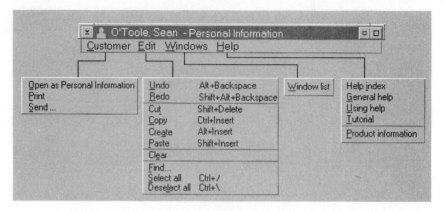

Figure 100. Menus for the Personal Information View of the Customer Object

Figure 101 (Page 1 of 3). Menus for the Customer Object		
Menu	**Choice**	**Purpose**
Customer	**Open as Personal Information**	Allows a salesperson to open another window for the same customer object. Because there is only one view for the customer object, the name of the view (**Personal Information**) is part of the name of this choice.
	Print	Allows the salesperson to print the information about the customer
	Send...	Allows the salesperson to send customer information to another user

Menu	Choice	Purpose
Edit	**Undo**	Undoes the salesperson's last action
	Redo	Redoes the last action that the salesperson undid
	Cut	Removes the selected object from the window and stores it on the clipboard
	Copy	Stores a copy of the selected object on the clipboard
	Create	Makes a new object from the selected object and stores the new object on the clipboard
	Paste	Places a copy of the contents of the clipboard into the customer object at a user-specified location
	Clear	Removes the selected object from the customer object without compressing the space the object occupied
	Find...	Displays a window that contains controls that allow a salesperson to search for specific customer information
	Select all	Selects all of the information in the window
	Deselect all	Deselects all of the information in the window
Windows	**Window list**	Displays a window containing a list of other windows that have been opened from this customer object, from other objects associated with this customer object, and from other windows associated with the car dealership product

Figure 101 (Page 2 of 3). Menus for the Customer Object

Menu	Choice	Purpose
Figure 101 (Page 3 of 3). Menus for the Customer Object		
Help	**Help index**	Displays a window containing an index of all of the help information available for the customer object
	General help	Displays a window containing help information about the tasks a salesperson can accomplish in the window for the customer object
	Using help	Displays a window containing an explanation of how to retrieve and use help information
	Tutorial	Displays a window containing help information about how to use the product
	Product information	Displays a window containing information such as the product's version number and copyright notice.

Menus for the Customer List Object

Figure 102 on page 127 illustrates the menus and choices for the **Icons** view of the customer list object. The menu bar choices are the same for the **Details** and **Settings** views, so those views are not shown here. The menu choices are described in the following table. For an illustration of the complete window, see Figure 128 on page 157.

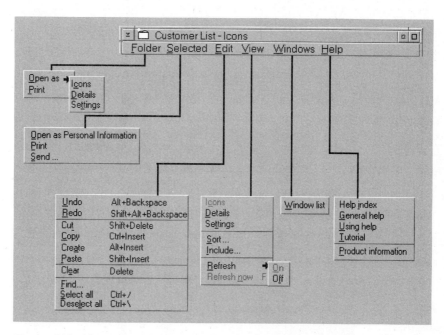

Figure 102. Menus for the Icons View of the Customer List Object

Figure 103 (Page 1 of 4). Menus for the Customer List Object		
Menu	**Choice**	**Purpose**
Folder	**Open as →**	Allows a salesperson to open a new window containing a different view of the customer list object. The **Open as →** choice leads to a cascaded menu that contains the names of the views available.
	Print	Allows a salesperson to print a list of customers in the customer list
Selected	**Open as Personal Information**	Opens a new window containing the personal information view of the selected customer. Because this is the only view available for the customer object, the choice does not appear in a cascaded menu.
	Print	Allows the salesperson to print the general information for the selected customer
	Send...	Allows the salesperson to send customer information to another user

Figure 103 (Page 2 of 4). Menus for the Customer List Object		
Menu	**Choice**	**Purpose**
Edit	**Undo**	Undoes the salesperson's last action
	Redo	Redoes the last action that the salesperson undid
	Cut	Removes the selected object from the window and stores it on the clipboard
	Copy	Stores a copy of the selected object on the clipboard
	Create	Makes a new object from the selected object and stores the new object on the clipboard
	Paste	Places a copy of the contents of the clipboard into the customer list at a user-specified location
	Clear	Removes the selected object from the customer list without compressing the space the object occupied
	Find...	Displays a window that contains controls that allow a salesperson to search for specific information in the customer list
	Select all	Selects all of the information in the window
	Deselect all	Deselects all of the information in the window

Figure 103 (Page 3 of 4). Menus for the Customer List Object		
Menu	**Choice**	**Purpose**
View	**Icons**	Displays the contents of the customer list as icons
	Details	Displays the contents of the customer list as rows and columns of related information
	Settings	Displays the settings for the customer list
	Sort	Displays a window that allows a salesperson to specify the criteria that determine the order in which the customers are displayed
	Include...	Displays a window that allows a salesperson to specify the criteria that determine which customers are displayed
	Refresh→	Displays a cascaded menu containing the choices **On** and **Off,** which allow the salesperson to choose whether to continually update the view of the customer list
	Refresh now	Causes the view of the customer list to be updated immediately to reflect any changes in the customers since the last time the view was refreshed
Windows	**Window list**	Displays a window containing a list of other windows that have been opened from this customer list, from other objects associated with this customer list, and from other windows associated with the car dealership product

Figure 103 (Page 4 of 4). Menus for the Customer List Object		
Menu	**Choice**	**Purpose**
Help	**Help index**	Displays a window containing an index of all of the help information available for the customer list
	General help	Displays a window containing help information about the tasks a salesperson can accomplish in the window for the customer list
	Using help	Displays a window containing an explanation of how to retrieve and use help information
	Tutorial	Displays a window containing help information about how to use the product
	Product information	Displays a window containing information such as the product's version number and copyright notice.

Menus for the Worksheet Object

Figure 104 illustrates the menus and choices for the **Worksheet** view of the worksheet object. The menu choices are described in the following table. For an illustration of the complete window, see Figure 133 on page 162.

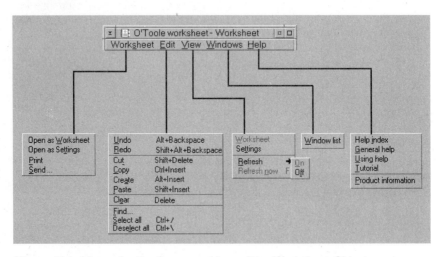

Figure 104. Menus for the Summary View of the Worksheet Object

Figure 105 (Page 1 of 2). Menus for the Worksheet Object

Menu	Choice	Purpose
Worksheet	**Open as Worksheet**	Allows a salesperson to open another window for the same worksheet object. The window opens to a worksheet view.
	Open as Settings	Allows a salesperson to open another window for the same worksheet object. The window opens to a settings view.
	Print	Allows the salesperson to print the worksheet information
	Send...	Allows the salesperson to send worksheet information to another user
Edit	**Undo**	Undoes the salesperson's last action
	Redo	Redoes the last action that the salesperson undid
	Cut	Removes the selected object from the window and stores it on the clipboard
	Copy	Stores a copy of the selected object on the clipboard
	Create	Makes a new object from the selected object and stores the new object on the clipboard
	Paste	Places a copy of the contents of the clipboard into the worksheet object at a user-specified location
	Clear	Removes the selected object from the worksheet object without compressing the space the object occupied
	Find...	Displays a window that contains controls that allow a salesperson to search for specific worksheet information
	Select all	Selects all of the information in the window
	Deselect all	Deselects all of the information in the window

Menu	Choice	Purpose
		Figure 105 (Page 2 of 2). Menus for the Worksheet Object
View	Worksheet	Displays the worksheet object opened to the worksheet section of the notebook
	Settings	Displays the settings for the worksheet object
	Refresh→	Displays a cascaded menu containing the choices **On** and **Off,** which allow the salesperson to choose whether to continually update the view of the worksheet object
	Refresh now	Causes the view of the worksheet object to be updated immediately to reflect any changes in the worksheet since the last time the view was refreshed
Windows	Window list	Displays a window containing a list of other windows that have been opened from this worksheet object, from other objects associated with this worksheet object, and from other windows associated with the car dealership product
Help	Help index	Displays a window containing an index of all of the help information available for the worksheet object
	General help	Displays a window containing help information about the tasks a salesperson can accomplish in the window for the worksheet object
	Using help	Displays a window containing an explanation of how to retrieve and use help information
	Tutorial	Displays a window containing help information about how to use the product
	Product information	Displays a window containing information such as the product's version number and copyright notice.

Menus for the Worksheet List Object

Figure 106 on page 133 illustrates the menus and choices for the **Icons** view of the worksheet list object. The menu bar choices are the same for the **Details** and **Settings** views, so those views are not shown here.

The menu choices are described in the following table. For an illustration of the complete window, see Figure 132 on page 161.

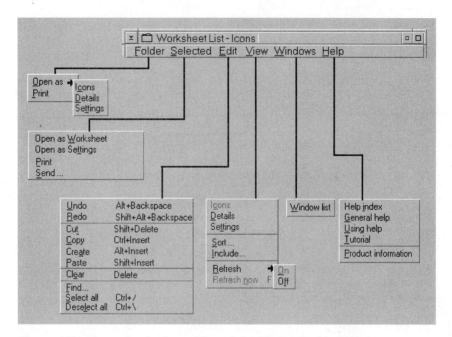

Figure 106. Menus for the Icons View of the Worksheet List Object

Figure 107 (Page 1 of 4). Menus for the Worksheet List Object		
Menu	**Choice**	**Purpose**
Folder	**Open as** →	Allows a salesperson to open a new window containing a different view of the worksheet list. The **Open as** → choice leads to a cascaded menu that contains the names of the views available.
	Print	Allows a salesperson to print a list of worksheets in the worksheet list

Figure 107 (Page 2 of 4). Menus for the Worksheet List Object

Menu	Choice	Purpose
Selected	**Open as Worksheet**	Allows a salesperson to open a window or windows for the selected worksheet object or objects.. The window or windows open to a worksheet view.
	Open as Settings	Allows a salesperson to open a window or windows for the selected worksheet object or objects. The window or windows open to a settings view.
	Print	Allows the salesperson to print the selected worksheet
	Send...	Allows the salesperson to send a copy of a worksheet to another user
Edit	**Undo**	Undoes the salesperson's last action
	Redo	Redoes the last action that the salesperson undid
	Cut	Removes the selected object from the window and stores it on the clipboard
	Copy	Stores a copy of the selected object on the clipboard
	Create	Makes a new object from the selected object and stores the new object on the clipboard
	Paste	Places a copy of the contents of the clipboard into the worksheet list at a user-specified location
	Clear	Removes the selected object from the worksheet list without compressing the space the object occupied
	Find...	Displays a window that contains controls that allow a salesperson to search for specific information in the worksheet list
	Select all	Selects all of the information in the window
	Deselect all	Deselects all of the information in the window

Menu	Choice	Purpose
Figure 107 (Page 3 of 4). Menus for the Worksheet List Object		
View	**Icons**	Displays the contents of the worksheet list as icons
	Details	Displays the contents of the worksheet list as rows and columns of related information
	Settings	Displays the settings for the worksheet list
	Sort	Displays a window that allows a salesperson to specify the criteria that determine the order in which the worksheets are displayed
	Include...	Displays a window that allows a salesperson to specify the criteria that determine which worksheets are displayed
	Refresh→	Displays a cascaded menu containing the choices **On** and **Off,** which allow the salesperson to choose whether to continually update the view of the worksheet list
	Refresh now	Causes the view of the worksheet list to be updated immediately to reflect any changes in the worksheets since the last time the view was refreshed
Windows	**Window list**	Displays a window containing a list of other windows that have been opened from this worksheet list, from other objects associated with this worksheet list, and from other windows associated with the car dealership product

Figure 107 (Page 4 of 4). Menus for the Worksheet List Object		
Menu	**Choice**	**Purpose**
Help	**Help index**	Displays a window containing an index of all of the help information available for the worksheet list
	General help	Displays a window containing help information about the tasks a salesperson can accomplish in the window for the worksheet list
	Using help	Displays a window containing an explanation of how to retrieve and use help information
	Tutorial	Displays a window containing help information about how to use the product
	Product information	Displays a window containing information such as the product's version number and copyright notice.

Step 4. Designing the Windows

We consulted Part 2, "CUA Reference" to design the actual contents of the windows for our sample product.

The descriptions below do not contain all of the components possible in windows of products with a CUA interface; our product did not need all of them. Nor are the window designs definitive. A different group of designers might have designed windows with different components.

We considered three principle aspects of each window:

- The window frame (includes the window border, window title, the scroll bars, the system menu symbol, and the window sizing buttons)

- The menus (includes the menu bar, the pull-down menus, and any cascaded menus needed for choices in the pull-down menus)

- The contents of the window (the view).

Because our product is an example only, we did not design all of the windows for all of the objects. The designs described in the following sections are representative only; they are not comprehensive.

Window for the Car Object

We designed only one window for the car object, a window to display the general information view. A salesperson displays the window by opening a car object.

We used read-only fields to display the textual information, and we combined the textual information with a drawing of the car. We could have used some other kind of graphic representation, such as a video image or computer animation. Figure 108 shows the car object window.

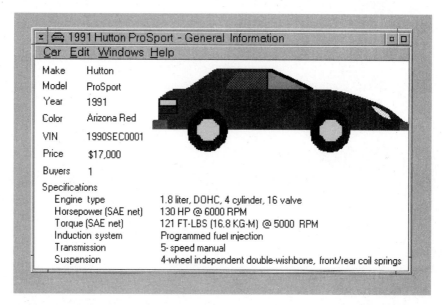

Figure 108. Car Object. A general information view of a car object displays textual and graphical information that both the salesperson and the customer want to see.

Windows for the Car Lot Object

We designed several windows for the car lot object, including windows for displaying the contents views (icons view and details view), windows from routing choices, and a window for the composed view (the map view).

The Window for the Icons View: A salesperson displays this window by opening the car lot object. The window contains icons representing car objects. The car icon is a generic representation of a car. We considered creating a separate icon for each car model, one that closely resembled the model it represented, but we knew that many of the distinguishing features would not be easy to see even on icons of a normal size and would be indiscernible in views, such as the details view, that display small icons.

Because salespeople are competitive, we knew that we should provide a way to indicate when a car has a potential buyer. We designed a small graphic of a human figure to augment the car icon when a salesperson has an interested customer. When a car icon is augmented with the buyer figure, a salesperson can decide to speed the close of a sale so that his or her customer can make the purchase before another customer does, or the salesperson can decide to steer a customer to a different car that is not being considered by another customer. The car icon is augmented automatically by the system when a salesperson transfers car information to a worksheet or when a customer takes a car for a test drive. Figure 109 shows the window for the icons view of the car lot object. The icons of the Hutton Sapphire, the Hutton GT, and the Watson Faser are augmented.

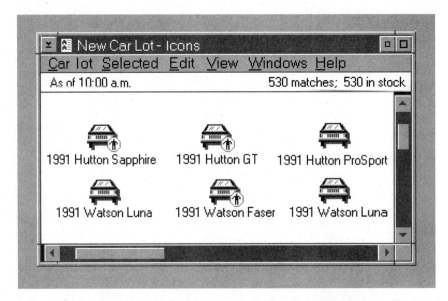

Figure 109. Window Displaying the Icons View of the Car Lot Object. Each icon represents one car in the car lot. Three of the six icons are augmented.

The Window for the Details View: This window can be displayed by opening the car lot object to a details view or by selecting the **Details** choice from the **View** menu.

In the details view we wanted to display the most frequently used information about each car, so we arranged the year, make, model, price, number of buyers, and vehicle identification number (VIN) in columns. Then we placed a column heading over each column of data to identify the items in that column. We designed the window so that the column headings are in a different part of the window than the list of cars. This design allows a salesperson to scroll the list of cars vertically without losing sight of the headings. However, when the salesperson scrolls the list horizontally, the headings scroll with the columns. Otherwise the headings would be displayed over the wrong columns.

We designed the window to scroll in both directions. The horizontal scrolling is helpful when the salesperson makes the window small enough that not all of the columns are displayed. The vertical scrolling is helpful when the salesperson makes the window small enough that not all of the lines are displayed.

We included a status area at the top of the window to tell the salesperson when the window had last been refreshed and whether the view had been filtered. Figure 110 shows the window for the details view of the car lot object. Each line represents one car in the car lot.

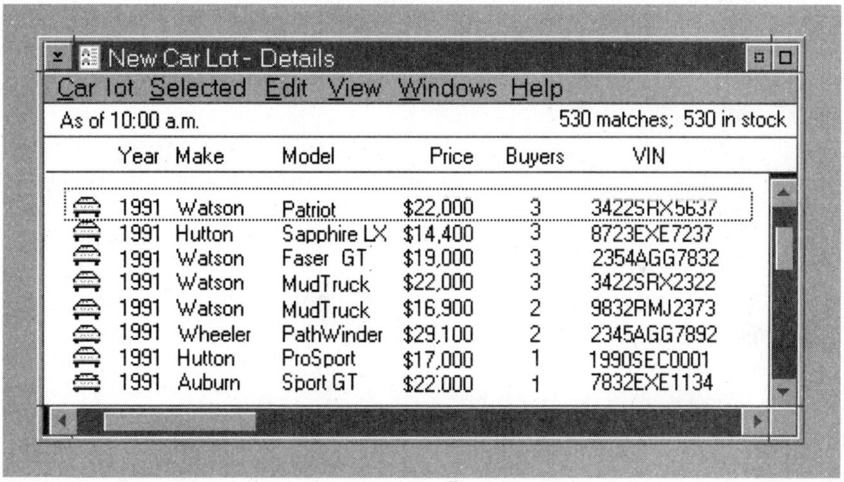

New Car Lot - Details
Car lot Selected Edit View Windows Help
As of 10:00 a.m.
530 matches; 530 in stock
Year Make Model Price Buyers VIN
1991 Watson Patriot $22,000 3 3422SRX5637
1991 Hutton Sapphire LX $14,400 3 8723EXE7237
1991 Watson Faser GT $19,000 3 2354AGG7832
1991 Watson MudTruck $22,000 3 3422SRX2322
1991 Watson MudTruck $16,900 2 9832RMJ2373
1991 Wheeler PathWinder $29,100 2 2345AGG7892
1991 Hutton ProSport $17,000 1 1990SEC0001
1991 Auburn Sport GT $22,000 1 7832EXE1134

Figure 110. Window Displaying the Details View of the Car Lot Object. Each line of information in the window represents one car in the car lot.

The Window for the Filtering Feature: We named the filtering feature **Include...** because it allows a salesperson to specify which cars are to be included in the view of the car lot. The **Include...** choice is a routing choice that appears in the pull-down menu from the **View** choice on the menu bar of the icons and details views of the car lot object. The

Include Cars window appears when a salesperson selects the **Include...** choice. It is a secondary window.

Our first design of the **Include Cars** window for appears in Figure 111. Although we subsequently changed the design of the window, we have included our original design here to illustrate how we used the iterative design process to improve our product.

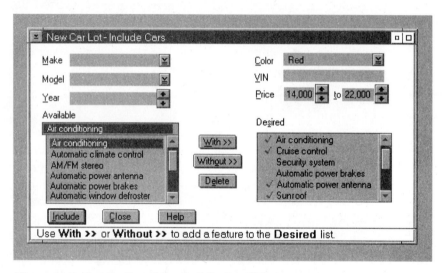

Figure 111. First Design of the Include Cars Window

To allow a salesperson to specify the filter criteria, we provided several types of controls. For the **Model, Make,** and **Color** fields, we used drop-down combination boxes. The drop-down characteristic saves space in the window, the entry field portion of the control allows a salesperson to type the appropriate information, and the list box portion of the control allows a salesperson to select the desired information without having to type it.

We used two spin buttons for the **Price** field, and we provided a ring of values in $1,000 increments. The spin buttons allow the salesperson to specify a minimum and maximum price for the cars to be displayed in the contents views (icons and details).

To allow a salesperson to specify the features of the cars to be displayed in the contents views, we used a pair of list boxes with three associated push buttons. The list box on the left contains the features that are available for a particular make, model, and year of car. The list box on the right is where the salesperson creates a list of the features that the customer does and does not want. To create the list in the list box on the right, the salesperson selects a feature from the list box on the left, then selects the **With >>** push button if the customer wants that feature. The salesperson selects the **Without >>** push button if the customer does not want that feature.

Features added to the list box on the right appear with a check mark if they were added with the **With** push button.

When a salesperson wants to remove a feature from the list, the salesperson selects the feature in the list box on the right, then selects the **Delete** push button.

At the bottom of the window we placed some standard CUA-defined push buttons: **Include, Close,** and **Help.** When a salesperson selects the **Include** push button, the window containing the contents view of the car lot displays all of the cars that match the criteria specified in the Include Cars window, and the Include Cars window remains open.

The **Close** push button closes the Include Cars window without changing the display in the Icons or Details window of the car lot.

A salesperson can select the **Help** push button to display contextual help for the control or choice that the cursor is on.

To assist salespeople in learning to use our product, we provided an information area at the bottom of the Include Cars window. When a salesperson moves the cursor to a control, the information area displays information about how to use that control. For example, when the cursor is on the **Available** list box, the information area displays a message that says something like this:

```
Select a feature from this list.
Then use With >> or Without >> to add the feature to the Desired list.
```

During a usability test, we discovered that the **Available** and **Desired** list boxes and the **With >>** and **Without >>** push buttons didn't make sense to our users. Consequently we redesigned the Include Cars window to make it easier to understand and to reduce the number of decisions that salespeople had to make. In particular, we added two fields that contain the features customers ask for most often. Figure 112 on page 142 shows the redesigned Include Cars window.

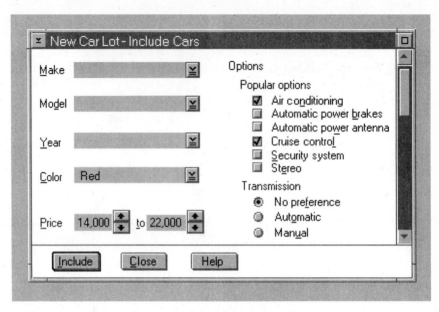

Figure 112. New Version of the Include Cars Window

To alleviate the confusion that resulted when salespeople had to transfer a feature from one control to another, we used check boxes and radio buttons instead of the list boxes. The check boxes are appropriate for most of the options because the salespeople can easily understand the implications of checking an option or not—that is, a salesperson realizes that checking the **Air conditioning** choice means that the customer wants air conditioning, and not checking it means that the customer does not want air conditioning. For the **Transmission** choices, however, check boxes were not appropriate because a car must have some kind of transmission. Therefore, we used radio buttons so that a salesperson has to select which kind of transmission the car should have. To accommodate customers who will accept either kind of transmission, we provided a **No preference** choice.

The Window for the Sorting Feature: We named the sorting feature **Sort...,** aptly enough. The **Sort...** choice is a routing choice that appears in the pull-down menu from the **View** choice on the menu bar of the car lot object. The Sort Cars window appears when a salesperson selects the **Sort...** choice. It is a secondary window.

A salesperson can select the **Sort...** choice to specify the order in which the cars should appear in the details view of the car lot object. We used drop-down lists to display the names of the sorting categories so that a salesperson would not have to remember the names of the appropriate sorting values. The values correspond to the column headings shown in the details view.

We designed two alternatives for the Sort Cars window. In the first version, we used radio buttons and text as the mechanism for specifying the sort order. Figure 113 shows this version.

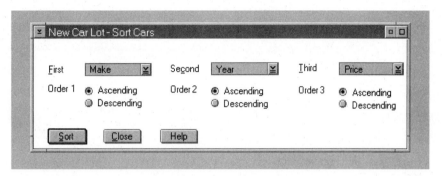

Figure 113. Version 1 of the Sort Cars Window. In this version of the window design, we used radio buttons as the mechanism for specifying the sort order.

In the second version, we used value sets containing graphics that depict the sort order. Figure 114 shows this version.

The push buttons in both versions operate much like the push buttons in the Include Cars window.

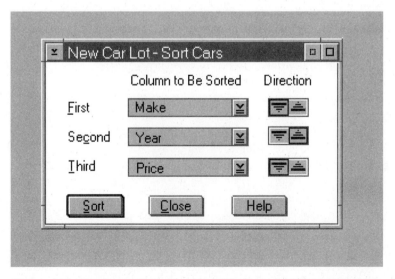

Figure 114. Version 2 of the Sort Cars Window. In this version of the window design, we used value sets as the mechanism for specifying the sort order.

It is not uncommon for designers to produce more than one proposed solution to a design problem. Usability testing is the only way to determine which design is superior.

When the salesperson selects the **Sort** push button the details view of the car lot object is sorted as shown in Figure 115. The sort order is indicated in the status area.

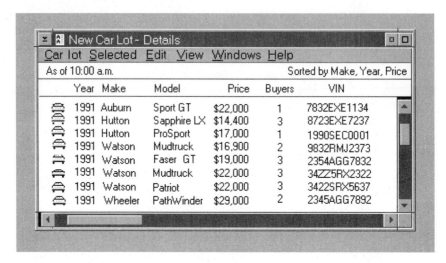

Figure 115. Sorted Details View of the Car Lot Object. The sort order is indicated in the status area.

The Window for the Map View: The map view is a pictorial display of the dealership's physical car lot. The view contains drawings of the showroom and the parking places in the car lot. Car icons in the parking places indicate where the corresponding cars are parked.

Car lot attendants are the primary users of this view of the car lot. As the lot attendants move cars into and out of the lot, they update the information displayed in this view. However, salespeople use the map view to find out the location of cars that customers want to test drive. Furthermore, a salesperson can drag a car icon to the showroom. By doing so, the salesperson signals a lot attendant to bring the car to the showroom so that a customer can take it for a test drive. When a sale is closed, the salesperson drags the car icon to the service building so that the service manager can schedule the pre-delivery prep work for the car.

Other dealership workers can also use the map view. Sales managers can analyze sales patterns by using the map view. If the map view were tied to the sales database, the sales managers might be able to learn, for example, that cars parked in the first two rows of the lot sell more quickly than cars parked at the back of the lot. The map view can also be used to take a physical inventory of the cars in stock.

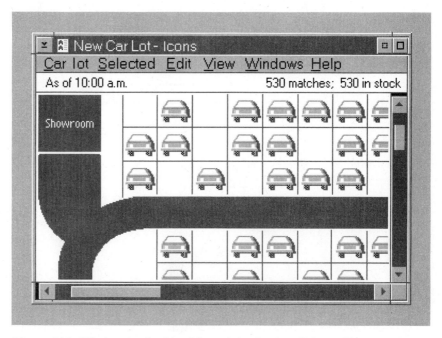

Figure 116. Window for the Map View of the Car Lot Object. The map view represents the dealership's physical car lot.

Windows for the Customer Object

A salesperson needs to be able to enter, view, and work with the customer information, so we decided to display these groups of information in two sections of a notebook control, one for general information and one for financial information. The notebook control was the obvious choice because the information can be grouped easily and because the design of the notebook control can be helpful in controlling access to certain information. For example, if we wanted to restrict access to a customer's financial information, we could include security measures that allow only the salesperson and the finance manager to have access to that section of the notebook. Figure 117 on page 146 shows the first page of the general information section of the customer object.

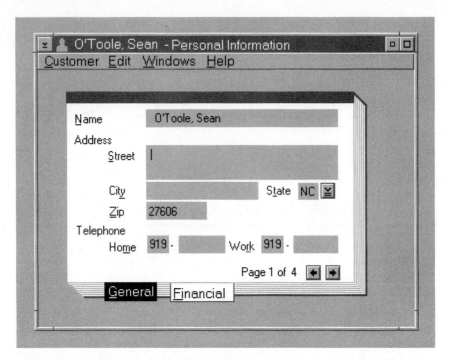

*Figure 117. Window for the Customer Object. A notebook control with divider tabs displays information about a customer. The divider tabs, labeled **General** and **Financial,** indicate the major groups of information.*

The general information section of the notebook has four pages. On the first page we provided entry fields for most of the information because entering the information is the only way to acquire the information. For the **Name, City, Zip, Home,** and **Work** fields, we used single-line entry fields. For the **Street** field we used a multiple-line entry field. We made the entry fields large enough to display a typical customer's information, so we did not provide scroll bars.

We provided a drop-down combination box for the **State** field. The drop-down combination box allows a salesperson either to type in the two-letter abbreviation for the state or to scroll through and select from a list of all of the abbreviations.

Because most of a car dealership's customers live in the vicinity of the dealership, we pre-filled some of the entry fields with the values most likely to appear in them. For example, because our dealership is in North Carolina, we pre-filled the **State** field with NC, and we pre-filled the **Home** and **Work** fields with the area code for the area where the dealership is located. Of course the salesperson can changes these values.

Each field has a field prompt, and some fields are grouped with a group heading. For example, the **Street, City, State,** and **Zip** fields are grouped under the **Address** group heading, and the **Home** and **Work** fields are grouped under the **Telephone** group heading.

A salesperson can move the cursor from one entry field to the next by pressing the Tab key or by moving the pointer and clicking the mouse button.

The second page of the general information section of the notebook looks like this:

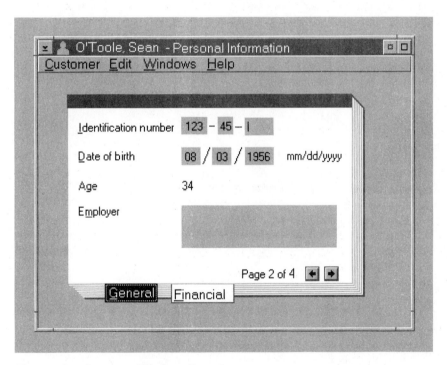

Figure 118. Customer Window, Page 2

Our product automatically calculates the value for the **Age** field, which is a read-only field, by reading the values the salesperson enters into the **Date of birth** field. Descriptive text appears to the right of the **Date of birth** field to let the salesperson know the correct format for the date of birth information.

Some of the customer information has inherent characteristics that we could use to help verify whether the salesperson has entered appropriate values. For example, state information must be two alphabetic characters, and the identification number must be nine numeric characters. When a salesperson enters a value for one of these pieces of information, our product checks the entered information to ensure that it has the correct characteristics. If it does not, the product alerts the salesperson.

We considered two methods for alerting a salesperson. First we considered changing the background color or contrast of the entry field as soon as the salesperson enters an inappropriate value. Then we considered displaying a message window that describes the problem and provides controls that allow the salesperson to correct the problem from within the message window. For example, if a salesperson enters fewer than nine digits for the identification number or enters alphabetic characters instead of numbers, our product would display a message like this:

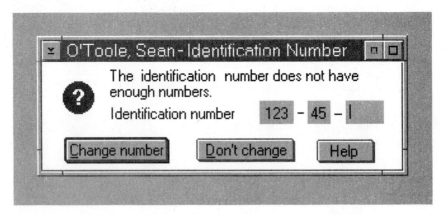

Figure 119. Message Window

We decided the first method might be too subtle for our intended users, so we settled on the message window.

The third and fourth pages of the general information section contain settings choices that pertain to the customer object itself rather than to the customer that the object represents. The pages are similar to the page shown in Figure 34 on page 52. We placed these pages behind the other pages in the section because a salesperson will use the customer object information less often than the customer information found on the first two pages.

Windows for the Worksheet Object

The worksheet object is the most important because it is where all of the elements of the sale come together: the customer, the car, and the money. However, if we had tried to display all of the information about the car, customer, and money at once, a salesperson would have had difficulty reading and working with the information. We used a notebook control to organize the information into sections that are meaningful to a salesperson and that reflect the tasks the salesperson wants to accomplish. A salesperson can get to any section of the notebook by selecting the tab for that section.

Figure 120 on page 150 shows the worksheet window. The page displayed is the actual worksheet that the salesperson uses when negotiating the sale. Several of the entry fields are filled in automatically when the salesperson transfers the customer and car information to the worksheet. For example, the **Vehicle, VIN,** and **Retail** fields are filled according to information from the car object. The values for some of the other fields are based on defaults suggested by the dealership. For example, the **License fee** field automatically displays the standard licensing fee for the state in which the dealership is located. If a customer plans to license the vehicle in a different state, the salesperson can type a different value into the field or can change the amount to $0. The **Net price** and **Balance** fields are read-only fields. The values they contain are calculated according to the values contained in other fields.

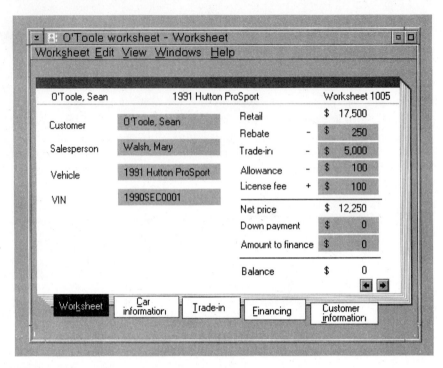

Figure 120. Worksheet Window

Using the Product

After completing the research and planning and the design of the product, we built a prototype and tested the product. As stated earlier, a discussion of prototyping and usability testing is beyond the scope of this book. However, we can provide a brief description of how the completed product is used.

Scenario of Use

Sean O'Toole walks into an automobile dealership looking for a particular kind of car. Mary Walsh, the dealership's top salesperson greets Sean and asks him what kind of car he is interested in.

"Do you have any Hutton ProSport cars?" Sean asks.

"Just a minute. Let me check," Mary responds.

Mary leads Sean to her desk, where she has a workstation. She moves her pointing device, a mouse, until the pointer is on an icon that represents the dealership's new car lot. She double-clicks on the icon and a window appears on her display screen. The window contains many icons that resemble cars. The color of each icon is the same as the color of the car it represents.

"This window shows me all the new cars we have in stock," she explains.

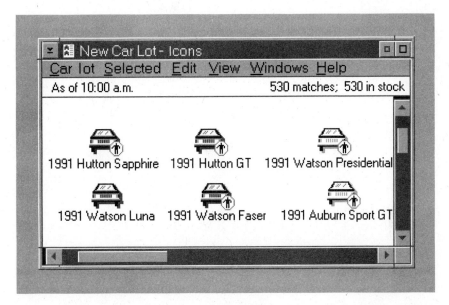

Figure 121. Icons View of the New Car Lot Object. By double-clicking on an icon labeled New Car Lot, Mary opens this window.

She moves the pointer to the **View** choice on the menu bar and clicks on the choice. A pull-down menu appears. Then she moves the pointer to the **Details** choice in the **View** menu and clicks on the choice.

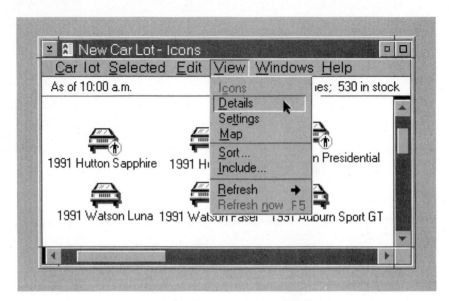

Figure 122. Changing from One View to Another. Mary changes from an icons view to a details view by clicking on the **Details** choice in the **View** menu.

The appearance of the contents of the window changes immediately.

	Year	Make	Model	Price	Buyers	VIN
	1991	Watson	Patriot	$22,000	3	3422SRX5637
	1991	Hutton	Sapphire LX	$14,400	3	8723EXE7237
	1991	Watson	Faser GT	$19,000	3	2354AGG7832
	1991	Watson	MudTruck	$22,000	3	3422SRX2322
	1991	Watson	MudTruck	$16,900	2	9832RMJ2373
	1991	Wheeler	PathWinder	$29,100	2	2345AGG7892
	1991	Hutton	ProSport	$17,000	1	1990SEC0001
	1991	Auburn	Sport GT	$22,000	1	7832EXE1134

New Car Lot - Details — Car lot Selected Edit View Windows Help — As of 10:00 a.m. — 530 matches; 530 in stock

Figure 123. Details View of the New Car Lot Object. Mary changes to this view by clicking on the **Details** choice in the **View** menu.

The title of the window is now **New Car Lot - Details**, and the window contains smaller icons along with columns of text that indicate each car's year, make, model, price, prospective buyers, and vehicle identification number (VIN).

"Let's see if we have the model you're looking for."

Mary moves the pointer to the **View** choice on the menu bar again. When the pull-down menu appears, she clicks on the **Include...** choice. Another window appears on the screen.

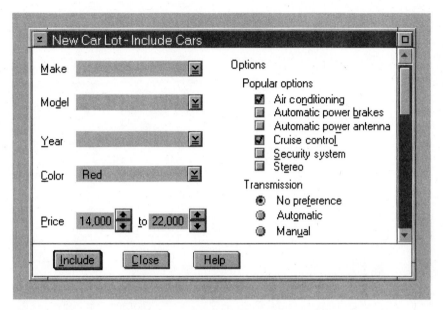

*Figure 124. Include Cars Window for the New Car Lot. Mary opens this window by clicking on the **Include...** choice in the **View** menu. By using the controls in this window, Mary can indicate which cars she wants to see in the New Car Lot window.*

Its title is **New Car Lot - Include Cars,** and it contains controls that allow Mary to specify which kinds of cars are to be included in the view of the new car lot.

"Let's see. You wanted a Hutton ProSport, right? This year's model?" Mary asks.

"Yes."

"What color and what kinds of options do you want?"

"Red, and I want air conditioning and cruise control. I don't care whether the transmission is automatic or manual."

"How much do you want to spend?"

"Well, I don't want a plain car, but I don't need the top-of-the-line option package either."

After filling in the entry fields of the drop-down combination boxes and checking the appropriate options, Mary adjusts the price field based on her knowledge of the range of prices for the ProSport model. Then she clicks on the **Include** push button. The **New Car Lot - Include Cars** window closes, and the contents of the **New Car Lot - Details** window change.

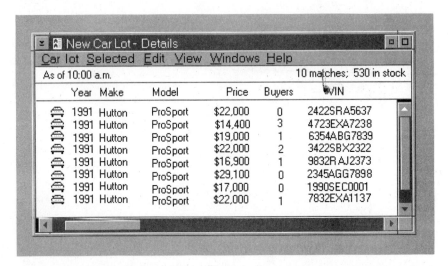

Figure 125. Filtered Details View of the Car Lot. The details view of the car lot now displays only the cars that matched the criteria that Mary specified in the **New Car Lot - Include Cars** window.

"Does that ProSport have a four-cylinder engine?" Sean asks.

"Let's see," Mary replies.

Mary moves the pointer to the icon for the car Sean indicated and double-clicks. A window displaying general information about the car appears. Mary reads the information and says, "No, it has a six-cylinder engine. Let's try another one." She double-clicks on the system-menu symbol and the window closes.

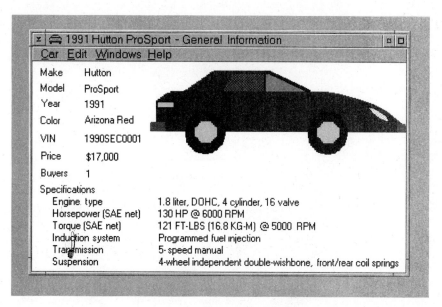

Figure 126. General Information View of a Car Object. Mary opens this window by double-clicking on a car icon.

"Here's another red one. Let's see if it has a more economical engine."

She double-clicks on the icon of a different car. When the window appears, she sees that the car does have a four-cylinder engine.

"Would you like to see the car? Maybe take it for a test drive?" Mary asks.

"Yes," Sean replies, "but where is it? I didn't see any ProSports on the lot when I came in."

"No problem," Mary says. "I'll find it on the map."

Mary moves the pointer to the title bar of the new car lot window and clicks on it to make the window active. Then she moves the pointer to the icon of the car Sean is interested in. She clicks on it to select it. Then she selects the **Map** choice from the **View** menu. The content of the window changes to show a map of the car dealership. The car Sean is interested in is highlighted.

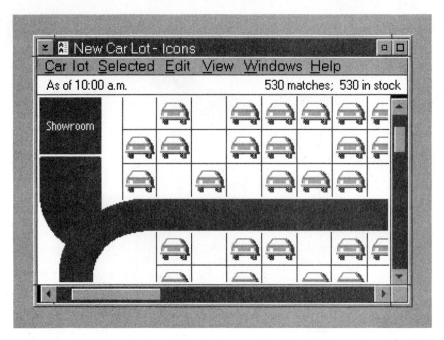

Figure 127. Map View of the New Car Lot. Mary displays this view by clicking on the **Map** *choice in the* **View** *menu.*

"There it is," Mary says. She drags the icon to the showroom. "The lot attendant will bring the car around front. You can take it for a test drive."

After driving the car, Sean returns and tells Mary he would like to buy it.

"Have you purchased a car here before?" Mary asks.

"No, I haven't."

"Then I need to get some information from you."

They return to Mary's workstation, where Mary double-clicks on an icon labeled **Customer List.** A window appears. It contains icons representing the dealership's customers. Mary moves the pointer to an existing customer icon and clicks to select the icon. Then she moves the pointer to the **Edit** menu and clicks. A pull-down menu appears. Mary moves the pointer to the **Create** choice and clicks on it. A newly created customer object is stored on the clipboard.

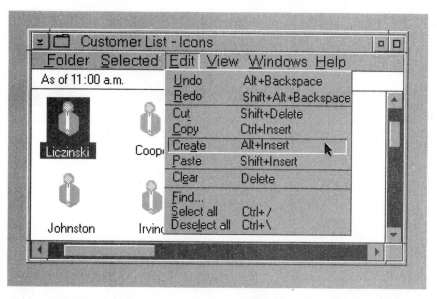

Figure 128. The Customer List Window. *To create a new customer object from the Customer List window, Mary clicks on the* **Create** *choice in the* **Edit** *menu.*

Then Mary clicks on the **Paste** choice in the **Edit** menu. The newly created customer object on the clipboard is placed in the customer list. Mary moves the pointer to the icon of the new customer object and double-clicks. A window opens containing a notebook. The **Name** field is highlighted and it contains the words "New customer."

"How do you spell your last name?" Mary asks.

"O-T-O-O-L-E." Mary types as Sean speaks, and Sean's name replaces the words "New customer." Mary presses the Tab key to move the cursor to the **Street** field.

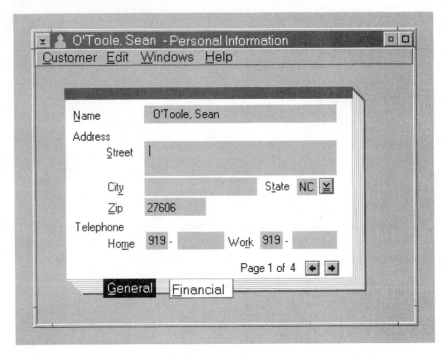

Figure 129. Window for the Customer Object

Sean tells her his address and telephone number and Mary fills in the rest of the entry fields.

"I think you forgot to change the state. I live in Virginia, not North Carolina," Sean says.

"Okay, I'll change it."

While pressing and holding the Alt key, Mary presses the T key, which is the mnemonic for the **State** field. The cursor moves to the **State** field. She types in the abbreviation for Virginia. Once the customer information is entered correctly, Mary moves the pointer to an icon labeled **Worksheet List.** She double-clicks on the icon and a window opens. The worksheet list contains all of the worksheets in progress for various customers, and the window opens to an icons view.

To create a new worksheet object, Mary could follow the same procedure she used to create a new customer object—that is, by indirect manipulation. However, she chooses to create a new worksheet by direct manipulation. She double-clicks on a folder icon labeled **New Things.** The folder opens. It contains templates of standard objects in the car dealership product. Figure 130 on page 159 shows an icons view of the **New Things** folder.

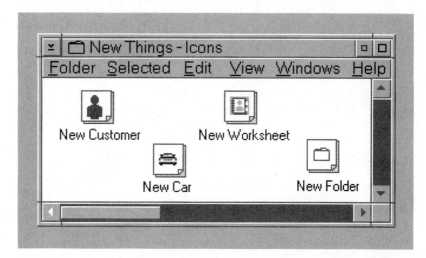

Figure 130. Templates of Standard Objects. The **New Things** *folder contains templates of standard objects in the car dealership product. Mary can use these templates to create new customer objects, worksheet objects, and folder objects. A lot attendant can use the* **New Car** *template to create car objects when new inventory arrives at the dealership.*

Mary moves the pointer to the icon labeled **New Worksheet** and drags a new worksheet from the template to the **Worksheet List** window. When she releases the mouse button, the newly created worksheet remains in the **Worksheet List** window, and the worksheet template remains in the **New Things** window. Figure 131 on page 160 illustrates creating by direct manipulation.

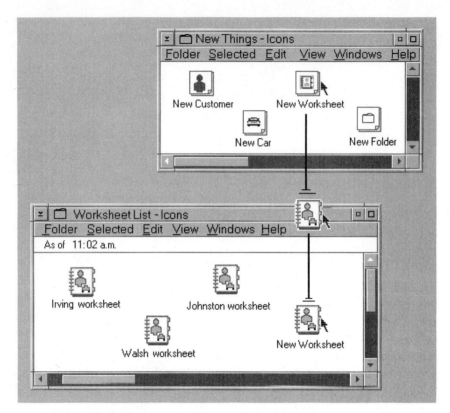

Figure 131. Creating a New Object by Direct Manipulation. Mary opens a folder containing templates of objects. She places the pointer on the **New Worksheet** *object and creates a new worksheet by dragging a copy of the worksheet from the template to the* **Worksheet List** *window.*

Mary drags Sean's customer icon to the new worksheet icon. A copy of Sean's customer information is transferred to the worksheet object.

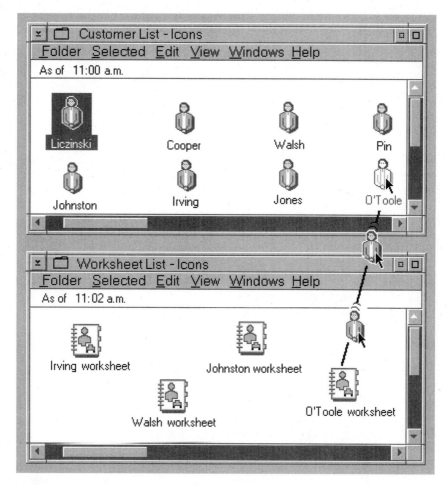

Figure 132. Transferring Data by Direct Manipulation. Mary copies information from Sean's customer object to Sean's worksheet object by dragging the customer icon to the worksheet icon.

Mary does the same with the icon of the car Sean is interested in. The car information is copied and transferred to the worksheet object.

Mary opens Sean's worksheet object by double-clicking on its icon. A window appears containing a notebook with several tabbed divider pages. The top page is a worksheet form that has some fields already filled in according to the information that Mary transferred to the worksheet object. The entire set of Sean's customer information is in a section of the notebook called **Customer information.** Likewise, the information that Mary transferred from the car object appears together in a section called **Car information.**

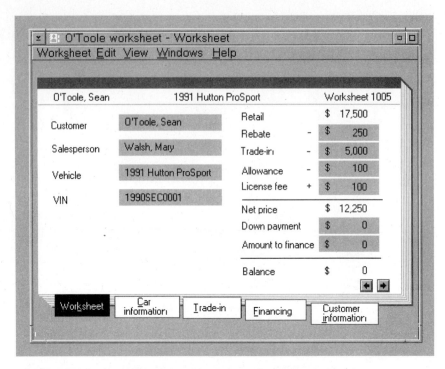

Figure 133. Sean's Worksheet. Mary opens Sean's worksheet by double-clicking on the worksheet's icon. Some of the entry fields are already filled in when Mary opens the worksheet. For example, the fields for the customer's name and the salesperson's name, and the fields for the vehicle information, are already filled in because Mary transferred that information to the worksheet by dragging the customer and car icons to the worksheet icon. Other fields are read-only fields that the product calculates automatically. For example, the Net price field is calculated according to the figure automatically displayed in the Retail field and the figures Mary enters in the Rebate, Trade-in, Allowance, and License fee fields.

"Do you want to trade in a car?" Mary asks.

"I'm not sure. I'd like to see the difference in financing if I do," Sean replies.

"Okay, I'll make two worksheets, one with a trade-in and one without. Then you can decide which is better for you."

Mary selects Sean's worksheet, then copies it and pastes the copy into the worksheet list.

Mary and Sean then discuss the prices and conditions of the sale. As they agree on prices, Mary enters them into the appropriate fields on the worksheets. Sean decides he will trade in his old car. The worksheets automatically calculate the net price and balance due. Finally, Mary says, "You're a tough bargainer. I need to ask my sales manager, Peter Liczinski, if he will agree to these figures."

Mary drags the icon for the worksheet containing the trade-in information to an icon that represents an electronic mail out-basket. The icon is labeled **To Liczinski.**

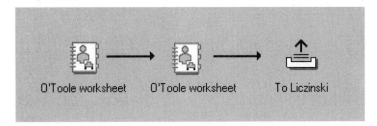

O'Toole worksheet   O'Toole worksheet   To Liczinski

Figure 134. Using Electronic Mail to Send Information. Mary sends a worksheet to the sales manager by dragging the worksheet's icon to an icon that represents an electronic mail out-basket.

"He'll look over the figures we've proposed and let us know if we've got a deal. Would you like some coffee while we wait?"

After a few minutes, Mary's terminal makes a sound and her electronic mail in-basket flashes to indicate that a message has arrived. Mary double-clicks on the in-basket and a window opens showing the contents of the in-basket. Mary double-clicks on the icon of the single message in the in-basket, and another window opens. It contains a message from Peter Liczinski saying that he accepts the figures she proposed.

"It seems that you've got yourself a car, Sean," Mary says. "I'll send this information to the finance manager, Rachel Green. She'll help you finish the transaction. In the meantime, I'll get your car ready for you."

Mary drags the icon for the completed worksheet to another out-basket icon labeled **To Green.** Then she takes Sean to Rachel's office. After introducing them, she returns to her terminal to tidy up the windows.

She wants to get rid of the unused worksheet, so she drags the icon to an icon labeled **Delete Folder.** The delete folder will delete the worksheet for her.

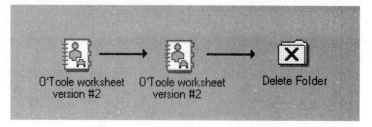

Figure 135. Deleting Unwanted Information. *Mary deletes the unused worksheet by dragging its icon to the delete folder icon.*

Then she double-clicks on the system menu symbol on Sean's worksheet window, on Sean's customer window, on the worksheet list window, on the customer list window, and on the car window. Each window closes in turn because closing is the default action for double-clicking on the system menu symbol. Then, with her workplace in order, Mary goes to prepare Sean's new car.

Part 2. CUA Reference

Chapter 7. Overview

This overview provides a brief description of the major components covered by the CUA guidelines. It summarizes many of the topics covered in "Common User Access Interface Components" beginning on page 203 and provides comparative information about when and how components are used. If you are unfamiliar with the CUA guidelines and terminology, specific related topics are identified to help you determine which topics should be referred to for more detailed product-development information.

Operating Environment

The CUA guidelines support the development of products that are to be used in application-oriented operating environments and object-oriented operating environments. The operating environment establishes a basic framework of function that products can utilize. The environment typically includes such basic functions as management functions for windows, files, printers, and configuration options.

An application-oriented environment is one in which users must first start applications in order to work with objects. The CUA graphical model, first published in 1989, defines a graphical user interface for products that are designed to be used in an application-oriented operating environment. The IBM Operating System/2* (OS/2*) 1.3 operating system is an example of an application-oriented operating environment.

In an application-oriented environment, groups of available applications are initially represented in application-manager windows as small graphic images called icons. A user can start an application which then displays its own window (or group of windows) from which a user performs tasks related to the application. While an application is running, a user can reduce the size of its window to a minimum size and position it in a handy place on the screen, which is typically referred to as the desktop. The desktop is the screen in an application-oriented operating environment. Figure 136 on page 170 is an example of an application-oriented operating environment.

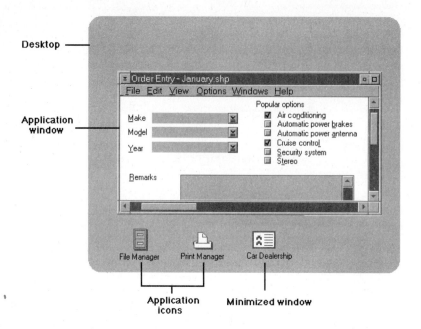

Figure 136. Example of an Application-Oriented Environment

In OS/2 1.3 a minimized window appears as an icon on the desktop but represents a running application. A user can manipulate running applications on the desktop, but cannot place objects on the desktop. Data transfer within and between applications is typically accomplished by using the **Cut, Copy,** and **Paste** menu choices associated with a system-provided clipboard.

Also introduced in 1989 was the workplace extension to the graphical model. The desktop in an object-oriented environment is called the workplace. The workplace extension defines an object-oriented user interface to support the development of products that are to be used in an object-oriented operating environment. In this environment, icons represent objects rather than running applications. A user no longer must start an application before selecting the object to work with. Instead, the user opens the object which automatically causes a window to be displayed that contains a view of the object. In addition to choosing actions from menus, a user can drag objects—represented as icons on the workplace—to perform some operations. For example, a text object can be printed by dragging its icon to the icon of a printer object. Figure 137 on page 171 is an example of the workplace in an object-oriented operating environment.

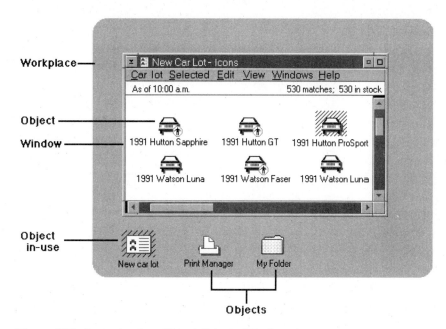

Figure 137. Example of an Object-Oriented Environment

An object, such as a document, often contains other objects, such as graphs, charts, and tables. The workplace extension defines techniques that allow a user to perform actions on an object as a whole and on objects that are contained within other objects.

Because interfaces are evolving to support an object-oriented environment, the CUA guidelines in this book emphasize object-orientation. However, many of the CUA guidelines apply equally to both application-oriented and object-oriented environments. For example, dragging techniques and pop-up menus can be supported within and between product windows on the workplace even if they are not supported on the desktop of an application-oriented environment. By defining interface features useful in both application-oriented and object-oriented environments, the CUA guidelines allow you to position your products advantageously for the evolution to an object-oriented interface while maintaining compatibility with many aspects of an existing application-oriented interface.

Types of Objects

Objects are the focus of a user's attention. The CUA guidelines define three types of objects: device, data, and container.

The CUA guidelines do not define particular types of data objects. However, guidelines are provided for interacting with data objects, such as text objects.

The CUA guidelines define four types of container objects that other objects can be placed into: folders, delete folders, work areas, and workplaces.

Each product defines the objects and properties necessary for that product, and the object-specific actions that can be applied only to those objects. The CUA guidelines define how the objects are displayed on the desktop or workplace, such as in windows, and how the actions are presented to a user, such as in menus.

Related Topics

- "Folder (Object)" on page 287
- "Device (Object)" on page 260
- "Object" on page 366
- "Delete Folder (Object)" on page 256
- "Work Area (Object)" on page 512
- "Workplace" on page 514

Creating New Objects

There are several methods available to a user to create new objects. In an application-oriented environment, new objects are created by opening an application window and either selecting the **New** choice to create a new object or by selecting the **Save as** choice to copy an existing object.

The **New** choice is used to create a new object in the window where **New** was selected. The new object is typically of the same class as the existing object in the window, but unique information can be automatically generated for it when it is created. This unique information may be simple, such as a new form number, or it can be more elaborate information taken from the current context. The newly created object reuses the same window from which the **New** choice was selected. The location of the new object is not determined when the object is created; instead, it is specified by the user from the **Save As** window when the **Save as** choice is selected or when the window is closed.

The **Save as** choice is used in an application-oriented environment to create a new object based on an existing object. When this choice is selected while working with an existing named object in a window, a copy of the object is made and the **Save As** window is displayed to allow the user to specify a name and location for the new object. The original object in the window is not affected.

Two other choices, **Create** and **Copy,** are provided in both application-oriented and object-oriented environments from menus, or their function can be provided through direct manipulation. In an object-oriented environment, new objects are created by finding another object of the desired type and requesting that a new one either be created from this object or copied from this object. In an application-oriented environment, **Create** and **Copy** are typically used to create or copy objects within the window. In an object-oriented environment, **Create** and **Copy** can be used for objects within a window, as well as objects on the workplace.

When using menus the **Create** choice is selected from the **Edit** menu or from the pop-up menu of an object. The **Create** choice uses the clipboard. Like the **New** choice, this choice may generate unique information for the new object. A default name is usually generated for the new object, although the user could change this name later. The location of the new object is determined by the user when the **Paste** choice is selected.

Like the **Create** choice, the **Copy** choice is selected from the **Edit** menu or from the pop-up menu of an object and uses the clipboard. The new object can have the same name as the original object if unique names are not required. The location of the new object is determined by the user when the **Paste** choice is selected.

When using direct manipulation, the default operation when a user drags an object can be either a move or a copy. A user can override a default operation, for example, to request that an object be copied instead of moved by pressing a mouse button. In addition, an object may have a create-on-drag setting that allows the user to specify whether when overriding the move default a create operation should be performed instead of the **Copy.** When this setting is on, the appearance of the object's icon is changed to reflect that the create operation will occur instead of the copy.

In many situations it may be convenient for users to create a folder containing sample objects from which users can create new objects. Each object in this folder would have the create-on-drag setting on to allow the user to easily create new objects by dragging objects out of this folder (using the override key) to the desired location.

In addition to creating new objects a user can create a reflection of an object. Objects that support reflections will have cascaded choices off the **Create** choice to specify that a reflection is desired. In addition, a user could create a reflection during direct manipulation.

Elements of the User Interface

Elements of the user interface, as opposed to objects, are unique to the computer environment. User-interface elements provide the means of representing and interacting with user objects on the desktop or workplace. Windows, icons, choices, and controls are examples of user-interface elements that are commonly found in products using the CUA guidelines.

Views of Objects

Opening a window on an object displays a view of the object. An object may have more than one view to allow a user to see other aspects of the same object. The CUA guidelines define four common types of views: composed, contents, settings, and help. The appearance of composed and contents views are object-specific. A user can change the view of an object by selecting another view from a menu. The CUA guidelines recommend that the settings view for an object be displayed using a notebook control and help views be displayed by opening another window.

A user can display multiple, simultaneous views of an object in multiple windows by opening the same object multiple times. To see different parts of a view in the same window, a **Split** choice could be provided to allow a user to split the window into different sections. In Figure 138 on page 175 a contents view and a settings view of the same object are displayed.

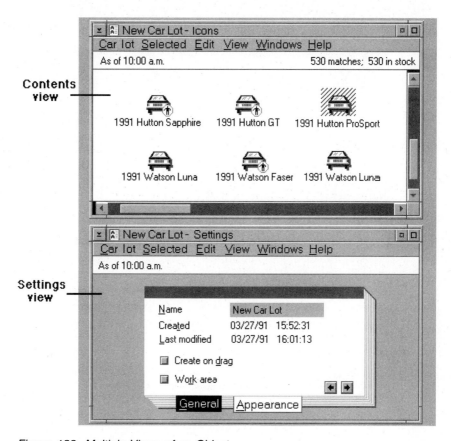

Contents
view

Settings
view

Figure 138. Multiple Views of an Object

Help

While using a product, a user occasionally requires additional information about choices, fields, or how to proceed with a task. This type of information is displayed when a user requests help.

Help can be accessed from the menu bar. The choices in the menu give specific kinds of help information, such as an index of the help topics, or help about the window or task. Help can also be accessed from a push button or a key assigned to contextual help on the indicated item. Contextual help can also be accessed from the pop-up menu of an object.

Figure 139 shows an example of the help menu.

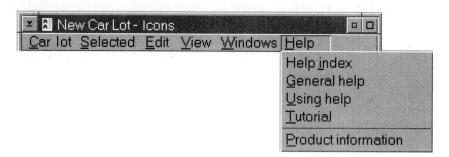

Figure 139. Help Menu

Users can get contextual help for a choice or object. Contextual help provides specific help information about the choice or object with respect to its current state. For example, getting contextual help on a choice displayed with unavailable-state emphasis might explain why that choice is currently unavailable and what a user would have to do to select the choice. Figure 140 shows an example of contextual help for the Make field in the window.

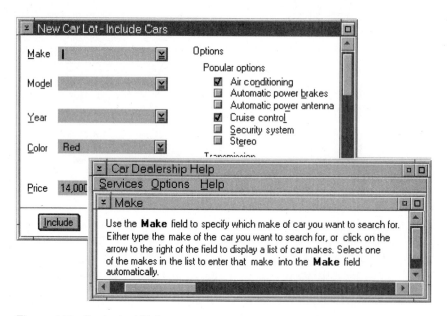

Figure 140. Contextual Help

Related Topics

Providing Help for Users
- "Contextual Help" on page 233
- "General Help (Choice)" on page 289
- "Help Menu" on page 296
- "Help Index (Choice)" on page 294
- "Keys Help" on page 323
- "Product Information (Choice)" on page 395
- "Tutorial (Choice)" on page 484
- "Using Help (Choice)" on page 489

Icons

In an application-oriented operating environment, a user's first encounter with icons is usually with icons that represent applications. Icons that represent applications appear in containers used to group such objects. Users can manipulate these icons to accomplish tasks such as moving the object to a new container. Also, users can start applications by opening the icon for that application.

In OS/2 1.3, for example, icons on the desktop also represent minimized windows of running applications. When a user double-clicks or restores a minimized window's icon, the icon disappears from the desktop and is replaced by an open window.

In an object-oriented operating environment, icons represent objects. When a user opens an icon, the icon remains visible but is visually augmented to indicate that it is currently in use. This augmentation, or emphasis, is called in-use emphasis.

When a user opens an object, a window is opened to display a view of the object. Figure 141 on page 178 shows an icon being moved from one container to another container. It also shows an icon displayed with in-use emphasis in the container.

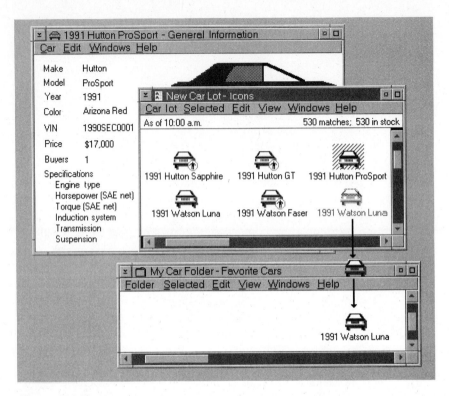

Figure 141. Icons

Related Topics

- "Icon" on page 300

Windows

Windows are used to present views of objects. In an application-oriented operating environment, users typically open a window and then specify the object they wish to interact with. In an object-oriented operating environment, a view of an object is displayed in the window when the window is opened. This is one difference between an application-oriented operating environment and an object-oriented operating environment: users can display views of objects directly without first specifying the application used to display that view. Another key difference is that in an application-oriented operating environment, the same window could be used to display other objects. In an object-oriented operating environment there is a one-to-one relationship between objects and windows. When a window is open on an object, in order to view another object, the object is displayed in a separate window.

Windows are also used to present messages, progress indicators, help information, and choices that further clarify actions.

In both application-oriented and object-oriented operating environments, multiple windows can be shown on the screen at the same time. If windows overlap, the active window (the window the user is interacting with) is usually placed on top of any overlapping windows. The two basic types of windows are: primary windows and secondary windows.

Primary window

A primary window is used to present a view of an object or group of objects when the information displayed about the object or group of objects is not dependent on any other object. A view of an object is typically displayed in a primary window.

Object information is presented in the area of the window below the menu bar (Figure 142 shows the components of a primary window). A user can control the size and position of primary windows on the screen.

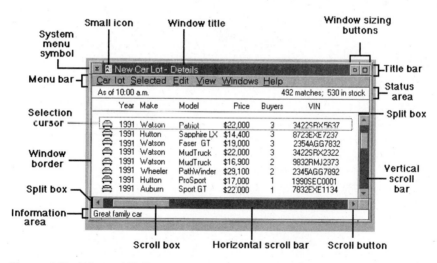

Figure 142. Primary Window

Secondary window

Secondary windows look very much like primary windows. For example, both have window borders and title bars. The important distinction between primary and secondary windows is based on how they are used. Secondary windows are always associated with a primary window and contain information that is dependent on an object in the primary window. Secondary windows are used, for example, to allow a user to further clarify action requests. Secondary windows are removed when the primary window is closed or minimized, and redisplayed when the primary window is opened or restored. Figure 143 on page 180 shows a typical secondary window.

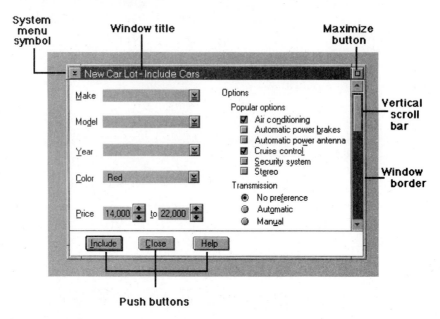

Figure 143. Secondary Window

Related Topics

Designing Windows

Designing Window Layout

Action Windows

Some actions require additional information from the user before they can be completed. In these situations, a choice, such as on a menu or push button, leads to a secondary window containing additional choices that clarify the action requested. Such a window is called an action window.

The **Open** and **Save as** choices are examples of menu choices that result in an action window. Figure 144 on page 182 shows an example of the action window displayed as a result of selecting the **Save as** choice.

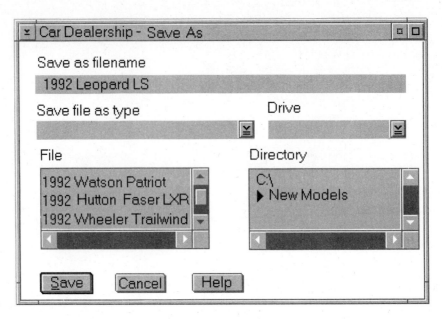

Figure 144. Save As Action Window

Messages

Messages are feedback to the user that occur because of a condition the operating environment or an object in the operating environment has detected. Messages tell a user that something has happened because of a request or that something undesirable or unexpected could occur. The CUA guidelines define three types of messages: information message, warning message, and action message. These three message types are based on the user actions that can be performed, not on the severity of the message.

Messages should clearly indicate why the message appeared and what actions can be taken. You can always provide access to help information in any kind of message to further aid a user in determining the problem or to learn how to correct the situation.

Information Message: An information message appears when a situation occurs that a user can do nothing about. The only actions a user can take when an information message is displayed is to dismiss the message window or request help information. Figure 145 on page 183 shows an example of an information message.

Figure 145. Information Message

Information regarding the normal completion of a process can be
displayed in an information area instead of as an information message.

Warning Message: Use a warning message when a user can continue
the original request without modification, though a situation exists that
the user should be aware of. Other actions may be provided to allow a
user to modify the original request or cancel it. Figure 146 shows an
example of a warning message.

Figure 146. Warning Message

Action Message: Use an action message when a situation arises in
which the user must take some explicit action to correct the situation or
choose an alternative action.

When an action message is displayed, a user can choose to retry the
request after correcting the situation, choose some other action that
redirects the request, or cancel the request. An action message can
also contain controls, such as an entry field, that allow a user to attempt
to correct data that is not valid or not correct. Figure 147 on page 184
and Figure 148 on page 184 show examples of action messages.

Figure 147. Action Message - Immediate User Attention Not Required

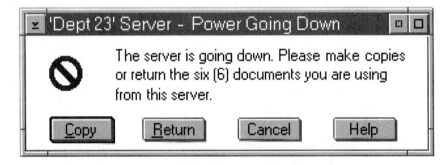

Figure 148. Action Message - Immediate User Attention Required

Progress Indicators

When a user requests a lengthy process, a progress indicator is used to indicate that the process is running and to provide information about the status of the process, such as how far it is from completion. A progress indicator is continually updated to reflect the latest status. Progress indicators may be displayed in the window where the process was requested or in a separate window. When displayed in a separate window, the window may also contain information that may otherwise have been displayed in an information message.

Figure 149 shows an example of a progress indicator in a window.

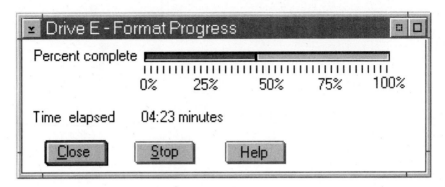

Figure 149. Progress Indicator in a Window

Related Topics

Informing a User
- "Action Message" on page 206
- "Information Area" on page 307
- "Information Message" on page 310
- "Message" on page 337
- "Progress Indicator" on page 396
- "Warning Message" on page 494

Choices

Choices are used to act on indicated objects. There are three types of choices:

- Action choices for performing actions on objects
- Routing choices that lead to another menu or window from which additional selections can be made
- Settings choices to specify properties of objects.

Figure 150 shows some examples of choices.

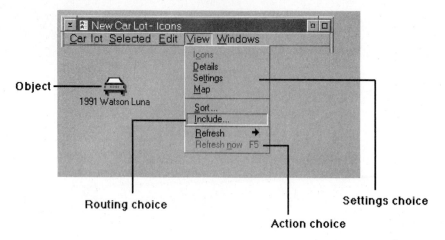

Figure 150. Choices

Related Topics

Action Choices

- "Action Choice (Choice Type)" on page 204
- "Clear (Choice)" on page 222
- "Close (Choice)" on page 225
- "Copy (Choice)" on page 240
- "Create (Choice)" on page 242
- "Cut (Choice)" on page 246
- "Delete (Choice)" on page 254
- "Maximize (Choice)" on page 329
- "Minimize (Choice)" on page 342
- "Move (Choice)" on page 357
- "New (Choice)" on page 361
- "Open As (Choice)" on page 371
- "Paste (Choice)" on page 376
- "Print (Choice)" on page 393
- "Refresh and Refresh Now (Choice)" on page 415
- "Restore (Choice)" on page 418
- "Save (Choice)" on page 423
- "Select All and Deselect All (Choice)" on page 435
- "Size (Choice)" on page 459
- "Split (Choice)" on page 469
- "Undo and Redo (Choice)" on page 487
- "Window List (Choice in Windows Menu)" on page 506
- "Window List (Choice in System Menu)" on page 505

Routing Choices
- "Find (Choice)" on page 284
- "Include (Choice)" on page 305
- "Open (Choice)" on page 369
- "Open As (Choice)" on page 371
- "Print (Choice)" on page 393
- "Routing (Choice Type)" on page 421
- "Save As (Choice)" on page 427
- "Sort (Choice)" on page 463

Settings Choices
- "Settings (Choice Type)" on page 448
- "Short Menus and Full Menus (Choice)" on page 454

Controls

Controls are components of the interface that allow a user to select choices and to type information. Menus are one type of control that is commonly used to contain choices. Other controls are used, for example, in settings views of objects and in windows that clarify an action request. However, controls may also be used in any view of an object.

Some controls can perform the same function, but are better suited for certain tasks or presentation schemes. For example, list boxes, combination boxes, drop-down list boxes, and drop-down combination boxes all perform similar functions. However, some of these controls allow a user to type values not provided by the control or require less space in a window. Because there are many different ways of allowing a user to interact with the interface, the CUA guidelines provide different controls to allow a user to work most efficiently. Figure 151 on page 188 shows some examples of controls.

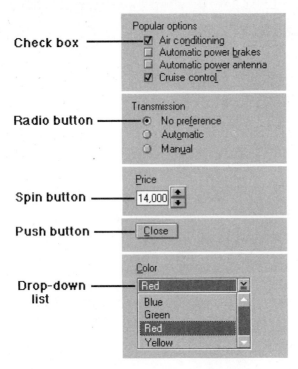

Check box

Radio button

Spin button

Push button

Drop-down list

Figure 151. Examples of Some Controls Defined by the CUA Guidelines

Related Topics

Using Controls

Menus

The types of menus defined by the CUA guidelines are:

- Menu bars
- Pull-down menus
- Cascaded menus
- Pop-up menus.

Menu Bar and Pull-Down Menu Contents: Menu bars are displayed at the top of a window, under the window title. Each choice in the menu bar is a routing choice that leads to an associated pull-down menu. Choices in the pull-down menus are typically action or routing choices that relate to the contents of the window, though settings choices are also allowed. When routing choices are used, they lead to other windows or to cascaded menus.

The CUA guidelines define the common contents of the **File, Selected, Edit, View, Options, Windows,** and **Help** menu bar choices. In addition, the contents of the system menu pull-down are also defined. The system menu is shown as a graphical choice in the top, left-hand corner of the window, in the title bar.

The menu bar choices and contents defined in this version of the CUA guidelines provide an evolutionary step towards an object-oriented menu scheme. Below is a brief description of these choices, along with a description of the system menu and its contents. Figure 152 on page 191 and Figure 153 on page 192 show the layout of the predefined menu choices on the menu bar and title bar and also shows the predefined choices within those pull-down menus. Additional information about these choices is found in "Common User Access Interface Components" beginning on page 203.

File
        The **File** menu contains choices that affect the overall object in the window. There are two types of **File** menus: application-oriented and object-oriented.

Application-Oriented
        Contains choices that affect the underlying object presented in the application-oriented window. For example, the **File** menu could contain an **Open** choice that allows a user to change the object presented in the window.

Object-Oriented

Contains choices that affect the underlying object presented in the object-oriented window. The label of this choice is the class name of the underlying object that is shown in the window. For example, in the **File** pull-down menu for a window displaying a view of a folder, the label of the menu-bar choice would be **Folder,** and its pull-down menu could contain the **Open as** choice that would allow a user to open new windows displaying views of the same underlying object.

Selected

The **Selected** menu is used for containers and data objects where objects within the window can be selected and actions applied to them. If the objects in the window are not homogeneous, then the available choices in this menu may vary widely, depending on which object is selected. For example, the names of the views listed from the **Open as** choice, may be very different depending on the views available for the selected object. The **Selected** menu has the same contents as the **File** menu for the selected object if a window was opened on that object.

Edit

The **Edit** menu contains choices that are standard across many different object types, such as the choices that provide access to the clipboard.

View

The **View** menu contains choices that change the view type or some aspects of the view, such as the **Include, Sort,** and **Refresh** choices.

Options

The **Options** menu contains choices that allow a user to tailor the behavior and appearance of an application-oriented product.

Windows

The **Windows** menu contains choices that provide access to other windows that are related to the same task.

Help

The **Help** menu contains choices that provide access to help information.

System menu   The system menu contains choices that change the visual characteristics of a window and other operating-environment-specific functions. Included in this menu is a **Close** choice for closing the window.

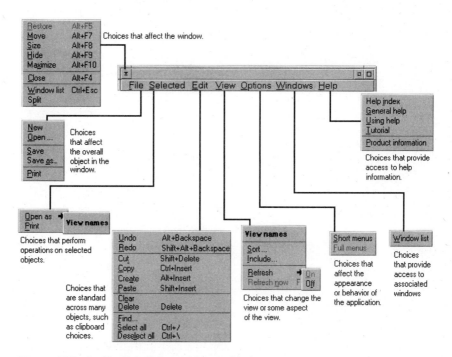

Figure 152. Application-Oriented Menu Choices

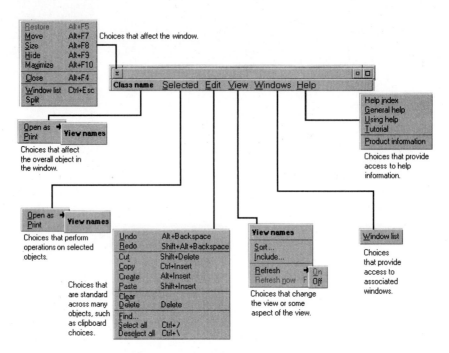

Figure 153. Object-Oriented Menu Choices

Pop-Up Menu Contents: Pop-up menus provide choices specific to an object. Pop-up menus are not visible until a user requests the pop-up menu be displayed. Unlike the choices in the menu bar and pull-downs, choices on a pop-up menu for a particular object vary depending on the state of the object. That is, only the choices that are currently valid are displayed in the pop-up menu.

Figure 154 on page 193 shows the content and layout that the CUA guidelines define for pop-up menus. In the top portion of the menu is the **Help** choice and other choices that open a view of the object. In the center of the pop-up menu are the choices that access the clipboard. In the lower area of the pop-up menu are object-specific choices provided for convenience to users. The CUA guidelines define such choices as **Undo, Print,** and **Clear,** that may appear in the lower area of the pop-up menu. Other choices defined by the product may appear in this area as well.

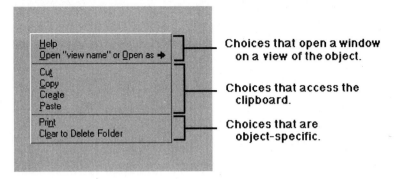

Figure 154. Pop-Up Menu

Related Topics

Designing Menus
- "Cascaded Menu" on page 214
- "Choice" on page 218
- "Menu (Control)" on page 331
- "Menu Bar" on page 334
- "Mnemonic" on page 344
- "Pop-Up Menu" on page 388
- "Pull-Down Menu" on page 398
- "Short Menus and Full Menus (Choice)" on page 454

User Interaction

Selection

A user interacts with an object by identifying the desired object and indicating actions to apply to that object. CUA interface guidelines define that a user must indicate an object or group of objects first, and then choose actions to apply to the object or group of objects.

A user can implicitly or explicitly indicate, or select, an object. An object that is implicitly selected does not require a specific selection action by a user and does not display selected-state emphasis. For example, a user does not need to first explicitly select an object in order to request its pop-up menu. Pointing at an object and requesting its pop-up menu will implicitly select the object. However, to request a pop-up menu for a group of objects, the user must explicitly select all objects to be included in the group.

An object that is explicitly selected is put into a selected state. This selected state is indicated with selected-state emphasis. Because an object stays selected until it is deselected, multiple actions can be applied to the same object without selecting that object multiple times.

Selecting an object does not imply an action, affect the object itself, or commit a user to some action. A user can select or deselect the object without changing the object in any way. In contrast to selecting an object, selecting an action causes something to happen to the selected object. For example, when the **Delete** choice is applied to a selected object, that object is deleted.

Selection Types

The CUA guidelines define three types of selection based on the number of objects that can be selected:

- The first type, single selection, allows at most one object to be selected at any time in a scope.

- Multiple selection allows a user to select one or more objects at any time in a scope.

- Extended selection allows a user to select only one object at a time or to extend the selection to more than one object.

One of these types of selection must be defined for each group of objects. For each of the controls discussed in "Controls" on page 187, one or more of these types of selection are already defined.

Selection Techniques

Selection techniques are the interaction mechanisms used for selecting objects. The CUA guidelines define techniques for both the keyboard and the mouse. Of the techniques specified, some are appropriate for selecting one object at a time, and others are appropriate for selecting multiple objects.

All selection techniques defined by the CUA guidelines are either point selection, point-to-endpoint selection, or random-point selection. The specific behavior of the selection technique depends on the selection type used, the type of object being selected, and the view of that object.

Point selection allows a user to select one object at a time. For example, the user moves the cursor to the object and presses the spacebar or clicks on the object with the mouse.

Point-to-endpoint selection allows a user to select all objects between two or more specified points. For example, a user can define two ends of a rectangle to select all objects fully contained within that rectangle;

however, in a different type of view, any object or part of an object that falls within the defined area might be selected.

Random-point selection allows a user to select objects as the pointer passes over them, in whatever order the user chooses.

Related Topics

- "Automatic Selection" on page 213
- "Extended Selection" on page 275
- "Marquee Selection" on page 327
- "Multiple Selection" on page 358
- "Point Selection" on page 383
- "Point-to-Endpoint Selection" on page 385
- "Random-Point Selection" on page 411
- "Select All and Deselect All (Choice)" on page 435
- "Selection Types and Techniques" on page 440
- "Shortcut Key" on page 450
- "Single Selection" on page 457

Data Transfer

Users can transfer data within an object, or from one object to another by dragging with the pointing device or by using the clipboard choices (**Cut, Copy, Create,** and **Paste**). Data-transfer operations allow a user to move data, copy data, or create a new object.

When a mouse is used, a user first identifies the object to be transferred. The object is identified by pressing the mouse manipulation button while the pointer is over the object. If more than one object is to be dragged, then the objects must be selected before the transfer. While holding the mouse manipulation button down, the user moves the mouse and drags the object or group of objects until it is at the desired location. The characteristics of the source and target object determine what the default operation for the object will be, such as a move or copy. The user can be allowed to override this default operation by pressing a key before dropping the object at the desired location.

The user can also transfer data by using the clipboard. The clipboard provided by the operating environment can be accessed by any object that provides the **Cut, Copy, Create,** and **Paste** choices.

To retrieve the contents of the clipboard, the user selects the **Paste** choice. A copy of the contents of the clipboard is pasted at the cursor position. Because the clipboard contents are preserved, the paste action can be repeated to get additional copies or, for the **Create** choice, to paste additional new objects.

Direct Manipulation

Direct manipulation allows a user to perform actions on objects by interacting directly with the objects. Dragging an object with a mouse and dropping it on another object is one form of direct manipulation. Moving, copying, printing, and deleting are examples of actions that can be accomplished using direct-manipulation techniques.

Using direct-manipulation techniques is usually an easier method of performing actions than performing the equivalent actions from menu bars and pull-downs. For example, with direct manipulation a user can move a document from one container to another by dragging it to the new container. Using the pull-downs requires that a user first select the document, then select the **Copy** choice from a pull-down menu to copy the object to the clipboard and then paste the clipboard contents into the new folder.

The user can perform other actions on objects by requesting a pop-up menu for an object. Pop-up menus can be thought of as a form of direct manipulation because they allow a user to more directly interact with an object, rather than through an intermediate control, such as a pull-down menu in a window that contains a choice that acts on a view of an object.

Related Topics

- "Contextual Help" on page 233
- "Data Transfer" on page 248
- "Direct Manipulation" on page 261
- "Object" on page 366
- "Source Emphasis (Cue)" on page 465
- "Split Window" on page 471
- "Target Emphasis (Cue)" on page 477

Scrolling

Scrolling is used to display information in a view that does not fit within the current size of the window or the part of the window allocated for that information. For example, a long list of document names displayed in a window, or in a list box within a window, may require scroll enabling to allow a user to see all the names in the list.

A scroll bar is used as a visual indication that information may be scrolled. A user can interact with a scroll bar using the pointing device to scroll the information. In addition the CUA guidelines define techniques for scrolling information using the keyboard.

Related Topics

- "Column Heading" on page 227
- "Cursor" on page 244
- "Keyboard" on page 315
- "Mouse" on page 350
- "Scroll Bar" on page 428
- "Scrolling Increment" on page 431

Pointers and Cursors

A visible cue is provided for both the pointing device (such as a mouse) and the keyboard to show where interaction will occur. The visual cue for the pointing device is the pointer; the visual cue for the keyboard is the cursor. To avoid confusion as to where input will occur, only one pointer and one cursor are visible at a time.

The user moves the pointer freely on the screen. Users can move the cursor to only valid cursor positions. For example, the cursor can be moved to the menu bar choices and push buttons, but not to field prompts or headings. When a user clicks the pointing device, the cursor is placed at the indicated position, if possible. A cursor never affects the pointer location.

The CUA guidelines define the following types of pointers: an arrow pointer, an arrow pointer with augmentations, a wait pointer, and an I-beam pointer. Their descriptions follow in Figure 155.

Figure 155. Predefined Pointers

Arrow pointer	▲	The pointer that the user sees most of the time and that is used to select choices and objects. The arrow pointer is also used during a direct-manipulation operation on an object to indicate that the object will be moved.
Arrow pointer — While copying or creating	▲	The arrow pointer is modified when a user performs a direct-manipulation operation on an object that results in a copy of that object being created.
Arrow pointer — Do not	⊘	When an object is not a valid target for a direct-manipulation operation, the arrow pointer is augmented with a circle with a slash through it. The source object will not be dropped at the current pointer location.
Wait pointer	🕐 ⧗	A pointer that indicates to a user that the computer is performing a process and cannot receive input at the current pointer location. A user can move the wait pointer, but the wait pointer cannot be used to perform any operation.
I-beam pointer	I	A pointer that indicates that the pointer is positioned over an area where text can be typed or selected.

Products may change the appearance of the pointer to indicate a product- specific action. A tool palette may be provided by a product to allow easy access to several actions. When a user selects a tool from a tool palette, the pointer shape changes and pointer interaction is determined by the tool. For example, selecting a line-drawing tool causes a line to be drawn as users drag the pointing device.

CUA-interface guidelines define two types of cursors:

Selection cursor   A selection cursor is used for settings choices and for all objects. This cursor typically appears as a dotted outline box around the settings choice or the object. The cursor is usually seen even when other types of emphasis are displayed.

For example, the selection cursor is visible on an object that is displayed with in-use emphasis.

Text cursor   A text cursor is used for keyboard text input. Two visuals are typically used for text cursors: a vertical bar to indicate insert mode and a colored background behind a character to indicate replace mode.

Related Topics

Designing Keyboard and Cursor Usage
- "Cursor" on page 244
- "Entry Field (Control)" on page 272
- "Input Focus" on page 312
- "Keyboard" on page 315
- "Keys Help" on page 323
- "Mnemonic" on page 344
- "Selection Types and Techniques" on page 440
- "Shortcut Key" on page 450

Designing Mouse and Pointer Usage
- "Direct Manipulation" on page 261
- "Mouse" on page 350
- "Pointer" on page 378
- "Pointing Device" on page 382
- "Selection Types and Techniques" on page 440
- "Tool Palette" on page 482

Cues

Cues provide information to users and help to orient them as they interact with the interface. Cues can be used to direct a user's attention to a part of the screen or to indicate a particular state of an object. The two kinds of cues are visible and audible.

Visible Cues

Visible cues allow users to immediately see the results of their interaction with the interface. We only discuss emphasis here, but arrow pointers, cursors, even animation, can be used as visible cues as well.

The type of emphasis used is determined by the type of interaction a user has with an object or choice. More than one type of emphasis may be valid on an object or choice at the same time, and therefore may be seen simultaneously. The CUA guidelines define these types of emphasis:

In-Use Emphasis: Indicates that a window is currently open on an object; users can still interact with the object as they normally would.

Selected-State Emphasis: Indicates that a choice or an object is selected.

Unavailable-State Emphasis: Indicates that a choice cannot be selected at that time.

Target Emphasis: Indicates the object that is the receiver of a direct-manipulation action. Target emphasis is used in conjunction with different pointer visuals to indicate the type of action that will be performed. Target emphasis can also indicate where the source object will be placed in the target object.

Source Emphasis: Indicates that an object is the source for a direct manipulation action. Source emphasis remains in effect until the direct manipulation action is complete.

Audible Cues

Audible cues are provided when a user attempts to perform an action that is not valid or when an event or state of the operating environment requires the user's attention. For example, when a user tries to select a choice displayed with unavailable-state emphasis, an audible cue should be generated. However, users can always specify in their operating environment that they want audible cues turned off.

Audible cues can be anything from a beep to a recorded message. The only limit is the hardware your product runs on and the usefulness of the cue for your users.

Related Topics

Providing Cues

- "Audible Feedback" on page 212
- "In-Use Emphasis (Cue)" on page 314
- "Selected-State Emphasis (Cue)" on page 439
- "Source Emphasis (Cue)" on page 465
- "Target Emphasis (Cue)" on page 477
- "Unavailable-State Emphasis (Cue)" on page 485

Chapter 8. Common User Access Interface Components

How to Use the CUA Reference

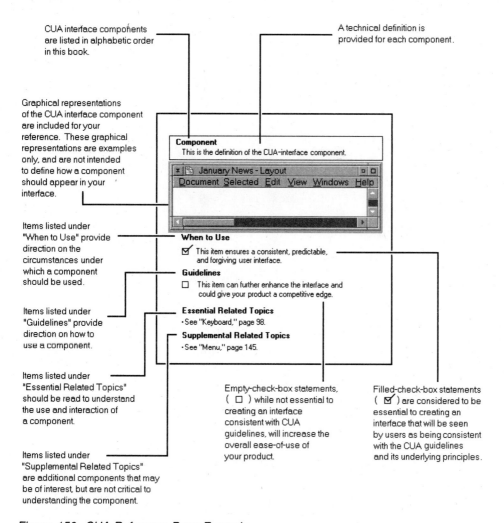

CUA interface components are listed in alphabetic order in this book.

A technical definition is provided for each component.

Graphical representations of the CUA interface component are included for your reference. These graphical representations are examples only, and are not intended to define how a component should appear in your interface.

Items listed under "When to Use" provide direction on the circumstances under which a component should be used.

Items listed under "Guidelines" provide direction on how to use a component.

Items listed under "Essential Related Topics" should be read to understand the use and interaction of a component.

Items listed under "Supplemental Related Topics" are additional components that may be of interest, but are not critical to understanding the component.

Component
This is the definition of the CUA-interface component.

January News - Layout
Document Selected Edit View Windows Help

When to Use
☑ This item ensures a consistent, predictable, and forgiving user interface.

Guidelines
☐ This item can further enhance the interface and could give your product a competitive edge.

Essential Related Topics
• See "Keyboard," page 98.

Supplemental Related Topics
• See "Menu," page 145.

Empty-check-box statements, (☐) while not essential to creating an interface consistent with CUA guidelines, will increase the overall ease-of-use of your product.

Filled-check-box statements (☑) are considered to be essential to creating an interface that will be seen by users as being consistent with the CUA guidelines and its underlying principles.

Figure 156. CUA Reference Page Example

Action Choice (Choice Type)

A choice that immediately begins to perform an action, such as the **Close** or **Copy** choice.

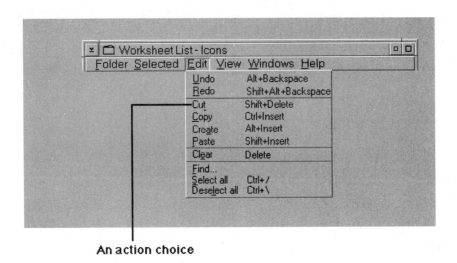

An action choice

When to Use

☑ Use an action choice for actions on objects that occur immediately after the choice is selected.

Guidelines

☑ When a user selects an action choice, immediately begin to perform the action.

☑ Provide access to all action choices through menus or push buttons, or both.

☑ Do not use an action choice to open an action window, to display a cascaded menu, or to display a pull-down menu; instead, use a routing choice.

Essential Related Topics

• "Choice" on page 218

• "Message" on page 337

- "Progress Indicator" on page 396

Supplemental Related Topics

- "Routing (Choice Type)" on page 421
- "Settings (Choice Type)" on page 448

Action Message

Action Message

A message that indicates that a condition has occurred that requires a response from the user. The user can correct the condition and then continue, withdraw the request, or get help.

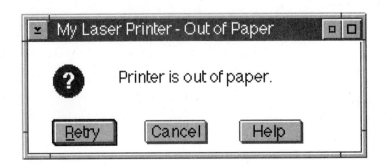

When to Use

Display an action message when a situation occurs in which a user must correct the situation and retry, take some related alternative action, or withdraw the request.

Guidelines

☐ Provide controls in the message window that allow a user to correct the situation that caused the message to appear or to request a related alternative action. For example, provide an entry field in which a user can correct a value.

☐ Provide a push button that allows a user to retry the request after correcting the situation that caused the message to appear. For example, provide a push button labeled **Retry** that a user can select after adding paper to the printer.

☐ If your product can determine that the situation that caused the message to appear has been corrected so that the process can continue, immediately remove the message. For example, if the user puts paper in the printer and the product can determine that paper has been added, immediately remove the message.

☐ Provide a push button that allows a user to withdraw the request. For example, provide a push button labeled **Cancel.**

☐   When a user withdraws a request, leave the objects in a form that is meaningful to a user. For example, when a user requests to copy a group of objects, and an error occurs that causes the user to withdraw the request while the fifth object is being copied, leave the first four copied objects where they are and remove the partially copied fifth object.

☐   In the message text, suggest possible actions that a user can take to correct the situation that caused the message to appear.

☑   Display the appropriate symbol in each action message as Figure 157 indicates:

Figure 157. Symbols That Appear in Action Messages

Symbol	When to use
?	When a user's immediate attention is not required, such as when a user's data will not worsen with time.
🚫	When a user's immediate attention is required.

☑   Provide an audible cue when an action message is displayed.

Essential Related Topics

- "Information Message" on page 310
- "Message" on page 337
- "Push Button (Predefined)" on page 404
- "Warning Message" on page 494

Supplemental Related Topics

- "Audible Feedback" on page 212

Action Window

A secondary window that is used to allow a user to further specify settings that are needed to complete the user's request.

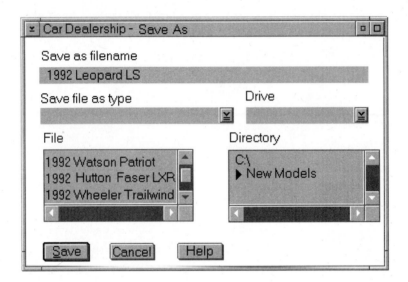

When to Use

☐ Provide an action window when a user makes a request and more information is required in order to complete the request.

☑ Provide an action window when a user selects a routing choice that leads to a window.

Guidelines

☐ Provide push buttons in the action window that continue the request, cancel the request, and allow user to request help.

☐ Make the default push button continue the request with the information in the window.

☐ Use a secondary window to display an action window.

Essential Related Topics

• "Push Button (Predefined)" on page 404

- "Routing (Choice Type)" on page 421

- "Secondary Window" on page 433

Supplemental Related Topics

- "Settings (Choice Type)" on page 448

Active Window

The window that currently has the input focus. The active window is indicated by emphasis displayed on its title bar and border, as specified by the operating environment.

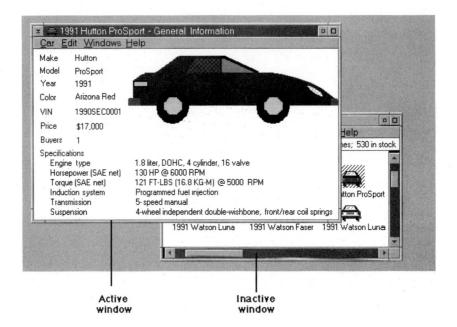

Active window   Inactive window

When to Use

☑ Make the window that can currently receive keyboard input the active window.

Guidelines

☑ When a window receives input focus, change the color of the active window's title bar and border to the color the user has specified for the operating environment.

☐ When an inactive window becomes active as a result of a technique that does not explicitly specify the position of the cursor, redisplay the cursor in the position it was in when the window was last active.

☐   When a window is reopened and information about the previous position of the cursor has been saved, redisplay the cursor in its saved position. Otherwise, display the cursor in a default position, for example on the top left-most item on which the cursor can be positioned.

☐   Place a window on top of all other primary windows and make it the active window when a user:

- Selects an object in the window

- Selects the title bar or window border of that window

- Presses the key assigned to the switch between unassociated windows function

- Presses the key assigned to the switch between associated windows function.

☐   Design a window so that a user can interact with it or make it active when it is not the topmost window. For example, when a user begins a process that searches a text object, allow the user to interact with the text object while continuing to display the **Find** action window on top of the text window.

Essential Related Topics

- "Inactive Window" on page 303

- "Input Focus" on page 312

Supplemental Related Topics

- "Window" on page 496

Audible Feedback

A sound generated by the computer to draw a user's attention to, or provide feedback about, an event or state of the computer. Audible feedback enhances and reinforces visible feedback.

When to Use

☑ Provide audible feedback when a warning message or action message is displayed.

☑ Provide audible feedback when a user types a character that is not a mnemonic for the window in which the cursor is positioned, and the control on which the cursor is positioned does not accept text input. For example, if mnemonics are supported but no choice has "L" assigned as the mnemonic, provide audible feedback when "L" is typed. If mnemonics are not supported, do not provide audible feedback when the user types a character.

☑ Provide audible feedback when a user attempts to select a choice that is displayed with unavailable-state emphasis.

Guidelines

☑ If a user has turned off the audible feedback option for the operating environment and a situation arises in which the system would normally generate audible feedback, do not generate audible feedback. For example, if a user has turned off audible feedback for the operating environment, do not generate audible feedback when an action message is displayed.

☐ Allow a user to take advantage of audio-generation capabilities of hardware and software. For example, allow a user to specify different sounds to different events. At a minimum, generate a beep as audible feedback.

Essential Related Topics

- "Message" on page 337
- "Unavailable-State Emphasis (Cue)" on page 485

Automatic Selection

A selection technique in which moving the keyboard cursor automatically changes the current selection. Provided as a convenience so that a user does not have to explicitly select an object, automatic selection occurs as the cursor moves among the objects or choices.

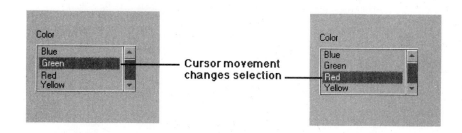

When to Use

☐ Provide automatic selection when at least one object must always be selected.

☐ Provide automatic selection as the initial technique in extended selection when using the keyboard.

Guidelines

☑ Always display selected-state emphasis on the object on which the cursor is currently positioned.

Essential Related Topics

• "Extended Selection" on page 275

• "Selection Types and Techniques" on page 440

• "Single Selection" on page 457

Supplemental Related Topics

• "Selected-State Emphasis (Cue)" on page 439

Cascaded Menu

A menu that appears when a cascading choice is selected. It contains a set of choices that are related to the cascading choice. Cascaded menus are used to reduce the length of a menu.

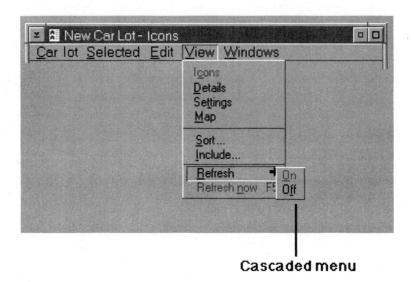

Cascaded menu

When to Use

☐ Use a cascaded menu to reduce the length of a menu. For example, place a related set of choices in a cascaded menu rather than placing them individually on a pull-down menu.

Guidelines

☑ When a user selects a cascading choice, display the cascaded menu associated with that choice.

☑ Display a right-pointing arrow to the right of a cascading choice and align the right edge of the arrow with the right edge of the menu displaying the cascading choice.

☐ Avoid displaying more than two levels of cascaded menus from a menu.

Essential Related Topics

- "Control" on page 235
- "Menu (Control)" on page 331
- "Routing (Choice Type)" on page 421

Check Box (Control)

A control used to display a settings choice that has two clearly distinguishable states, for example, on and off. Check boxes are typically used in a group to provide a multiple-choice field.

Check box ——————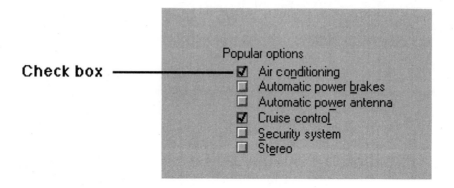

When to Use

☑   Use a check box to display an individual settings choice that can be set to on or off.

☑   Use a group of check boxes for settings choices that are not mutually exclusive and can each be set to on or off.

☐   Use a check box only if a user will clearly understand the meaning of the choice when it is selected or not selected. For example, use a check box for a choice labeled **Locked.** A user can clearly understand that when the check box is selected, the associated object is locked, and when the check box is not selected, the associated object is not locked. Otherwise, use a control that clearly identifies the two choices, such as two radio buttons.

Guidelines

☑   Display a check box to the left of its associated choice text.

☐   Arrange the check boxes in a group, in rows or columns, or both.

☑   If a check box choice is currently unavailable, display it with unavailable-state emphasis.

☑ When a user selects a check box from a group of check boxes, do not change the state of any other check boxes within the group.

☑ When a check box represents a setting shared by more than one selected object:

  • Display a mark in the check box if all of the selected objects have that setting turned on. For example, if two selected objects are both locked, display a mark in the **Locked** check box.

  • Fill the box with shading if some, but not all, of the selected objects have that setting turned on. For example, if only one of two selected objects is locked, fill the **Locked** check box with shading.

  • Do not display anything in the box if none of the selected objects has that setting turned on. For example, if neither of two selected objects is locked, leave the **Locked** check box empty.

☐ Assign a mnemonic to each check box choice.

☐ If a check box has a mnemonic assigned to it, provide access to the mnemonic by allowing a user to press the Alt key and that mnemonic.

☐ Capitalize only the first letter of the first word of a label of a check box choice unless the label contains an abbreviation, acronym, or proper noun that should be capitalized.

Essential Related Topics

• "Control" on page 235

Supplemental Related Topics

• "Choice" on page 218

• "Mnemonic" on page 344

• "Window Layout" on page 500

Choice

Text or graphics in a control that a user can select. Examples of choices are push buttons, radio buttons, and menu items. The three kinds of choices are action, routing, and settings.

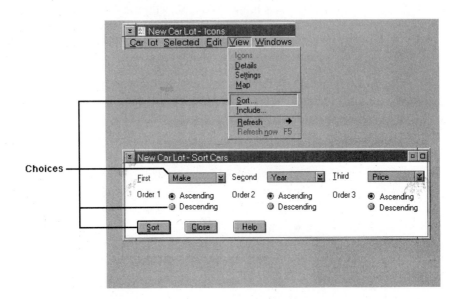

When to Use

☑ Provide a choice for any item in a window that a user can select.

Guidelines

☑ When a choice is not currently available, display it with unavailable-state emphasis, except in pop-up menus. Do not include unavailable choices in pop-up menus.

☐ In a menu that contains a group of mutually exclusive choices, display unavailable-state emphasis on the choice that is in effect.

☐ If choices in a group of mutually exclusive choices must show that they are unavailable and must indicate that one of those choices is currently in effect, then do not use a menu to display these choices: display these choices in a window instead.

☐ If a user attempts to select a choice that is currently unavailable, indicate in the information area that the choice cannot be selected and that **Help** will indicate why the choice is unavailable.

☐ Identify a choice with graphics or text, or both, depending on which best identifies the choice. For example, choices for a drawing product could consist of graphic fill patterns rather than text.

☐ Dynamically change the name of a choice by adding text or graphics, or both, to the name of a choice to make the meaning of that choice clearer in a given context. For example, changing the name of the **Undo** choice to **Undo typing** clarifies the meaning and differentiates the choice from **Undo delete.**

☐ Do not change the function of a choice because of a given context. For example, do not provide a push button labeled "Pause/Resume" that would have the function of either pausing or resuming a process depending on the current context. In that case, provide a push button labeled **Pause** and a push button labeled **Resume** and display unavailable-state emphasis on the one that is not available in the current context.

☐ Capitalize only the first letter of the first word of a name of a choice unless the name contains an abbreviation, acronym, or proper noun that should be capitalized.

☑ Use the predefined label for each predefined choice.

☑ Provide the predefined mnemonic for each predefined textual choice.

☑ Provide a unique mnemonic for each product-specific textual choice in a menu, unless no meaningful unique mnemonic can be found.

☑ Use Figure 158 to determine the appropriate choice types for each control. For example, use a check box control, rather than a menu or push button, for a settings choice that allows a user to choose whether or not lines are displayed in a table.

Choice

Menu or Control	Action choice	Routing choice	Settings choice
Figure 158. Recommended Choice Usage			
Menu	Yes	Yes	Yes, but recommend using a notebook instead.
Push button	Yes	Yes	No
Check box	No	No	Yes
Radio button	No	No	Yes
Value set	No	No	Yes
List box	No	No	Yes
Drop-down list box	No	No	Yes
Combination box	No	No	Yes
Drop-down combination box	No	No	Yes
Spin button	No	No	Yes
Slider	No	No	Yes

Essential Related Topics

Supplemental Related Topics

Clear (Choice)

An action choice that removes a selected object or group of objects without compressing the visible space it occupied.

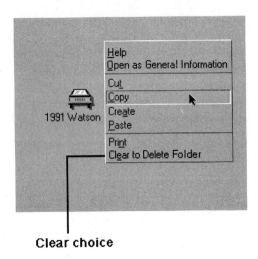

Clear choice

When to Use

☐ Provide a **Clear** choice to allow a user to remove an object or group of objects from a window without compressing the visible space the object or group of objects occupied. For example, provide a **Clear** choice to allow a user to remove information from selected cells of a spreadsheet without removing the cells that contained the information.

Guidelines

☑ If you provide a **Clear** choice, and you provide an **Edit** menu, place the **Clear** choice in the **Edit** menu.

☐ If you provide the **Clear** choice for an object, place the **Clear** choice in the pop-up menu for the object when the object can currently be removed without compressing the visible space it occupied.

☑ If you provide the **Clear** choice, display it with unavailable-state emphasis when the selected object or group of objects cannot be removed without compressing the visible space the object or group of objects occupied or when nothing is selected.

☐ Use the default delete folder provided by the operating environment as the destination of the **Clear** choice for objects represented by icons.

☐ If the destination of the **Clear** choice is a delete folder, append the label of the **Clear** choice with the name of the associated delete folder. For example, modify the choice to read **Clear to Trash1** when "Trash1" is the name assigned to the delete folder into which the **Clear** choice will place cleared objects.

☐ If a user changes the name of the delete folder to which cleared choices are placed, immediately update the label of the **Clear** choice to display the new name of the delete folder.

☑ Assign the Delete key as the shortcut key for the **Clear** choice when the **Delete** choice is not provided.

☑ Assign "E" as the mnemonic for the **Clear** choice.

Essential Related Topics

• "Delete (Choice)" on page 254

• "Edit Menu" on page 270

Supplemental Related Topics

• "Delete Folder (Object)" on page 256

Clipboard

A data storage area used during transfer of information within an object or between objects. A clipboard is typically provided by the operating environment.

When to Use

☑ Provide access to the clipboard for all objects that support data transfer.

Guidelines

☐ Provide access to the clipboard through the **Cut, Copy, Create,** and **Paste** choices.

☐ Support as many formats of the object as is practical given the different views in which the object can be pasted.

Essential Related Topics

Close (Choice)

An action choice that removes a window and all of the secondary windows associated with it.

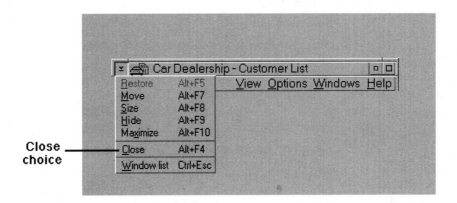

Close choice

When to Use

☐ Provide a **Close** choice for each window.

Guidelines

☑ If a **Close** choice is provided, place it on the system menu only, or on both the system menu and a push button in the window.

☑ If an object's information could be lost when the user selects the **Close** choice, display a warning message. For example, display a warning message if information in a table will be lost when a user closes the window in which a view of that table is displayed.

☐ If information in an action window could be lost when the user selects the **Close** choice, do not display a warning message. For example, do not display a warning message if information in a **Find** action window will be lost when a user closes the **Find** action window.

☐ When closing a window, save its state, including its position, size, and associated information, action, and warning messages that are currently displayed, so that they can be restored if the window is opened at a later time.

Close (Choice)

☐   When closing a work area, save the position and size of each open window associated with that work area, so that they can be restored if the work area is opened at a later time.

☑   When a user selects the **Close** choice, remove the window and any associated secondary windows from the workplace.

☑   When a user closes a work area, remove from the workplace all windows associated with that work area.

☑   Assign "C" as the mnemonic for the **Close** choice.

☑   Assign Alt+F4 as the shortcut key combination for the **Close** choice.

Essential Related Topics

- "Push Button (Predefined)" on page 404
- "System Menu" on page 475

Column Heading

A label above a column of information that serves to identify the contents of the column.

Column Headings ———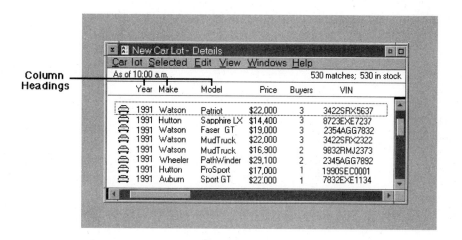

When to Use

☐ Provide a column heading for each column unless there is only one column and that column is identified by the window title.

Guidelines

☑ Place a column heading above the column it identifies.

☐ If information can be scrolled vertically, place the column heading in a separate area that does not scroll so that the heading will remain visible.

☑ If information can be scrolled horizontally, allow the column heading to scroll along with the column it is associated with.

☐ Use a separator to distinguish a column heading from the information in a column.

☐ Capitalize the first letter of the first and last words of a column heading, and all other words except articles, coordinating conjunctions, prepositions, and the "to" in infinitives.

Column Heading

☐   If a column heading is wider than the widest item in its associated column, center the column heading over the column.

☐   If a column heading is narrower than the widest item in its associated column, and the items in the column are left-aligned and of various lengths, align the column heading with the left edge of the column.

☐   If a column heading is narrower than the widest item in its associated column, and the items in the column are right-aligned and of various lengths, align the column heading with the right edge of the column.

☐   If information in a column is of fixed length, center the column heading over the column.

☐   Allow a user to directly edit a column heading in the place where it is displayed.

☑   If you allow a user to directly edit a column heading, allow the user to edit the column heading by clicking on the text with the mouse selection button.

Supplemental Related Topics

- "Field Prompt" on page 278
- "Group Heading" on page 292
- "Window Layout" on page 500

Combination Box (Control)

A control that combines the functions of an entry field and a list box. A combination box contains a list of objects or settings choices that a user can scroll through and select from to complete the entry field. Alternatively, a user can type text directly into the entry field. The typed text does not have to match one of the objects or settings choices contained in the list.

Combination box

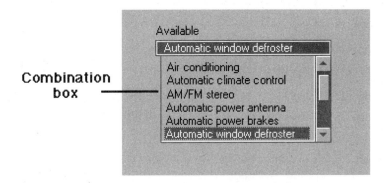

When to Use

☐ Provide a combination box when a user may have to type values that cannot be provided by the product and a set of commonly used settings choices or objects can be provided to assist the user in completing the entry field.

Guidelines

☐ Display the settings choices or objects in an order that is meaningful to a user, such as alphabetic order, numeric order, or chronological order. For example, display a list of printers in alphabetic order.

☑ In a list that can be scrolled, such as a scrollable list box, do not allow the cursor to wrap.

☐ Make the combination box large enough to display a minimum of six settings choices or objects at a time.

☐ When a user increases the size of the window in which the combination box is displayed, increase the number of settings choices or objects displayed in the combination box.

Combination Box (Control)

☐   When a user decreases the size of the window in which the combination box is displayed, decrease the number of settings choices or objects displayed in the combination box to a minimum of six. If the window is sized so that six settings choices or objects cannot be displayed, clip the combination box.

☐   Capitalize only the first letter of the first word of a settings choice or object unless the settings choice or object contains an abbreviation, acronym, or proper noun that should be capitalized.

☐   Display an initial value from the list in the entry field and display the initial value with selected-state emphasis so that typed text will replace the value.

☑   Provide horizontal or vertical scroll bars, or both, when some of the data is not visible in the combination box.

Essential Related Topics

- "Control" on page 235
- "Drop-Down Combination Box (Control)" on page 266
- "Drop-Down List (Control)" on page 268
- "Entry Field (Control)" on page 272
- "List Box (Control)" on page 325
- "Scroll Bar" on page 428

Supplemental Related Topics

- "Spin Button (Control)" on page 467

Container (Control)

A control used to create product-specific containers whose specific purpose is to hold other objects. The operating system provides general purpose containers, such as folders, for use by all products. Products can provide specific containers where needed.

Container ——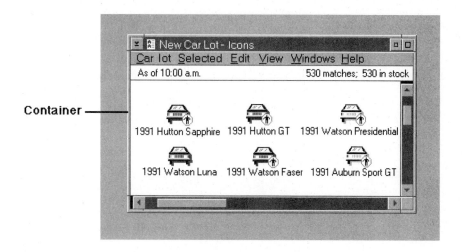

When to Use

☐ Provide a product-specific container to allow a user to group and view objects in ways that are not provided by the system-provided containers.

Guidelines

☐ Provide data transfer for the objects in a container.

☐ When appropriate, provide additional views, layout, and behavior for a product-specific container.

☐ Allow a container to hold any other object, including other containers.

☐ Provide an **Include** choice for each view of a container.

☐ Provide a **Sort** choice for each view of a container.

☐ Provide a status area for contents views of containers.

Container (Control)

□   Display the number of objects in a container near the bottom-lefthand corner of the container's icon, so that both the number and graphic are visible. For example, show the number on a small square background that has a different color than the icon.

□   Allow a user to turn off the display of the count.

Essential Related Topics

- "Control" on page 235
- "Selection Types and Techniques" on page 440

Supplemental Related Topics

- "Column Heading" on page 227
- "Data Transfer" on page 248
- "Folder (Object)" on page 287
- "Extended Selection" on page 275
- "Include (Choice)" on page 305
- "In-Use Emphasis (Cue)" on page 314
- "Object" on page 366
- "Primary Window" on page 391
- "Sort (Choice)" on page 463
- "Status Area (Cue)" on page 473
- "Work Area (Object)" on page 512

Contextual Help

Help information that is adapted to the current context of a choice, object, or group of choices or objects.

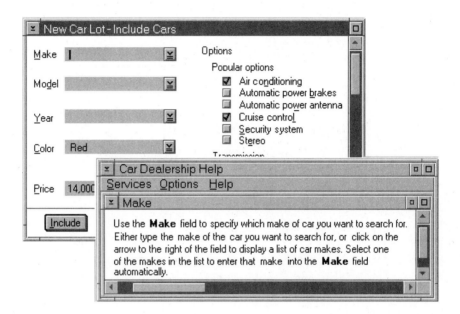

When to Use

☐ Provide contextual help for each choice or object that the cursor can be positioned on.

☐ Provide contextual help for each direct-manipulation operation.

☐ Provide contextual help for each object that has a pop-up menu.

Guidelines

☑ If you provide contextual help for a choice or object, display contextual help for that choice or object when the cursor is on it and a user presses the Help key.

☑ When a user selects the **Help** choice from a pop-up menu, display contextual help for the object from which the pop-up menu was requested.

Contextual Help

☐ While a user is performing a direct-manipulation operation and presses the Help key, cancel the direct-manipulation operation and display contextual help for that direct-manipulation operation. For example, if a user presses the Help key while moving an object from one container to another by dragging it, display contextual help for the direct-manipulation operation, such as the result of dropping the object on that container.

☑ If a choice is displayed with unavailable-state emphasis and contextual help is provided, describe in the help why the choice is unavailable and how the user might make the choice available.

☑ Assign F1 as the Help key.

Essential Related Topics

- "Direct Manipulation" on page 261

Supplemental Related Topics

- "Help Menu" on page 296
- "General Help (Choice)" on page 289
- "Help Index (Choice)" on page 294
- "Keyboard" on page 315
- "Keys Help" on page 323
- "Mouse" on page 350
- "Using Help (Choice)" on page 489

Control

A visual user-interface component that allows a user to interact with data. Controls are usually identified by text; for example, headings, labels in push buttons, field prompts, and titles in windows.

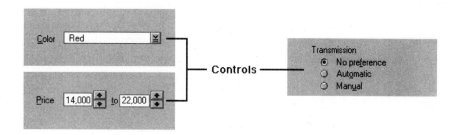

When to Use

☐ Provide a control in a window to allow a user to interact with information.

Guidelines

☑ Identify each control or field of controls with a field prompt, a column heading, or a window title, whichever is most appropriate.

☐ Use a label that clearly indicates the control's function.

☐ Immediately update a control when the value it represents changes. For example, if a slider and an entry field are provided to represent the same numerical value, immediately change the slider to represent the value entered into the entry field.

☐ Use the controls provided by the operating environment rather than creating new ones.

☐ Avoid changing the function, interaction technique, or appearance of controls provided by the operating environment.

☐ When a window is sized, adjust the size of the controls. For example, make the entry fields longer or shorter as the window is sized larger or smaller. At some minimal useful size, clip the controls instead of adjusting the size.

Control

☐   See Figures 159 and 160 on page 237 and Figure 161 on page 238 for the recommended usage of text and non-text controls.

Figure 159. Recommended Usage of Text-Entry Controls

Control	Number of Selectable Choices	Length of Entry Field (characters)	Types of Selectable Choices	Shown As	Relative Space Used	Selection Type Supported
Entry field (single line)	None	60 or fewer	None	Alphanumeric	Low	Text
Entry field (multiple-line)	None	Any	None	Alphanumeric	Medium - high	Text
Combination box	Any number	60 or fewer	Variable settings choices or objects	Alphanumeric	High	Single choice in list and text in entry field
Drop-down combination box	Any number	60 or fewer	Variable settings choices or objects	Alphanumeric	Low	Single choice in list and text in entry field
Spin button with entry field	20 or fewer	20 or fewer	Settings choice from an ordered list	Alphanumeric	Low	Single choice in list and text in entry field

Figure 160 (Page 1 of 2). Recommended Usage of Non-Text-Entry Controls

Control	Number of Selectable Choices	Types of Choices	Shown As	Relative Space Used	Selection Type Supported
Push button	1 for each push button, 6 or fewer per field	Fixed action or routing choices	Alphanumeric, Graphic	Low	Single
Radio button	1 for each radio button, 6 or fewer per field	Fixed setting choices	Alphanumeric	Medium	Single
Value set	20 or fewer	Fixed settings choices	Short alphabetic, Numeric, Graphic	Medium	Single
List box	Any number	Variable settings choices or objects	Alphanumeric, Graphic	Medium - High	Single, Multiple
Drop-down list	Any number	Variable settings choices or objects	Alphanumeric, Graphic	Low	Single

Control

Figure 160 (Page 2 of 2). Recommended Usage of Non-Text-Entry Controls

Control	Number of Selectable Choices	Types of Choices	Shown As	Relative Space Used	Selection Type Supported
Check box	1 for each check box, 6 or fewer per field	Fixed settings choices	Alphanumeric, Graphic	Medium	Multiple
Menu bar	6 or fewer	Fixed routing choices	Alphabetic, Graphic	Low	Single
Pull-down menu	10 or fewer	Fixed action or routing choices	Alphanumeric, Graphic	Low	Single
Cascaded menu	10 or fewer	Fixed action or routing choices	Alphanumeric, Graphic	Low	Single
Pop-up menu	10 or fewer	Fixed action or routing choices	Alphanumeric, Graphic	Low	Single
Slider	60 or fewer visible increments	Fixed setting in a range	Numeric, Graphic	Low	Single
Spin button without entry field	20 or fewer	Setting choice from an ordered list	Alphanumeric	Low	Single
Container	Any number	Objects	Alphanumeric, Graphic	High	Extended

Figure 161. Recommended Usage of Notebook Control

Control	Number of Objects and Controls	Types of Objects and Controls	Shown As	Relative Space Used	Selection Type Supported
Notebook	Any number	Any (except another notebook)	Alphanumeric, Graphic	Medium - high	As appropriate for each object or control

Supplemental Related Topics

- "Check Box (Control)" on page 216
- "Choice" on page 218
- "Column Heading" on page 227
- "Combination Box (Control)" on page 229
- "Container (Control)" on page 231

Copy (Choice)

An action choice that copies a selected object from the object in which it is contained and places the copy on the clipboard.

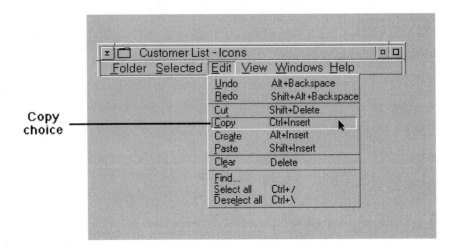

Copy choice

When to Use

☐   Provide a **Copy** choice for all objects for which the user can create a new object of that same type.

Guidelines

☑   If you provide a **Copy** choice, and you provide an **Edit** menu, place the **Copy** choice in the **Edit** menu.

☐   If you provide the **Copy** choice for an object, place the **Copy** choice in the pop-up menu for the object when the object can currently be copied.

☐   When the **Copy** choice is selected, create a new object on the clipboard that is an exact copy of the indicated object.

☐   When a user copies an object to the clipboard, do not change the state of the source object.

☐   When a user copies an object to the clipboard, do not change the state of the copied object on the clipboard. For example, do not change the selection state of the object as a result of copying that object to the clipboard.

☑ Display the **Copy** choice with unavailable-state emphasis when the selected object cannot be copied to the clipboard or when nothing is selected.

☑ Assign Ctrl+Insert as the shortcut key combination for the **Copy** choice.

☑ Assign "C" as the mnemonic for the **Copy** menu choice.

Essential Related Topics

- "Clipboard" on page 224
- "Create (Choice)" on page 242
- "Cut (Choice)" on page 246
- "Edit Menu" on page 270
- "Paste (Choice)" on page 376

Supplemental Related Topics

- "Data Transfer" on page 248
- "Pop-Up Menu" on page 388

Create (Choice)

An action choice that creates a new object and places it on the clipboard. The newly created object will be of the same class as the selected object, and it can contain new information generated during creation.

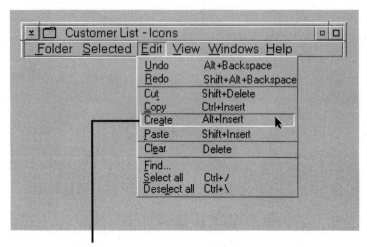

Create choice

When to Use

☐ Provide a **Create** choice for all objects in an object-oriented environment. For example, provide a **Create** choice for a printer object in a container to allow a user to create one or more additional printers.

Guidelines

☑ If you provide a **Create** choice, and you provide an **Edit** menu, place the **Create** choice in the **Edit** menu.

☐ If you provide the **Create** choice for an object, place the **Create** choice in the pop-up menu for the object when a copy of the object can currently be created.

☐ When a user selects the **Create** choice, create a new object of the same type on the clipboard, copy to it all relevant information from this object, and generate new information if necessary.

☐   If the object for which the **Create** choice was requested supports reflections, display the **Create** choice as a routing choice that leads to a cascaded menu with choices for selecting a new object or another appearance of the same object.

☐   When a user creates an object on the clipboard, do not change the state of the source object.

☑   Display the **Create** choice with unavailable-state emphasis when a new object cannot be created from the selected object or when nothing is selected.

☑   Assign Alt+Insert as the shortcut key combination for the **Create** choice.

☑   Assign "A" as the mnemonic for the **Create** menu choice.

Essential Related Topics

- "Clipboard" on page 224
- "Copy (Choice)" on page 240
- "Cut (Choice)" on page 246
- "Data Transfer" on page 248
- "Edit Menu" on page 270
- "Paste (Choice)" on page 376

Supplemental Related Topics

- "Direct Manipulation" on page 261
- "Pop-Up Menu" on page 388
- "Reflection (Object)" on page 413

Cursor

The symbol cue that indicates the current position of the keyboard-input focus. The keyboard cursors are the selection cursor and the text cursor.

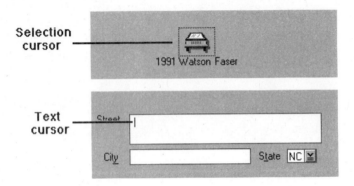

When to Use

☑ Display a text cursor in text that can be edited or selected and currently has input focus.

☑ Display a selection cursor in any component (other than text that can be edited) that a user can interact with using the keyboard.

Guidelines

☑ Display only one cursor at a time.

☐ Show the selection cursor as a dotted outline box around the current object.

☐ Display the text cursor as a vertical bar between characters when a user is in insert mode.

☐ Display the text cursor as background shading behind a character when a user is in replace mode.

☑ Move the cursor to the pointer position when a user presses the mouse selection button on an object, choice, or text.

☐ Make the cursor visible in addition to any other forms of emphasis that are currently visible on an object while the cursor is on that object. For example, display the cursor and selected-state emphasis on a selected object when the cursor is moved to that object.

☐ Except when scrolling by using the cursor-movement keys, scroll the cursor along with the information, even if that means scrolling the cursor out of sight.

☐ When a user presses any cursor-movement key, keep the cursor in sight, scrolling the information if necessary. For example, if a user is viewing a document and presses the End of Data key, keep the cursor visible while scrolling to the end of the document.

☐ When moving the cursor to a control causes the control to be scrolled into view, scroll as much of the control into view as possible. For example, if moving the cursor to a radio-button field causes scrolling, scroll as much of the radio-button field into view as possible.

☑ In a component that can be scrolled, such as a scrollable list box, do not allow the cursor to wrap.

☑ In a component that cannot be scrolled, such as a menu, allow the cursor to wrap at the top and bottom of the component.

Supplemental Related Topics

- "Choice" on page 218
- "Entry Field (Control)" on page 272
- "Pointer" on page 378
- "Text Entry" on page 479

Cut (Choice)

Cut (Choice)

An action choice that removes a selected object from the object in which it is contained and places it onto the clipboard.

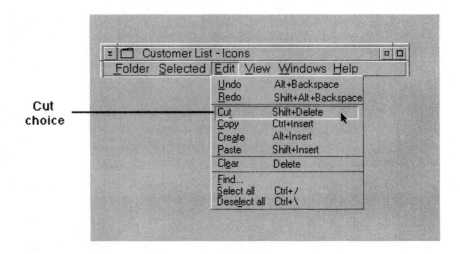

Cut
choice

When to Use

☐   Provide a **Cut** choice for all objects.

Guidelines

☑   If you provide a **Cut** choice, and you provide an **Edit** menu, place the **Cut** choice in the **Edit** menu.

☐   If you provide the **Cut** choice for an object, place the **Cut** choice in the pop-up menu for the object when the object can currently be cut.

☑   When a user cuts an object, remove it from the object it was in and place it on the clipboard.

☑   Display the **Cut** choice with unavailable-state emphasis when the selected object cannot be cut or when nothing is selected.

☑   Assign Shift+Delete as the shortcut key combination for the **Cut** choice.

☑   Assign "T" as the mnemonic for the **Cut** menu choice.

Essential Related Topics

- "Clipboard" on page 224
- "Copy (Choice)" on page 240
- "Create (Choice)" on page 242
- "Data Transfer" on page 248
- "Edit Menu" on page 270
- "Paste (Choice)" on page 376

Supplemental Related Topics

- "Clear (Choice)" on page 222
- "Delete (Choice)" on page 254
- "Pop-Up Menu" on page 388

Data Transfer

The transmission of data from one object to another. Clipboard operations (cut, copy, create and paste) and direct-manipulation techniques, like dragging, are data-transfer operations.

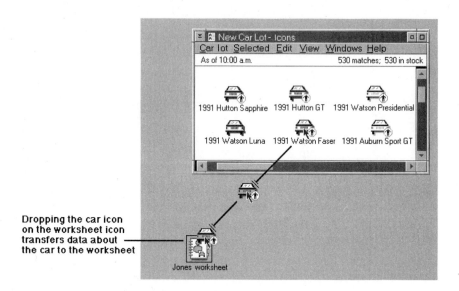

Dropping the car icon on the worksheet icon transfers data about the car to the worksheet

Guidelines

☐ Do not change the state of a source object or group of objects as a result of a data-transfer operation. For example, if a user copies selected text to the clipboard, do not remove selected-state emphasis from the text when the copying operation is complete.

☐ If the target of a data-transfer operation is an object or group of objects of a different type from the source, then add, insert, or combine the source object into the target object.

☑ When a container is transferred by dragging the container's icon, transfer the contents of the container along with the container. For example, when a folder is moved or copied to another container, move or copy the folder's contents to that container as well.

Essential Related Topics

- "Clipboard" on page 224
- "Direct Manipulation" on page 261

Supplemental Related Topics

- "Copy (Choice)" on page 240
- "Cut (Choice)" on page 246
- "Paste (Choice)" on page 376
- "Pop-Up Menu" on page 388

Default Action

A default action is an action that is performed when a user presses the Enter key, double-clicks the selection button on an object, or performs a direct-manipulation operation. The default action is intended to be the action that a user would most likely want in the given situation.

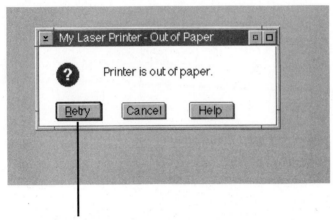

Default push button : Pressing Enter retries printing the object, anticipating that a user has refilled the printer with paper.

When to Use

☐   Provide a default action:

- For double-clicking and dragging of icons
- For a frequently-used action on a view of an object
- Whenever a predefined push button is provided in a window.

Guidelines

☑   Assign default actions as in Figure 162.

Figure 162. Default Actions

Context	User action	Default action
System-menu symbol	Double-click mouse selection button	Close window
Minimized window	Double-click mouse selection button	Restore the minimized window to its previous size and position
Cursor positioned on minimized window	Enter key	Restore the minimized window to its previous size and position

Default Action

☐   Assign default actions as in Figure 163.

Figure 163. Recommended Default Actions		
Context	**User action**	**Recommended default action**
Icon	Double-click mouse selection button	Open a new window containing the last displayed view of an object. If the icon is currently displayed with in-use emphasis, surface the existing window or open a new window, depending on the type of behavior the user has specified for the operating environment.
Icon	Drag using pointing device	**Move** or **Copy,** depending on source and target objects
Cursor positioned on icon	Enter key	Open a new window containing the last displayed view of an object
Window containing a frequently-used push button choice	Enter key	Perform action assigned to the frequently-used push button
Window not containing a frequently-used push button choice	Enter key	Perform default action assigned for object on which the cursor is positioned
Information message	Enter key	Close information message window (using the **OK** push button)
Warning message	Enter key	Perform non-destructive action
Action message	Enter key	Retry if supported; otherwise, perform a non-destructive action.

☑   Provide a visible cue to indicate which push button in a window performs the default action for that window. For example, place a dark border around the push button that performs the default action for that window.

☐   When the cursor is on a push button, make that push button the default for that window.

☐ When the cursor is moved from a field of push buttons, reset the default push button to be the same as it was before the cursor entered that field of push buttons. For example, if a user moves the cursor from the **OK** push button (the default) to the **Help** push button (the new default), then moves the cursor to a field of radio buttons, the default push button should again be the **OK** push button.

Essential Related Topics

- "Data Transfer" on page 248

- "Push Button (Control)" on page 400

- "Push Button (Predefined)" on page 404

Supplemental Related Topics

- "Direct Manipulation" on page 261

- "Icon" on page 300

- "System Menu" on page 475

- "Window" on page 496

Delete (Choice)

Delete (Choice)

An action choice that removes a selected object or group of objects and compresses the space it occupied.

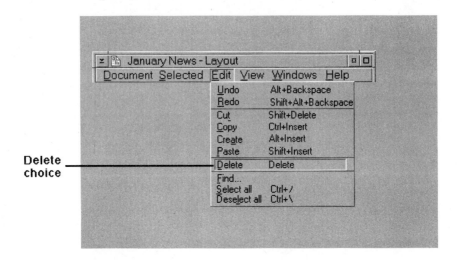

Delete choice

When to Use

☐   Provide a **Delete** choice if an object or group of objects can be removed and the space it occupied in the window can be compressed.

Guidelines

☑   If you provide a **Delete** choice, and you provide an **Edit** menu, place the **Delete** choice in the **Edit** menu.

☐   If you provide the **Delete** choice for an object, place the **Delete** choice in the pop-up menu for the object when the object can currently be deleted.

☑   If you provide the **Delete** choice, display it with unavailable-state emphasis when the selected object or group of objects cannot be removed, the space the selected object or group of objects occupied in the window cannot be compressed, or nothing is selected.

☐   If the object for which the **Delete** choice is requested supports reflections, display the **Delete** choice as a routing choice that leads to a cascaded menu with choices for deleting just this reflection or deleting the entire object and all reflections on it.

☑   When a user selects the **Delete** choice, move the remaining information closer together so that it closes the space previously occupied by the removed information. For example, if characters are removed from an entry field, move the remaining characters closer together.

☐   Use the default delete folder provided by the operating environment as the destination of the **Delete** choice for objects represented by icons.

☐   If the destination of the **Delete** choice is a delete folder, append the label of the **Delete** choice with the name of the associated delete folder. For example, modify the choice to read **Delete to Trash1** when "Trash1" is the name assigned to the delete folder into which the **Delete** choice will place cleared objects.

☐   If a user changes the name of the delete folder to which deleted choices are placed, immediately update the label of the **Delete** choice to display the new name of the delete folder.

☑   If you provide the **Delete** choice, assign Delete as the shortcut key.

☑   Assign "D" as the mnemonic for the **Delete** choice.

Essential Related Topics

*   "Clear (Choice)" on page 222

*   "Edit Menu" on page 270

Supplemental Related Topics

*   "Delete Folder (Object)" on page 256

Delete Folder (Object)

A folder that holds objects and that will remove the objects it holds from a user's system. A delete folder could delete objects immediately, or it could allow the user to specify when the objects are to be deleted.

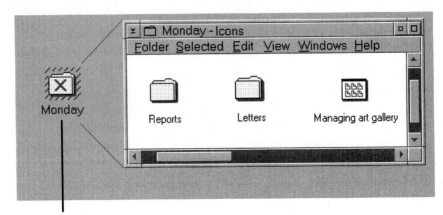

Delete Folder

When to Use

☐ Provide access to the delete folder provided by the operating environment to allow a user to remove objects from the operating environment.

Guidelines

☐ If a delete folder is provided by the operating environment, support it. For example, allow a user to place your objects in the delete folder provided by the operating environment.

☑ When a container is placed in a delete folder, place the contents of the container in the delete folder along with the container.

Essential Related Topics

• "Container (Control)" on page 231

Delete

Delete Folder (Object)

Supplemental Related Topics

- "Clear (Choice)" on page 222
- "Delete (Choice)" on page 254
- "Folder (Object)" on page 287

Descriptive Text

Text used in addition to a field prompt to provide information about a field.

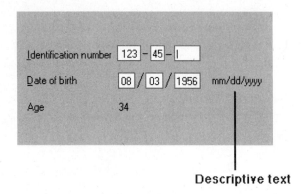

Descriptive text

When to Use

☐ Use descriptive text to provide additional information about a control or field of controls when other labels are not sufficient to explain its function. For example, describe the required date format for an entry field that will contain a date.

Guidelines

☐ If you provide descriptive text, place it to the right or below the control it describes.

☐ Place descriptive text so that it cannot be confused with a field prompt or column heading. For example, in two columns of controls, align the second column of field prompts to the right of the left edge of the longest descriptive text in the first column of controls as in Figure 164 on page 259.

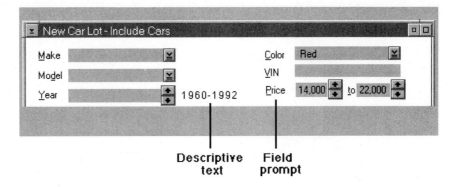

Descriptive   Field
text   prompt

Figure 164. Columns of Controls with Descriptive Text

☐　　　For controls that support more than one type of selection,
provide information about the number of items that can be
selected. For example, provide descriptive text for list boxes
that provide multiple selection, and show in the descriptive
text that more than one item can be selected.

Supplemental Related Topics

- "Column Heading" on page 227
- "Control" on page 235
- "Field Prompt" on page 278
- "Group Heading" on page 292
- "Window Layout" on page 500

Device (Object)

An object that represents a physical or logical device, such as a printer, mouse, or scanner, that is connected to a user's system. Device objects can be provided by products or by the operating environment.

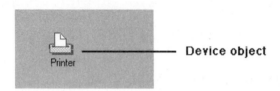

Device object

When to Use

☐ Provide a device object for each device to which a user has access.

Guidelines

☐ Allow each device object to support data-transfer operations. For example, allow a user to drag and drop objects onto printer, plotter, and film-recorder device objects.

☑ If you provide access to a device object from a menu and there is more than one device that a user has access to through that device object, allow the user to designate the device to be used. For example from a **Print** choice, provide a list of printers in a cascaded menu or in a window.

Supplemental Related Topics

• "Data Transfer" on page 248

• "Object" on page 366

Direct Manipulation

A set of techniques that allow a user to work with an object by dragging it with a pointing device or interacting with its pop-up menu.

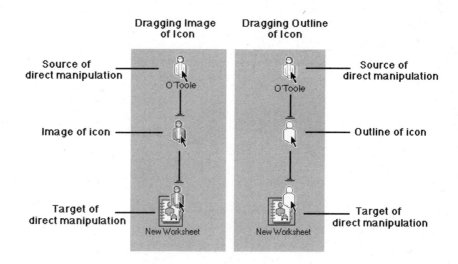

When to Use

☑   Provide direct manipulation for all objects represented as icons on the workplace.

Guidelines

☑   When a user presses the Cancel key or when a user drops an object onto the same position it currently occupies, cancel the direct-manipulation operation.

☐   Avoid changing the input focus as a result of a direct-manipulation operation.

☑   Do not change which window is the active window when a direct-manipulation operation is performed.

☐   Provide contextual help for direct-manipulation operations.

☑   If you provide contextual help for a direct-manipulation operation, allow a user to display contextual help about the direct-manipulation operation by pressing the Help key.

Direct Manipulation

☐ Allow a user to transfer data through direct manipulation. For example, when a user drags a document to a printer, prepare the document to be printed and schedule it to be printed on that printer.

☑ During a direct-manipulation operation, display source emphasis on the source object.

☑ During a direct-manipulation operation, if a target object is in a state where it can receive data as a result of the direct-manipulation operation, display target emphasis on the target object when the pointer is on that object.

☑ During a direct-manipulation operation, if a target object is in a state where it can receive data as a result of the direct manipulation operation, but cannot receive the object being directly manipulated, display target emphasis and change the pointer when the pointer is over that object. For example, change the pointer to the "do not" pointer.

☐ During a direct-manipulation operation on a single object, drag a copy of the icon or an outline of the object. If an identical image of an icon for that object is not available, substitute an outline of the object's icon.

☐ During a direct-manipulation operation on a group of objects where the spatial relationship between the objects in the group is not relevant for positioning in the view of the target object, such as on the workplace and in folders, drag a generic image of three overlapped objects.

☐ If a direct-manipulation operation is performed on a group of objects and the requested action cannot be performed on all of the objects, perform the requested action on the valid objects and display a message giving completion information.

☐ During a direct-manipulation operation on a group of objects where the spatial relationship between the objects in the group is relevant for positioning in the view of the target object, such as in a composed view of an object, drag the objects while maintaining their relative positions.

☐ When a user drags an image or an outline of an object to perform a copy operation, dim the image or outline as in Figures 165 and 166 on page 262.

Figure 165. Dragging an Image of an Object

	Single object	Multiple objects
Move operation		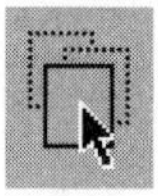
Copy operation		

Figure 166. Dragging an Outline of an Object

	Single object	Multiple objects
Move operation		
Copy operation		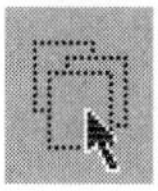

☐   When a user drags an object or group of objects, attach an image or outline of the object or group of objects to the pointer at the spot on the object or within the group of objects where the direct-manipulation operation was initiated.

☑   When a direct-manipulation operation will result in a predefined action, augment the pointer using the predefined pointer visuals.

☐   When a direct-manipulation operation will result in a product-specific action, augment the pointer to indicate what the resulting action will be.

☐   Provide a create-on-drag setting in the settings view of each object. For example, provide a **Create on drag** check box choice in an object's settings notebook. When this setting is set on, change the keyboard override of a direct-manipulation operation from the copy function to the create function.

☑   When the create-on-drag setting is set on, change the object's icon to show this setting by showing the small icon on a notepad background as in Figure 167 on page 264.

Direct Manipulation

Figure 167. Small Icon on a Notepad Background

☐   If a user drags an object to a device or from a device that is external to the user's environment, such as floppy disk, a printer, or a mail outbasket, assign the data transfer default for a direct-manipulation operation so that the source object's location is left unchanged.

☑   Allow a user to override the default data transfer for a direct-manipulation operation by pressing a key during a direct-manipulation operation, as listed in Figure 168.

Figure 168. Keyboard Overrides for Direct-Manipulation Operations	
Move	Shift+Mouse manipulation button
Create or Copy	Ctrl+Mouse manipulation button
Note: Ctrl+Mouse manipulation button will perform the create function when the create-on-drag setting is set on for the object; otherwise it will perform a copy operation.	

Essential Related Topics

- "Contextual Help" on page 233

- "Copy (Choice)" on page 240

- "Move (Choice)" on page 357

- "Pointer" on page 378

- "Source Emphasis (Cue)" on page 465

- "Target Emphasis (Cue)" on page 477

Supplemental Related Topics

- "Data Transfer" on page 248

- "Keyboard" on page 315

- "Mouse" on page 350
- "Pointing Device" on page 382
- "Pop-Up Menu" on page 388

Drop-Down Combination Box (Control)

A control that is a combination box in which the list is hidden until a user takes an action to make it visible. A drop-down combination box contains a list of objects or settings choices that a user can scroll through and select from to complete the entry field. Alternatively, a user can type text directly into the entry field. The typed text does not have to match one of the objects or settings choices contained in the list.

Drop-down combination boxes

When to Use

☐ Use a drop-down combination box when a window does not have enough space to use a combination box.

Guidelines

☐ Display an initial value from the list in the entry field.

☐ Display the initial value in the entry field with selected-state emphasis so that typed characters will replace the value.

☐ Display the choices or objects in the list in an order that is meaningful to a user, such as alphabetic order, numeric order, chronological order, or some other order. For example, display dates in chronological order.

☑ In a list that can be scrolled, such as a scrollable list box, do not allow the cursor to wrap.

☐ Display no more than six choices or objects at a time in a drop-down combination box.

☑ Provide horizontal or vertical scroll bars, or both, when some of the data is not visible in the drop-down combination box.

☐ Capitalize only the first letter of the first word of a choice or object name unless the choice or object name contains an abbreviation, acronym, or proper noun that should be capitalized.

Essential Related Topics

- "Combination Box (Control)" on page 229
- "Control" on page 235
- "Drop-Down List (Control)" on page 268
- "List Box (Control)" on page 325

Supplemental Related Topics

- "Entry Field (Control)" on page 272
- "Keyboard" on page 315
- "Mouse" on page 350
- "Text Entry" on page 479

Drop-Down List (Control)

Drop-Down List (Control)

A control that is a variation of a list box. A drop-down list only displays one item until the user takes an action to display the other objects or choices. Like a list box, the drop-down list does not allow a user to type information into it.

Drop-down lists

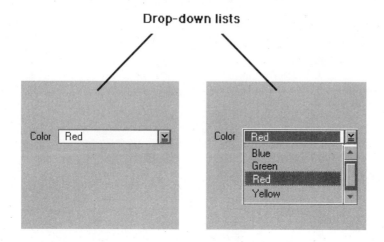

When to Use

☐ Use a drop-down list instead of a single selection list box when a choice or object is not changed frequently or when space is so limited that the window does not have enough space to display a list box.

Guidelines

☑ Display an initial value from the list in an entry field that contains read-only text.

☐ Display the choices or objects in a drop-down list in an order that is meaningful to a user, such as alphabetic order, numeric order, chronological order, or some other order. For example, display modem baud rates in numeric order.

☑ In a list that can be scrolled, such as a scrollable list box, do not allow the cursor to wrap.

☐ Display no more than six choices or objects at a time in a drop-down list.

☑ Provide horizontal or vertical scroll bars, or both, when some of the information is not visible in the drop-down list.

☐ Capitalize only the first letter of the first word of a choice or object name unless the choice or object name contains an abbreviation, acronym, or proper noun that should be capitalized.

Essential Related Topics

Supplemental Related Topics

Edit Menu

A pull-down menu from the **Edit** choice on a menu bar that contains the undo choices, the clipboard choices, and choices that affect which objects are selected. The choices in the *Edit* pull-down menu are common across a wide range of objects.

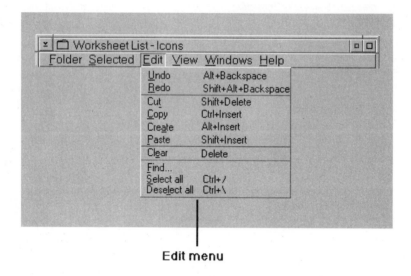

Edit menu

When to Use

☑ Provide the **Edit** menu when a menu bar is provided in a window and at least two of the following choices are provided: **Undo, Redo, Cut, Copy, Create, Paste, Clear, Delete, Find, Select all,** and **Deselect all.**

☐ Provide an **Edit** menu if you provide undo choices, clipboard choices, or choices that affect the number of objects that are selected.

Guidelines

☑ When any of the following choices are provided, place them in the following relative order in the **Edit** menu:

- **Undo**
- **Redo**
- --Separator--
- **Cut**

- **Copy**
- **Create**
- **Paste**
- --Separator--
- **Clear**
- **Delete**
- --Separator--
- **Find**
- **Select all**
- **Deselect all**

☐ Provide additional product-specific choices in the **Edit** menu grouped with other related choices.

☑ Assign "E" as the mnemonic for the **Edit** choice.

Essential Related Topics

- "Clear (Choice)" on page 222
- "Copy (Choice)" on page 240
- "Create (Choice)" on page 242
- "Cut (Choice)" on page 246
- "Delete (Choice)" on page 254
- "Find (Choice)" on page 284
- "Paste (Choice)" on page 376
- "Select All and Deselect All (Choice)" on page 435
- "Undo and Redo (Choice)" on page 487

Supplemental Related Topics

- "Selected Menu" on page 437

Entry Field (Control)

A control into which a user can type one or more lines of text. Entry fields can be scrolled if more information is available than is currently visible.

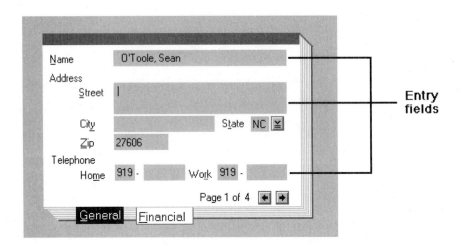

When to Use

☐ Provide an entry field to allow a user to type values that cannot be supplied by the product in a list of choices.

☐ Provide an entry field containing read-only text when a value is displayed that a user cannot change.

Guidelines

☐ When the length of the data is predictable, such as a date, time, or telephone number, make the entry field wide enough and tall enough to show all of the data of average length.

☐ Display an entry field with a background color different from the background color of the underlying window or an outline color specified by a user for the operating environment. Use the user-specified color setting for entry fields if provided by the operating environment; otherwise, use another related component setting.

☐ To indicate a required entry field, display along the bottom edge of the entry field a thin unbroken line of a solid color specified by the user for the operating environment. For example, with VGA resolution use a one-pel solid green line along the bottom of an entry field.

☐   To indicate an error in the information entered in an entry field, display, along the bottom, left, and right edges of the entry field, a thin unbroken line of a solid color specified by the user for the operating environment. For example, with VGA resolution use a one-pel solid red line on the bottom, left, and right edges of an entry field.

☐   To indicate an entry field containing read-only text, display the entry field text against the normal window background and do not display an outline box around the text. That is, display the entry field text against the normal window background.

Figure 169. Different Types of Entry Fields

Description	Example
Entry field with outline box	Text
Entry field with background color of entry field	Text
Entry field with background color of entry field— Required	Text
Entry field with background color of entry field— Error	Text
Entry field with background color of the underlying window— Read-only	Text
Entry field with background color of entry field— Scrollable	◀ a very long line of text ▶

☑   Allow a user to scroll data in an entry field when more text can be typed or when more information is available than can be displayed in the entry field at any one time.

☐   When information can be scrolled in an entry field, provide a visible cue to indicate that the information can be scrolled. For example, provide left and right arrow scroll push buttons on an entry field of one line or provide a scroll bar for an entry field of more than one line.

☐   If an entry field allows tabs within the field, allow a user to press Ctrl+Tab to exit the entry field and to move the cursor to the next control in the window.

Entry Field (Control)

□   If an entry field must contain a value, provide an appropriate initial value.

□   If a user will typically accept the initial value in the entry field or replace it by typing, display the initial value with selected-state emphasis so that the text is replaced by the first typed character.

Essential Related Topics

- "Control" on page 235
- "Text Entry" on page 479

Supplemental Related Topics

- "Combination Box (Control)" on page 229
- "Drop-Down Combination Box (Control)" on page 266
- "Spin Button (Control)" on page 467
- "Window Layout" on page 500
- "Window Navigation" on page 507

Extended Selection

A type of selection optimized for the selection of a single object. A user can extend selection to more than one object, if required.

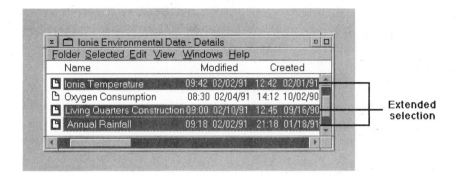

When to Use

☐ Provide extended selection when a user typically performs actions on one object at a time, but can perform actions on more than one object at a time.

Guidelines

☑ Allow a keyboard user to press Shift+F8 to establish a mode in which the initial deselection is bypassed and the new selected objects are added or removed from the current group of selected objects.

☑ Allow a user to modify the extended selection by pressing and holding down the Ctrl key while selecting an object or group of objects.

☑ Design your product so that the results listed in Figure 170 on page 276 occur during extended selection.

Extended Selection

Figure 170 (Page 1 of 2). Extended Selection Techniques			
Technique	**Mouse**	**Keyboard**	**Result**
Point selection	Click mouse selection button with pointer on object to be selected.	With cursor on object to be selected, press Ctrl+Spacebar; also spacebar if spacebar is not used to type a space.	Deselects all other objects in selection scope; selects single identified object.
Point-to-endpoint selection			
Area (Marquee)	Press mouse selection button at the start point and move the pointer to the end point; release the mouse selection button at the end point.	Not applicable.	Deselects all other objects in selection scope; selects all objects contained within the identified area.
Range (Swipe)	Press mouse selection button at the start point and move the pointer to the end point; release the mouse selection button at the end point.	Press Shift at the start point and hold while using cursor-movement keys to move the cursor to the end point; release Shift at end point.	Deselects all other objects in selection scope; selects all objects in order from the identified start point to the identified end point.
Range (Click)	Click mouse selection button at the start point; press Shift and click the mouse selection button at the end point, then release Shift key.	Not applicable.	Deselects all other objects in selection scope; selects all objects in order from the identified start point to the identified end point.
Random-point selection			

Technique	Mouse	Keyboard	Result
Random (Swipe)	Press mouse selection button with pointer on first object to be selected; move the pointer over other objects to be selected; release mouse selection button.	Not applicable.	Deselects all other objects in selection scope; selects individual objects in the order the user identified the objects to be selected.

Figure 170 (Page 2 of 2). Extended Selection Techniques

Note:

Modifying extended selection

When a user is using a mouse, pressing the Ctrl key while performing a selection technique allows the user to add objects to and remove objects from the current group of selected objects by bypassing the initial deselection.

In point selection and random-point selection, pressing the Ctrl key while selecting an object or group of objects toggles the selection state of the first object or group of objects selected and that new state becomes the selection state of all objects selected thereafter until the Ctrl key is released.

In point-to-endpoint selection, the selection state of the start point is toggled first and that new state becomes the selection state of all objects within the range or area.

In point selection and random-point selection, pressing spacebar toggles the selection state of the identified object.

Essential Related Topics

- "Multiple Selection" on page 358

- "Selection Types and Techniques" on page 440

- "Single Selection" on page 457

Supplemental Related Topics

- "Automatic Selection" on page 213

- "Descriptive Text" on page 258

- "Information Area" on page 307

- "Marquee Selection" on page 327

- "Point-to-Endpoint Selection" on page 385

- "Point Selection" on page 383

- "Status Area (Cue)" on page 473

Field Prompt

Text that identifies a field, such as a field of check boxes or an entry field.

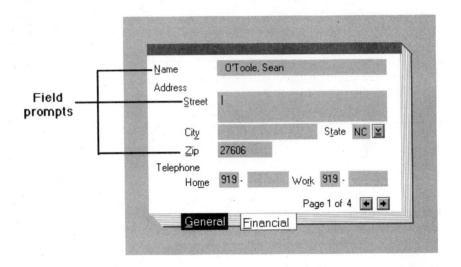

When to Use

☐ Provide a field prompt for each field unless there is only one field in the window and the window title serves as the field prompt.

☐ Provide a field prompt for each field unless the fields appear in columns and the column headings serve as the field prompts.

Guidelines

☐ Place a field prompt above or to the left of the field it is associated with.

☐ If a field prompt is displayed above a field, align the prompt with the left edge of the field.

☐ In high-volume data-entry windows, consider using right-aligned edges of field prompts next to left-aligned entry fields so that a narrow vertical column of space is left between the field prompts and their associated entry fields to allow a user to quickly scan the choices in the window.

☐   If a field prompt is displayed under a group heading, indent the field prompt to the right of the group heading.

☐   Capitalize only the first letter of the first word of a field prompt unless the prompt contains an abbreviation, acronym, or proper noun that should be capitalized.

☐   Use descriptive text to provide additional information.

☐   Left-align fields of controls along a margin to the right of the longest field prompt in a column.

Supplemental Related Topics

File Menu (Application-Oriented)

A pull-down menu from the **File** choice on a menu bar that contains choices that affect the object presented in that window.

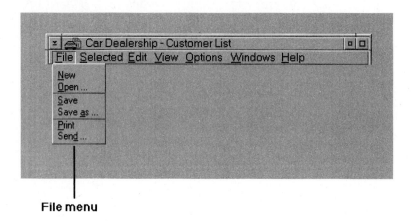

File menu

When to Use

Provide a **File** menu choice in all application-oriented windows that provide a menu bar if any of the **File** menu choices are provided.

Guidelines

☑ When the following choices are provided, place them in the following relative order in the **File** menu:

- **New**
- **Open**
- --Separator--
- **Save**
- **Save as**
- --Separator--
- **Print**

☐ Add any product-specific choices, as needed, grouped with other related choices.

☑ Assign "F" as the mnemonic for the **File** menu choice.

Essential Related Topics

- "Menu (Control)" on page 331

- "New (Choice)" on page 361

- "Open (Choice)" on page 369

- "Print (Choice)" on page 393

- "Save (Choice)" on page 423

- "Save As (Choice)" on page 427

Supplemental Related Topics

- "File Menu (Object-Oriented)" on page 282

- "Menu Bar" on page 334

File Menu (Object-Oriented)

A pull-down menu from a choice labeled with the class name of the object in the window, that contains choices that affect the underlying object presented in that window.

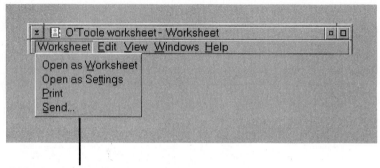

Object-oriented File menu

When to Use

☑ Provide a **File** menu choice, object-oriented version, in all object-oriented windows that provide a menu bar if any of the **File** menu choices are provided.

Guidelines

☑ Label the menu bar choice with the class-name of the object in the window. For example, for a worksheet object, label the menu-bar choice **Worksheet.**

☑ When the following choices are provided, place them in the following relative order in the **File** menu:

- **Open as**
- --Separator--
- **Save** (use only if the save function is not immediate)
- --Separator--
- **Print**

☐ Add any product-specific choices, as needed, grouped with other related choices.

☑   Assign a unique mnemonic for the class name choice.

Essential Related Topics

•   "Menu (Control)" on page 331

•   "Open As (Choice)" on page 371

•   "Print (Choice)" on page 393

•   "Save (Choice)" on page 423

Supplemental Related Topics

•   "File Menu (Application-Oriented)" on page 280

•   "Menu Bar" on page 334

Find (Choice)

A routing choice that displays an action window that allows a user to search an object displayed in a window. A user can specify the criteria to be used for the search. The find operation searches the current view of the object from which the **Find** choice was selected.

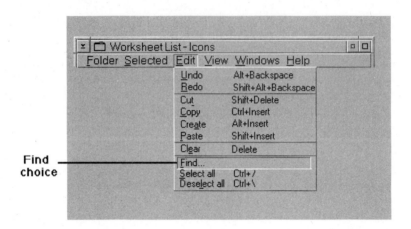

Find choice

When to Use

☐ Provide a **Find** choice for each object.

Guidelines

☑ If you provide a **Find** choice, and you provide an **Edit** menu, place the **Find** choice in the **Edit** menu.

☐ If you provide the **Find** choice for an object, place the **Find** choice in the pop-up menu for the object when the object can currently be searched.

☑ If you provide the **Find** choice, provide an action window that allows a user to specify the parameters of the search. For example, allow a user to specify the text to be found, the direction of the search, or sensitivity to text capitalization.

☐ Avoid changing the contents of a window as a result of a find operation, except to scroll the next matching object into sight and to indicate that it matches the search criteria, such as by selecting the matching word.

☐   Avoid removing the **Find** action window unless a user explicitly requests to remove it, such as by selecting a **Close** push button.

☐   Always display the **Find** action window on top of the primary window it is dependent on, even when the **Find** action window is not the active window.

☐   Avoid opening a new window to display the results of the find operation.

☑   Assign "F" as the mnemonic for the **Find** choice.

Essential Related Topics

•   "Edit Menu" on page 270

Supplemental Related Topics

•   "Include (Choice)" on page 305

First-Letter Cursor Navigation

A selection technique in which users select an object in a list by typing the first character of the object they want to select.

When to Use

☑ Provide first-letter cursor navigation in all lists of objects or settings choices, such as details views, list boxes, and drop-down lists.

Guidelines

☑ When a user types a letter, move the cursor to the next object or settings choice that starts with that letter.

☑ When a user types a letter that has no valid match, do not move the cursor.

☑ Allow a user to press either the uppercase or lowercase character to gain access to first-letter cursor navigation.

Essential Related Topics

- "Audible Feedback" on page 212
- "Cursor" on page 244

Supplemental Related Topics

- "Drop-Down List (Control)" on page 268
- "List Box (Control)" on page 325

Folder (Object)

A container object used to store and organize objects.

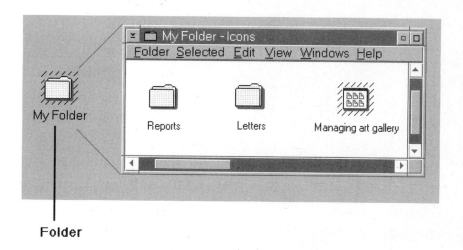

Folder

When to Use

☐   Provide a folder to allow a user to store and group objects.

Guidelines

☑   When a user closes or minimizes a folder, continue to display
      any window opened on an object contained in that folder.

☐   If folders are provided by the operating environment, support
      them. For example, allow a user to place your objects into
      the folders provided by the operating environment and use
      the folders provided by the operating environment to create
      product-specific folders.

☐   Provide a settings choice that allows a user to change
      between a folder and a work area. For example, provide a
      choice on a check box in the settings view of a folder that
      allows a user to change the folder into a work area.

☐   If a user changes a folder into a work area, immediately
      change its icon to that of a work area.

☐   Allow a user to place any object into a folder.

Folder (Object)

☐ Provide a folder containing sample objects from which users can create new objects. Make the create-on-drag setting the initial setting for the objects in the folder. For example, provide a folder named "New Forms" containing initialized versions of frequently-used forms.

Essential Related Topics

- "Container (Control)" on page 231
- "Work Area (Object)" on page 512

Supplemental Related Topics

- "Delete Folder (Object)" on page 256

General Help (Choice)

An action choice that displays a window containing a brief overview of the function of the window from which the **General help** choice was selected.

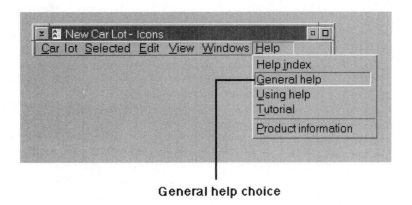

General help choice

When to Use

☑   Provide a **General help** choice for each **Help** menu.

Guidelines

☑   When a user selects the **General help** choice, display a window containing general help information.

☑   Assign "G" as the mnemonic for the **General help** choice.

Essential Related Topics

•   "Help Menu" on page 296

Group Box

A rectangular box drawn around a group of fields to indicate that the fields are related and to provide a label for the group.

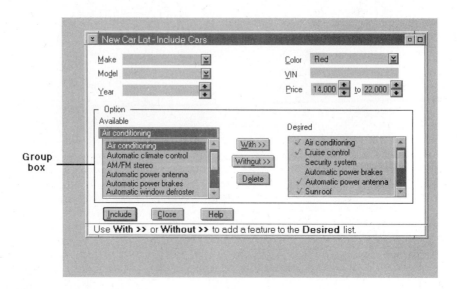

When to Use

☐ Use a group box only when a group heading or white space does not visually distinguish groups of fields in a window.

Guidelines

☑ Provide a label for each group box.

☐ Capitalize only the first letter of the first word of a label of a group box unless the label contains an abbreviation, acronym, or proper noun that should be capitalized.

☐ Avoid using a group box around a field of push buttons.

☐ Avoid using a group box around a single field. For example, avoid using a group box around a single list box.

Supplemental Related Topics

- "Control" on page 235

- "Group Heading" on page 292

- "Separator" on page 446

- "Window Layout" on page 500

Group Heading

Text that identifies a set of related fields.

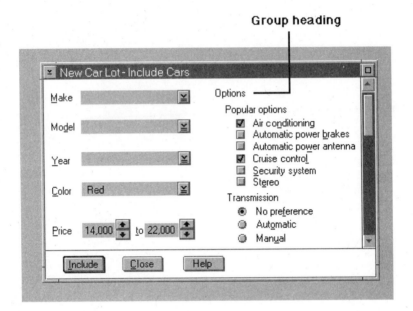

Group heading

When to Use

☐   Use a group heading rather than a group box to identify a group of related fields.

Guidelines

☐   Place a group heading above each group of fields.

☐   Indent the fields in each group under their associated group heading.

☐   Left-align group headings vertically with the left edge of other group headings.

☐   Capitalize the first letter of the first and last words of a group heading, and all other words except articles, coordinating conjunctions, prepositions, and the "to" in infinitives.

☐   If a group heading appears in a window that can be scrolled, scroll the heading with the group it identifies.

Supplemental Related Topics

- "Control" on page 235

- "Field Prompt" on page 278

- "Window Layout" on page 500

Help Index (Choice)

An action choice that displays an alphabetic listing of all help topics within the product or application.

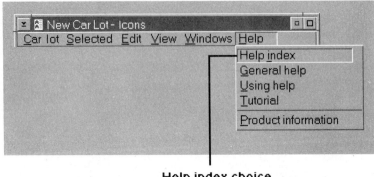

Help index choice

When to Use

☑ Provide a **Help index** choice in each help menu.

Guidelines

☑ Provide access to keys help from the help index window. For example, provide a **Keys help** choice in a menu or on a push button in the help index window that allows a user to get keys help.

☑ Provide access to the help index from every help window.

☐ Follow appropriate indexing conventions (such as printed material conventions) to create a help index.

☐ Indicate which entries in a help index lead to task-oriented help and tutorial help. For example, provide entries for the **Copy task** and the **Copy tutorial.**

☐ Place in the help index an entry for each help topic about an object.

☐ Place in the help index an entry for each help topic about a window or choice.

☐ Provide synonyms for each help index entry.

Help Index (Choice)

☑ Allow a user to search the help index. For example, provide a **Search** routing choice in a menu or on a push button.

☐ When a user specifies a synonym as a search criterion, find the corresponding help topic and display it in a secondary window with a title bar containing the name of the help topic that was found as a match to the synonym. For example, if a user specifies the topic "action bar" as a search criterion, and you've provided help for the topic "menu bar," display help for menu bar in a window entitled "Menu Bar - Help."

☐ Do not include the words "Help for" in index entries. For example, do not label an entry "Help for Cut."

☑ Assign "I" as the mnemonic for the **Help index** choice.

Essential Related Topics

- "Help Menu" on page 296
- "Keys Help" on page 323

Help Menu

A pull-down menu from the **Help** choice on a menu bar that contains choices that provide information about a window, choice, object, or a task.

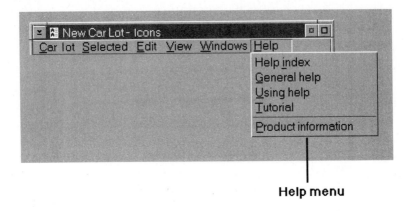

Help menu

When to Use

☑ Provide a **Help** choice in the menu bar of all windows that have a menu bar and provide help.

Guidelines

☑ When the following choices are provided, place them in the following relative order in the **Help** menu:

- **Help index**
- **General help**
- **Using help**
- **Tutorial**
- --Separator--
- **Product information**

☑ If you provide other **Help** choices, place them between the **Using help** choice and the **Product information** choice in the **Help** menu. For example, if you provide a **Getting started** choice, place it below the **Using help** choice and above the **Product information** choice.

☑ Place a **Help** choice on a push button in a window if that window does not have a menu bar.

☐   Display help information in a secondary window.

☐   Create the title of a **Help** window by naming the object or action about which help was requested followed by a dash (–) and the word **Help.**

☐   If additional wording is helpful in identifying the window, place the extra words after the dash (to the right, left, or both sides of the word **Help**). For example, label the window **MyObject – General Help.**

☐   Do not place the title of a help window in the text of the help information; instead, rely on the title bar.

☐   When a user selects a Help choice or presses the Help key, do not change the state or appearance of the object about which help was requested. For example, if a user requests help about a check-box choice, do not select the check-box choice because help was requested.

☐   Place a help window so that it does not cover the object for which help was requested.

☐   Provide help in the form most appropriate and useful to a user. For example, use text, graphics, animation, audio, video, or any other technique or combination of techniques that conveys the information clearly and concisely.

☑   Assign "H" as the mnemonic for the **Help** menu choice.

Essential Related Topics

Help Menu

Supplemental Related Topics

- "Contextual Help" on page 233
- "Keyboard" on page 315
- "Keys Help" on page 323
- "Window Title" on page 510

Hide (Choice)

An action choice that removes the window and all associated windows from the workplace.

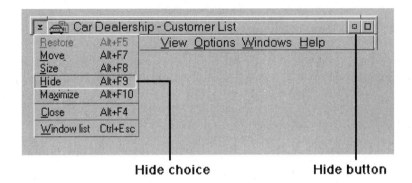

Hide choice   Hide button

When to Use

☐   Provide a **Hide** choice for windows in an operating environment that supports the hide function.

Guidelines

☑   When a **Hide** function is provided, place a hide button on the title bar of each window that can be hidden.

☐   When a user selects the **Hide** choice or the hide button, remove the window and all associated windows from the workplace and indicate its hidden status in a window list.

☑   Assign Alt+F9 as the shortcut key combination for the **Hide** choice.

☑   Assign "H" as the mnemonic for the **Hide** choice.

Essential Related Topics

•   "Window List" on page 503

Supplemental Related Topics

•   "System Menu" on page 475

Icon

Icon

A pictorial representation of an object, consisting of an image, image background, and a label. Small icons can be substituted for regular icons. The small icon in the title bar of a window is another icon for the object that is displayed in the window.

1991 Watson Luna

When to Use

☑ When a user places an object on the workplace, use an icon to represent that object.

Guidelines

☐ Display a small icon in the title bar of each window that displays a view of an object.

☑ If you provide a small icon in the title bar of a window, place it immediately to the right of the system-menu symbol.

☑ If you provide a small icon in the title bar of a window, provide the same direct manipulation functions for it as are available for the object's icon. For example, allow a user to print the object by dragging the small icon in the title bar to a printer.

☑ If you provide a small icon in the title bar of a window, display target emphasis on the small icon in the title bar during a direct manipulation operation when the object in the window is a valid target of the direct-manipulation operation.

☑ Provide a label for each icon, except for the small icon in the title bar; in that case, the window title serves as the label for the small icon in the title bar.

☑ Use the name of the object as the label for the icon.

☐　　　Design an icon so that it shows the important characteristics of the object it represents and important states of the object. Such characteristics might include:

- Needs attention, for example, when a printer is out of paper

- Threshold reached, for example, when a mailbox is full

- Read-only, for example, when a user does not have the ability to edit a document.

- Security classification, for example, confidential or restricted

- Urgency, for example, when a piece of urgent electronic mail arrives

- Quantity, for example, the number of objects a container holds.

☐　　　When an icon displays the state or settings of the object it represents, immediately update the icon to indicate changes to the state or settings. For example, if a user selects an object, immediately display selected-state emphasis on the icon that represents the selected object.

☐　　　If a user changes a folder into a work area or changes a work area into a folder, immediately update the icon of that container to indicate the change.

☐　　　Allow a user to customize the appearance of an icon. For example, allow a user to change an icon to make it more meaningful, recognizable, or personal.

☑　　　Display appropriate emphasis, such as source emphasis, target emphasis, selected-state emphasis, and in-use emphasis, when a user interacts with an icon. For example, display an object's icon with in-use emphasis when a user displays a view of that object in a window.

☑　　　Do not show in-use emphasis on small icons used in the title bar.

☑　　　Do not display a count of the number of objects in a container on a small icon.

☐　　　Do not use an algorithmically reduced copy of the original icon as a small icon. Instead, use a separate graphic to display a small icon that shows fewer characteristics so that the characteristics can be more easily distinguished.

Icon

☐ Allow a user to rename an object where that object is displayed.

☐ If you allow a user to edit an icon's label, provide text entry techniques that allow the user to type, select, and manipulate the text of the icon's label.

Supplemental Related Topics

Inactive Window

A window that does not have the input focus. The inactive window is indicated by the type of emphasis displayed on its title bar and border, as specified by the operating environment.

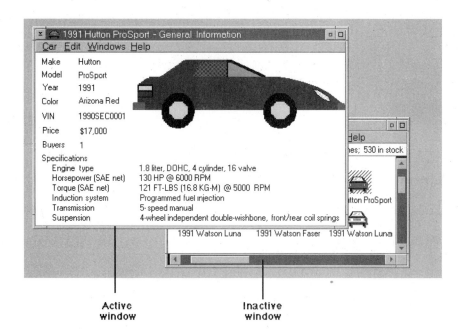

Active   Inactive
window   window

When to Use

☑   Make any window that does not currently have the input focus an inactive window.

Guidelines

☑   Change the color of the title bar and window border of an inactive window to the color specified in the operating environment.

☑   Do not continue to display the cursor an inactive window.

☑   Display any appropriate emphasis types in an inactive window. For example, display selected-state emphasis for selected objects displayed in an inactive window.

Inactive Window

Essential Related Topics

- "Active Window" on page 210

- "Input Focus" on page 312

Supplemental Related Topics

- "Window" on page 496

Include (Choice)

A routing choice that displays an action window that allows a user to specify characteristics of a subset of objects so that only the subset is displayed in the window.

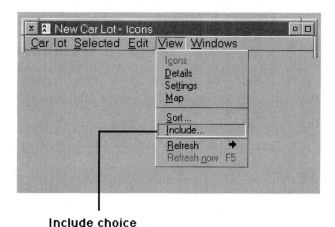

Include choice

When to Use

⊓ Provide an **Include** choice when it is useful to identify subsets of objects contained within the object from which the **Include** choice is selected.

Guidelines

☑ If you provide an **Include** choice, and you provide a **View** menu, place the **Include** choice in the **View** menu.

☐ If you provide the **Include** choice for an object, place the **Include** choice in the pop-up menu for the object when the object can currently be included.

☑ Allow a user to specify the objects that are to be shown in the view.

☑ Display the **Include** settings in an action window that is dependent on the window from which the **Include** choice is selected.

Include (Choice)

☑ Display the results of the **Include** operation in the window from which the **Include** choice was selected.

☐ In the window in which the results of the **Include** operation will be displayed, provide a status area to list the criteria used to create the subset. For example, indicate the number of objects displayed, as well as the total number of objects in the container.

☐ When an object is added to another object on which an included view is displayed and in which the include criteria are being maintained for that view, and the object being added matches the include criteria for the subset, place the object being added in its correct position in the subset. For example, if a document is added to a folder and that document matches the current include criteria for that folder, the document will be visible in the current view; if the document does not match the include criteria, the document is added to the folder, but the document will not be visible in the current view.

☐ When a user performs an include operation on an object, apply the include criteria to the entire object, not just the contents of the current view of the object.

☑ Assign "I" as the mnemonic for the **Include** choice.

Essential Related Topics

- "View Menu" on page 492

Supplemental Related Topics

- "Find (Choice)" on page 284
- "Status Area (Cue)" on page 473

Information Area

A part of a window where information appears about the object or choice that the cursor is on. Information about the normal completion of a process can also appear in the information area.

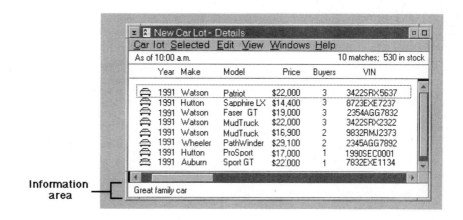

Information area

When to Use

☐ Provide an information area for each window.

Guidelines

☐ When the cursor is on a choice, briefly describe in an information area what will happen when a user selects that choice.

☐ When the cursor is on an object, briefly suggest in an information area:

- The default action, if any.
- The most appropriate action, if any.
- How to perform available actions on the object.

☐ Place information about the normal completion of a process in the information area. For example, indicate in an information area that a file was successfully saved.

☐ For contents views that provide a selection type other than extended selection, place in the information area information about the number of items that can be selected. For example, for single selection display text saying, "Select at most one."

☐ Make the information area the same width as the window.

☐ Make the information area no taller than necessary to accommodate brief, but meaningful, information. For example, when using text, accommodate only two lines of text.

☐ If you provide an information area, place it at the bottom of a window.

☐ If you provide an information area and there is a horizontal scroll bar in the window, place the information area below the scroll bar and above the window border.

☐ Use a separator to separate the information area from the rest of the window. For example, use a solid line or a horizontal scroll bar to separate the information area from the rest of the window.

☐ If you provide an information area, do not scroll the information area when the window's contents are scrolled.

☐ If a user attempts to select a choice that is currently displayed with unavailable-state emphasis, indicate in the information area that the choice cannot be selected and that requesting help will explain why it is unavailable.

☑ If you provide an information area, allow a user to turn the display of the information area on or off. For example, provide a settings choice in the **View** pull-down menu or on a page in a settings notebook that allows a user to turn the display of the information area on or off.

☐ Remove information from the information area as soon as it is no longer relevant to the current state of the window or the current position of the cursor.

☐ Do not allow a user to interact with the information area, except to copy information from the information area.

☐ Do not use an information area to display information that a user must see; display that type of information in a message.

☐ If a user reduces the width of a window with an information area and the information can wrap in the information area, wrap the information; otherwise, clip the information area.

☐ Do not provide scroll bars for an information area and do not allow a user to scroll information in the information area.

Essential Related Topics

• "Information Message" on page 310

• "Separator" on page 446

Supplemental Related Topics

• "Choice" on page 218

• "Clipboard" on page 224

• "Progress Indicator" on page 396

• "Status Area (Cue)" on page 473

• "Window Layout" on page 500

Information Message

A message that indicates that a condition has occurred that the user can do nothing about. The only actions available to the user are to acknowledge the message or get help.

When to Use

☑   Display an information message when a situation has occurred that the user can do nothing about or when there is additional information about the status of normal completion. If a progress indicator is currently displayed in its own window, display the message information in the progress indicator window.

Guidelines

☑   Provide an **OK** push button that allows a user to acknowledge the information displayed in the information message and remove the message.

☑   Display the *i* symbol in each information-message window.

Essential Related Topics

-     "Action Message" on page 206
-     "Message" on page 337
-     "Progress Indicator" on page 396
-     "Push Button (Predefined)" on page 404

- "Warning Message" on page 494

Supplemental Related Topics

- "Information Area" on page 307

Input Focus

A state of a component, identified by the existence of a cursor that indicates where the results of a user's interaction with the keyboard will appear.

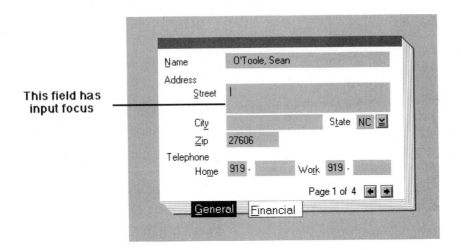

This field has input focus

When to Use

☑ Provide input focus for the component that can currently receive input from the keyboard.

Guidelines

☐ When a user selects a choice that displays a window, move the input focus to that window unless the user has switched input focus to another window. When a window is closed, return the input focus to where it was before that window was opened, if possible.

☐ When a user opens a window but switches input focus to another window before the requested window is displayed, do not display the previously requested window on top of the window that currently has focus.

☐ When a user presses the mouse selection button, move the input focus to the pointer position or to the closest part of the window that can receive the input focus.

☐ When an inactive window becomes active as a result of a technique that does not explicitly specify the position of the cursor, redisplay the cursor in its previous position.

☐ When a user presses the mouse menu button, move input focus to the pop-up menu.

☐ Avoid changing the input focus as a result of a direct-manipulation operation.

☐ When a user presses the Switch Between Associated Windows key, move the input focus between windows displayed from the same object. For example, when a user presses Alt+F6, move the input focus from a primary window to an associated secondary window.

☐ When a user presses the Switch Between Unassociated Windows key, move the input focus between the groups of associated windows displayed from different objects. For example, when a user presses Alt+Esc, move the input focus from a window to an unassociated window.

Essential Related Topics

- "Active Window" on page 210
- "Inactive Window" on page 303

Supplemental Related Topics

- "Cursor" on page 244
- "Keyboard" on page 315
- "Mouse" on page 350
- "Window Navigation" on page 507

In-Use Emphasis (Cue)

A visible cue that indicates that a window is open on an object.

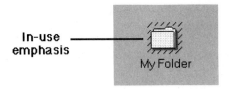

In-use emphasis — My Folder

When to Use

☑ When a user opens a window on an object represented by an icon, display in-use emphasis on that object's icon.

Guidelines

☑ Remove in-use emphasis from an object's icon when all windows containing a view of that object have been removed from the user's workplace.

☐ Display in-use emphasis as diagonal stripes behind each appearance of an object's icon.

☑ Do not display in-use emphasis on the small icon when it is on the title bar.

☑ Do not change the behavior of an object when it is in use. For example, allow a user to open additional windows by double-clicking its icon with the pointing device.

Supplemental Related Topics

• "Icon" on page 300

Keyboard

A device, consisting of systematically arranged keys, that allows a user to type information, move the cursor, or select functions assigned to keys.

When to Use

☑ Provide access to all functions of an object using equivalent, though not necessarily identical, keyboard and pointing device techniques.

Guidelines

☑ Use the Ctrl, Shift, and Alt keys only to modify the function of other keys or key combinations on the keyboard.

☐ Use the Alt key only to provide access to mnemonics.

☑ If the functions listed in Figure 171 and Figure 172 on page 319 are provided, assign them to the keys listed in the table. Do not assign these functions to other keys unless a user reassigns them.

Figure 171 (Page 1 of 5). Keyboard Functions and Key Engravings

Function	Key Engraving (US Keyboard)	Description
Backspace	←(Backspace)	Deletes one character to the left of the cursor.
Backtab	Shift+Tab | ← (Backtab)	Moves the cursor to the previous field. The cursor is positioned either on the previous choice in that field or on the currently set choice in that field. The cursor moves from right to left and bottom to top. At the top-leftmost field, the cursor moves to the bottom-rightmost field. Within an entry field, backtab moves the cursor to the character position defined by the previous tab stop.
Beginning of data	Ctrl+Home	Moves the cursor to the top-leftmost position in the current field.
Beginning of line	Home	Moves the cursor to the leftmost choice in a group of choices, or to the beginning of the current line in an entry field.
Cancel	Esc	Removes the window without applying any changes that were not previously applied in that window.

Keyboard

Figure 171 (Page 2 of 5). Keyboard Functions and Key Engravings

Function	Key Engraving (US Keyboard)	Description
Cancel direct manipulation	Esc	Cancels the direct manipulation operation.
Create	Alt+Insert	Creates a new object, similar to the selected object, and places it on the clipboard
Clear	Delete or no assignment (see Note)	Removes selected object or group of objects from view without compressing the space previously occupied by the object or group of objects.
Close	Alt+F4	Closes active window.
Contextual help	F1	Displays contextual help for the choice, object, control, or group of choices, objects, or controls relative to the current context, such as the cursor position or the process currently in progress.
Copy	Ctrl+Insert	Produces a duplicate of the selected object or group of objects and places it on the clipboard.
Cut	Shift+Delete	Removes the selected object or group of objects and copies it to the clipboard.
Default action	←⏎ Enter or Enter (on numeric keypad), depending on the control the cursor is on	Performs the default action for the control the cursor is positioned on.
Delete	Delete (see Note)	Removes selected object or group of objects from view and compresses the space previously occupied by the object or group of objects.
Deselect all	Ctrl+\	Removes selected-state emphasis from all objects in the active window.
Display drop-down list or drop-down combination box	Alt+↓ (Down Arrow)	Displays the list for the drop-down list or the drop-down combination box.
End of data	Ctrl+End	Moves the cursor to the bottom-rightmost position in the current field.
End of line	End	Moves the cursor to the rightmost choice in a group of choices, or to the end of the current line in an entry field.
Extend selection	Shift+cursor-movement key	Extends the selection in the direction in which the cursor is moved.

Figure 171 (Page 3 of 5). Keyboard Functions and Key Engravings

Function	Key Engraving (US Keyboard)	Description
General help	F2 (in a **Help** window)	Displays a brief overview of each action or task, or both, that a user can perform within the window.
Help index	F11 (in a **Help** window)	Displays an alphabetic listing of help topics for an object or a product.
Hide	Alt+F9	Removes the window and all associated windows from the screen.
Keys help	F9 (in a **Help** window)	Displays a listing of all the key assignments for an object or a product.
Maximize	Alt+F10	Enlarges the window to its largest possible size.
Minimize	Alt+F9	Reduces the window to its smallest possible size and removes all of the windows associated with that window from the screen.
Move	Alt+F7	Allows a user to move a window to a different location.
Move cursor	Arrow keys	Moves the cursor left, right, up, or down. At the last choice, the cursor wraps. For example, at the bottom-most choice, the cursor wraps to the top-most choice to the right.
New line	←⏎ Enter	Performs the default action for the control the cursor is positioned on.
Page down	Page Down	A scrolling action that displays information below the currently visible window area.
Page left	Ctrl+Page Up	A scrolling action that displays information to the left of the currently visible window area.
Page right	Ctrl+Page Down	A scrolling action that displays information to the right of the currently visible window area.
Page up	Page Up	A scrolling action that displays information above the currently visible window area.
Paste	Shift+Insert	Copies the contents of the clipboard into an object at the specified location.
Pop-up menu	Shift+F10	Displays a pop-up menu for the indicated object or group of selected objects.
Redo	Shift+Alt+ ←(Backspace)	Reverses the effect of the last applied undo action.
Refresh now	F5	Updates the window to reflect the underlying data.
Restore	Alt+F5	Returns the window to the size it was and the position it was in before the user minimized or maximized the window.

Keyboard

Function	Key Engraving (US Keyboard)	Description
Figure 171 (Page 4 of 5). Keyboard Functions and Key Engravings		
Select all	Ctrl+/	Selects all objects in active window.
Select object or choice on which cursor is positioned	Use Spacebar if it is not assigned to any other function; otherwise, use Ctrl+Spacebar	Selects object or choice on which cursor is positioned.
Size	Alt+F8	Allows a user to change the size of the window.
Switch between associated windows	Alt+F6	Changes the active window within a group of related windows.
Switch between insert and replace modes in text entry	Insert	Toggles between insert and replace modes.
Switch between unassociated windows	Alt+Esc	Changes the input focus between the groups of associated windows displayed from different objects (if more than one object is displayed by an object).
Switch to and from menu bar	F10	Moves the cursor from within a window to its menu bar or from the menu bar to within the window.
Switch window pane	F6	Moves the cursor in a clockwise direction from one window pane to the next.
System menu	Shift+Esc	Displays system menu.
Tab	Tab→|	Moves the cursor to the next field. The cursor is positioned either on the first choice in that field or on the currently set choice in that field. The cursor moves from left to right and top to bottom. At the bottom-rightmost field, the cursor moves to the top-leftmost field. Within an entry field, tab moves the cursor to the character position defined by the next tab stop.
Toggle in or out of add mode when in extended selection mode	Shift+F8	Toggles in or out of add mode when extended selection is provided for a view. The initial deselection is bypassed and the new selected objects are added or removed from the current group of selected objects.
Tutorial	Shift+F2 (in a **Help** window)	Displays online educational information.

Figure 171 (Page 5 of 5). Keyboard Functions and Key Engravings

Function	Key Engraving (US Keyboard)	Description
Undo	Alt+Backspace	Reverses the action of the most recently performed user action.
Using help	Shift+F10 (in a **Help** window)	Displays help information that describes how to use the help facility.
Window list	Ctrl+Esc	Displays the window list window from the system menu.
Word left	Ctrl+← (Left Arrow)	Moves the cursor to the beginning of the word to the left of the cursor.
Word right	Ctrl+→ (Right Arrow)	Moves the cursor to the end of the word to the right of the cursor. Includes any trailing space characters.

Note: Assign the Delete key to either the Delete or Clear function, if only one is provided. If both Delete and Clear functions are provided, assign the Delete key to the Delete function.

Figure 172 (Page 1 of 4). Keys to Functions

Key Engraving	Key Only	Alt+Key	Ctrl+Key	Shift+Key
F1	Display contextual help			
F2	In a **Help** window, display **General help**			In a **Help** window, display **Tutorial**
F4		Close		
F5	Refresh now	Restore		
F6	Switch window pane	Switch from a window to an associated window		
F7		Move		
F8		Size		Toggles between in or out of add mode, when in extended selection mode
F9	In a **Help** window, display **Keys help**	Minimize or Hide		

Keyboard

Figure 172 (Page 2 of 4). Keys to Functions				
Key Engraving	**Key Only**	**Alt+Key**	**Ctrl+Key**	**Shift+Key**
F10	Switch to menu bar. Places the cursor on the menu bar.	Maximize		Display pop-up menu. In a **Help** window, display **Using help** window instead.
F11	In a **Help** window, display **Help index** window			
\ (Backslash)			Deselect all	
← (Backspace)[1]	Backspace	Undo		
Delete	Delete or Clear			Cut
↓ (Down Arrow)	Moves cursor down, if possible	Display drop-down list or drop-down combination box. Moves from notebook tab or page push button to notebook page.		Extends selection to the current character position on the line below the current line
End	End of line		End of data	Extend selection
← Enter	Default action or new line (when in text)		Default action	New line
Enter (on numeric keypad)	Default action. Never new line.			
Esc	Cancel or cancel direct manipulation	Switch from a window to an unassociated primary window	Window list	Display system menu
Home	Beginning of line		Beginning of data	Extend selection
Insert	Switch between insert and replace modes in text entry	Create	Copy	Paste

Figure 172 (Page 3 of 4). Keys to Functions

Key Engraving	Key Only	Alt+Key	Ctrl+Key	Shift+Key
← (Left Arrow)	Moves cursor left, if possible		Word left	Extends selection one character position to the left
Page Down	Page down	Move to next page in notebook	Page right	Extend selection
Page Up	Page up	Move to previous page in notebook	Page left	Extend selection
→ (Right Arrow)	Moves cursor right, if possible		Word right	Extends selection one character position to the right
Spacebar[2]	Toggles the selection state of the object or choice on which the cursor is positioned	Display system menu	Always toggles the selection state of the object or choice on which the cursor is positioned	Inserts a space where space is allowed
/ (Slash)			Select all	
Tab→|[3]	Moves cursor to next control; in an entry field, moves to next tab position.		Moves to the next control when the cursor is currently in an entry field or in a notebook.	Moves to the previous tab position or to the previous control.

Keyboard

Figure 172 (Page 4 of 4). Keys to Functions				
Key Engraving	**Key Only**	**Alt+Key**	**Ctrl+Key**	**Shift+Key**
↑ (Up Arrow)	Moves cursor up, if possible	Moves focus from notebook page to notebook tab or page push button.		Extends selection to the current character position on the line above the current line
Note:				
1. Pressing Shift+Alt+← (Backspace) performs the Redo action.				
2. Use Spacebar if it is not assigned to any other function; otherwise, use Ctrl+Spacebar.				
3. Ctrl+Shift+Tab→| moves to the previous control when the cursor is currently in an entry field.				

Supplemental Related Topics

- "Clear (Choice)" on page 222
- "Control" on page 235
- "Copy (Choice)" on page 240
- "Cursor" on page 244
- "Delete (Choice)" on page 254
- "Menu (Control)" on page 331
- "Mnemonic" on page 344
- "Selection Types and Techniques" on page 440
- "Shortcut Key" on page 450
- "Text Entry" on page 479
- "Window Navigation" on page 507

Keys Help

An entry in the help index that displays a window containing a listing of key assignments and pointing-device button assignments, if applicable, for the object or application from which keys help was requested.

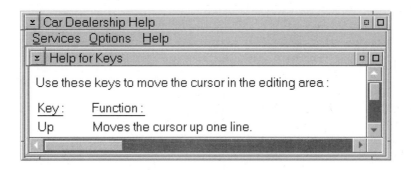

When to Use

☑ Provide a **Keys help** choice in the help index.

Guidelines

☐ List in keys help all key assignments for the window from which the user requested help.

☐ Indicate to a user which keys are available in the current state of the window.

☐ If a pointing device is attached to a user's system, list in keys help the functions assigned to the pointing device buttons.

☐ List shortcut key assignments in keys help.

☐ If a user adds or changes key assignments, list the new or changed assignments in keys help along with any unchanged assignments.

Essential Related Topics

• "Help Index (Choice)" on page 294

• "Help Menu" on page 296

Keys Help

Supplemental Related Topics

- "Keyboard" on page 315
- "Shortcut Key" on page 450

List Box (Control)

A control that contains a list of objects or settings choices that a user can select. List boxes support single or multiple selection.

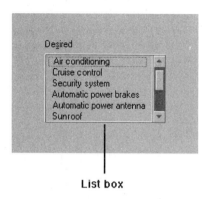

List box

When to Use

☐ Use a list box to display a list of settings choices or objects, but not both, in which the number of choices or objects may vary.

Guidelines

☐ Display the settings choices or objects in a list box in an order that is meaningful to a user, such as alphabetic order, numeric order, chronological order, or some other order. For example, display modem baud rates in numeric order.

☐ Make a list box large enough to display six to eight settings choices or objects at a time, or all settings choices or objects if fewer than six.

☑ In a list that can be scrolled, such as a scrollable list box, do not allow the cursor to wrap.

☑ Provide horizontal or vertical scroll bars, or both, when some information is not visible in the list box.

☐ Make list boxes at least wide enough to display the choices or objects of average width.

List Box (Control)

☐ When a user increases the size of the window in which the list box is displayed, increase the number of settings choices or objects displayed in the list box.

☐ When a user decreases the size of the window in which the list box is displayed, decrease the number of settings choices or objects displayed in the list box to a minimum of six. If the window is sized so that six settings choices or objects cannot be displayed, clip the list box.

☐ When a list box provides multiple selection, place in the descriptive text for the list box information about the number of items that can be selected. For example, add text and a counter near the list box that dynamically shows the number of items selected, such as "3 selected."

☐ Capitalize only the first letter of the first word of a choice or object name unless the choice or object name contains an abbreviation, acronym, or proper noun that should be capitalized.

Essential Related Topics

- "Control" on page 235

- "Drop-Down List (Control)" on page 268

Supplemental Related Topics

- "Column Heading" on page 227

- "Combination Box (Control)" on page 229

- "Drop-Down Combination Box (Control)" on page 266

- "Field Prompt" on page 278

- "First-Letter Cursor Navigation" on page 286

- "Scroll Bar" on page 428

- "Selection Types and Techniques" on page 440

Marquee Selection

A technique that allows a user to select objects by drawing a rectangle around them with a pointing device.

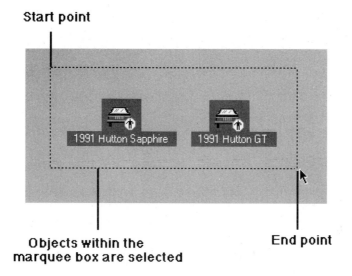

Start point

Objects within the
marquee box are selected

End point

When to Use

☐   Provide marquee selection for all multiple selection and extended selection lists.

Guidelines

☑   In multiple or extended selection:

  • Using the mouse, when the user presses the mouse selection button on white space and moves the pointer, begin drawing a marquee rectangle that starts at the point where the mouse selection button was pressed and extends to the current mouse pointer location. As objects are encompassed by the marquee rectangle they are selected. Marquee selection is completed when the mouse selection button is released.

☑   Display the marquee box only during selection.

Marquee Selection

☑   Display selected-state emphasis on each object as soon as the object is completely contained within the marquee box.

☑   Display selected-state emphasis on each icon as soon as the icon's graphic is completely contained within the marquee box.

Supplemental Related Topics

- "Point-to-Endpoint Selection" on page 385
- "Selection Types and Techniques" on page 440

Maximize (Choice)

An action choice that enlarges a window to the largest size possible for that view or to the size of the workplace.

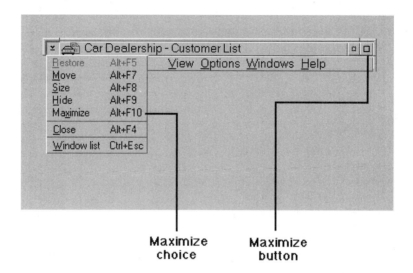

Maximize choice   Maximize button

When to Use

☑ Provide a **Maximize** choice when a user can change the size of a window.

Guidelines

☑ Place the **Maximize** choice in the system menu.

☑ Display the **Maximize** choice with unavailable-state emphasis when the window is maximized.

☑ Provide a maximize button on the title bar when the size of a window can be changed and the window is not currently maximized.

☑ When a user selects the **Maximize** choice or clicks on the maximize button, enlarge the window to the largest size possible for the current view or to the size of the workplace, whichever is smaller.

Maximize (Choice)

☑   Change a maximize button to a restore button when a window is currently maximized.

☑   Before maximizing a window, save its state, including its size and position for use when the window is restored.

☑   Assign Alt+F10 as the shortcut key combination for the **Maximize** choice.

☑   Assign "X" as the mnemonic for the **Maximize** choice.

Essential Related Topics

- "System Menu" on page 475

Supplemental Related Topics

- "Minimize (Choice)" on page 342
- "Restore (Choice)" on page 418
- "Size (Choice)" on page 459

Menu (Control)

A list of action, routing, and settings choices. The types of menus are the menu bar, pull-down menu, cascaded menu, and pop-up menu.

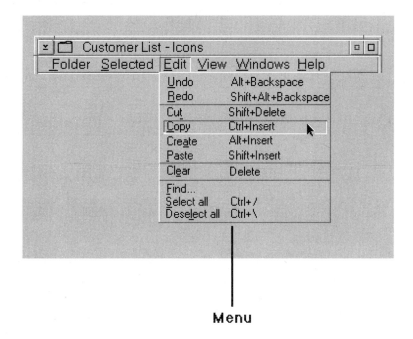

Menu

When to Use

☐ Use a menu to present action, routing, or settings choices that a user can select while performing tasks.

Guidelines

☑ When a user selects a routing choice that leads to a menu, always display the menu even if all of the choices in it are unavailable.

☑ Do not display unavailable-state emphasis on routing choices that lead to pull-down menus or cascaded menus.

☑ Display unavailable-state emphasis on action and settings choices that cannot be selected in the current context.

☑ Allow the cursor to wrap at the top and bottom of a menu.

Menu (Control)

☑   Except in the **Selected** menu, a pop-up menu, or when a user switches between **Full menus** and **Short menus,** do not add or remove choices from a menu to indicate availability of choices. Instead, display unavailable choices with unavailable-state emphasis.

☑   If a choice is never available to a particular user, do not display it in a menu, and do not save space for it in a menu.

☐   Place related choices together.

☐   Use separators to distinguish groups of related choices.

☐   Place product-specific choices either following a group of related predefined choices or at the bottom of a menu.

☐   Keep the relative order of identical choices the same among different menus. For example, keep the order of the **Cut, Copy, Create** and **Paste** choices the same in the **Edit** pull-down menu and the pop-up menu for an object.

☐   Use graphics, text, or both for each choice in a menu depending on which best identifies the choice. For example, a menu for a drawing product could be made up of graphic fill-patterns rather than text.

☐   Dynamically add text or graphics to a choice to make the meaning of that choice clearer in a given context. For example, change the name of the **Undo** choice to **Undo typing.** This clarifies the meaning and differentiates the choice from **Undo delete.**

☐   Capitalize only the first letter of the first word of a name of a choice in a menu unless the name contains an abbreviation, acronym, or proper noun that should be capitalized.

☐   Avoid using settings choices in menus unless a user specifically requests to place settings choices in menus. Put settings choices in a notebook control in a settings view for the object instead.

☐   If a menu contains a group of settings choices that are not mutually exclusive, display a check mark to the left of each choice that has been selected. Remove the check mark when the choice is deselected.

☐   If a menu contains a group of settings choices that are mutually exclusive, display unavailable-state emphasis on the choice that currently applies to the object. Remove the unavailable-state emphasis when the choice no longer applies to the object.

☐ Place at least two choices in a menu.

☐ Avoid placing more than 10 choices in a menu. Use cascaded menus to reduce the number of choices in a menu.

☐ Provide a shortcut key for each frequently used choice in a pull-down menu or cascaded menu.

☑ Provide the predefined mnemonic for each predefined textual choice in a menu.

☑ Provide a unique mnemonic for each product-specific textual choice in a menu, unless no meaningful unique mnemonic can be found.

Essential Related Topics

Menu Bar

The area near the top of a window, below the title bar and above the rest of the window, that contains routing choices that display pull-down menus. Typically, a menu-bar choice is a single word.

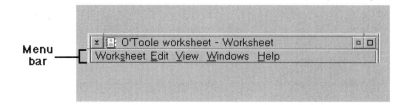

Menu bar

When to Use

☐ Provide a menu bar when a window will provide more than six action choices or routing choices. Also provide a menu bar if you provide the functions available in the **File, Selected, Edit,** or **View** menus.

Guidelines

☑ If you provide a menu bar, place on it only routing choices that lead to pull-down menus.

☑ If a menu bar is not provided in a window displaying a view of an object, place all action and routing choices on push buttons in that window, except for those choices that appear on the system menu.

☐ Allow a user to turn the display of the menu bar on and off.

☑ Provide the following choices on the menu bar, in the relative order shown, if you provide any of the choices listed in their associated menus:

- **File** (Object-oriented) or **File** (Application-oriented)
- **Selected**
- **Edit**
- **View**
- **Options** (Application-oriented)
- **Windows**
- **Help**

☐   If you provide choices that do not logically fit within any of the predefined menus, such as the **Edit** menu or the **View** menu, provide product-specific menu bar choices that lead to menus that logically group your product-specific choices.

☑   Add any product-specific menu bar choices between the **View** and **Help** menu-bar choices. If a **View** choice is not provided, place product-specific menu-bar choices between the last standard menu-bar choice that is provided and the **Help** choice.

☑   If a menu-bar choice can never be selected by a particular user, do not display it on the menu bar, and do not save space for it on the menu bar.

☑   When a user selects a choice on a menu bar, display the pull-down menu associated with that choice.

☐   When a window contains push buttons that affect the entire window and the window contains a menu bar, place choices in the pull-down menus that provide function equivalent to the push button functions in that window.

☐   Use graphics, text, or both, for each choice in a menu bar, as appropriate to the product. For example, choices on a menu bar for a drawing product could be graphical rather than textual.

☐   Capitalize only the first letter of the first word of a name of a choice on a menu bar unless the name contains an abbreviation, acronym, or proper noun that should be capitalized.

☑   Assign a unique mnemonic to each product-specific textual choice on a menu bar, unless no meaningful mnemonic can be found.

☑   Provide the predefined mnemonic assignments for the standard menu bar choices.

Essential Related Topics

- "Choice" on page 218
- "Control" on page 235
- "Menu (Control)" on page 331
- "Mnemonic" on page 344

Menu Bar

- "Pull-Down Menu" on page 398
- "Routing (Choice Type)" on page 421

Supplemental Related Topics

- "Edit Menu" on page 270
- "File Menu (Application-Oriented)" on page 280
- "Help Menu" on page 296
- "Options Menu" on page 375
- "Push Button (Control)" on page 400
- "Selected Menu" on page 437
- "System Menu" on page 475
- "View Menu" on page 492
- "Window" on page 496
- "Windows Menu" on page 509

Message

Information displayed in a window in response to an unexpected event, a situation in which something undesirable could occur, or when there is additional status information on a process that has completed. The three types of messages are information message, warning message, and action message.

When to Use

☐ Use a message to report unexpected or undesirable situations to the user.

☐ Use a message to indicate that a process has completed successfully, but there is additional information about the status of the completion that the user must see.

Guidelines

☑ Display a warning message to indicate that an undesirable situation could occur but that the user can allow the process to continue.

☑ Display an action message to indicate that a condition has occurred and that the user must correct the situation and retry, choose an alternative action, or withdraw the request.

☑ Display an information message to indicate that a condition has occurred that the user can do nothing about or that the user must see additional information about the status of normal completion.

☑ If a progress indicator is displayed in a separate window, display information about the status of a process in the progress-indicator window.

☐ Phrase message text so that a user clearly understands what caused the message as well as what action, if any, can be taken to correct the situation that caused the message.

☐ Avoid phrasing messages in a way that requires a "Yes" or "No" response from the user. For example, do not use the message, "Are you sure you don't want to save the file?" Instead, use, "File has been modified. Select 'Discard' to throw away changes or select 'Save' to save the file and then quit." If **Yes** and **No** push buttons are used, avoid using negatives in the message text.

☐ Provide access to help information from each message window by providing a push button labeled **Help.**

☐ If an associated window is open, display a message in a secondary window that is dependant on the associated window.

☐ If no associated window is open for which a message must be displayed, augment that object's icon with a small version of the message symbol. For example, if a note could not be successfully sent and no associated window is open, augment the mail basket icon with an appropriate message symbol, such as an "i" or "?."

☐ If no associated window is open for which a message must be displayed and the object's icon is not currently visible, augment the container that is visible with a small version of the message symbol. For example, if an object's icon is contained in a folder that is currently visible, augment the folder's icon with an appropriate message symbol. If that folder's icon were not visible because it was contained in a closed work area, augment the work area's icon with an appropriate message symbol.

☑ Use Figure 173 to determine which symbol to use to visually identify each type of message.

Figure 173. Message Symbols and Message Types	
Symbol	**Message Type**
	Information Message
	Warning Message
	Action Message (When a user's immediate attention is not required, such as when the situation will not worsen with time.)
	Action Message (When a user's immediate attention is required.)

☐   Display the message symbol to the left of the message text.

☐   Include in the window title the name of the object and the action or situation that caused the message to appear. For example, "Drive A: – Format Diskette" might be used for a message title for a message displayed during a format operation.

☐   Make messages as modeless as possible. For example, if a message is associated with an entry field in a window, make the message modeless.

☐   If you provide a message identifier in a message window, place it in the bottom right-most corner of the message and display it in a smaller font than the rest of the message text.

☐   Use Figure 174 on page 340 to determine when and how to display messages.

Message

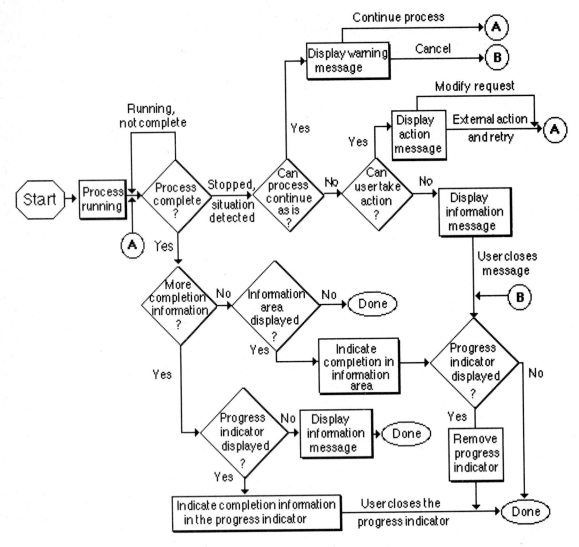

Figure 174. Message and Progress Indicator Flowchart

Essential Related Topics

- "Action Message" on page 206
- "Information Area" on page 307
- "Information Message" on page 310

- "Progress Indicator" on page 396

- "Push Button (Predefined)" on page 404

- "Warning Message" on page 494

Supplemental Related Topics

- "Audible Feedback" on page 212

- "Information Area" on page 307

Minimize (Choice)

An action choice that removes a window and all of its secondary windows from the workplace. A minimized-window visual, such as an application-defined icon, is placed on the workplace to represent a minimized window.

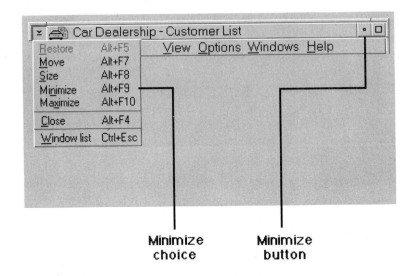

Restore	Alt+F5	
Move	Alt+F7	
Size	Alt+F8	
Minimize	Alt+F9	
Maximize	Alt+F10	
Close	Alt+F4	
Window list	Ctrl+Esc	

Car Dealership - Customer List

View Options Windows Help

Minimize
choice

Minimize
button

When to Use

☐ Provide a **Minimize** choice for windows that contain views of objects.

Guidelines

☑ If you provide the **Minimize** choice, place it in the system menu.

☑ Display the **Minimize** choice with unavailable-state emphasis when the window is currently minimized.

☑ If you provide the **Minimize** choice, place a minimize push button on the title bar if the window is not currently minimized.

☐ When a user minimizes a window that has not been minimized previously, place the minimized-window visual near the bottom of the workplace.

☐ When a user minimizes a window that has been minimized previously, place the minimized-window visual where it had been before being restored previously.

☑ When a user minimizes a work area, remove from the workplace all windows associated with that work area and save the open state of each associated window for use when the work area is restored.

☐ Before minimizing a window, save its state, including its size and position, along with the state of each of its associated windows, to be used when the window is restored.

☑ Assign Alt+F9 as the shortcut key combination for the **Minimize** choice.

☑ Assign "N" as the mnemonic for the **Minimize** choice.

Essential Related Topics

• "System Menu" on page 475

Supplemental Related Topics

• "Maximize (Choice)" on page 329

• "Restore (Choice)" on page 418

• "Size (Choice)" on page 459

Mnemonic

A single, easy-to-remember alphanumeric character that moves the cursor to a choice and selects the choice.

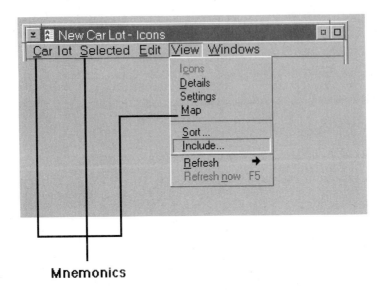

Mnemonics

When to Use

☑ Provide the predefined mnemonic for each predefined choice.

☑ Provide a unique mnemonic for each product-specific textual choice in a menu, unless no meaningful unique mnemonic can be found.

☐ Provide a unique mnemonic for each choice in a field of choices, except for push buttons that have a specific key assignment.

Guidelines

☐ When a user presses a mnemonic character, move the cursor to the choice in that scope that corresponds with that mnemonic and selects that choice; otherwise, generate an audible cue to indicate that the mnemonic is not valid within that scope.

☑ Make mnemonics unique:

- Within each pull-down menu, cascaded menu, and pop-up menu.

- For all choices, field prompts, controls that allow typing, push buttons, and menu bar choices within a window.

☐ In a window with a menu bar, when a user presses Alt+mnemonic character, move the cursor to a menu-bar choice that has that mnemonic.

☐ In a control that allows typing, when a user presses Alt+mnemonic character, move the cursor to a choice that has that mnemonic outside the control.

☑ Identify each mnemonic with an underline.

☑ If a mnemonic is an alphabetic character, allow a user to press either the uppercase or lowercase character.

☐ Provide a mnemonic for the default push button if the default push button is not always a push button at the bottom of the window.

☐ For push buttons that do not open a new window or close the current window, avoid moving the cursor when a user types a mnemonic to select a push button.

☑ If you provide the following choices, assign unique mnemonics to them as in 175 through 185 on pages 345 through 348.

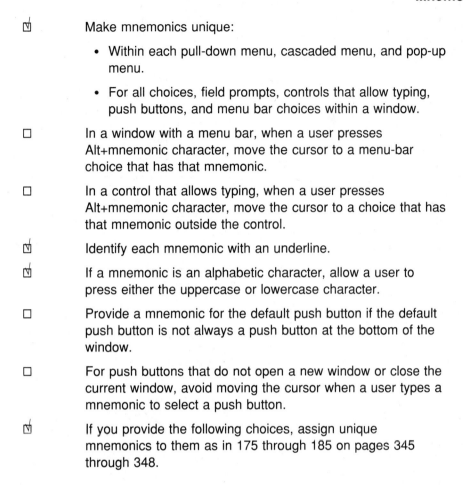

Figure 175. Mnemonic Assignments for the Title Bar and Menu Bar

Choice	Mnemonic
System menu	Spacebar
File menu	F
Selected menu	S
Edit menu	E
View menu	V
Options menu	O
Windows menu	W
Help menu	H

Mnemonic

Figure 176. Mnemonic Assignments for a Field of Push Buttons

Push button	Mnemonic
Apply	A
OK	O
Reset	R
Retry	R
Stop	S
Close	C
Continue	C
Pause	P
Resume	R

Note:

1. Reset, Retry, and Resume will not appear within the same field of push buttons.

2. Close and Continue will not appear within the same field of push buttons.

Figure 177. Mnemonic Assignments for the System Menu

System Menu Choice	Mnemonic
Restore	R
Move	M
Size	S
Minimize	N
Hide	H
Maximize	X
Close	C
Window list	W
Split	P

Figure 178 (Page 1 of 2). Mnemonic Assignments for the File Menu

File Menu Choice	Mnemonic
New	N
Open (Application-oriented)	O
Open as (Object-oriented)	O

Figure 178 (Page 2 of 2). Mnemonic Assignments for the File Menu	
File Menu Choice	**Mnemonic**
Save	S
Save as	A
Print	P
Note: Open and Open as will not appear within the same menu	

Figure 179. Mnemonic Assignments for the Selected Menu	
Selected Menu Choice	**Mnemonic**
Open as	O
Print	P

Figure 180. Mnemonic assignments for the Edit Menu	
Edit Menu Choice	**Mnemonic**
Undo	U
Redo	R
Cut	T
Copy	C
Create	A
Paste	P
Clear	E
Delete	D
Find	F
Select all	S
Deselect all	L

Figure 181 (Page 1 of 2). Mnemonic Assignments for the View Menu	
View Menu Choice	**Mnemonic**
Icon	C
Details	D
Settings	T
Sort	S

Mnemonic

Figure 181 (Page 2 of 2). Mnemonic Assignments for the View Menu	
View Menu Choice	**Mnemonic**
Include	I
Refresh	R
Refresh now	N

Figure 182. Mnemonic Assignments for the Refresh Cascade Choices	
Choice	**Mnemonic**
On	O
Off	F

Figure 183. Mnemonic Assignments for the Options Menu	
Options Menu Choice	**Mnemonic**
Short menus	S
Full menus	F

Figure 184. Mnemonic Assignments for the Windows Menu	
Windows Menu Choice	**Mnemonic**
Window list	W

Figure 185. Mnemonic Assignments for the Help Menu	
Help Menu Choice	**Mnemonic**
Help index	I
General help	G
Using help	U
Tutorial	T
Product information	P

For choices other than those listed in the preceding tables, assign mnemonic characters by applying the first applicable guideline that follows:

1. Use the first character of the choice name, or the first character of one of the words in a multiple-word choice,

unless those characters have been assigned as
mnemonics for other choices.

2. If the first character of a choice name has been used as
   the mnemonic for another choice, use a consonant in the
   choice name.

3. If all consonants in a choice name have been used as
   mnemonics for other choices, use any other character in
   the choice name.

4. If all characters in a choice name have been used as
   mnemonics for other choices, add a unique character to
   the choice text and make it the mnemonic. Display the
   character in parentheses after the choice.

Supplemental Related Topics

- "Audible Feedback" on page 212

- "First-Letter Cursor Navigation" on page 286

- "Keyboard" on page 315

- "Shortcut Key" on page 450

Mouse

A commonly used pointing device, containing one or more buttons, that allows a user to interact with a product or the operating environment. A mouse button is mapped to one of three functions: selection, manipulation, and displaying a pop-up menu.

Guidelines

☐ Assign mouse button one as the mouse selection button as the initial default for a two-button mouse.

☐ Assign mouse button two as the mouse manipulation button as the initial default for a two-button mouse.

☐ Assign the chording of mouse buttons one and two as the mouse menu button as the initial default for a two-button mouse.

☑ When a user clicks a mouse button, perform the function assigned to a click of that button.

☑ Design your product so that when a user double-clicks a mouse button, only the function assigned to a double-click of that button is performed. Do not allow the function assigned to a single click of that mouse button to be performed. For example, if a user double-clicks on an object, the object's selection state should remain unaffected, and the object should be opened.

☑ Do not assign double-click as the only way to select a choice and perform an action. Provide a keyboard alternative, such as a menu choice or push button.

☐ Do not assign double-click functions to choices on which users will typically perform multiple single clicks, such as on scroll bar buttons.

☑ Perform the function assigned to a chord when a user presses more than one mouse button in such a way that the buttons are down and the mouse moves no more than the distance that the user has specified for the operating environment. Do not perform the functions assigned to clicking each mouse button individually.

☐ When a user presses the mouse selection button, move the input focus to the pointer position or to the closest part of the window that can receive the input focus.

☐ Avoid moving input focus to the pointer position when a user presses the mouse menu button.

☑ If pop-up menus are provided, allow a user using a 3-button mouse to select a choice from the pop-up menu with either the mouse selection button or mouse menu button.

☑ Provide access to all functions of an object using equivalent, though not necessarily identical, mouse and keyboard techniques.

☑ Assign the mouse-button functions for a one-button, two-button, and three-button mouse as in the following tables:

Figure 186 (Page 1 of 2). Mouse Techniques for Selection

Selection technique	Mouse button pressed	Key pressed	User action to begin selection	User action to end selection	Result
Point selection	Selection	None	Click on any object or choice that can be selected.	Not applicable	Selected-state emphasis is displayed on object or choice.
Begin point-to-endpoint range (click) selection	Selection	None	Click in list of objects or choices that can be selected.	Not applicable	Anchor point is set.
End point-to-endpoint range (click) selection	Selection	Shift	Click elsewhere in list of objects or choices that can be selected.	Not applicable	All objects in range are selected.
Point-to-endpoint area (marquee) selection	Selection	None	Press and hold mouse button in blank space, then drag until all desired objects are within the marquee box.	Release mouse button.	All objects that are fully within the marquee box are selected.
Random-point selection	Selection	None	Press mouse button while pointer is on an object, then move mouse while holding mouse button down.	Release mouse button when pointer is on last object to be selected.	All items passed over by mouse while mouse button was down are selected.

Mouse

Figure 186 (Page 2 of 2). Mouse Techniques for Selection					
Selection technique	**Mouse button pressed**	**Key pressed**	**User action to begin selection**	**User action to end selection**	**Result**
Deselect all	Selection	None	Click in blank space.	Not applicable	Selection emphasis is removed from all objects or choices

Figure 187 (Page 1 of 2). Mouse Techniques for Direct Manipulation for a One-Button Mouse					
Direct manipulation technique	**Mouse button pressed**	**Key pressed**	**User action to begin direct manipulation**	**User action to end direct manipulation**	**Result**
Move	Selection	None	Press mouse button while pointer is on an object, then move mouse while holding the button down.	Release mouse button when pointer is on target object.	Object is moved from source to target.
Cause Move (override default)	Selection	Shift	Press mouse button while pointer is on an object, then move mouse while holding the button down.	Release mouse button when pointer is on target object.	Object is moved from source to target.
Copy	Selection	None	Press mouse button while pointer is on an object, then move mouse while holding the button down.	Release mouse button when pointer is on target object.	A copy of the source object is placed at the target position.
Cause Copy (override default)–when create-on-drag is set off	Selection	Ctrl	Press mouse button while pointer is on an object, then move mouse while holding button down	Release mouse button when pointer is on target object	A copy of the source object is placed at the target position
Cause Create (override default)–when create-on-drag is set on	Selection	Ctrl	Press mouse button while pointer is on an object, then move mouse while holding button down	Release mouse button when pointer is on target object	A new object is placed at the target position
Incremental scrolling	Selection	None	Click on scroll button in scroll bar.	Not applicable	Contents of window are scrolled one smallest scrolling increment.
Page scrolling	Selection	None	Click in scroll shaft between scroll button and scroll box.	Not applicable	Contents of window are scrolled one page increment.

Figure 187 (Page 2 of 2). Mouse Techniques for Direct Manipulation for a One-Button Mouse

Direct manipulation technique	Mouse button pressed	Key pressed	User action to begin direct manipulation	User action to end direct manipulation	Result
Direct positioning	Selection	None	Drag scroll box to a different position on scroll shaft.	Not applicable	Contents of window are scrolled to display information at relative position indicated by scroll box.
Split window	Selection	None	Drag split bar.	Not applicable	Window is divided into multiple panes.

Figure 188 (Page 1 of 2). Mouse Techniques for Direct Manipulation for a Two-Button or Three-Button Mouse

Direct manipulation technique	Mouse button pressed	Key pressed	User action to begin direct manipulation	User action to end direct manipulation	Result
Move	Manipulation	None	Press mouse button while pointer is on an object, then move mouse while holding the button down.	Release mouse button when pointer is on target object.	Object is moved from source to target.
Cause Move (override default)	Manipulation	Shift	Press mouse button while pointer is on an object, then move mouse while holding the button down.	Release mouse button when pointer is on target object.	Object is moved from source to target.
Copy	Manipulation	None	Press mouse button while pointer is on an object, then move mouse while holding the button down.	Release mouse button when pointer is on target object.	A copy of the source object is placed at the target position.
Cause Copy (override default)–when create-on-drag is set off	Manipulation	Ctrl	Press mouse button while pointer is on an object, then move mouse while holding button down	Release mouse button when pointer is on target object	A copy of the source object is placed at the target position
Cause Create (override default)–when create-on-drag is set on	Manipulation	Ctrl	Press mouse button while pointer is on an object, then move mouse while holding button down	Release mouse button when pointer is on target object	A new object is placed at the target position
Incremental scrolling	Selection	None	Click on scroll button in scroll bar.	Not applicable	Contents of window are scrolled one smallest scrolling increment.

Mouse

Figure 188 (Page 2 of 2). Mouse Techniques for Direct Manipulation for a Two-Button or Three-Button Mouse

Direct manipulation technique	Mouse button pressed	Key pressed	User action to begin direct manipulation	User action to end direct manipulation	Result
Page scrolling	Selection	None	Click in scroll shaft between scroll button and scroll box.	Not applicable	Contents of window are scrolled one page increment.
Direct positioning	Selection	None	Drag scroll box to a different position on scroll shaft.	Not applicable	Contents of window are scrolled to display information at relative position indicated by scroll box.
Split window	Manipulation	None	Drag split bar.	Not applicable	Window is divided into multiple panes.

Figure 189. Mouse Techniques for Miscellaneous Actions for a One-Button Mouse

Action	Mouse button pressed	Key pressed	User action to begin action	User action to end action	Result
Create Reflection	Selection	Ctrl+Shift	Press mouse button while pointer is on an object, then move mouse while holding button down	Release mouse button	Create a reflection of the object.
Default action	Selection	None	Double-click on an object or choice.	Not applicable	Default action for that object or choice is carried out.
Pop-up menu	Selection	Alt	Click or button-down	Not applicable	Pop-up menu is displayed.

Figure 190 (Page 1 of 2). Mouse Techniques for Miscellaneous Actions for a Two-Button Mouse

Action	Mouse button pressed	Key pressed	User action to begin action	User action to end action	Result
Create Reflection	Manipulation	Ctrl+Shift	Press mouse button while pointer is on an object, then move mouse while holding button down	Release mouse button	Create a reflection of the object.

Figure 190 (Page 2 of 2). Mouse Techniques for Miscellaneous Actions for a Two-Button Mouse

Action	Mouse button pressed	Key pressed	User action to begin action	User action to end action	Result
Default action	Selection	None	Double-click on an object or choice.	Not applicable	Default action for that object or choice is carried out.
Pop-up menu	Selection and Manipulation	None	Chord mouse buttons	Not applicable	Pop-up menu is displayed.
reserved	Manipulation	Alt	Press mouse button while pointer is on an object, then move mouse while holding button down	Release mouse button	This combination is reserved for future releases of the CUA interface.

Figure 191. Mouse Techniques for Miscellaneous Actions for a Three-Button Mouse

Action	Mouse button pressed	Key pressed	User action to begin action	User action to end action	Result
Create Reflection	Manipulation	Ctrl+Shift	Press mouse button while pointer is on an object, then move mouse while holding button down	Release mouse button	Create a reflection of the object.
Default action	Selection	None	Double-click on an object or choice.	Not applicable	Default action for that object or choice is carried out.
Pop-up menu	Menu	None	Click or button down	Not applicable	Pop-up menu is displayed.
reserved	Manipulation	Alt	Press mouse button while pointer is on an object, then move mouse while holding button down	Release mouse button	This combination is reserved for future versions of the CUA interface.

Essential Related Topics

- "Data Transfer" on page 248
- "Pointing Device" on page 382

Mouse

Supplemental Related Topics

- "Default Action" on page 250
- "Pointer" on page 378

Move (Choice)

An action choice that allows a user to move a window to a different location.

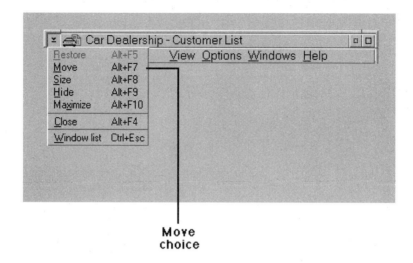

Move
choice

When to Use

☑   Provide a **Move** choice for each window.

Guidelines

☑   Place the **Move** choice in the system menu.

☑   When a user selects the **Move** choice, use the operating environment's mechanism that allows a user to change the position of a window.

☑   Assign Alt+F7 as the shortcut key combination for the **Move** choice.

☑   Assign "M" as the mnemonic for the **Move** choice.

Essential Related Topics

•   "System Menu" on page 475

Supplemental Related Topics

•   "Direct Manipulation" on page 261

Multiple Selection

A type of selection in which a user can select any number of objects or settings choices, or not select any.

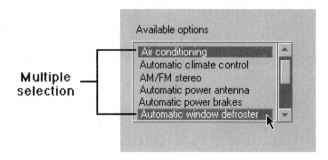

When to Use

☐ Provide multiple selection when more than one object can be operated on at a time and a user will typically select more than one object.

☐ Provide multiple selection when more than one settings choice can be applied to an object or group of objects at a time and a user will typically select more than one settings choice.

Guidelines

☑ For the following selection techniques, provide the mouse and keyboard access mechanisms as listed in Figure 192 on page 359.

Figure 192 (Page 1 of 2). Multiple Selection Techniques

Technique	Mouse	Keyboard	Result
Point selection	Click mouse selection button with pointer on object to be selected or deselected.	With cursor on object to be selected or deselected, press Ctrl+Spacebar; also spacebar if spacebar is not used to type a space.	Toggles the selection state of the single identified object; does not affect the state of other objects.
Point-to-endpoint selection			
Area (Marquee)	Press mouse selection button at the start point and move the pointer to the end point; release the mouse selection button at the end point.	Not applicable.	Toggle the selection state of the first object and make the selection state of all objects within the identified area the same as the new selection state of the first object.
Range (Swipe)	Press mouse selection button at the start point and move the pointer to the end point; release the mouse selection button at the end point.	Press Shift at the start point and hold while using cursor-movement keys to move the cursor to the end point; release Shift at end point.	Toggle the selection state of the first object and make the selection state of all other objects in order from the identified start point to the identified end point the same as the new selection state of the first object.
Range (Click)	Click mouse selection button at the start point; press Shift and click the mouse selection button at the end point, then release Shift key.	Not applicable.	Toggle the selection state of the first object and make the selection state of all other objects in order from the identified start point to the identified endpoint the same as the new selection state of the first object.
Random-point selection			

Multiple Selection

Figure 192 (Page 2 of 2). Multiple Selection Techniques

Technique	Mouse	Keyboard	Result
Random (Swipe)	Press mouse selection button with pointer on first object to be selected; move the pointer over other objects to be selected; release mouse selection button.	Not applicable.	Toggle the selection state of the first object and make the selection state of all identified objects in the order the user identified the objects the same as the new selection state of the first object.

Essential Related Topics

- "Extended Selection" on page 275
- "Marquee Selection" on page 327
- "Selection Types and Techniques" on page 440
- "Single Selection" on page 457

Supplemental Related Topics

- "Descriptive Text" on page 258
- "Information Area" on page 307
- "Keyboard" on page 315
- "Mouse" on page 350
- "Status Area (Cue)" on page 473

New (Choice)

An action choice that allows a user to create a new object.

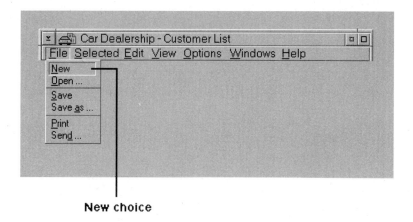

New choice

When to Use

☐ Provide a **New** choice for any application for which a user can create a new object from and replace the current window's contents with that new object.

Guidelines

☑ If you provide a **New** choice, and you provide an application-oriented **File** menu, place the **New** choice in the application-oriented **File** menu.

☑ When a user selects the **New** choice, do the following:

- Prompt the user with a message to save any unsaved data in the object displayed in the window.

- Remove the existing information from the current window and replace it with the new object.

New (Choice)

☐   Generate a name for each newly created object. Make the name unique if the operating environment requires a unique name, for example, create a unique name by appending a number to the name of the object it was created from.

☑   Assign "N" as the mnemonic for the **New** menu choice.

Essential Related Topics

•   "File Menu (Application-Oriented)" on page 280

•   "Window Title" on page 510

Notebook (Control)

A control that resembles a bound notebook that contains pages separated into sections by tabbed divider-pages. It allows a user to turn the pages of the notebook and to move from one section to another.

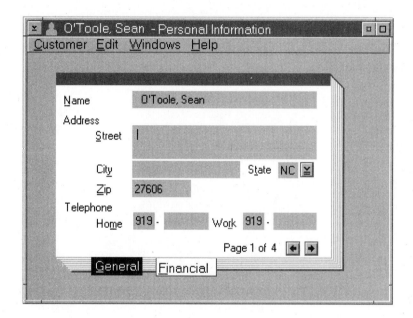

When to Use

☐ Use a notebook to present settings choices to be applied to an object.

☐ Use a notebook to present data that can be logically organized into groups. For example, use a notebook to present a clip-art library that is organized alphabetically or by subject.

Guidelines

☐ Place within a single tabbed section information that is related.

☑ If a section has more than one page, indicate the page number within that section.

Notebook (Control)

☑ Label tabbed-divider pages with either text or graphics, or a combination of both.

☐ Order tabs so that they initially appear to go deeper from left to right, and top to bottom.

☐ Assign a mnemonic to a tabbed-divider page that is labeled with text.

☐ Design each tabbed-divider page to have approximately the same proportions, to present a balanced appearance.

☐ Do not place a notebook within a notebook.

☐ Place at the bottom of the window, outside of the notebook, push buttons that affect the entire notebook. For example, provide a **Reset** push button to allow a user to return all settings choices on every page of a notebook to their last applied state.

☐ Place on the page of a notebook push buttons that affect only that page. For example, provide a **Reset** push button to allow a user to return all settings choices on the currently displayed page to their last applied state.

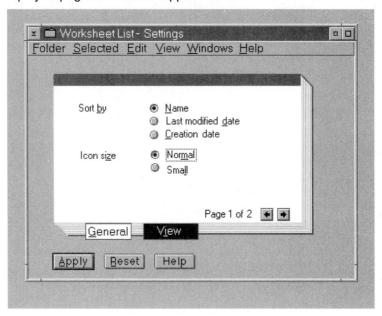

Essential Related Topics

Supplemental Related Topics

Object

An item that can be manipulated as a unit and that a user works with to perform a task. An object can be represented as text, image, graphic, video, or audio.

When to Use

☐   Provide an object to allow a user to manipulate a group of information as a unit to perform a task.

Guidelines

☑   When a user places an object on the workplace, use an icon to represent that object.

☐   Allow each object to support interaction with the standard objects provided by the operating environment. For example, allow each object to interact with a printer.

☐   Allow each object to support standard data-transfer operations, such as **Cut, Copy,** and **Paste,** with objects provided by other products.

☐   Allow a user to display a view of an object in a window.

☐   Allow a user to display more than one view of an object at the same time. For example, allow a user to see an icons view of a container in one window and a settings view of the same container in another window.

☐   Design each object to support direct manipulation.

☐   Provide a pop-up menu for each object.

☐   If an object can be placed on the workplace, do not prevent that object from being placed in other containers that can contain any type of object. For example, if an object can be placed on the workplace, allow a user to place that object in a system-provided folder that can contain any type of object.

☑   If you want a view of an object to be displayed in a window that is opened, closed, minimized, maximized, restored, or moved independently of all other windows on the workplace, use a primary window to display a view of the object.

☑   If you want a view of an object to be displayed in a window that is opened, closed, minimized, maximized, restored, or moved when another window (other than a work area window) is opened, closed, minimized, maximized, restored, or moved, use a secondary window to display a view of the object and make the secondary window dependent on a primary window.

☐   When a user closes a window that contains a view of an object, save the state of the object and the state of the view. For example, save the size and position of the window as well as the scrolling location, cursor position, and selection state of the contents.

☐   When a user opens a window to a particular view of an object or restores a minimized window, restore the window to its previous state, if state information is available, regardless of the amount of time that has elapsed since the user last opened or restored the window, and regardless of whether the user's system has been turned off and on again.

☐   Provide product information about each object.

☐   Provide access from both the keyboard and the pointing device to product-specific functions that can be performed on an object.

☐   If you provide a name for an object, allow a user to change that name.

☐   Allow all objects that can appear on the workplace to have reflections.

Object

☐   Generate a name for each newly created object. Make the name unique if the operating environment requires a unique name, for example, create a unique name by appending a number to the name of the object it was created from.

☐   Provide a folder containing sample objects from which users can create new objects. Make the create-on-drag setting the initial setting for the objects in the folder. For example, provide a folder named "New Forms" containing initialized versions of frequently-used forms.

Supplemental Related Topics

- "Container (Control)" on page 231
- "Data Transfer" on page 248
- "Direct Manipulation" on page 261
- "Icon" on page 300
- "Keyboard" on page 315
- "Mouse" on page 350
- "Pop-Up Menu" on page 388
- "Product Information (Choice)" on page 395
- "Work Area (Object)" on page 512

Open (Choice)

A routing choice that displays a window that allows a user to specify an object to be opened in the window from which the **Open...** choice was selected.

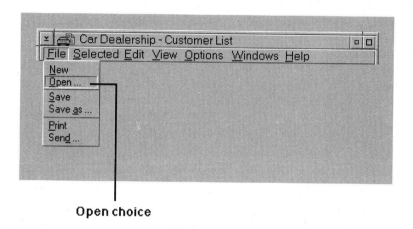

Open choice

When to Use

☐ Provide an **Open** choice for objects designed for application-oriented environments to allow a user to display another object of the same type in the window from which the **Open** choice was selected.

Guidelines

☑ If you provide an **Open** choice, and you provide an application-oriented **File** menu, place the **Open** choice in the application-oriented **File** menu.

☑ When a user selects the **Open** choice, display the **Open** action window.

☑ Assign "O" as the mnemonic for the **Open** menu choice.

Open (Choice)

Essential Related Topics

- "File Menu (Application-Oriented)" on page 280

- "Open (Action Window)" on page 373

Supplemental Related Topics

- "Window" on page 496

Open As (Choice)

An action choice that displays a window containing the named view, for example, **Open as (view)**. Or, when several views are available, it is a routing choice that leads to a cascaded menu containing the names of the view choices.

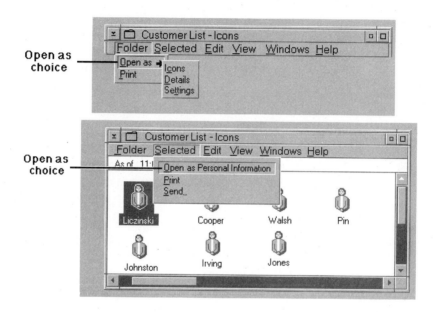

When to Use

☐   Provide an **Open as** choice to allow a user to open a selected object or group of selected objects in a new window to a specific view.

☐   Provide an **Open as** choice to allow a user to open the underlying object in a window to another view in a new window.

☐   If a settings view is displayed with a notebook, provide a cascaded menu from the **Open as settings** choice that provides direct access to each tabbed-divider page in the notebook.

Open As (Choice)

Guidelines

☑ If you provide the **Open as** choice, place it in the **Selected** menu if the **Selected** menu is provided to allow a user to open a selected object or group of objects to a specified view.

☑ If at least one view for an object is available and if a pop-up menu is provided, place the **Open as** choice in the pop-up menu for that object.

☐ Place the **Open as** choice in the object-oriented **File** menu if the object-oriented **File** menu is provided and your users must frequently open new windows on the underlying object and require the flexibility to open a user-specified view.

☐ If an object has more than three views, make the **Open as** choice a cascading choice and place the view names in the cascaded menu.

☐ If a cascaded menu is not used to list the names of the available views, then for each view, label a choice in the menu with the name of the view appended to the **Open as** choice. For example, show a choice labeled **Open as settings.**

☑ Assign "O" as the mnemonic for the **Open as** cascaded menu choice.

Essential Related Topics

- "File Menu (Object-Oriented)" on page 282
- "Selected Menu" on page 437

Supplemental Related Topics

- "Cascaded Menu" on page 214
- "Notebook (Control)" on page 363
- "Pop-Up Menu" on page 388
- "Primary Window" on page 391
- "Secondary Window" on page 433
- "Window" on page 496

Open (Action Window)

A window that appears from the routing choice **Open** that allows a user to select an object to open.

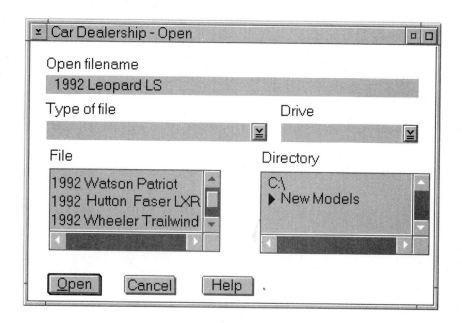

When to Use

Display the **Open** window when a user selects the **Open** choice in the application-oriented **File** menu.

Guidelines

☐ Display the **Open** window in a secondary window that is dependent upon the window from which the **Open** choice was selected.

☐ Provide an entry field to allow a user to type the name of an object to be opened.

☐ Provide a drop-down list that allows a user to display a list of file types that can be opened.

☐ Provide a drop-down list that allows a user to specify the storage device, such as the A:, B:, or C: drive.

Open (Action Window)

☐   Provide a list box of appropriate containers, such as directories. Use a filled in greater-than symbol (▸) to the left of the current container, and show the containment hierarchy by indenting containers that are within another container.

☐   Provide in a list box the names of all objects that are in the specified container, and on the specified storage device, that match the specified type.

☐   Assign the default action, such as double-click, for an object in the list of objects to open the selected object into the same window from which the **Open** choice was selected.

☑   Assign the default action, such as double-click, for a container in the list of containers to display or refresh the list of objects.

☐   When a user selects an object from the list of objects, insert the name of the selected object into the entry field that displays the object name.

☑   Provide a **Cancel** push button to allow a user to close the **Open** window without opening a new object.

☑   Provide an **Open** push button to allow a user to open the specified object.

☑   Provide a push button labeled **Help.**

Essential Related Topics

- "Open (Choice)" on page 369

Supplemental Related Topics

- "Default Action" on page 250
- "Drop-Down List (Control)" on page 268
- "Entry Field (Control)" on page 272
- "File Menu (Application-Oriented)" on page 280
- "List Box (Control)" on page 325
- "Push Button (Predefined)" on page 404

Options Menu

A pull-down menu from the **Options** choice on a menu bar that contains choices that allow a user to customize the functions of an application.

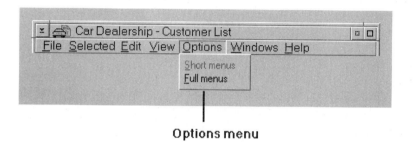

Options menu

When to Use

☐ Provide an **Options** choice on the menu bar in each window that provides a menu bar and a user can tailor the appearance or behavior of the product.

Guidelines

☐ Provide choices that are specific to a product, not specific to a particular view or object. For view-specific options, use the **View** pull-down. For object-specific options, provide an object setting.

☑ Assign "O" as the mnemonic for the **Options** choice.

Essential Related Topics

• "View Menu" on page 492

Supplemental Related Topics

• "Short Menus and Full Menus (Choice)" on page 454

• "Tool Palette" on page 482

Paste (Choice)

An action choice that places a copy of the contents of the clipboard into an indicated object.

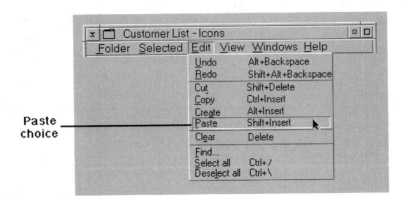

Paste
choice

When to Use

☐ Provide a **Paste** choice for all objects that can be modified by a user.

Guidelines

☑ If you provide a **Paste** choice, and you provide an **Edit** menu, place the **Paste** choice in the **Edit** menu.

☐ If you provide the **Paste** choice for an object, place the **Paste** choice in the pop-up menu for the object when the object on the clipboard can currently be copied into the object with the **Paste** choice.

☐ When a user selects the **Paste** choice from a pop-up menu, then add, insert, or combine the source object into the target object as appropriate.

☐ When a user selects the **Paste** choice in a window, place the source object at the current location of the cursor in the target object.

☐ When a user selects the **Paste** choice in a window, and no cursor is provided, place the source object at the current position of the pointer in the target object.

☐   When a user selects the **Paste** choice in a window and the cursor is positioned on or adjacent to selected text, replace the selected text with the source object; otherwise, insert the source object at the current position of the cursor.

☑   Display the **Paste** choice with unavailable-state emphasis when the clipboard is empty or when the contents cannot be pasted at the indicated position.

☐   Generate a name for each newly created object. Make the name unique if the operating environment requires a unique name, for example, create a unique name by appending a number to the name of the object it was created from.

☑   Assign "P" as the mnemonic for the **Paste** choice.

☑   Assign Shift+Insert as the shortcut key combination for the **Paste** choice.

Essential Related Topics

Supplemental Related Topics

Pointer

The symbol, usually in the shape of an arrow, that is displayed on the screen and is moved by a pointing device, such as a mouse. It is used to point to choices and objects that a user wants to select or otherwise interact with. A position on the pointer called the hot spot indicates where interaction will occur.

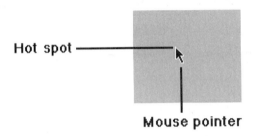

Hot spot

Mouse pointer

When to Use

☑ Display a pointer whenever pointing device support is enabled by the operating environment.

Guidelines

☑ When no other object-specific or task-specific pointer is displayed, display the arrow pointer.

☑ Move the pointer only when a user moves the pointing device.

☐ Display a pointer that a user can associate with an action or set of actions that can be performed within the current context. For example, augment the pointer with a rectangle when a user selects a rectangle-drawing tool from a tool palette.

☐ Place the pointer hot spot as follows:

- Place the pointer hot spot in the upper left-hand corner of the pointer image.

- If a user would typically expect the pointer hot spot in a position other than the upper-lefthand corner of the pointer image, place the pointer hot spot where the user would typically expect it. For example, if you provide a crosshair pointer, place the hot spot at the intersection of the two lines, rather than in the upper-lefthand corner of the pointer image.

☑ Use the predefined pointer when a user performs a predefined operation.

Essential Related Topics

• "Pointer (Predefined)" on page 380

Supplemental Related Topics

• "Direct Manipulation" on page 261

• "Mouse" on page 350

• "Pointing Device" on page 382

Pointer (Predefined)

Pointers used for predefined operations.

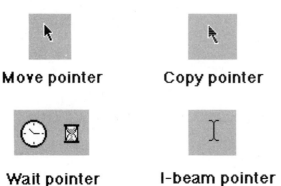

Move pointer   Copy pointer

Wait pointer   I-beam pointer

Do-not pointer

When to Use

          Display the move pointer to indicate that the result of the direct-manipulation operation will be a move.

Display the copy pointer to indicate that the result of the direct-manipulation operation will be a copy.

Display the do-not pointer to indicate that the target object is not a valid target for the direct-manipulation operation.

☐   Display the I-beam pointer to indicate that the pointer is over an area where text can be typed or selected.

Display a wait pointer to indicate that the user cannot currently interact with the component the pointer is over.

Guidelines

Make the move pointer the default pointer.

□   If a user cannot interact with a component because a process is affecting that component, display the wait pointer while the pointer is over that component. Do not prevent a user from interacting with components that are not affected by the process that is running.

□   When the user uses a pointing device for selection in text that can be edited, place the text cursor at the pointer position when the user clicks the selection button.

Essential Related Topics

*   "Cursor" on page 244

*   "Pointer" on page 378

*   "Progress Indicator" on page 396

Supplemental Related Topics

*   "Entry Field (Control)" on page 272

*   "Text Entry" on page 479

Pointing Device

A device, such as a mouse, trackball, or joystick, used to move a pointer on the screen.

When to Use

☑   Provide support for a pointing device.

☐   Support one-button, two-button, and three-button mouse pointing devices.

Guidelines

☑   Provide access to all functions of an object using equivalent, though not necessarily identical, pointing device and keyboard techniques.

Supplemental Related Topics

- "Cursor" on page 244
- "Keyboard" on page 315
- "Mouse" on page 350
- "Pointer" on page 378

Point Selection

A selection technique that allows a user to select a single object.

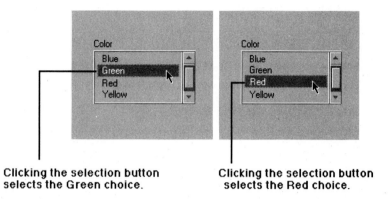

Clicking the selection button
selects the Green choice.

Clicking the selection button
selects the Red choice.

When to Use

☑ Provide point selection for single, multiple, and extended selection.

Guidelines

☑ In single selection mode:

- Using the mouse, when the user presses the mouse selection button, deselect the currently-selected object and select the object the pointer is on.

- Using the keyboard, when the user presses Spacebar, deselect the currently-selected object and select the object the cursor is on.

☑ In multiple selection mode:

- Using the mouse, when the user presses the mouse selection button, toggle the selection state of the object or group of objects the pointer is on. The selection state of all other objects are not affected.

- Using the keyboard, when the user presses Spacebar, toggle the selection state of the object or group of objects the cursor is on. The selection state of all other objects are not affected.

Point Selection

In extended selection mode:

- Using the mouse, when the user presses the mouse selection button, deselect the currently-selected object or group of objects and select the object the pointer is on.

- Using the mouse while holding the Ctrl key, when the user presses the mouse selection button, toggle the selection state of the object or group of objects the pointer is on. The selection state of all other objects are not affected.

- Using the keyboard, when the user presses Spacebar, deselect the currently-selected object or group of objects and select the object the cursor is on.

- Using the keyboard after pressing Shift+F8, when the user presses spacebar, toggle the selection state of the object or group of objects the cursor is on. The selection state of all other objects are not affected.

Essential Related Topics

- "Selection Types and Techniques" on page 440

Supplemental Related Topics

- "Point-to-Endpoint Selection" on page 385
- "Random-Point Selection" on page 411

Point-to-Endpoint Selection

Selection techniques in which a user selects objects by specifying a beginning point and an end point. The three implementations of point-to-endpoint selection are range (click), range (swipe), and area (marquee).

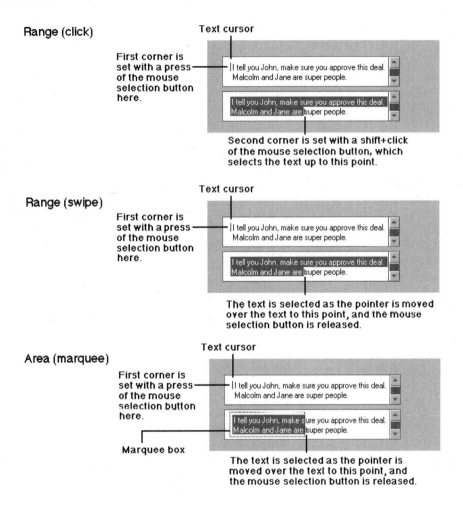

Range (click)

Text cursor

First corner is set with a press of the mouse selection button here.

II tell you John, make sure you approve this deal.
Malcolm and Jane are super people.

I tell you John, make sure you approve this deal.
Malcolm and Jane are super people.

Second corner is set with a shift+click of the mouse selection button, which selects the text up to this point.

Range (swipe)

Text cursor

First corner is set with a press of the mouse selection button here.

II tell you John, make sure you approve this deal.
Malcolm and Jane are super people.

I tell you John, make sure you approve this deal.
Malcolm and Jane are super people.

The text is selected as the pointer is moved over the text to this point, and the mouse selection button is released.

Area (marquee)

Text cursor

First corner is set with a press of the mouse selection button here.

II tell you John, make sure you approve this deal.
Malcolm and Jane are super people.

I tell you John, make sure you approve this deal.
Malcolm and Jane are super people.

Marquee box

The text is selected as the pointer is moved over the text to this point, and the mouse selection button is released.

When to Use

☑ Provide one or more point-to-endpoint-selection techniques in extended selection and multiple selection.

Point-to-Endpoint Selection

Guidelines

☑ Allow a keyboard user to press Shift+F8 to establish a mode in which the new selected objects are added or removed from the current group of selected objects.

☑ In extended selection mode:

- Using the mouse for an area, the user presses the mouse selection button to deselect all other objects in the selection scope and to select all objects contained within the identified area.

- Using the mouse for a range while holding the Ctrl key, the user presses the mouse selection button to deselect all other objects in the selection scope and select all objects in order from the start point to the identified end point.

- Using the keyboard for a range, the user presses Shift at the start point and moves the cursor to the end point to deselect all other objects in the selection scope and to select all objects in order from the start point to the identified end point.

- Using the mouse and keyboard for a range, the user presses the mouse selection button at the start point and presses Shift and the mouse selection button at the end point to deselect all other objects in the selection scope and to select all objects in order from the identified start point to the identified end point.

- Using the keyboard after pressing Shift+F8, the user presses Spacebar to toggle the selection state of the object the cursor is on.

☑ Display the marquee box only during selection.

☑ Display selected-state emphasis on each object as soon as it is completely contained within the marquee box.

☑ Display selected-state emphasis on each icon as soon as the icon's graphic is completely contained within the marquee box.

☑ Display selected-state emphasis on each object as soon as the pointer passes over it when performing range (swipe) selection.

Essential Related Topics

Supplemental Related Topics

Pop-Up Menu

A menu that is displayed next to, and contains choices appropriate for, a given object or set of objects in their current context, such as the container it is contained in, what other objects are selected, and what it contains.

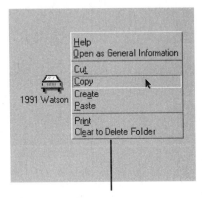

Pop-up menu

When to Use

☐ Provide a pop-up menu for each object.

Guidelines

☑ Do not change the state of a window or an object when a pop-up menu is displayed. For example, do not change the selection state of any object.

☑ If pop-up menus are provided, allow a user to display the pop-up menu:

- Using the keyboard by pressing Shift+F10 when the cursor is on the object.

- Using a one-button mouse by pressing Alt+mouse selection button when the pointer is over the object.

- Using a two-button mouse by chording the mouse selection and manipulation buttons when the pointer is over the object.

- Using a three-button mouse by pressing the mouse menu button when the pointer is over the object.

☐ When a user requests a pop-up menu using the keyboard, place the pop-up menu centered and to the right of the object from which it was requested, if possible; otherwise, place it near the object as space allows, but not covering the object.

☐ When a user requests a pop-up menu using a pointing device, place the pop-up menu centered and to the right of the pointer, if possible; otherwise, place it near the pointer as space allows, but not covering the object.

☐ Place the cursor on a choice near the middle of a pop-up menu when the menu is first displayed.

☑ Continue to display a pop-up menu until a user selects a choice (other than a cascading choice) from the pop-up menu, presses the cancel key, or until a user initiates an action outside the scope of the pop-up menu, such as displaying a pop-up menu for another object or clicking a button on the pointing device while the pointer is not over the pop-up menu.

☑ When a user requests a pop-up menu from one of a group of selected objects, display in the pop-up menu only those choices that are applicable to all of the selected objects in the group. When a user selects a choice in the pop-up menu, apply the selected choice to each of the selected objects.

☐ If pop-up menus are provided for an object, allow a user to display the pop-up menu on an object whether or not the object is selected.

☐ If a choice in a pop-up menu is not currently available, do not include it in the menu.

☑ Place choices in a pop-up menu in the following order:

- Choices that open a window on an object, such as **Open as** or **Help.**
- --Separator--
- Choices that provide access to the clipboard, such as **Cut, Copy, Create,** and **Paste.**
- --Separator--
- Choices provided as a convenience to users, such as **Print** and **Delete.**

Pop-Up Menu

☐   When possible, use the order of choices in pull-down menus to determine the order of related choices in pop-up menus. For example, if you provide the **Save** and **Print** choices in a pop-up menu, place them in the same relative order as they appear in the **File** menu.

☑   When a user cancels a pop-up menu by pressing the Cancel key, remove the menu and return input focus to where it was prior to displaying the menu.

☐   Allow a user to customize a pop-up menu by adding or removing choices.

Essential Related Topics

*   "Control" on page 235
*   "Menu (Control)" on page 331

Supplemental Related Topics

*   "Cascaded Menu" on page 214
*   "Keyboard" on page 315
*   "Mouse" on page 350

Primary Window

A window in which the main interaction between a user and an object takes place. A primary window is used to present information that is used independently from information in all other windows.

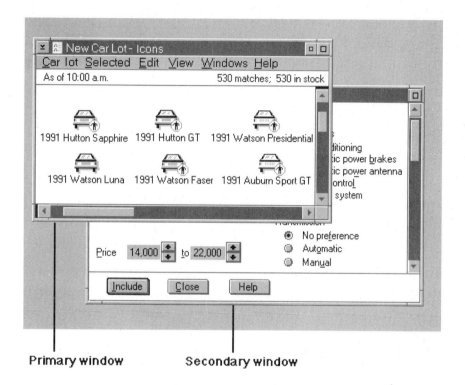

Primary window   Secondary window

When to Use

☑ Use a primary window to display a view of an object that is independent of all other windows (except work areas) with respect to the closing, opening, minimizing, and restoring actions.

☑ Use a primary window to display all views of objects opened from the workplace.

Guidelines

☑ When a primary window is opened or restored, restore its associated secondary windows.

Primary Window

☑ When a primary window is closed or minimized, remove its secondary windows.

☐ Allow a view of an object to be displayed in multiple primary windows.

Essential Related Topics

- "Secondary Window" on page 433
- "Window" on page 496

Print (Choice)

An action or routing choice that causes an object to be printed.

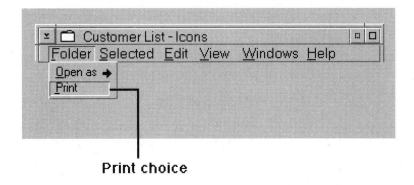

Print choice

When to Use

☐   Provide a **Print** choice for all printable objects.

Guidelines

☑   If you provide a **Print** choice and you provide a **File** menu, place the **Print** choice in the **File** menu if the underlying object can be printed.

☑   If you provide a **Print** choice and you provide a **Selected** menu, place the **Print** choice in the **Selected** menu if the selected object can be printed.

☐   If more than one printer is connected to a user's system, allow the user to designate the printer to be used. For example, provide a list of printers in a cascaded menu or in an action window.

☐   If additional information is required before an object can be printed, allow a user to specify that information.

☐   Provide access from any object to any printer object through direct manipulation.

Print (Choice)

☐   When a user selects the **Print** choice in the:

- **File** menu, print the view in the window.
- **Selected** menu, print the default print view.
- Pop-up menu, print the default print view.

☐   When a user drags an icon (other than the small icon in the title bar) to a printer object, print the default print view for the object.

☐   When a user drags the small icon in the title bar to a printer object, print the view in the window.

☐   Allow a user to specify which view is the default print view for an object.

☑   Assign "P" as the mnemonic for the **Print** choice.

Supplemental Related Topics

- "Data Transfer" on page 248

- "Direct Manipulation" on page 261

- "File Menu (Application-Oriented)" on page 280

- "Selected Menu" on page 437

Product Information (Choice)

An action choice that displays a window containing product information, such as a copyright notice, a logo, or both.

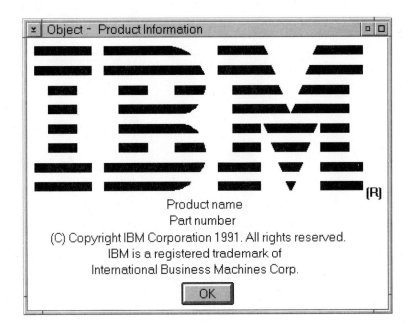

When to Use

☐   Provide a **Product information** choice in each **Help** menu.

Guidelines

☑   If the **Product information** choice is provided, place it in the **Help** menu.

☐   Use a secondary window to display product information.

☑   Provide a centered **OK** push button that removes the window.

☑   Assign "P" as the mnemonic for the **Product information** choice.

Essential Related Topics

•   "Help Menu" on page 296

Progress Indicator

One or more controls that inform the user about the status of a process. If a progress indicator appears in a dedicated window, information normally presented in an information message can be displayed in that window.

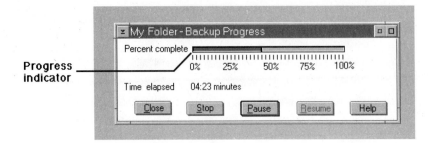

Progress indicator

When to Use

☐ When a wait pointer has been displayed for more than five seconds, display a progress indicator in addition to the wait pointer.

Guidelines

☐ Place a progress indicator in the same window as the process is requested from to reduce the number of windows the user must interact with.

☑ Close a progress-indicator window when a request made by a user completes normally.

☑ If information that would have been displayed in an information message is displayed in the progress-indicator window, do not close the window until the user explicitly requests to close it, such as by selecting the **Close** push button.

☑ When a progress indicator is displayed, continually update the progress indicator to accurately represent the known progress of a request made by a user.

☐ Provide a push button that allows a user to end the process and close the window. For example, provide a push button labeled **Stop** to allow a user to end the process and close the window.

☑ Provide a push button that allows a user to close the progress-indicator window without affecting the process. For example, provide a push button labeled **Close** to allow a user to close the progress indicator window without affecting the process. Do not use a **Close** push button to end a process.

☐ Provide a push button that allows a user to suspend a process and provide a push button that allows a user to resume the process that has been suspended. For example, provide one push button labeled **Pause** and another labeled **Resume.** Display unavailable-state emphasis on one or the other depending on whether the process is running or has been suspended.

☐ Provide access to help information from each progress-indicator window. For example, provide a push button labeled **Help.**

☐ Include the name of the object followed by a hyphen, the name of the process, and the word "Progress" in the title bar when a separate window is used to display the progress indicator.

Essential Related Topics

- "Action Message" on page 206
- "Information Message" on page 310
- "Message" on page 337
- "Pointer (Predefined)" on page 380
- "Push Button (Predefined)" on page 404
- "Slider (Control)" on page 461
- "Warning Message" on page 494

Pull-Down Menu

A menu of related choices that extends from a selected choice on a menu bar or from the system-menu symbol.

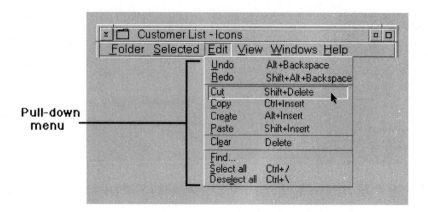

When to Use

☑ Provide a pull-down menu for each choice on a menu bar and for the system menu.

Guidelines

☐ If you provide choices that do not logically fit within any of the predefined menus, such as the **Edit** menu or the **View** menu, provide product-specific menu bar choices that lead to menus that logically group your product-specific choices.

☑ Provide the predefined mnemonic for each predefined textual choice in a pull-down menu.

☑ Provide a unique mnemonic for each product-specific textual choice in a menu, unless no meaningful unique mnemonic can be found.

☑ Provide the predefined shortcut key assignment for each predefined choice in a pull-down menu.

☐ Provide a unique shortcut key assignment for each frequently-used product-specific choice in a pull-down menu.

Essential Related Topics

Supplemental Related Topics

Push Button (Control)

A control containing text or graphics, or both, representing an action choice or routing choice that will be activated when a user selects it.

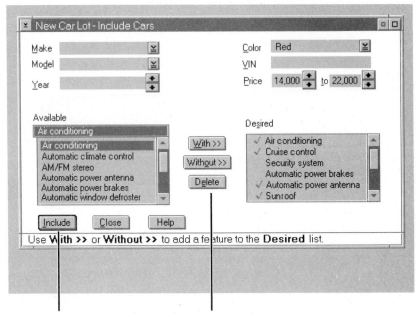

Push buttons at the bottom of the window affect the entire window.

Push button next to the field it affects.

When to Use

☐   Use a push button in a window with a menu bar to provide convenient access to a frequently-used action choice or routing choice.

☑   If a menu bar is not provided in a window displaying a view of an object, place all action and routing choices on push buttons in that window, except for those choices that appear on the system menu.

Guidelines

- ☐ Avoid placing settings choices on push buttons.

- ☐ If one push button in a field is typically used most frequently by users, make that push button the default push button for the field.

- ☐ If the cursor is on a push button, make that push button the default push button.

- ☐ Assign the default push button according to the position of the cursor. For example, when a user moves the cursor to a control with associated push buttons, assign one of the associated push buttons as the default push button.

- ☑ Assign a unique mnemonic to each textual push button choice that does not have a specific keyboard access mechanism, such as Esc for the **Cancel** push button or F1 for the **Help** push button, unless no meaningful unique mnemonic can be found.

- ☐ When a user types a mnemonic assigned to a push button, perform the action assigned to that push button.

- ☐ For push buttons that do not open a new window or close the current window, avoid moving the cursor when a user types a mnemonic to select a push button.

- ☑ If two push button choices are mutually exclusive, for example, **Undo** and **Redo,** use two push buttons and display unavailable-state emphasis on whichever one is unavailable given the current state of the object. Do not change the label or the function of a push button.

- ☐ Capitalize only the first letter of the first word of a choice appearing on a push button unless the choice contains an abbreviation, acronym, or proper noun that should be capitalized.

- ☑ When you provide a push button with the function of one of the predefined push buttons, use the predefined push-button label for that push button.

- ☐ Label a product-defined action push button to indicate the action that will be applied to an object.

- ☐ Label a product-specific routing push button to indicate the window or menu that the user will be routed to.

Push Button (Control)

☑ When a push button is used for a routing choice, use an ellipsis following the choice text.

☑ Place push buttons that affect the entire window horizontally at the bottom of the window and justified from the left edge.

☐ If a window that can be scrolled contains push buttons that affect the entire window, scroll the area above the push buttons, keeping the push buttons visible.

☐ If the action indicated by the label on a push button adjusts or is associated with a component within the same window as the push button, place the push button near that component. For example, if the function of a push button is to restore the initial value in an entry field, place that push button beside the entry field that it affects.

☐ If a window contains a push button that affects a component in the window, scroll the push button along with the component when a user scrolls the window.

☐ If a push button adjusts (or is associated with) a component within a window (rather than the entire window), do not close the window when a user selects the push button.

☐ Avoid using a push button to change the size of a window; instead, allow a user to change the size of the window using the size borders and the maximize push button. For example, do not provide a push button labeled **More>>** to allow a user to enlarge a window.

☐ When a window contains push buttons and a menu bar, place, in the pull-down menus, choices that provide function that is equivalent to the push button functions that affect the entire window so that the push buttons provide convenient access to frequently-used choices in the pull-down menus.

☐ Combine existing menu choices to create new push-button choices for frequently-used combinations of choices. For example, the **Save** and **New** choices could be combined into a new push-button choice called **Save and new** that would perform the **Save** action followed by the **New** action.

☐ If push buttons contain choices that are also available through another mechanism, such as the menu bar or scroll bar, allow a user to hide or remove the push buttons.

☐   Clip the push buttons at the bottom of the window when a user decreases the width of the window rather than reflowing the push buttons into multiple lines.

☐   Avoid using a group box around a field consisting only of push buttons.

☐   For push buttons that provide choices that can be used repeatedly, repeat the action as long as the user presses and holds the mouse selection button. Stop repeating the action when the user moves the pointer away from the push button and resume repeating the action if the user moves the pointer back over the push button without having released the mouse selection button.

Essential Related Topics

- "Choice" on page 218

- "Control" on page 235

- "Default Action" on page 250

- "Mnemonic" on page 344

- "Push Button (Predefined)" on page 404

Push Button (Predefined)

Push buttons that provide predefined functions. The predefined push buttons are **OK, Close, Stop, Continue, Retry, Apply, Reset, Cancel, Pause, Resume** and **Help.**

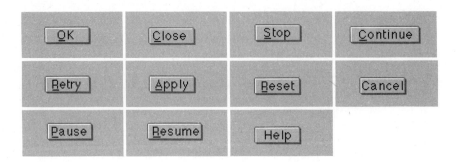

When to Use

Use a push button with the predefined label when you provide the function defined in Figure 193.

Figure 193. Predefined Push Buttons

Label	Function
OK	Accepts any changes that have been made in the window and removes the window. Also used to indicate that the user should acknowledge information in the window before removing the window.
Close	Removes the window without affecting a process. Close does not change the information in the window.
Stop	Ends a process and removes the window.
Continue	Resumes a process that has been interrupted by the operating environment when the user may proceed as originally requested.
Retry	Tries a process again that has been interrupted by the operating environment because of a situation that the user can attempt to correct.
Apply	Applies changes made to settings choices without removing the window in which the changes were made.
Reset	Returns the values of changed settings choices to their last saved state.
Cancel	Removes the window without applying any changes that were not previously applied in that window.
Pause	Temporarily suspends a process without ending the process.
Resume	Continues a process that was paused.
Help	Displays a window containing contextual help information.

Push Button (Predefined)

Guidelines

☑ If you provide the **Cancel** and **Help** push buttons, place them to the right of all other push buttons.

☑ Provide a **Reset** push button whenever an **Apply** push button is provided.

☐ If **Reset** is selected, return the values of settings that were changed only in the window where **Reset** was selected.

☑ If **Reset** is selected, return the object to the state it was in prior to any uncommitted changes. Changes that have been previously committed, for example using **Apply** or **OK** are not reset.

☑ Do not use both a **Close** push button and a **Cancel** push button in the same window.

☐ See Figure 194 to determine window usage for standard push buttons and the corresponding functions for the **Close** choice on the system menu, the Enter key, and the Esc key.

Figure 194 (Page 1 of 2). Use of Predefined Push Buttons

Type of Window	Push Buttons (Listed in the relative order they would appear in)	Result of Close Choice in System menu	Result of Enter Key	Result of Esc Key
Object views	Any actions (for example, **Print** or **Undo**)	**Close** (Optionally, provide a warning message for Save or Don't Save changes.)	Any action	**Cancel,** if used
Settings (not immediately saved)	**OK** **Apply**[1] **Reset**[2] **Cancel** **Help**	**Cancel** (Does a **Reset**, then **Close**)	**OK**	**Cancel** (Does a **Reset**, then **Close**)
Settings (immediately saved)	**Close** **Help**	**Close**	**Close**	**Close**
Action Window	Action name[3] **Cancel** or **Close** **Help**	**Cancel** or **Close**[4] (Withdraw action request)	Default action[5]	**Cancel** or **Close**[4] (Withdraw action request)
Information message	**OK** **Help**	**OK**	**OK**	**OK**

Figure 194 (Page 2 of 2). Use of Predefined Push Buttons

Type of Window	Push Buttons (Listed in the relative order they would appear in)	Result of Close Choice in System menu	Result of Enter Key	Result of Esc Key
Progress indicator	**Close** **Stop** (optional) **Pause** and **Resume** (both optional) **Help**	**Close**	**Pause** if supported, otherwise **Close**	**Stop** if supported, otherwise **Close**
Warning message	Action name[3] (optional) **Continue**[8] **Cancel** **Help**	**Cancel** (if supported, or else a non-destructive action)	Non-destructive action	**Cancel** (if supported, or else a non-destructive action)
Action message (general case)	Action name[3] (optional) **Retry**[9] **Cancel**[7] **Help**[10]	**Cancel** (if supported, otherwise a non-destructive action)	**Retry** (if supported, otherwise a non-destructive action)	**Cancel** (if supported, otherwise a non-destructive action)
Action message (simple case)	**Yes**[6] **No** **Help**	Choice of **Yes/No** that does not lose data	Choice of **Yes/No** that does not lose data	Choice of **Yes/No** that does not lose data

Notes:

1. **Apply** is typical when a large number of settings is possible, and when a user might want to apply a few at a time.

2. Both **Reset** and **Apply** are provided together.

3. One or more push buttons that contain the names of the actions must be available.

4. **Cancel** must remove the action window and return to the window from which the action was requested.

5. This assignment is optional; provide it for a useful, non-destructive action.

6. **Yes** and **No** each represent an action, or **Yes** represents an action and **No** is **Cancel.**

7. Use **Cancel** if it is practical. Affected user data must be returned to its original state or left in a useful state.

8. The window must have at least one action that continues the request and one action that cancels the request.

9. Use **Retry** if it is practical.

10. The window must have at least two from the set: "action," **Retry, Cancel.**

Essential Related Topics

- "Push Button (Control)" on page 400

Push Button (Predefined)

Supplemental Related Topics

Radio Button (Control)

A control used to display mutually exclusive textual settings choices.

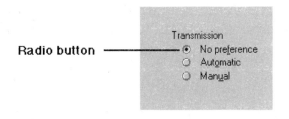

When to Use

☐ Use a field of radio buttons to display mutually exclusive settings choices.

Guidelines

☑ Use radio buttons for settings choices. Do not use radio buttons to represent action choices or routing choices.

☐ Avoid using a radio button for graphical choices, instead use a value set for graphical choices.

☑ Use at least two radio buttons in each field.

☑ Assign one of the choices in a radio-button field as the default except when the radio buttons represents a setting for more than one selected object and no single choice applies to all the objects.

☐ If a user can choose not to select any of the choices, provide a radio button labeled **None** or equivalent appropriate text.

☐ Arrange the radio buttons in a group in rows, columns, or both.

☐ If a radio button choice is currently unavailable, display it with unavailable-state emphasis.

☐ Assign a mnemonic to each radio-button choice.

☐ If a radio button has a mnemonic, provide access to the mnemonic by allowing a user to press the Alt key and that mnemonic.

Radio Button (Control)

☐　　　　　Capitalize only the first letter of the first word of a radio button choice unless the choice contains an abbreviation, acronym, or proper noun that should be capitalized.

☑　　　　　When a field of radio buttons represents a setting shared by more than one selected object:

- Do not display a dot in any of the radio buttons if some, but not all, of the selected objects have the setting turned on.

- Display a dot in one of the radio buttons if that setting applies to all of the selected objects.

Essential Related Topics

- "Control" on page 235

- "Mnemonic" on page 344

Supplemental Related Topics

- "Check Box (Control)" on page 216

- "Choice" on page 218

- "Field Prompt" on page 278

- "Group Heading" on page 292

- "Value Set (Control)" on page 490

Random-Point Selection

A selection technique that allows a user to select objects as the pointer touches them, while the selection button on a mouse is pressed. The implementation of random-point selection is random (swipe).

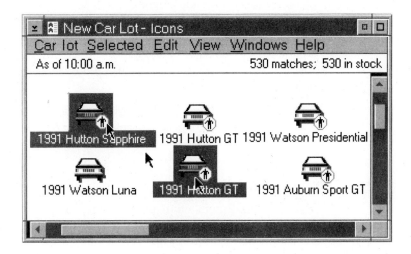

When to Use

☐ Provide random point selection techniques when multiple objects can be selected, in any order, not necessarily contiguously. For example, this provides a user with a technique to select any documents in a folder and then print those documents in the order they were selected with one action request.

Guidelines

☑ In extended selection:

- Using the mouse, when the user presses the mouse selection button on the first object to be selected and moves the pointer over other objects to be selected, deselect all other objects in the selection scope and select the individual objects in the order the user identified them.

Random-Point Selection

☑ In multiple selection:

- Using the mouse, when the user presses the mouse selection button on the first object to be selected and moves the pointer over other objects to be selected, select the individual objects in the order the user identified them.

☑ Toggle the selection state of objects that the pointer touches when a user is using random-point selection. Objects that were not already in the same selection state as the first object then take on the selection state of the first object. In extended selection, all previously selected objects are deselected.

☐ Provide sufficient space between objects for a user to move the mouse around and not touch objects they do not wish to select.

Essential Related Topics

- "Selected-State Emphasis (Cue)" on page 439

- "Selection Types and Techniques" on page 440

Reflection (Object)

An object that is represented by more than one icon. If a user changes an object's reflection, all other reflections of the object are changed. If a user deletes a reflection, other reflections of the object are not necessarily deleted.

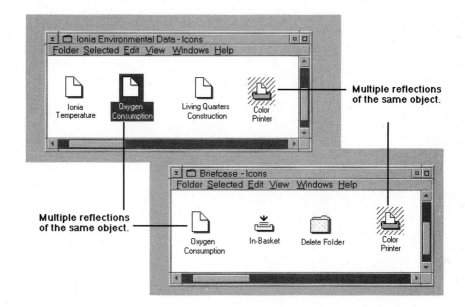

Multiple reflections of the same object.

Multiple reflections of the same object.

When to Use

☐   Provide reflections for all objects to provide access to an object from more than one location.

Guidelines

☐   If you provide a choice that allows a user to create a reflection of an object and you provide an **Edit** menu, place the choice that creates the reflection in the **Edit** menu.

☐   If you provide a choice that allows a user to create a reflection of an object, place the choice that creates the reflection in the pop-up menu for the object when a reflection of the object can be created.

Reflection (Object)

☐   When a user presses the reflection override key and performs a direct-manipulation operation on an object or group of selected objects, create a reflection of the indicated object or group of selected objects.

☐   If the object for which the **Delete** choice is requested supports reflections, display the **Delete** choice as a routing choice that leads to a cascaded menu with choices for deleting just this reflection or deleting the entire object and all reflections of the object.

Essential Related Topics

- "Create (Choice)" on page 242
- "Delete (Choice)" on page 254
- "Direct Manipulation" on page 261
- "Mouse" on page 350
- "Object" on page 366

Refresh and Refresh Now (Choice)

Choices that allow a user to control whether changes made to underlying data are immediately displayed in the current view or are displayed upon user request at a later time. **Refresh** is a routing choice that leads to a cascaded menu or an action window that allows the user to select refresh options. **Refresh now** is an action choice that causes the current view to be immediately updated to match the underlying information.

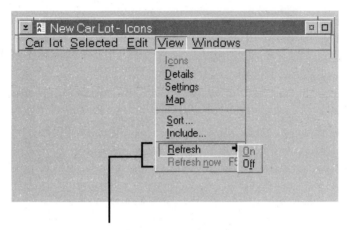

Refresh and Refresh now choices

When to Use

☐ Provide the **Refresh** and **Refresh now** choices to allow a user to control when a view will be updated to reflect changes in the underlying data. For example, provide **Refresh** and **Refresh now** choices:

- To increase a user's control over the display of data when the data can be changed by another user or by another process.

- When the time it takes to redisplay the data could interfere with a user's ability to interact with the data.

- When the data of interest to a user is located on another system and subject to communications performance constraints.

Refresh and Refresh Now (Choice)

Guidelines

☑   If you provide the **Refresh** or **Refresh now** choices, and you provide a **View** menu, place the **Refresh** or **Refresh now** choices in the **View** menu.

☐   If you provide the **Refresh** or **Refresh now** choices for an object, place the **Refresh** or **Refresh now** choices in the pop-up menu for the object when the object can currently be refreshed.

☐   Provide at least the **On** and **Off** choices to allow a user to specify if the view will be updated.

☐   Provide object-specific choices as appropriate. For example, provide a short list of time intervals, such as **5 minutes, 10 minutes,** or **30 minutes** in a cascaded menu or provide more choices in an action window.

☐   If you provide the **On,** and **Off** choices, place them in a cascaded menu from the **Refresh** choice.

☑   When a user selects the **Refresh now** choice, immediately update the view to display the current data.

☑   When a user selects the **On** choice, continually update the view to display the most current data in the view.

☑   When a user selects the **Off** choice, do not continue to update the view until a user selects the **Refresh now** or **On** choice.

☐   If you provide the **On** choice, make it the default setting unless a user has specified otherwise.

☑   Display unavailable-state emphasis on the **Refresh now** choice if the current display is known to match the underlying data.

☐   If you provide the **Refresh now** choice and you do not currently know or can never know if the current display matches the underlying data, make the **Refresh now** choice available.

☑   Display the **Refresh now** choice with unavailable-state emphasis if **On** is currently selected.

☑   Assign "R" as the mnemonic for the **Refresh** choice.

☑   Assign "N" as the mnemonic for the **Refresh now** choice.

☑   Assign "O" as the mnemonic for the **On** choice.

☑   Assign "F" as the mnemonic for the **Off** choice.

Essential Related Topics

- "View Menu" on page 492

Restore (Choice)

Restore (Choice)

An action choice that returns a window to the size it was and the position it was in before it was previously minimized or maximized.

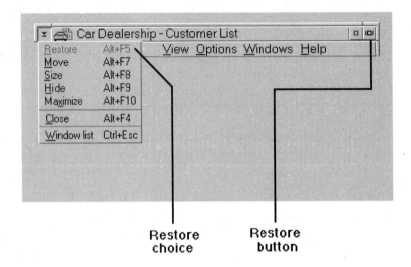

Restore
choice

Restore
button

When to Use

☑ If a window can be minimized, provide a **Restore** choice to allow a user to return the window from the minimized state to its last saved size and position prior to being minimized.

☑ If a window can be maximized, provide a **Restore** choice to allow a user to return the window from the maximized state to its last saved size and position prior to being maximized.

Guidelines

☑ If you provide the **Restore** choice, place it in the system menu.

☑ Display the **Restore** choice with unavailable-state emphasis when the window is not maximized or minimized.

☑ Change the maximize button to a restore button in the title bar when the size of a window can be changed and the window has been maximized.

☑ When a user selects the **Restore** choice from the minimized state, return the window to the size it was and the position it was in before it was last minimized. For example, if a window was maximized prior to being minimized, display the window in the maximized state when a user selects the **Restore** choice.

☑ When a user selects the restore button from the maximized state, return the window to the size it was and the position it was in before it was last maximized. For example, if a window was at a user-defined size prior to being maximized, return the window to the user-defined size when the user selects the **Restore** choice.

☑ When a user selects the **Restore** choice from a minimized work area, restore any associated windows that were open when the work area was last minimized.

☐ When a user restores a minimized work area, restore the work area window and any associated windows to their previous states, regardless of the amount of time that has elapsed since a user last restored the work area, and regardless of whether the user's system has been turned off and on again.

☑ When a user selects the **Restore** choice from a minimized primary window, restore any secondary windows that were open when the primary window was last minimized.

☐ When a user restores a minimized primary window, restore the primary window and any secondary windows to their previous states, regardless of the amount of time that has elapsed since a user last restored the primary window, and regardless of whether the user's system has been turned off and on again.

☑ Change the restore button to the maximize button after a window has been restored to a state other than maximized.

☑ Assign Alt+F5 as the shortcut key combination for the **Restore** choice.

☑ Assign "R" as the mnemonic for the **Restore** choice.

Restore (Choice)

Essential Related Topics

- "System Menu" on page 475

Supplemental Related Topics

- "Maximize (Choice)" on page 329
- "Minimize (Choice)" on page 342
- "Size (Choice)" on page 459

Routing (Choice Type)

A choice that displays a pull-down menu, a cascaded menu, or a window that contains additional choices used to further specify or clarify the routing choice.

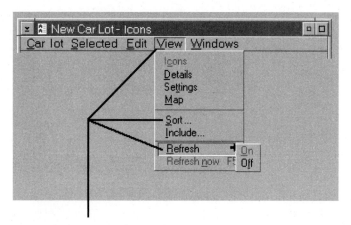

Routing choices

When to Use

☑ Use a routing choice to display a pull-down menu or cascaded menu or to display an action window.

Guidelines

☑ Use a right-pointing arrow (→) after a pull-down menu choice, cascaded menu, or pop-up menu choice that causes a cascaded menu to be displayed.

☑ Use ellipses (...) after a choice in a pull-down menu, cascaded menu, pop-up menu, or on a push button that causes an action window to be displayed.

☑ Do not use ellipses (...) or a right-pointing arrow (→) after a menu bar choice.

Routing (Choice Type)

Essential Related Topics

- "Action Choice (Choice Type)" on page 204
- "Choice" on page 218
- "Settings (Choice Type)" on page 448

Supplemental Related Topics

- "Menu (Control)" on page 331
- "Push Button (Control)" on page 400

Save (Choice)

An action choice that stores the object in the window on a storage device, such as a disk or diskette.

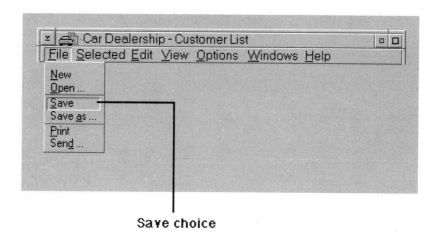

Save choice

When to Use

☐ Provide a **Save** choice for each object that is not automatically saved when changed.

Guidelines

☑ If you provide a **Save** choice, and you provide a **File** menu, place the **Save** choice in the **File** menu.

☑ Do not close the window when a user selects the **Save** choice.

☑ Do not change the appearance or position of the object in a window when a user selects the **Save** choice. For example do not scroll the object in the window.

☐ If the object being saved does not have a user-assigned name, display the **Save as** window.

☑ Assign "S" as the mnemonic for the **Save** choice.

Save (Choice)

Essential Related Topics

- "File Menu (Application-Oriented)" on page 280
- "File Menu (Object-Oriented)" on page 282
- "Save As (Choice)" on page 427

Save As (Action Window)

A window from the **Save as** choice that allows a user to save a copy of an object by giving it a different name.

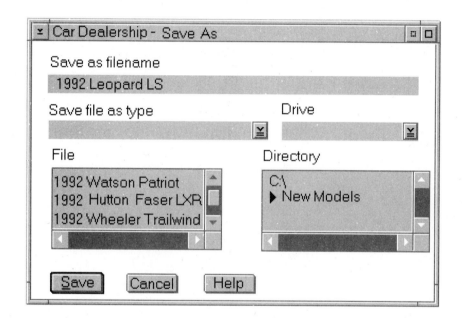

When to Use

☑ Display the **Save As** window when a user selects the **Save as** choice.

Guidelines

☐ Display the **Save As** window in a secondary window that is dependent upon the window from which the **Save as** choice was selected.

☐ Provide an entry field to allow a user to type the name of the new object.

☐ Provide a drop-down list that allows a user to display a list of the file types that can be saved.

☐ Provide a drop-down list that allows a user to specify the storage device, such as the "A:," "B:," or "C:" drive.

Save As (Action Window)

☐   Provide a list box of the appropriate containers. Use a filled in greater-than symbol (►) to the left of the current container, and show the containment hierarchy by indenting containers that are within another container.

☐   Provide in a list box the names of all objects in the specified container and on the specified storage device that match the specified type.

☐   Do not provide a default action, such as a double-click, that allows a user to select an object within the list of existing objects. Use this list only to present the names of existing objects; not as an easy way to overwrite an existing object. To overwrite an existing object, allow a user to type its name into the entry field that presents the new object name.

☐   Assign the default action, such as double-click, for a container in the list of containers to display or refresh the list of objects.

☑   Provide a **Cancel** push button to allow a user to close the **Save As** window without saving the current object.

☑   Provide a **Save** push button to allow a user to save the current object under the specified name.

☑   Provide a push button labeled **Help.**

Essential Related Topics

- "Save (Choice)" on page 423

Supplemental Related Topics

- "Default Action" on page 250
- "Drop-Down List (Control)" on page 268
- "Entry Field (Control)" on page 272
- "File Menu (Application-Oriented)" on page 280
- "List Box (Control)" on page 325
- "Open (Action Window)" on page 373
- "Push Button (Predefined)" on page 404

Save As (Choice)

A routing choice that presents a window that allows a user to specify a name for the object to be saved on a storage device, such as a disk or diskette. The original object remains unchanged if a different name is used.

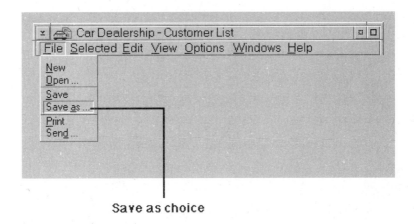

Save as choice

When to Use

☐ Provide a **Save as** choice for each object in an application-oriented environment for which a user can save with a specified name.

Guidelines

☑ If you provide a **Save as** choice, and you provide a **File** menu, place the **Save as** choice in the **File** menu.

☑ Display the **Save As** action window when the user selects the **Save as** choice.

☑ Assign "A" as the mnemonic for the **Save as** choice.

Essential Related Topics

• "File Menu (Application-Oriented)" on page 280

• "Save As (Action Window)" on page 425

Scroll Bar

A window component, associated with a scrollable area, that indicates to a user that more information is available or can be added in a particular direction and can be scrolled into view. The two types of scroll bars are: horizontal and vertical. The components of a scroll bar are the scroll box, shaft, and scroll buttons.

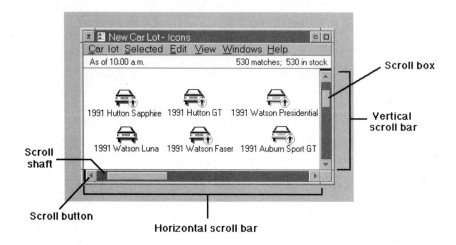

When to Use

☑ Provide a scroll bar if the information is not fully visible within a window in a particular direction.

☑ Provide a scroll bar if the information in a window can be extended to a size that is larger than the window. For example, provide scroll bars for a text object that can become smaller or larger as a user works with it.

Guidelines

☑ Provide a scroll bar along the dimension in which more information is available. For example, if an object is wider, provide a horizontal scroll bar, and if an object is taller, provide a vertical scroll bar.

☑ If the information in the window is extendable, but is not currently scrollable, display the scroll bar with unavailable-state emphasis.

☑ Use a scroll bar when scrolling windows. Use a slider to display a numeric value.

☐ When a user scrolls by dragging the scroll box, update the information in the window as the user drags the scroll box.

☐ If it is not possible to continually update information in a window as it is being scrolled, update the information in the window when the user pauses scrolling.

☑ Assign scrolling actions as in Figure 195.

Figure 195. User Actions and Scrolling Actions

User action	Scrolling action
Click once on up scroll button (↑)	Scroll one smallest vertical-scrolling-increment toward bottom of window
Click once on down scroll button (↓)	Scroll one smallest vertical-scrolling-increment toward top of window
Click once on right scroll button (→)	Scroll one smallest horizontal-scrolling-increment toward left of window
Click once on left scroll button (←)	Scroll one smallest horizontal-scrolling-increment toward right of window
Click once on scroll shaft above scroll box in vertical scroll bar	Scroll one vertical-page-scrolling-increment toward bottom of window
Click once on scroll shaft below scroll box in vertical scroll bar	Scroll one vertical-page-scrolling-increment toward top of window
Click once on scroll shaft to right of scroll box in horizontal scroll bar	Scroll one horizontal-page-scrolling-increment toward left of window
Click once on scroll shaft to left of scroll box in horizontal scroll bar	Scroll one horizontal-page-scrolling-increment right of window
Drag scroll box with selection button and release button when scroll box is in new location in scroll shaft	Scroll so that Information indicated by position of scroll box is visible in window

☐ When cursoring to a control causes the control to be scrolled into view, scroll as much of the control into view as possible. For example, if cursoring to a radio button field causes scrolling, scroll as much of the radio button field into view as possible.

☑ Display a scroll button with unavailable-state emphasis when there is no more information in the direction indicated on the button.

Scroll Bar

☑   Adjust the size of a scroll box so that it is proportional to the amount of information that can be visible in the scrollable area in relation to the total amount of information.

☑   Adjust the position of a scroll box so that it indicates the position of the information visible in the scrollable area in relation to the total amount of information.

☑   Do not change the size of a scroll box unless:

- Information is added to or removed from the object represented in the window
- The window's size changes

Essential Related Topics

- "Scrolling Increment" on page 431

Supplemental Related Topics

- "Mouse" on page 350
- "Size (Choice)" on page 459
- "Unavailable-State Emphasis (Cue)" on page 485
- "Window" on page 496

Scrolling Increment

The amount of information that can be scrolled with a single scrolling action.

Guidelines

☐ Allow a user to control the scrolling increment. For example, give the user an option of page scrolling text the entire height of the scrollable area, instead of the height of the scrollable area minus the height of one line.

☐ Make the initial scrolling increments equal to those shown in Figure 196.

Figure 196 (Page 1 of 2). Scrolling Increments

Type of data	Smallest Scrolling Increment		Page Scrolling Increment	
	Horizontal	Vertical	Horizontal	Vertical
Text	Width of em (M) character (1)	Bottom of one line to bottom of next line	Width of scrollable area minus width of one em (M) character	Height of scrollable area minus some portion of the area (for example, one line)
Icon	Width of smallest icon	Height of smallest icon	Width of scrollable area minus width of smallest icon	Height of scrollable area minus height of smallest icon

Scrolling Increment

Figure 196 (Page 2 of 2). Scrolling Increments

Type of data	Smallest Scrolling Increment		Page Scrolling Increment	
	Horizontal	Vertical	Horizontal	Vertical
Graphic	5% of the width of the view, or by units of a scale specified by the user	5% of the height of the view, or by units of a scale specified by the user	95% of the width of the view	95% of the height of the view

Note:

1. Smallest horizontal scrolling increment is the width of em (M) character when scrolling using the arrow keys or scroll bar. When typing, the increment should be a percentage of the entire field.

☐   When a user is scrolling, make the information being scrolled appear to be scrolling smoothly by actually moving the data in smaller increments than the smallest scrolling increment.

Essential Related Topics

- "Scroll Bar" on page 428

Supplemental Related Topics

- "Keyboard" on page 315
- "Mouse" on page 350

Secondary Window

A window that is used to supplement the interaction in the primary window it is dependent on.

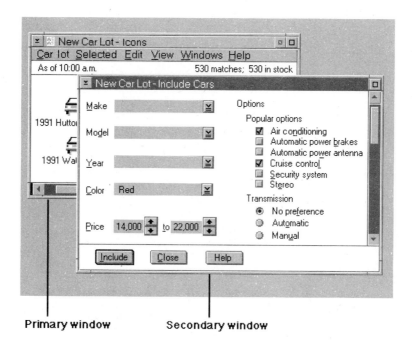

Primary window   Secondary window

When to Use

☐   Use a secondary window to display an action window. For example, use a secondary window to display an action window that allows a user to specify criteria associated with an **Include** choice.

☐   Use a secondary window to view an object only if the secondary window is used to support interaction with its associated primary window.

☐   Use a secondary window to display a message.

Guidelines

☑   Remove a secondary window when the primary window it is associated with is closed or minimized.

Secondary Window

☑   If a secondary window was open when its associated primary window was closed or minimized, display that secondary window when its associated primary window is opened or restored.

☐   Provide a sizing border that allows a user to change the size of a secondary window.

☐   Make secondary windows as modeless as possible. For example, when a user begins a process that searches a text object, allow the user to interact with the text object while continuing to display the **Find** action window on top of the text window.

☐   Allow a user to minimize a secondary window that displays a view of an object.

Essential Related Topics

- "Primary Window" on page 391

- "Window" on page 496

Supplemental Related Topics

- "Action Window" on page 208

Select All and Deselect All (Choice)

Action choices that allow a user to select all the objects in a view or deselect all of the selected objects in the view from which the choice was selected.

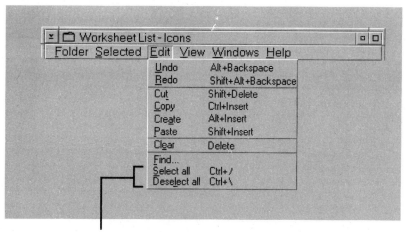

Select all and Deselect all choices

When to Use

☐   Provide the **Select all** choice to allow a user to select all objects in the view.

☐   Provide the **Deselect all** choice to allow a user to deselect all objects in the view.

Guidelines

☑   If you provide the **Select all** and **Deselect all** choices, and you provide an **Edit** menu, place the **Select all** and **Deselect all** choices in the **Edit** menu.

☑   Display the following choices with unavailable-state emphasis under the following conditions:

- **Select all** - when all objects in the view are selected.
- **Deselect all** - when no objects in the view are selected.

☑   When a user selects the **Select all** choice, select all the objects in the view, including all objects in the view that are not currently visible in the window.

Select All and Deselect All (Choice)

☑ When a user selects the **Deselect all** choice, cancel the selection of all objects in the view, including all object in the view that are not currently visible in the window.

☑ Assign Ctrl+/ as the shortcut key combination for the **Select all** choice.

☑ Assign Ctrl+\ as the shortcut key combination for the **Deselect all** choice.

☑ Assign "S" as the mnemonic for the **Select all** choice.

☑ Assign "L" as the mnemonic for the **Deselect all** choice.

Essential Related Topics

- "Edit Menu" on page 270

Supplemental Related Topics

- "Selection Types and Techniques" on page 440

Selected Menu

A pull-down menu from the **Selected** choice on a menu bar that contains choices that allow a user to work with the selected objects in the current view.

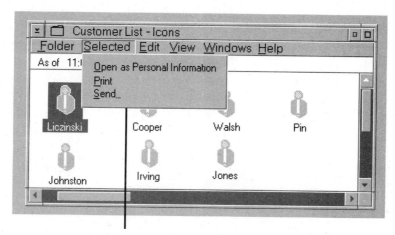

Selected menu

When to Use

Provide a **Selected** choice on the menu bar in each window that provides a menu bar if any objects in that window can be selected and displayed in another window, printed, or operated on by some other action other than those provided in the **Edit** menu, unless those choices are provided on push buttons in the window. For example, provide a **Selected** choice in a container to allow a user to open selected objects that are in that container.

Guidelines

☐ Include in the **Selected** menu choices that apply to the selected object or group of objects.

Selected Menu

☐   If nothing is currently selected, include in the **Selected** menu of a view only choices displayed with unavailable-state emphasis that apply to the object on which the cursor is currently positioned. For example, provide in the **Selected** menu of a folder choices that are specific to a document object if the object on which the cursor is currently positioned is a document.

☐   Do not display choices that can never apply to the selected object, or object on which the cursor is positioned if nothing is selected, even if those choices could apply to other objects in another context in the same view. For example, if a user moves the cursor from a container object to a data object, remove from the **Selected** menu those choices that can apply only to container objects and add choices that apply to data objects.

☑   If you provide an **Open as** choice for the selectable objects in a view, place it in the **Selected** menu.

☑   If you provide a **Print** choice for the selectable objects in a view, place it in the Selected menu.

☐   Provide other object-specific choices as needed. For example, provide a **Send** choice.

☑   Assign "S" as the mnemonic for the **Selected** menu choice.

Essential Related Topics

- "Edit Menu" on page 270
- "Menu Bar" on page 334
- "Open As (Choice)" on page 371
- "Print (Choice)" on page 393

Selected-State Emphasis (Cue)

Emphasis used on a choice or object to indicate that it is selected.

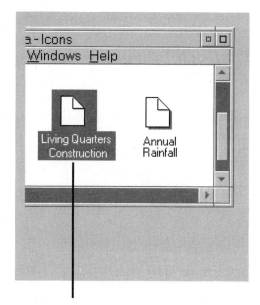

Selected-state emphasis

When to Use

☑ Display selected-state emphasis on all selected choices and objects.

Guidelines

☐ Display selected-state emphasis by changing the foreground and background colors of the selected object to those set in the operating environment.

☐ Display selected-state emphasis on all selected objects or groups of selected objects in all windows simultaneously.

Essential Related Topics

• "Selection Types and Techniques" on page 440

Selection Types and Techniques

Methods that a user can employ to identify objects to which actions are to be applied. The three types of selection are: single selection, extended selection, and multiple selection. The three techniques for selection are point selection, point-to-endpoint selection, and random-point selection.

When to Use

☐ Provide selection techniques to allow a user to identify objects and choices for subsequent interaction.

Guidelines

☑ Display selected-state emphasis on an object to indicate that it is currently selected.

☐ When an action or settings choice is applied to a selected object, do not change the selection state of that object, unless changing the selection state of the object is a part of the operation.

☑ Do not apply an action to an object as a result of selecting that object.

☑ When only one object can be in the selected state at any time, provide single selection.

☑ When any number of objects can be in the selected state at any time, provide multiple selection.

☐ When a user will typically operate on one object at a time but multiple objects can be operated on at the same time, provide extended selection.

☑ When extended selection is provided for a view, allow a keyboard user to press Shift+F8 to establish a mode in which the initial deselection is bypassed and the new selected objects are added or removed from the current group of selected objects.

☑ When extended selection is provided for a view, allow a user using a pointing device to modify extended selection by pressing the Ctrl key.

☐   When single selection is provided for a view, deselect all objects in the scope when a user clicks a button on blank space, unless selection is required on at least one object at all times.

☐   When multiple selection is provided for a view, do not affect the selection state of objects in the scope when a user clicks a button on blank space.

☐   When extended selection is provided for a view, deselect all objects in the scope when a user clicks a button on blank space.

☑   Refer to Figure 197 on page 442, Figure 198 on page 442, and Figure 199 on page 443 to determine which selection techniques to provide for a view.

Selection Types and Techniques

Figure 197. Single Selection Techniques

Technique	Mouse	Keyboard	Result
Point selection	Click mouse selection button with pointer on object to be selected.	With cursor on object to be selected, press Ctrl+Spacebar; also Spacebar if spacebar is not used to type a space.	Deselects currently-selected object in selection scope; selects single identified object.

Note: In zero-based single-selection mode, selecting the currently-selected object does not deselect the object. To deselect the currently-selected object, select the **Deselect all** choice.

Figure 198 (Page 1 of 2). Multiple Selection Techniques

Technique	Mouse	Keyboard	Result
Point selection	Click mouse selection button with pointer on object to be selected or deselected.	With cursor on object to be selected or deselected, press Ctrl+Spacebar; also spacebar if spacebar is not used to type a space.	Toggles the selection state of the single identified object; does not affect the state of other objects.
Point-to-endpoint selection			
Area (Marquee)	Press mouse selection button at the start point and move the pointer to the end point; release the mouse selection button at the end point.	Not applicable.	Toggle the selection state of the first object and make the selection state of all objects within the identified area the same as the new selection state of the first object.
Range (Swipe)	Press mouse selection button at the start point and move the pointer to the end point; release the mouse selection button at the end point.	Press Shift at the start point and hold while using cursor-movement keys to move the cursor to the end point; release Shift at end point.	Toggle the selection state of the first object and make the selection state of all other objects in order from the identified start point to the identified end point the same as the new selection state of the first object.

Figure 198 (Page 2 of 2). Multiple Selection Techniques

Technique	Mouse	Keyboard	Result
Range (Click)	Click mouse selection button at the start point; press Shift and click the mouse selection button at the end point, then release Shift key.	Not applicable.	Toggle the selection state of the first object and make the selection state of all other objects in order from the identified start point to the identified endpoint the same as the new selection state of the first object.
Random-point selection			
Random (Swipe)	Press mouse selection button with pointer on first object to be selected; move the pointer over other objects to be selected; release mouse selection button.	Not applicable.	Toggle the selection state of the first object and make the selection state of all identified objects in the order the user identified the objects the same as the new selection state of the first object.

Figure 199 (Page 1 of 2). Extended Selection Techniques

Technique	Mouse	Keyboard	Result
Point selection	Click mouse selection button with pointer on object to be selected.	With cursor on object to be selected, press Ctrl+Spacebar; also spacebar if spacebar is not used to type a space.	Deselects all other objects in selection scope; selects single identified object.
Point-to-endpoint selection			
Area (Marquee)	Press mouse selection button at the start point and move the pointer to the end point; release the mouse selection button at the end point.	Not applicable.	Deselects all other objects in selection scope; selects all objects contained within the identified area.

Selection Types and Techniques

Figure 199 (Page 2 of 2). Extended Selection Techniques

Technique	Mouse	Keyboard	Result
Range (Swipe)	Press mouse selection button at the start point and move the pointer to the end point; release the mouse selection button at the end point.	Press Shift at the start point and hold while using cursor-movement keys to move the cursor to the end point; release Shift at end point.	Deselects all other objects in selection scope; selects all objects in order from the identified start point to the identified end point.
Range (Click)	Click mouse selection button at the start point; press Shift and click the mouse selection button at the end point, then release Shift key.	Not applicable.	Deselects all other objects in selection scope; selects all objects in order from the identified start point to the identified end point.
Random-point selection			
Random (Swipe)	Press mouse selection button with pointer on first object to be selected; move the pointer over other objects to be selected; release mouse selection button.	Not applicable.	Deselects all other objects in selection scope; selects individual objects in the order the user identified the objects to be selected.

Note:

Modifying extended selection

When a user is using a mouse, pressing the Ctrl key while performing a selection technique allows the user to add objects to and remove objects from the current group of selected objects by bypassing the initial deselection.

In point selection and random-point selection, pressing the Ctrl key while selecting an object or group of objects toggles the selection state of the first object or group of objects selected and that new state becomes the selection state of all objects selected thereafter until the Ctrl key is released.

In point-to-endpoint selection, the selection state of the start point is toggled first and that new state becomes the selection state of all objects within the range or area.

In point selection and random-point selection, pressing spacebar toggles the selection state of the identified object.

Essential Related Topics

Supplemental Related Topics

Separator

A boundary, such as blank space, a line, or color change, that provides a visual distinction between two adjacent areas.

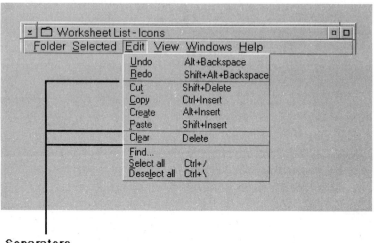

Separators

When to Use

☐　　　Use a separator to visually separate choices into distinct choice groups in menus and fields of controls into distinct groups in windows.

Guidelines

☐　　　Use blank space as a separator, except in menus.

☐　　　In menus, use a line as a separator.

Essential Related Topics

•　　　"Window Layout" on page 500

Supplemental Related Topics

- "Column Heading" on page 227
- "Group Box" on page 290
- "Group Heading" on page 292

Settings (Choice Type)

A choice that allows a user to change a property of an object.

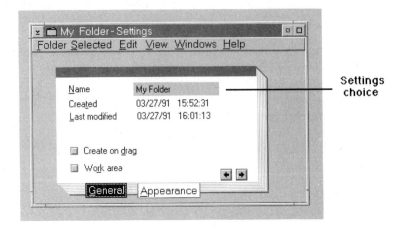

Settings choice

When to Use

☐ Use a settings choice to allow a user to change a property of an object.

Guidelines

☐ Display settings choices in a notebook.

☐ Avoid placing settings choices on push buttons or in menus.

☐ Allow a user to place settings choices in menus as a customization option.

☐ If a menu contains a group of settings choices that are not mutually exclusive, display a check mark to the left of each choice that has been selected. Remove the check mark when the choice no longer applies to the object.

☐ If a menu contains a group of settings choices that are mutually exclusive, display unavailable-state emphasis on the choice that currently applies. Remove the unavailable-state emphasis when the choice no longer applies.

☐ When a user selects a settings choice, immediately apply the choice to the selected object or group of objects.

☐　　　　If it is not practical to apply settings choices to an object immediately, provide a sample within the window that demonstrates the change that will occur when the settings are applied. For example, instead of applying a font change to a large document immediately, display sample text with the new font selection and provide an **Apply** push button that applies the selected font to the text in the document when the user makes a final decision.

Essential Related Topics

* "Action Choice (Choice Type)" on page 204

* "Choice" on page 218

* "Routing (Choice Type)" on page 421

Supplemental Related Topics

* "Notebook (Control)" on page 363

Shortcut Key

A key or combination of keys that a user can press to perform an action that is available from a menu.

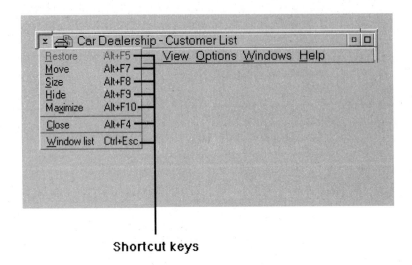

Shortcut keys

When to Use

☑ Provide the predefined shortcut key assignment for each predefined choice in a menu.

☐ Provide a unique shortcut key assignment for each frequently-used choice in a menu.

Guidelines

☐ If a choice in a menu has a shortcut key assignment, display it next to that choice in the menu.

☐ Left-align shortcut keys to the right of the choices in a menu.

☐ Allow a user to hide or display shortcut keys. For example, provide in a settings view of an object a check box choice labeled **Display shortcut keys.**

☐ Ship products with shortcut keys not displayed as the default.

☑ Include all shortcut key assignments in keys help.

☐ Allow a user to change shortcut key assignments.

☑ If a user can change shortcut key assignments, display the new assignments in menus and list the new assignments in keys help.

☑ When a user turns off the display of shortcut keys in menus, continue to provide access to the choices that are displayed in the menus using shortcut keys.

☑ When displaying shortcut keys, use a plus sign (+) between the key names to indicate that a user must press two or more keys at the same time. For example, use Alt+F4 for the **Close** choice.

☑ Perform the function assigned to a shortcut key only if it is assigned within the active window.

☑ If short menus are displayed, do not perform functions assigned to choices displayed only in full menus.

☑ Perform the identical function, whether a user presses the shortcut key or selects the associated choice.

☑ If a shortcut key uses an alphabetic character, apply the choice if a user presses either the uppercase or lowercase character.

☐ Identify shortcut keys by their actual key-top engravings.

☐ Do not assign more than one shortcut key to the same function.

☐ Assign the same shortcut key for the same choice in all windows that provide that choice.

☐ Use the Ctrl key as part of product-specific shortcut key assignments.

☐ Avoid using the Alt key as part of the shortcut key assignment. Alt should be used for mnemonic access only.

☑ Assign shortcut keys as in Figure 200:

Figure 200 (Page 1 of 2). Shortcut Key Assignments

Function	Shortcut key
Clear	Delete (unless a Delete choice is also provided)
Close	Alt+F4
Copy	Ctrl+Insert

Shortcut Key

Function	Shortcut key
Create	Alt+Insert
Cut	Shift+Delete
Delete	Delete
Deselect all	Ctrl+\
General help	F2 (in a Help window only)
Help index	F11 (in a Help window only)
Hide	Alt+F9
Keys help	F9 (in a Help window only)
Maximize	Alt+F10
Minimize	Alt+F9
Move	Alt+F7
Paste	Shift+Insert
Redo	Shift+Alt+←(backspace)
Refresh now	F5
Restore	Alt+F5
Select all	Ctrl+/
Size	Alt+F8
Tutorial	Shift+F2 (in a Help window only)
Undo	Alt+←(backspace)
Using help	Shift+F10 (in a Help window only)
Window list (in the system menu)	Ctrl+Esc

Essential Related Topics

Supplemental Related Topics

Short Menus and Full Menus (Choice)

Choices that allow a user to change the number of choices that appear in menus. Short menus contain a limited number of choices. Full menus contain all the possible choices for the window that they are associated with. When a user selects either the **Short menus** or the **Full menus** choice, any or all menus are affected.

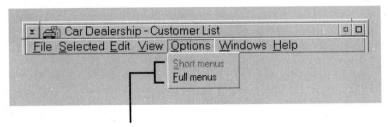

Short and Full menu choices

When to Use

☐ Provide both a **Short menus** choice and a **Full menus** choice for an object that has a large number of choices and there is a useful subset of choices for new users. This presents a simpler interface for the new user to learn.

Guidelines

☐ If you provide the **Short menus** and the **Full menus** choices and you provide settings views, place the **Short menus** and **Full menus** choices in the settings view of the object as radio buttons.

☐ If you provide the **Short menus** and **Full menus** choices and you do not provide settings views, place the **Short menus** and **Full menus** choices in the **Options** menu in the window displaying a view of that object.

☐ Include in the short menus the minimum number of choices necessary to accomplish useful work. For example, in making this decision, developers might consider which choices might be offered in higher-priced and lower-priced versions of the product and separate them along those lines.

☑ When displaying short menus, do not reserve space for choices that are included in the full menus but are not displayed in the short menus.

☑ When displaying short menus, do not support shortcut keys for choices that are included in the full menus but are not displayed in the short menus.

☑ If a user selects the **Full menus** choice from the **Options** menu, display the choice with unavailable-state emphasis until the user selects the **Short menus** choice.

☑ If a user selects the **Short menus** choice from the **Options** menu, display the choice with unavailable-state emphasis until the user selects the **Full menus** choice.

☑ Do not change the location of a choice from one pull-down menu to another when a user changes from full menus to short menus.

☑ When selecting the **Short menus** choice would remove all choices from a pull-down menu, remove that menu bar choice from the menu bar rather than displaying the menu bar choice with unavailable-state emphasis.

☑ When selecting the **Short menus** choice would remove all choices in a cascaded menu, remove the choice that causes the cascaded menu to be displayed rather than displaying that choice with unavailable-state emphasis.

☐ When selecting the **Short menus** choice would reduce a cascaded menu to only one choice, do not use a cascaded menu. Instead, replace the cascading choice with the choice from the cascaded menu. For example, if **Icons** is the only choice that would cascade from the **Open as** choice, change the name to **Open as Icons** and do not make it a cascading choice.

☐ Make the **Short menus** choice the default to allow new users to easily use a product to accomplish basic tasks.

☑ Assign "S" as the mnemonic for the **Short menus** choice that appears in the **Options** menu.

☑ Assign "F" as the mnemonic for the **Full menus** choice that appears in the **Options** menu.

Short Menus and Full Menus (Choice)

Essential Related Topics

- "Options Menu" on page 375

Supplemental Related Topics

- "Menu (Control)" on page 331
- "Radio Button (Control)" on page 409
- "Settings (Choice Type)" on page 448

Single Selection

A type of selection that allows a user to have only one object in the selected state at any one time.

When to Use

☐ Use single selection when only one object can be operated on at a time.

Guidelines

☑ See Figure 201 to determine which single selection techniques to use.

Figure 201. Single Selection Techniques

Technique	Mouse	Keyboard	Result
Point selection	Click mouse selection button with pointer on object to be selected.	With cursor on object to be selected, press Ctrl+Spacebar; also Spacebar if spacebar is not used to type a space.	Deselects currently-selected object in selection scope; selects single identified object.

Note: In zero-based single-selection mode, selecting the currently-selected object does not deselect the object. To deselect the currently-selected object, select the **Deselect all** choice.

☐ Use automatic selection as a convenience to a user when one object must always be selected, such as in a list box used to display a list of fonts.

Essential Related Topics

• "Automatic Selection" on page 213

• "Selection Types and Techniques" on page 440

Single Selection

Supplemental Related Topics

- "Extended Selection" on page 275
- "Keyboard" on page 315
- "Mouse" on page 350
- "Multiple Selection" on page 358

Size (Choice)

An action choice that allows a user to change the size of a window.

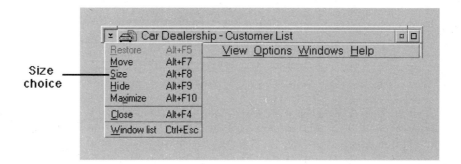

Size choice

When to Use

☑ Provide a **Size** choice when a user can change the size of a window.

Guidelines

☑ If you provide the **Size** choice, place it in the system menu.

☑ When a user selects the **Size** choice, use the operating environment's mechanism that allows a user to change the size of a window.

☑ Assign Alt+F8 as the shortcut key combination for the **Size** choice.

☑ Assign "S" as the mnemonic for the **Size** choice.

Essential Related Topics

• "System Menu" on page 475

Size (Choice)

Supplemental Related Topics

- "Direct Manipulation" on page 261
- "Maximize (Choice)" on page 329
- "Minimize (Choice)" on page 342
- "Restore (Choice)" on page 418
- "Window Layout" on page 500

Slider (Control)

A control that represents a quantity and its relationship to the range of possible values for that quantity. The control also allows a user to change the value of the quantity. The slider consists of a slider arm, slider shaft, and optionally, detents, a scale and slider buttons.

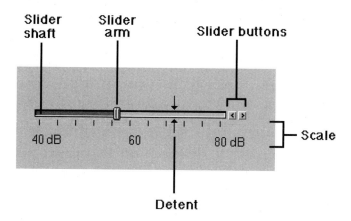

When to Use

☐　　　Use a slider when it is useful to see the current value relative to the range of possible values.

Guidelines

☑　　　If a user cannot change the value displayed in a slider, do not display a slider arm or slider buttons.

☐　　　Provide a scale to indicate the units of measure represented by the slider. For example, provide an incremental scale in units of millimeters to indicate length or provide an incremental scale in units of minutes to indicate time.

☐　　　Provide slider buttons to allow the user to move one smallest increment.

☐　　　Provide additional controls that can affect the slider setting. For example, provide a **Reset** push button.

Slider (Control)

☐   If a scale is displayed, allow a user to change the units of measure that the scale represents. For example, allow the user to change the scale from inches to millimeters.

☐   Allow a user to set the exact value represented by the detent, unless the slider is read-only.

☐   Provide detents to allow a user to easily set values that have special meaning. For example, on a slider used to set temperature for heating a room, provide a detent at 68 degrees.

☐   Allow a user to specify or change the value or values for which a detent will be displayed.

☐   If the exact value of the quantity represented is important to a user, provide a separate control in addition to the slider to display the value. For example, use an entry field to display the current value represented by the slider.

☐   Fill the slider shaft when the proportion of the value is more important than the value itself. For example, in a progress indicator to show relative amount of process completed and not completed.

☐   If you fill a slider shaft, fill horizontal sliders from the left to the slider arm and vertical sliders from the bottom to the slider arm.

Essential Related Topics

- "Control" on page 235
- "Progress Indicator" on page 396
- "Scroll Bar" on page 428

Sort (Choice)

A routing choice that displays an action window or a cascaded menu that allows a user to arrange the objects in a view into a specified order.

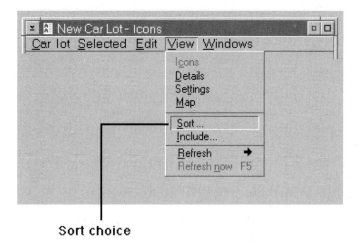

Sort choice

When to Use

☐   Provide a **Sort** choice for all objects whose contents can be sorted in a way that is meaningful to a user.

☐   Provide a **Sort** choice to allow a user to sort the contents of the current view into a particular order and to maintain that order as new objects are added to the object displayed in the window.

Guidelines

☑   If you provide a **Sort** choice, and you provide a **View** menu, place the **Sort** choice in the **View** menu.

☐   When the contents of a view are sorted, indicate the sorting order. For example, display "A–Z" in the status area to indicate that the view was sorted alphabetically.

☑   Display an action window or a cascaded menu to allow a user to specify the sort criteria.

Sort (Choice)

☐   When an object is added to a group of objects that are maintained in a specific order, place the new object in its correct position.

☐   If an object is added to a group of sorted objects, but its position is not currently visible, provide an indication that it was accepted. For example, increase the count displayed in the status area by one.

☑   Assign "S" as the mnemonic for the **Sort** choice.

Essential Related Topics

- "Status Area (Cue)" on page 473
- "View Menu" on page 492

Source Emphasis (Cue)

A visible cue that indicates the source object of a direct-manipulation operation.

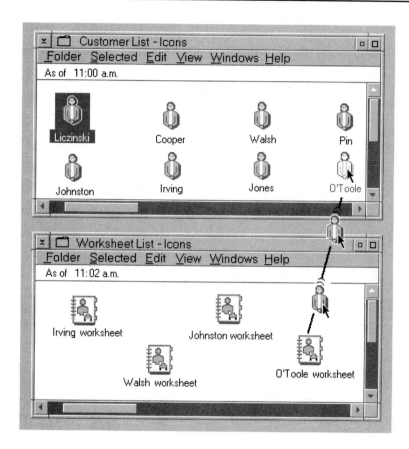

When to Use

Display source emphasis on an object during a direct-manipulation operation.

Source Emphasis (Cue)

Guidelines

☐ Display source emphasis by reducing the contrast of the object being manipulated. For example, change an object's icon by changing every other pel to the background color thus making the icon appear to dim.

Essential Related Topics

• "Direct Manipulation" on page 261

Spin Button (Control)

A control used to display, in sequence, a ring of related but mutually exclusive choices. It contains a field that can accept user input, which allows a user to make a selection by typing a valid choice, or a field that can display a value that the user can merely accept. The user can change the value by spinning through the ring of choices.

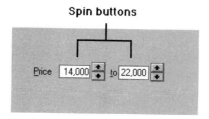

Spin buttons

When to Use

☐ Use a spin button to display a list of choices that have a logical consecutive order. For example, use a spin button for a list of the months of the year. When a list of choices does not have a logical consecutive order, use a drop-down list or drop-down combination box.

Guidelines

☐ When all the possible values are in the list of choices, make the spin button field a read-only field.

☐ When all the possible values are not included in the list of choices, make the spin button field an entry field.

☑ When using a spin button for alphabetical values, move down the order when a user selects the Down Arrow and back up the order when a user selects the Up Arrow. For example, if the letter "S" is currently displayed and a user selects the Up Arrow, display the letter "R;" if a user selects the Down Arrow, display the letter "T."

☑ When using a spin button for a value that represents magnitude, such as a list of numbers, display a larger value when a user selects the Up Arrow and a smaller value when a user selects the Down Arrow.

Spin Button (Control)

☑ Present the choices as a ring of choices that wrap. For example, if a user is at the largest number and presses the Up Arrow, the smallest number is displayed and vice versa so that the user can spin through the all the choices by pressing the same arrow.

Essential Related Topics

- "Control" on page 235
- "Entry Field (Control)" on page 272

Supplemental Related Topics

- "Drop-Down Combination Box (Control)" on page 266
- "Drop-Down List (Control)" on page 268

Split (Choice)

An action choice that allows a user to divide a window to display a view of an object in more than one pane of a window and to subsequently change the sizes of the panes.

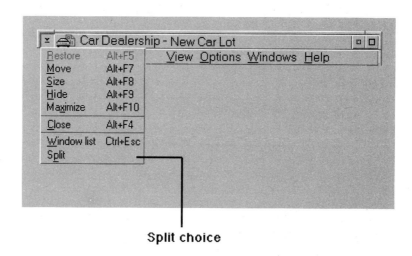

Split choice

When to Use

☑   Provide a **Split** choice for each window that can be split or is currently split.

Guidelines

☑   If you provide the **Split** choice, place it in the system menu.

☐   When a user selects the **Split** choice and the window has not previously been split, display a split bar and allow the user to position the split bar in the window.

☐   When a user selects the **Split** choice and the window has previously been split, allow the user to reposition the current split bar.

☑   Assign "P" as the mnemonic for the **Split** choice.

Split (Choice)

Essential Related Topics

- "Split Window" on page 471
- "System Menu" on page 475

Split Window

A window that contains a split bar that allows a user to display a view of an object in different panes of a window.

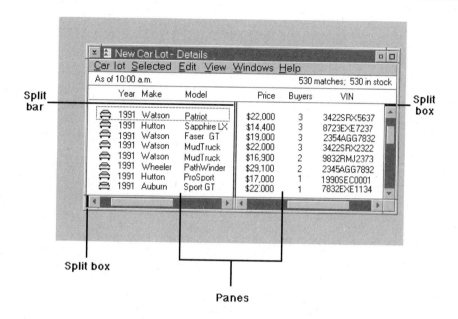

When to Use

☐ Provide a split window when it is useful for a user to display a view of an object in different panes of a window.

Guidelines

☑ Allow a user to change the size of a pane by selecting the **Split** choice or by directly manipulating a split bar.

☐ To split a window horizontally, provide a split box at the top of the topmost vertical scroll bar.

☐ To split a window vertically, provide a split box on the left of the leftmost horizontal scroll bar.

☐ Provide access to a split bar by allowing a user to directly manipulate a split box.

Split Window

☐ Allow a user to split a window multiple times vertically and horizontally. For example, use a pointing device to drag another split bar from the split box.

☐ Distinguish and separate the panes with horizontal or vertical split bars or scroll bars.

☐ Display the cursor only in the active pane.

☐ When an object is changed in one pane, immediately update the view of the object in other panes that display the same part of that object.

☐ Provide a horizontal scroll bar or vertical scroll bar, or both, for each pane.

☐ Do not move the cursor when a user splits a window. For example, when the cursor is on an object and the window is split, the panes display the part of the object that was displayed before the window was split. The cursor's location in the window does not change as a result of the split.

☐ Provide coordinated scrolling of related panes. For example, allow a user to scroll a single pane and have all other panes scroll with the first pane.

☐ Allow a user to switch input focus between active panes by pressing F6.

☐ Allow a user to switch input focus between active panes by pressing the mouse selection button.

Essential Related Topics

- "Split (Choice)" on page 469

Supplemental Related Topics

- "Input Focus" on page 312

Status Area (Cue)

A part of a window where information appears that shows the state of an object or the state of a particular view of an object.

Status area →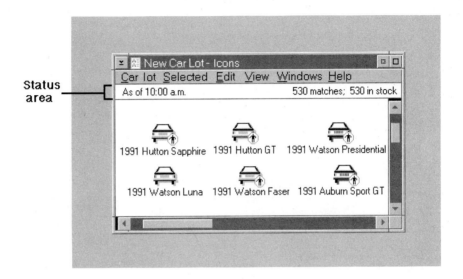

When to Use

☐   Provide a status area for the contents view of a container.

☐   Provide a status area for each window in which it is useful to display information about the current state of an object or view displayed in the window.

Guidelines

☐   If you provide a status area, place it below the title bar and below the menu bar, if a menu bar is provided, and above the rest of the window. For example, place a status area below the menu bar and above column headings in a window.

☐   If you provide a status area, do not scroll the status area when the window's contents are scrolled.

☐   Use a separator to separate the status area from the rest of the window. For example, use a gray line to separate the status area from the rest of the window.

Status Area (Cue)

- ☐ Update information in the status area to reflect the current state of the window or the current position of the cursor.

- ☐ If a window provides a selection type other than single selection, indicate in the window's status area the number of items currently selected. For example, place in the status area text saying, "2 cars selected."

- ☐ If only some objects are displayed in a window, indicate in that window's status area the number of objects to be displayed in proportion to the total number of objects. For example, place in a status area text that says "3 of 10 cars included."

- ☐ If only some objects are displayed in a window, indicate in that window's status area what criteria the objects met in order to be displayed in the window. For example, place in a status area text that says "Displaying documents created between 10/29/90 and 2/1/91" or if a view of an object has been sorted, indicate in a status area the criteria used for sorting.

- ☐ Provide only one status area in a window.

- ☐ If a user reduces the width of a window, compress the status area, if possible; otherwise, clip the status area.

- ☐ Make the status area the same width as the window.

- ☐ Make the status area no taller than necessary to accommodate brief, but meaningful, information. For example, when using text, accommodate only one line of text.

- ☑ If you provide a status area, allow a user to turn the display of the status area on or off. For example, provide a settings choice in the **View** pull-down menu or on a page in a settings notebook that allows a user to turn the display of the status area on or off.

Supplemental Related Topics

- • "Information Area" on page 307

- • "Window Layout" on page 500

System Menu

A pull-down menu, from the system menu symbol on the title bar of a window, that contains choices that affect the window and other operating-environment-specific functions.

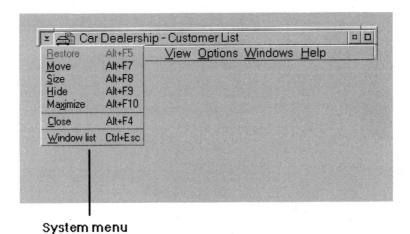

System menu

When to Use

☑ Provide a system menu for each window.

Guidelines

☑ Place the system-menu symbol in the leftmost corner of the title bar.

☑ Display the system menu when the user selects the system-menu symbol.

System Menu

☑   If any of the following choices are included in the system menu, place them in the following relative order:

- **Restore**
- **Move**
- **Size**
- **Minimize** or **Hide**
- **Maximize**
- --Separator--
- **Close**
- --Separator--
- **Window list**
- **Split**

☑   Assign Shift+Esc as the System-menu key.

☑   Assign spacebar as mnemonic for the system menu.

Essential Related Topics

- "Close (Choice)" on page 225

- "Maximize (Choice)" on page 329

- "Menu (Control)" on page 331

- "Minimize (Choice)" on page 342

- "Move (Choice)" on page 357

- "Restore (Choice)" on page 418

- "Size (Choice)" on page 459

- "Split (Choice)" on page 469

- "Window" on page 496

- "Window List (Choice in System Menu)" on page 505

Target Emphasis (Cue)

A visible cue that indicates that an object can act as a receiver of the source object in a direct-manipulation operation.

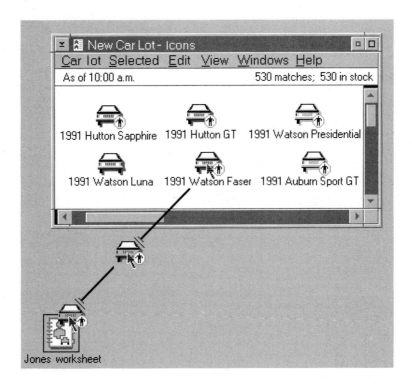

When to Use

Display target emphasis during a direct manipulation operation when the hot spot of the pointer is over an object that supports direct manipulation.

Guidelines

☐   When a target object is an icon, display target emphasis as a solid thin line around the icon image.

Target Emphasis (Cue)

☐ When a target object is an icon or small icon in the title bar of a window, do not display target emphasis on other icons of the object. For example, during a direct-manipulation operation, if multiple views of an object are displayed in separate windows, display target emphasis only on the small icon in the title bar of the window over which the icon is currently positioned. Do not display target emphasis on the small icon in the title bars of the other windows displaying views of that object.

☐ When a target object is a window containing a view of a container, display target emphasis as a solid thin line around the inside of the window adjacent to the border.

☐ When items in a window are maintained in an order, use a line between the items to indicate that an object being directly manipulated will be inserted between those items. The line indicates that the object will be added after the object that precedes the line and prior to the object following the line.

☐ Make target emphasis visible in addition to any other forms of emphasis that are currently visible on an object. For example, display target emphasis and selected-state emphasis on a selected object that is the target of a direct-manipulation operation.

Essential Related Topics

• "Direct Manipulation" on page 261

Text Entry

Techniques that a user employs for typing, selecting, and manipulating text.

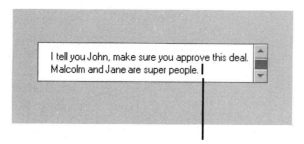

I tell you John, make sure you approve this deal. Malcolm and Jane are super people.

Typing text in a field.

Guidelines

☑   Provide insert and replace modes for all text entry. Allow a user to switch between these modes by pressing the Insert key.

☐   Allow a user to perform data-transfer operations on text by using direct manipulation. For example, allow a user to drag selected text from one position in a document to another, or from one window containing an entry field to a different window containing an entry field.

☐   Allow a user to perform data-transfer operations on text. For example, allow a user to transfer text using the clipboard.

☐   For each window that and allows text entry, provide a **Delete** choice.

☑   If a user moves or copies text to a target that is selected text, replace the selected text in the target object with the text from the source object.

☐   When text is selected and the cursor is in the selected text or adjacent to it, replace the selected text with the text typed by a user.

☑   If the cursor is in text and no text is selected, remove one character to the left of the cursor when a user presses the Backspace key, compressing the space occupied by that character.

Text Entry

☑   If the cursor is in text and nothing is selected, remove one character to the right of the cursor when a user presses the Delete key.

☑   When text is selected and the cursor is in the selected text or adjacent to it, remove the selected text when a user presses either the Backspace or the Delete key.

☑   See Figure 202 for selection techniques for text.

Figure 202. Extended Selection Techniques Used for Text	
Selection technique	**What to do**
Point selection	Position the text cursor and remove selected-state emphasis from all other text
Point-to-endpoint selection (Range)	Select all contiguous text in the range and remove selected-state emphasis from all other text
Point-to-endpoint selection (Area)	Select only the text in the marquee box and remove selected-state emphasis from all other text
Random-point selection	Not applicable

☐   Allow a user to double-click the mouse selection button in text, to select the entire word over which the pointer is positioned.

☐   Provide a margin that allows a user to click the mouse selection button to select an entire line of text and allows a user to double-click the mouse selection button to select an entire paragraph of text.

☐   When a user performs a direct-manipulation operation on text by dragging it, make the default for the direct-manipulation operation a move, unless the text can only be copied.

Essential Related Topics

- "Control" on page 235
- "Cursor" on page 244
- "Data Transfer" on page 248
- "Selection Types and Techniques" on page 440

Supplemental Related Topics

Tool Palette

One or more controls in a window, separate window, or menu that provide a set of graphical choices that represent tools. The tools redefine the set of operations possible with a pointing device.

When to Use

☐ Provide a tool palette when there are different modes of the pointer that the user can select. For example, provide a rectangle choice and a circle choice to allow the user to choose between drawing rectangles and circles in a graphics editor.

Guidelines

☑ Allow a user to select only one choice at a time from a tool palette.

☑ When the user selects a choice from the tool palette, change or augment the pointer to indicate the operation a user can perform with the pointing device. For example, display a rectangular pointer when a user selects a rectangle-drawing choice from a tool palette.

☑ When the pointer is moved to a position that is outside the scope of the mode change, return the pointer to the appropriate pointer for the action it is over. For example, change the pointer to an arrow pointer when a user moves the pointer to the menu bar to provide access to the menu bar choices.

☐ When choices are provided on a tool palette, also provide access to those choices from a menu. For example, provide access to the choices on a tool palette from a **Tools** menu bar choice.

☐ If you provide a tool palette as a menu, as well as in a window, allow a user to turn the display of the tool palette on or off. For example, provide a choice in the **Options** menu or on a page in a settings notebook that allows a user to turn the display of the tool palette in the window on or off.

☑ If a user selects a choice from a tool palette and the pointer will not be restored to the arrow pointer after the operation has been completed, provide an arrow-pointer choice on the tool palette.

☐ When displayed in its own window, display a tool palette in a secondary window.

☐ If there are settings that would be used with a tool palette and the tool palette is displayed in a secondary window, place those settings in the secondary window with the tool palette.

☐ Use a value set to display a tool palette.

Essential Related Topics

- "Control" on page 235

- "Pointer" on page 378

- "Value Set (Control)" on page 490

Supplemental Related Topics

- "Options Menu" on page 375

Tutorial (Choice)

An action choice that provides access to online educational information.

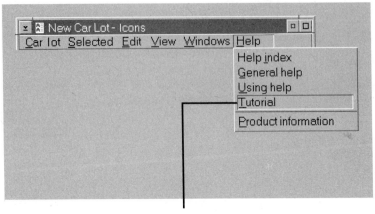

Tutorial choice

When to Use

☐ Provide online educational information for tasks and objects for users who require information that is not provided in general help or contextual help, or who require information that is structured in a different manner than is provided elsewhere.

Guidelines

☑ If you provide a tutorial, place the **Tutorial** choice in the **Help** menu.

☑ Assign "T" as the mnemonic for the **Tutorial** choice.

Essential Related Topics

• "Help Menu" on page 296

Supplemental Related Topics

• "Help Index (Choice)" on page 294

Unavailable-State Emphasis (Cue)

A visible cue that indicates that a choice cannot be selected.

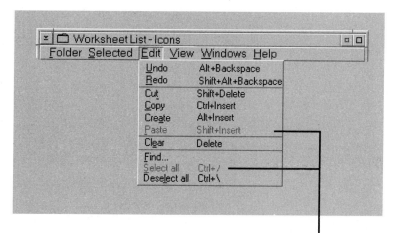

These choices cannot be
selected at this time.

When to Use

☑ Display unavailable-state emphasis on choices that represent
operations that cannot be selected in the current context.

Guidelines

☑ Display unavailable-state emphasis by dimming the choice
that cannot be selected. For example, indicate a menu
choice that is unavailable by changing every other pel to the
background color.

☐ When the contents of a list are variable from one presentation
to the next, such as a list of documents, avoid displaying
them with unavailable-state emphasis; instead, do not include
choices in the list that are unavailable.

☐ If a user attempts to select a choice that is currently displayed
with unavailable-state emphasis, indicate in the information
area that the choice cannot be selected and that requesting
help will explain why it is unavailable.

Unavailable-State Emphasis (Cue)

☑   Provide audible feedback when a user attempts to select a choice that is displayed with unavailable-state emphasis.

☑   If a choice is never available to a particular user, do not display the choice rather than displaying it with unavailable-state emphasis.

Supplemental Related Topics

- "Choice" on page 218

Undo and Redo (Choice)

The **Undo** choice is an action choice that reverses the effect of the last applied operation on an object, returning the object to the state it was in before the operation was applied. The **Redo** choice is an action choice that reverses the effect of the last applied undo action.

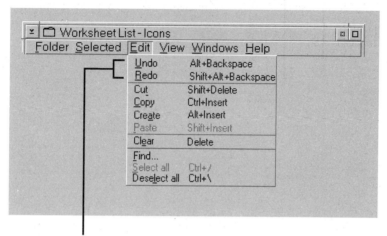

Undo and Redo choices

When to Use

☐ Provide the **Undo** and **Redo** choices for each object.

Guidelines

☑ If you provide the **Undo** and **Redo** choices and you provide the **Edit** menu, place the **Undo** and **Redo** choices in the **Edit** menu.

☐ If you provide the **Undo** and **Redo** choices for an object, place them in the pop-up menu for that object.

☐ If you provide the **Undo** choice, display it with unavailable-state emphasis if the user cannot undo the last operation.

☐ After a user selects the **Undo** choice, display it with unavailable-state emphasis until the user performs another operation that can be undone.

Undo and Redo (Choice)

☐   When a user selects the **Redo** choice, **Undo** becomes available and **Redo** becomes unavailable.

☐   Dynamically append to the name of the **Undo** choice to indicate the action that will be undone. For example, change **Undo** to **Undo typing** or **Undo delete**.

☐   Dynamically append to the name of the **Redo** choice to indicate the action that will be undone.

☐   When undoing an action, return all objects affected by the action to the state they were in before the action occurred.

☑   Assign "U" as the mnemonic for the **Undo** choice.

☑   Assign "R" as the mnemonic for the **Redo** choice.

☑   Assign Alt+Backspace as the shortcut key combination for the **Undo** choice.

☑   Assign Shift+Alt+Backspace as the shortcut key combination for the **Redo** choice.

Essential Related Topics

- "Edit Menu" on page 270

Supplemental Related Topics

- "Clear (Choice)" on page 222
- "Data Transfer" on page 248
- "Delete (Choice)" on page 254
- "Keyboard" on page 315

Using Help (Choice)

An action choice that displays a window containing information about how to use the help function.

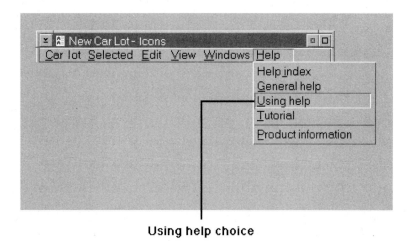

Using help choice

When to Use

☑ Provide the **Using help** choice in each **Help** menu.

Guidelines

☑ When a user selects the **Using help** choice, display a window containing information about how to use the help function.

☑ Assign "U" as the mnemonic for the **Using help** choice.

Essential Related Topics

• "Help Menu" on page 296

Value Set (Control)

A control that allows a user to select one choice from a group of mutually exclusive choices. A value set is used primarily for graphical choices.

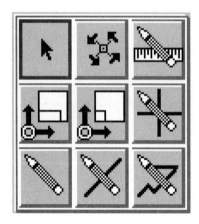

When to Use

☐ Use a value set for graphical choices that are mutually exclusive.

☐ Use a value set for short textual choices that are mutually exclusive; otherwise, use a field of radio buttons.

Guidelines

☑ Display only settings choices in a value set. Do not display action choices or routing choices in a value set.

☑ Use at least two choices when a value set is used.

☐ If a value set choice is currently unavailable, display it with unavailable-state emphasis.

☐ When a value set represents a setting shared by more than one selected object:

• Do not display selected emphasis on any of the value set choices if some, but not all of the objects, have the same setting selected.

- Display selected emphasis on one of the value set choices if all of the objects have the same setting selected.

☐   Capitalize only the first letter of the first word of a label for a value set choice unless the label contains an abbreviation, acronym, or proper noun that should be capitalized.

☐   Assign a mnemonic to each choice in a value set when all choices are textual.

☐   If a value set choice has a mnemonic assigned to it, provide access to the mnemonic by allowing a user to press the Alt key and that mnemonic.

☑   Assign one of the choices in a value set as the default choice.

Essential Related Topics

- "Control" on page 235
- "Mnemonic" on page 344
- "Radio Button (Control)" on page 409
- "Unavailable-State Emphasis (Cue)" on page 485

Supplemental Related Topics

- "Spin Button (Control)" on page 467
- "Tool Palette" on page 482

View Menu

A pull-down menu from the **View** choice on a menu bar that contains choices that affect the way an object is presented, for example, alternative formats, how much information is presented, what order it is presented in, and other related viewing choices.

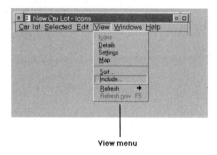

View menu

When to Use

Provide a **View** choice on the menu bar of each window that provides a menu bar when more than one view is available for an object or any of the following choices are provided: **Sort, Include, Refresh** or **Refresh now.**

Guidelines

When any of the following choices are provided place them in the following relative order in the **View** menu:

- view types - for example: icons, details, and settings
- --Separator--
- **Sort**
- **Include**
- --Separator--
- **Refresh** → **On/Off**
- **Refresh now**

☐   If you provide additional product-specific choices in the **View** menu, group them with related choices in the **View** menu.

☑   Indicate the current view of an object by displaying that view's choice with unavailable-state emphasis.

☐   If a settings view is displayed as a notebook that has more tabs than can be displayed at one time, provide a cascaded menu from the **Settings** choice that provides direct access to frequently used tabbed-divider pages in the notebook.

☑   Do not open a new window as a result of selecting a view; instead, display the new view of the object in the current window.

☑   Assign "V" as the mnemonic for the **View** choice.

Essential Related Topics

- "Include (Choice)" on page 305
- "Refresh and Refresh Now (Choice)" on page 415
- "Sort (Choice)" on page 463

Supplemental Related Topics

- "Information Area" on page 307

Warning Message

A message that indicates that an undesirable condition could occur but the user can allow the process to continue.

When to Use

☑ Display a warning message to indicate that an undesirable situation could occur but that the user can allow the process to continue.

Guidelines

☐ Provide controls in the message window that allow a user to correct the situation that caused the message to appear. For example, provide an entry field in which a user can correct a value.

☑ Provide a push button that allows a user to continue the request as originally requested. For example, in a message that warns a user copying multiple files that the diskette is 95% full, the user can continue with a push button labeled **Continue.**

☐ If your product can determine that the situation that caused the message to appear is changed so that it can continue, immediately remove the message.

☐ Provide a push button that allows a user to withdraw the request. For example, provide a push button labeled **Cancel.**

☐ When a user withdraws a request, leave the objects in a form that is meaningful to a user. For example, when a user requests to copy a group of objects, and an error occurs that causes the user to withdraw the request while the fifth object is being copied, leave the first four copied objects where they are and remove the partially copied fifth object.

☐ In the message text, suggest possible actions that a user can take to correct the situation that caused the message to appear.

☑ Display an exclamation mark symbol in each warning message.

☑ Provide an audible cue when a warning message is displayed.

Essential Related Topics

- "Action Message" on page 206

- "Information Message" on page 310

- "Message" on page 337

- "Push Button (Predefined)" on page 404

Supplemental Related Topics

- "Audible Feedback" on page 212

Window

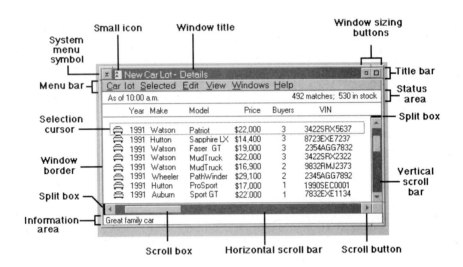

When to Use

☐   Use a window to display a view of an object or to conduct a dialog with a user.

Guidelines

☑   Provide a border, window title, and system-menu symbol for each window.

☐   Provide a small version of the object's icon in the title bar when a window displays a view of that object.

☐   Close a window when:

   • A user selects the **Close** choice from the system menu or from a push button labeled **Close.**

   • A user selects the **Cancel** choice from a push button.

   • A user selects a choice that completes the action represented in the window.

- The window has no further relevance. For example, close a progress-indicator window when the action the user has requested is complete.

☐ Allow a user to change the size and position of all windows.

☐ When a user closes , minimizes, or hides a window, save its current state, including its size and position, for use when the window is restored.

☐ When a user opens a window from an object to a particular view or restores a minimized or hidden window, restore the window and any dependent windows to their previous state, regardless of the amount of time that has elapsed since a user last opened or restored the window, and regardless of whether the user's system has been turned off and on again.

☐ If a user is opening or restoring a window on a screen of a different size than the screen on which the window was last viewed, and the window, when opened or restored, would otherwise be positioned outside the bounds of the user's current screen, ensure that at least part of the window's title bar is visible on the user's screen.

☐ When a user opens a window that has no previous state information:

- Place and size the window so that it is completely visible within the workplace.

- Make the window large enough for a user to perform useful work, but less than the full size of the user's workplace.

- Place the window so that it will draw a user's attention without impeding the user's work. For example, place a help window next to the window from which it was requested, not on top of that window.

- Place the window near where the user's attention was most likely focused when the user's request caused the window to appear. For example, place the window near the pointer or near the cursor.

☐ When a user opens a window but switches input focus to another window before the requested window is displayed, do not display the previously requested window on top of the window that currently has focus.

Window

☐   When a user opens another window from an object that already has open windows, do not completely cover the other windows associated with that object.

☐   If a user selects and opens more than one object, display each object in a separate window. Open the windows in the order that the objects were selected, so that the window for the object that was selected last has input focus and is not obscured by any other window.

☐   See Figure 203 on page 499 to determine the components to provide in a window based on the usage of that window.

Figure 203. Recommended Window Component Usage

Window Usage	System Menu	Small Icon in Title Bar	Title	Minimize Push Button	Maximize and Restore Push Button	Menu Bar	Sizing Border
Object	Yes	Yes	object name - view name:number	Yes	Yes	Yes	Yes
Messages	Yes	No	object name - action or situation	No	Yes	No	Yes
Progress Indicator	Yes	No	object name - process *Progress*	No	Yes	No	Yes
Help	Yes	No	object/action/field - *Help*	No	Yes	Yes	Yes
Action	Yes	No	object name - action	No	Yes	No	Yes
Application-oriented window	Yes	Yes	Application name - object name	Yes	Yes	Yes	Yes

Supplemental Related Topics

- "Active Window" on page 210
- "Inactive Window" on page 303
- "Input Focus" on page 312
- "Primary Window" on page 391
- "Secondary Window" on page 433
- "System Menu" on page 475
- "Window Layout" on page 500
- "Window Navigation" on page 507
- "Window Title" on page 510

Window Layout

The guidelines for the placement of controls in a window.

Guidelines

☐   Design the initial size and layout of an action window so that a user will not typically need to scroll the window. If the initial size of an action window is not large enough to display all of the controls, place less frequently used controls out of view.

☐   If more information is contained in a view than is visible in the initial size and layout of a window, ensure that the break between visible and hidden information is at a logical point. For example, avoid clipping an entry field so that only a portion of it is visible.

☐   Within a column of controls, left-align the edges of the controls to the right of the longest field prompt.

☐   If the contents of a window can be scaled when the window is sized, provide a user option to specify whether to scale or clip the contents.

☑   Place push buttons that affect the entire window horizontally at the bottom of the window and justified from the left edge.

☐   If a window that can be scrolled vertically contains push buttons that affect the entire window, scroll the area above the push buttons, keeping the push buttons visible.

☐   Avoid placing push buttons in more than two rows.

☐   If the action indicated by the label on a push button adjusts or is associated with a component within the same window as the push button, place the push button near that component. For example, if the function of a push button is to restore the initial value in an entry field, place that push button beside the entry field that it affects.

☐   Avoid using a push button to change the size of a window; instead, allow a user to change the size of the window using the size borders and the maximize push button or **Maximize** choice. For example, do not provide a push button labeled **More>>** to allow a user to enlarge a window.

☐ Use a notebook to organize groups of controls when they will not fit in a single window. Avoid placing related controls in separate windows connected by routing choices on push buttons.

☐ In high-volume data-entry windows, consider using right-aligned edges of field prompts next to left-aligned entry fields so that a narrow vertical column of space is left between the field prompts and their associated entry fields to allow a user to quickly scan the choices in the window.

☐ Allow a user to adjust the size of each column in a window, where appropriate. For example, provide column borders that a user can directly manipulate to change the size of columns.

☑ If a user cannot adjust the width of a column or scroll the column, make the column at least as wide as the widest item in the column or as wide as the column's heading, whichever is wider.

☐ If a user can adjust the width of a column, make the initial width of the column wide enough to display choices of average width.

☐ If the order of columns can be changed, allow a user to directly manipulate each column. For example, allow a user to drag column headings to change the order of columns.

☐ If you provide an information area, place it at the bottom of a window.

☐ If you provide an information area and there is a horizontal scroll bar in the window, place the information area below the scroll bar and above the window border.

☐ If you provide a status area, place it below the title bar and below the menu bar, if a menu bar is provided, and above the rest of the window. For example, place a status area below the menu bar and above column headings in a window.

Essential Related Topics

• "Window" on page 496

Window Layout

Supplemental Related Topics

- "Column Heading" on page 227
- "Control" on page 235
- "Field Prompt" on page 278
- "Group Box" on page 290
- "Group Heading" on page 292
- "Notebook (Control)" on page 363

Window List

A window that contains a list of the windows associated with the window from which the **Window list** choice was selected.

When to Use

☐ Display a window list window to show a user the organization of the windows, and to provide access to functions available for those windows.

Guidelines

☐ Display the window list window as a secondary window that is dependent on the window from which the **Window list** choice was selected.

☑ When the **Window list** choice in the **Windows** menu is selected, display a list of the windows associated with the window from which the **Window list** choice was selected.

☐ Indicate the state of each window listed in the window list window. For example, indicate which windows are minimized and maximized.

☐ Organize the names of the windows displayed in the window list window in a manner that helps users understand the relationships between windows. For example, indent names of secondary windows under their associated primary windows.

Window List

☐   Allow a user to condense or expand the number of window names that are displayed in the window list window. For example, provide a choice that displays only primary windows when the window list window is organized in a tree structure.

☐   Assign the default action for the window list window to switch to the selected window. For example, provide a default push button labeled **Show** that closes the window list and makes the selected window the active window.

☐   Provide access to common window functions such as **Minimize** and **Close** for the windows in the list.

☐   Support extended selection for the list of windows in the window list action window.

Essential Related Topics

- "Active Window" on page 210
- "Window List (Choice in System Menu)" on page 505
- "Window List (Choice in Windows Menu)" on page 506
- "Windows Menu" on page 509

Supplemental Related Topics

- "Close (Choice)" on page 225
- "Minimize (Choice)" on page 342

Window List (Choice in System Menu)

An action choice that displays a window containing a list of all of the active applications in an application-oriented environment or a list of all open windows in an object-oriented environment.

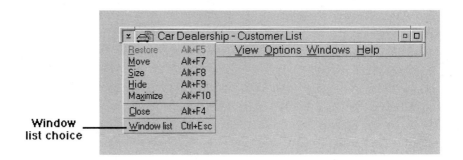

When to Use

☑ Provide a **Window list** choice for each window.

Guidelines

☑ Place a **Window list** choice in the system menu.

☐ When a user selects the **Window list** choice, use the mechanism provided by the operating environment that displays the **Window list** window.

☑ Assign Ctrl+Esc as the shortcut key combination for the **Window list** choice.

☑ Assign "W" as the mnemonic for the **Window list** choice.

Essential Related Topics

• "System Menu" on page 475

• "Window List (Choice in Windows Menu)" on page 506

Supplemental Related Topics

• "Window List" on page 503

Window List (Choice in Windows Menu)

An action choice that displays the window list window that allows a user to manage associated windows.

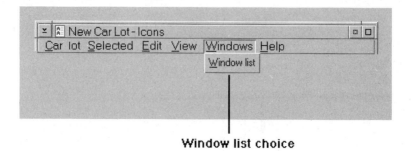

Window list choice

When to Use

☐ Provide a **Window list** choice to provide access to the window list window.

Guidelines

☑ If you provide the **Window list** choice that allows a user to manage associated windows, and you provide a **Windows** menu, place the **Window list** choice in the **Windows** menu.

☑ When a user selects the **Window list** choice, display the window list action window.

☑ Assign "W" as the mnemonic for the **Window list** choice.

Essential Related Topics

• "Active Window" on page 210

• "Window List" on page 503

• "Window List (Choice in System Menu)" on page 505

• "Windows Menu" on page 509

Window Navigation

Guidelines for the movement of the cursor in a window and access from a keyboard to any part of a window.

Guidelines

☐   Provide a mnemonic for each choice in a window.

☑   When a user presses the Alt key and types the mnemonic assigned to a push button, select that push button.

☑   When the cursor is positioned on a push button in a group of push buttons, allow a user to select a push button in that group by pressing the mnemonic character, if provided, assigned to that push button.

☑   When a user presses a key that moves the cursor to a field in which one of the choices is selected, place the cursor on the selected choice; otherwise, place the cursor on the first choice or on the default choice.

☑   When a user presses the Tab or Backtab key that moves the cursor to a group of push buttons, place the cursor on the default push button in that group.

☑   When the cursor is on a push button and a user presses the Tab or Backtab key, move the cursor to the next field in the window, not to another push button in the same field.

☐   When a user presses the Tab key, move the cursor between fields, from left-to-right and top-to-bottom in the window. When the cursor is on the bottom-rightmost field in the window, and a user presses the Tab key, move the cursor to the top-leftmost field in the window.

☐   When a user presses the Backtab key (Shift+Tab), move the cursor between fields, from right-to-left, and bottom-to-top in the window. When the cursor is on the top-leftmost field in the window, and a user presses the Backtab key, move the cursor to the bottom-rightmost field in the window.

☑   When the cursor is moved from a field of push buttons, reset the default push button to be the same as it was before the cursor entered that field of push buttons. For example, if a user moved the cursor off of the **OK** push button (the default) to the **Help** push button, then moved the cursor to a field of radio buttons, the default push button should again be the **OK** push button.

☐   Allow a user to interact with a field that is displayed with unavailable-state emphasis because of a setting elsewhere in that window. When a user changes a setting that makes that field available, apply the contents of the field.

Essential Related Topics

*   "Cursor" on page 244

*   "Mnemonic" on page 344

*   "Window Layout" on page 500

Supplemental Related Topics

*   "Control" on page 235

*   "Keyboard" on page 315

*   "Push Button (Predefined)" on page 404

*   "Window" on page 496

Windows Menu

A pull-down menu from the **Windows** choice on a menu bar that contains choices that allow a user to access the window list and other product-specific window-related choices.

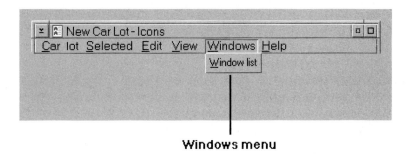

Windows menu

When to Use

☐ Provide a **Windows** choice on the menu bar in each window that provides a menu bar and has secondary windows that are used to display objects or other associated primary windows.

Guidelines

☐ Provide choices in the **Windows** menu that provide access to other associated windows without using the window list action window. For example, provide a **Close all** choice or a list of the last three windows that were active.

☑ Assign "W" as the mnemonic for the **Windows** menu choice.

Essential Related Topics

• "Menu (Control)" on page 331

• "Window List" on page 503

• "Window List (Choice in System Menu)" on page 505

• "Window List (Choice in Windows Menu)" on page 506

Window Title

The area in a title bar that identifies the window.

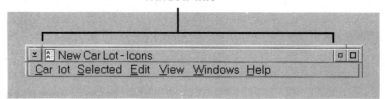

When to Use

☑   Provide a title for every window.

Guidelines

☐   Refer to Figure 204 to determine how to title a window:

Figure 204. Recommended Window Titling Formats	
Window usage	**Window title format**
Display view of an object	Object name - view name:n; for example, MyDoc - Settings:3
Note: where n is a number when multiple views of an object are provided	
Message	Object name - action or situation; for example, Drive A: - Format Diskette
Progress indicator displayed in separate window	Object name - action Progress; for example, MyDoc - Print Progress
Help	Object name, Action, or Field - xyz Help abc; for example, Font List - Help
Note: where xyz and abc are optional related identifying information	
Action window	Object name - action; for example, MyDoc - Find
Application-oriented window	Application name - file name; for example, Editor - MyDoc

☑   If more than one view of the same type has been opened from an object, append a colon (:) and unique number to the title of each of those windows. For example, if two icons views are opened on an object, label them "MyObject - Icons:1" and "MyObject - Icons:2."

☐   When a user opens more than one view of the same type on an object, begin numbering the window with "1" and continuing numbering with unique numbers. For the original window, change its title from "Object - View" to "Object - View:1" and label the next window displaying that same view "Object - View:2."

☐   Capitalize the first letter of the first and last words and the first letter of all other words except articles, coordinating conjunctions, prepositions, and the "to" in infinitives.

☐   If a user sizes a window so that all of the title cannot be displayed in the title bar, clip the window title from the right.

☐   Allow a user to directly edit a window title in the title bar.

☑   If you allow a user to directly edit a window title, allow the user to edit the window title by clicking on the text with the mouse.

Supplemental Related Topics

-        "Window" on page 496

Work Area (Object)

A container used to group windows and objects to perform a task.

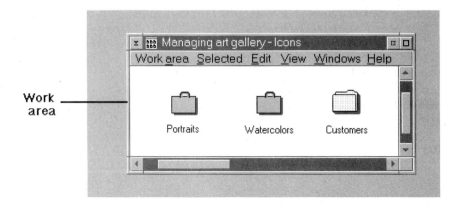

Work
area

When to Use

☐ Provide a work area to allow a user to group objects to perform a specific task or set of related tasks.

Guidelines

☑ When a user closes or minimizes a work area, remove any window that was opened from an object in that work area.

☑ If a window was open on an object in a work area when the work area was closed or minimized, restore that window when the work area is opened or restored.

☑ When a user closes or minimizes a work area, save the position and size of each open window associated with that work area.

☐ If you provide work areas, provide a settings choice that allows a user to change between a work area and a folder.

☐ If a user changes a work area into a folder, immediately change its icon to that of a folder.

☐ Allow a user to place any object into a work area.

Essential Related Topics

- "Container (Control)" on page 231

- "Folder (Object)" on page 287

Supplemental Related Topics

- "Close (Choice)" on page 225

- "Minimize (Choice)" on page 342

- "Window" on page 496

- "Workplace" on page 514

Workplace

A container provided by the operating environment where a user performs all tasks and where all user objects reside. The screen represents the workplace.

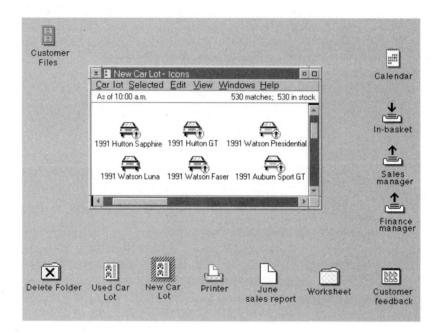

Guidelines

☑ Place all windows on the workplace.

☑ Represent all objects on the workplace as icons.

Essential Related Topics

• "Object" on page 366

• "Window" on page 496

Supplemental Related Topics

• "Icon" on page 300

Appendix A. Applying CUA Concepts to Touch Input and Multimedia User Interfaces

The following sections describe two areas of advanced development for CUA user interfaces: touch input and multimedia. Although the CUA guidelines do not yet provide detailed information about how to design touch and multimedia components of a product's interface, general information is provided here for designers and developers who want to add these features to their products.

Design Considerations for Touch Input

The CUA user interface has been designed to accommodate point-and-select interaction techniques. Although the CUA user interface is primarily intended for use with a pointing device such as a mouse, many CUA concepts and techniques can be incorporated in products that accept *touch input*—that is, input generated when a user places a finger on a display screen.

The design process for products that accept touch input is the same as for other kinds of products. However, a designer must be sure to accommodate the input device: a user's finger. Because a finger is larger than a cursor or pointer and can obscure objects and choices beneath it, a designer must pay special attention to a product's interaction techniques and visible cues to ensure that the result of a user's interaction is the result the user intended. A designer must ensure that a user knows which items can be selected. A designer must also ensure that a user is able to select items easily and accurately.

Deciding When Selection Occurs

When using a product that accepts touch input, a user can:

- Touch the display screen with a finger
- Lift a finger from the display screen
- Slide a finger while maintaining contact with the display screen.

Selection in a touch-input environment can occur at either the moment a user touches the screen or the moment a user lifts a finger from the screen.

Selection at the moment of the initial touch is the most intuitive method for selection and requires the least amount of training for users. However, this method of selection does not give a user the opportunity to cancel a selection once finger contact is made. If a designer chooses this method of selection, the designer should make the visual representations of a product's objects and choices relatively large. A designer should also provide mechanisms that make it easy for a user to identify errors and correct them.

Selection at the moment a user lifts a finger from the display screen allows a user to cancel an impending selection by sliding the finger away from an item before lifting the finger from the display screen. If a designer chooses this method of selection, the designer should provide some kind of visual highlighting on each object or choice that a user touches so that the user knows the item will be selected if the user lifts the finger. Users might require more training before they can use this method effectively to select objects and cancel selection.

In a variation of the second method of selection, a user touches the screen, slides the finger until the desired item is highlighted, then lifts the finger to select the highlighted item. This method works well for small or closely spaced items. If a designer chooses this method of selection, the designer should provide blank areas on the display screen so that a user can cancel an impending selection.

Some display screens can differentiate between a light touch and a heavier touch. For these displays a designer might specify a light touch for sliding a finger to an item and a heavier touch for selecting an item.

A designer can combine these different methods of selection. For example, a designer might specify that a user can select a choice on the menu bar at the moment the user touches the choice. Then, when the corresponding pull-down menu appears, the user could slide the finger up or down the pull-down menu until the desired choice is highlighted. The highlighted choice would be selected at the moment the user lifts the finger from the screen. This method is similar to the pointing device method used for selecting choices from menu bars and pull-down menus.

Making Selection Easy and Accurate

Several kinds of variables affect the ease and accuracy of touch input. These include:

- User variables—for example, user experience, height, position (sitting or standing), pointing acuity, left-handedness or right-handedness, and finger size

- Display variables—for example, image quality, height and angle of display screen, and physical support for the user's finger

- Product variables—for example, the number, size, and types of objects and choices, the frequency of use of objects and choices, and the types of interaction required.

Obviously, a software interface designer has no control over user variables and display variables, but a designer can control product variables to make it easy for a typical user to select items accurately. Several techniques for improving ease and accuracy are discussed in the following sections.

Providing Visible Cues

By providing obvious and consistent visible cues, a designer can make sure a user knows which items can be selected and which cannot. By giving special consideration to the design of items that can be selected, a designer can increase a user's accuracy in selecting items. Typically, a designer would use visible cues to help a user identify and select items, although audible cues can be appropriate for some products and some groups of users.

To make an interface component more obvious to a user, a designer can strengthen its visual representation. For example, a designer could specify a distinctive border for each item that can be selected. A designer can also provide special highlighting when a user touches an object that can be selected.

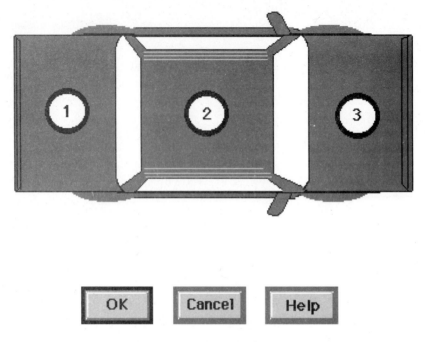

Figure 205. Distinctive Visual Cues. A designer can accentuate some of the visual characteristics of an object or choice to indicate to a user that the item can be selected.

Providing a Touch Pointer

A designer can provide a *touch pointer,* which is a smaller version of the arrow pointer (see "Pointer" on page 378). A touch pointer helps a user be more accurate in selecting a particular item.

A designer can provide a touch pointer when items on a screen are small or are closely spaced. A touch pointer can be displayed continuously or only when a user's finger is in contact with the screen. In either case, a touch pointer should be displayed only in a small area near the point where a user's finger is in contact with a screen, and it should be placed so that it is not obscured by the user's finger. When a user's finger moves to a new position on the screen, the touch pointer should also move.

If an item is particularly small and is likely to be completely obscured by a user's finger, a designer can choose to display visual highlighting on the touch pointer (rather than on the item to be selected) when the user touches the small item.

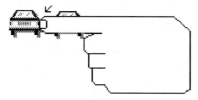

Figure 206. Touch Pointer. A touch pointer helps a user be more accurate when selecting objects or choices that are small or are close together.

Providing Adequate Visual Targets and Detection Zones

Items that can be selected have two components:

- Visual target—the graphic or text representation of the object or choice
- Detection zone—the area in which the touch of a user's finger is recognized as input.

The detection zone should encompass at least the entire area occupied by the visual target. In many cases, a designer will find it helpful to users to provide a detection zone that extends somewhat beyond the visual target.

The CUA guidelines do not specify a minimum size for objects or choices. Instead, a designer should determine the appropriate size by considering a product's users and the tasks the users will want to accomplish. Usually, the more varied and less experienced the users, the larger a product's visual targets and detection zones should be.

Design Considerations for Multimedia

Conventional user interfaces allow a user to work with textual information or with textual and graphical information. A multimedia user interface allows a user to work with more complex types of information, such as synchronized audio and video information. In addition to text and simple graphics, a multimedia user interface typically makes use of:

- Images, both static and moving, recorded and synthesized
- Audio, both recorded and synthesized.

The CUA environment allows the use of multimedia information. Products with a CUA interface can include:

- Enhanced visible cues, such as animated icons
- Enhanced audible cues, such as speech or music
- Animated objects, such as charts and graphs

- Video images, such as product demonstrations
- Computer visualizations, such as images based on data gathered from sensors.

Multimedia information can enrich and improve communication between people and between users and their computers.

However, designing a product that uses multimedia information is more challenging than designing a product that uses only text and graphics. To create a product with a multimedia user interface, a designer must be well versed in graphic design and in audio and video production, or must have access to people skilled in these areas.

Displaying and Manipulating Multimedia Information

A multimedia object has certain unique characteristics that affect the way a designer should display the object in a product. A multimedia object is typically a collection of data presented to a user in succession. To be displayed correctly, the data in a multimedia object must be presented to a user in the correct sequence and at the correct time. For example, an animation sequence is presented to a user as a series of images rather than as a single image. For the sequence to play correctly, each frame must appear in the correct relative order, and the interval from the appearance of one frame to the appearance of the next must be constant and must match the interval at which the sequence was developed. Otherwise, the motion in the sequence will seem jerky.

Multimedia objects can be combined. For example, a video object can be combined with an audio object. To achieve the desired effect, however, a designer must synchronize the objects. That is, a designer must link segments of data from each object so that the two segments will be displayed at the same point in time.

A designer can use standard components of the CUA interface, such as windows and controls, to display a multimedia object. For example, a product could display the waveform for an audio signal in a window. A user could see different parts of the waveform by scrolling the contents of the window.

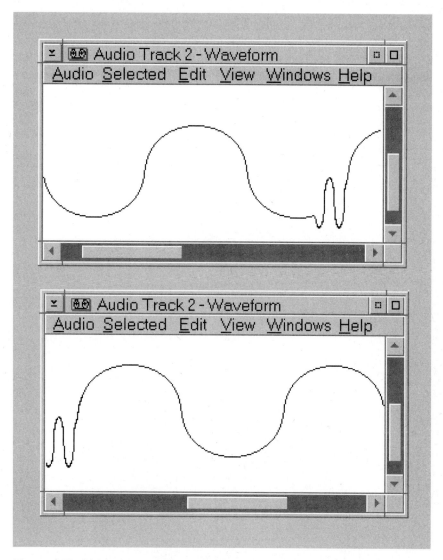

Figure 207. Displaying a Multimedia Object. A multimedia object can be displayed in a window. In the example above, the two windows display the same object, but they represent different segments of the object that correspond to different points in time. To view or work with a particular segment of the multimedia object, a user can scroll the window.

However, a designer should keep in mind that a scroll bar indicates the position and quantity of the information visible in a window only in relation to the quantity of information in the entire object being displayed. A scroll bar does not represent an absolute position or quantity.

Therefore, a scroll bar can be used to adjust the view of the object displayed in the window, but it should not be used to represent or adjust a specific quantity, such as time.

Instead, a designer should use a slider to represent a specific quantity. For example, in a product used for video editing, a designer could use a slider to indicate the total length (or time) of a "master tape" object. The slider arm would indicate the specific position or point in time of a single frame of the tape. To view the preceding (earlier) or following (later) frames, a user could manipulate the slider arm.

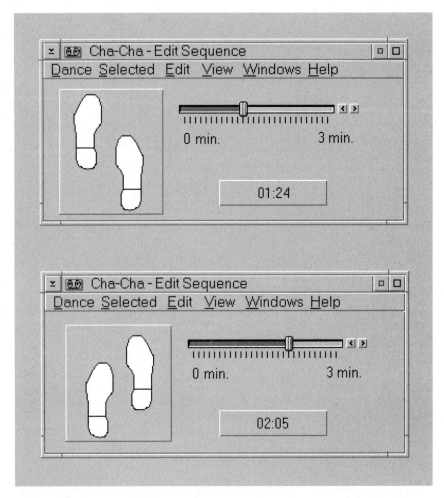

Figure 208. Slider. A slider can be used to represent a quantitative aspect of a multimedia object.

A designer can modify the visuals for controls when appropriate. For example, in a product used for video recording, the push buttons could be designed to resemble the Record, Pause, and Play buttons on an actual video recorder.

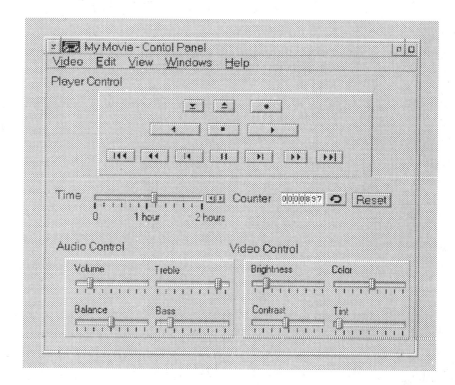

Figure 209. Multimedia Control Panel. The standard CUA controls can be used in multimedia products. The visuals for the controls can be modified as needed.

A designer could use a notebook to display the settings choices for audio or video equipment. Each section of the notebook could represent a different piece of equipment.

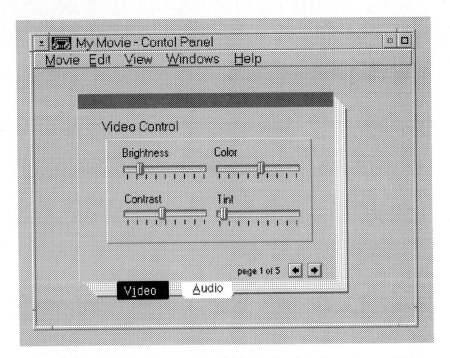

Figure 210. Notebook for Multimedia Objects. A notebook can be used to display settings choices for multimedia objects.

When deciding which controls and which visuals to use to display a multimedia object, a designer should keep a user's conceptual model in mind and, when possible, should mimic real-world objects that the user is accustomed to.

Accommodating Different System Configurations

A multimedia user interface can place considerable demands on a user's computer system. Factors that affect a user's ability to manage and manipulate multimedia objects include:

- Size, color, and resolution of a user's display screen
- Adapter cards and peripheral hardware, such as video or audio players or recorders
- System memory and storage capacity.

A designer should be aware that some users of a product might not have all the hardware necessary for an ideal installation. To accommodate a wider range of users, a product should include options for users with various system configurations. For example, a product developed on an elaborate system might contain an animation sequence that makes use of the system's high resolution and many colors. The product should also include a mechanism that allows a user to view the sequence on a less elaborate system that has lower resolution and fewer colors.

Appendix B. Design Considerations for the Use of Color

Color serves as a visible cue that can draw a user's attention to—or away from—a particular component of an interface. By using color, a designer can improve the appearance and effectiveness of a product's user interface. However, a designer should use color with care. If the colors in an interface are poorly chosen and poorly applied, the usability of the interface can be diminished.

Because some users might not have access to a color display screen, and because some users might have varying degrees of color blindness, a designer shouldn't rely solely on color to distinguish one interface component from another. Color should be used in combination with other cues, such as tonal value (contrast), size, shape, placement, and overlap. In fact, designers should design the interface in black and white first and should add color only after achieving a satisfactory design in black and white.

In general, a designer should use fewer colors and should apply them sparingly. Certain color combinations should be avoided. A red image on a green background, or a green image on a red background, can be difficult to see, particularly if the colors are of the same intensity. A designer should be aware that many users have red-green color blindness. Also, because saturated red and blue lines can appear to have depth, a designer should use them with care. Lighting conditions can also affect the visibility of colors. Before specifying colors for a user interface, a designer should consult someone skilled in the application of color to user interfaces.

Because users seek meaning in colors, a designer should take special care to learn what a particular color represents to a product's intended users. For example, in many Western cultures the color red means "stop" or "unsatisfactory conditions," the color yellow means "caution," and the color green means "go" or "satisfactory conditions." If a designer is certain that the users of a product will ascribe those meanings to those colors, the designer can use the colors to convey those meanings. However, if a product will be used by an international audience, a designer should not assume that red, yellow, and green will mean the same things to all users.

A designer should use the same color to convey the same meaning within a particular scope. For example, if the border of an entry field in a notebook changes to red when a user places an inappropriate value in the entry field, the border colors of other controls in the notebook should also change to red when a user supplies an inappropriate value. A designer could use red to convey a different meaning in the same product as long as the red appears in a different scope. For example, if a designer uses a slider to represent temperature, the designer could make one end of the slider red and the other blue to represent hot and cold, respectively.

Finally, whenever a designer includes color in a user interface, the designer should also provide mechanisms that allow a user to change the color. A designer should also provide a default set of colors that a user can revert to after changing to other colors.

Appendix C. Comparison of 1989 and 1991 Rules and Recommendations

This section provides information for designers migrating products from the *graphical model* defined in 1989 to the application-oriented and object-oriented models described in this guide. Not every rule is discussed in this section. Its intent is to point out some particularly important rules that have been changed and to make the reader aware of the new or changed topics. For specific implementation rules and guidelines refer to the appropriate component in Chapter 8, Common User Access Interface Components beginning on page 203.

Section	CUA Guidelines — 1989	CUA Guidelines — 1991
Accelerator	Accelerator term used.	Terminology change — called a Shortcut key.
Action bar	Action bar term used.	Terminology change — called a Menu bar.
	Used if more than one action available.	Used if more than six actions available, or when any of the predefined menu bar actions are available.
Action message	Stop-sign symbol always used.	Question mark or stop-sign symbol may be used.
Audible feedback	Beep recommended.	Recommend using available audio capabilities as feedback.
Column heading	Alignment of columns and headings not addressed.	Alignment of columns and headings are defined based on length.
	Use of separators not addressed.	Recommend separators between columns and headings.
	Required headings not addressed.	Column headings not required if there is only one column.
Combination box	Default choices not addressed.	Recommend displaying a default choice.
Container	Addressed at a direction level only.	A new control. An object used to hold other objects.

Section	CUA Guidelines — 1989	CUA Guidelines — 1991
Contents of menus	May contain action, routing, or settings (properties) choices. **Short menus** and **Full menus:** Not addressed.	May contain action or routing choices. Encourages using a notebook control for settings choices. **Short Menus** and **Full Menus** — the contents and techniques are defined.
Contextual help	Contextual help for direct-manipulation tasks not addressed.	Defined for direct-manipulation tasks.
Delete folder	Not addressed.	A container used to remove objects from the operating environment.
Dialog box	Dialog boxes used to continue users requests (movable, but not sizable).	Secondary windows used to continue users requests. Recommend they are movable and sizable. Terminology change - dialog box term no longer used.
Direct manipulation	Direct manipulation discussed briefly. Direct manipulation of split bar not addressed	Direct manipulation discussed as a pervasive technique. Recommendation to provide direct manipulation for all objects. Manipulation button drags split bar.
Do-not pointer	Not addressed.	Defines do-not pointer for use during direct-manipulation operations.
Drop-down combination box	Order and number of choices not addressed.	Recommend placing choices in numeric, alphabetic, or chronological order and display at least six choices in a box.
Drop-down list	Order and number of choices not addressed.	Recommend placing choices in numeric, alphabetic, or chronological order and display at least six choices in a box.

Section	CUA Guidelines — 1989	CUA Guidelines — 1991
Edit menu	**Redo:** Not addressed.	**Redo** choice used to reverse the effect of an undo action.
	Create: Not addressed.	**Create** choice used to create a new object or a reflection of the current object using the clipboard.
	Find: Not addressed.	**Find** choice allows a user to search for an object or a part of an object.
Field prompts	Left-align field prompts only.	Allow left-aligned or right-aligned field prompts.
	Field prompts followed by colons shown in many examples.	Field prompts followed by colons no longer suggested or used in examples.
File menu	**File:** Name used for first menu choice on the menu bar.	File — used for application-oriented windows; "class name" used for first menu choice of object-oriented windows.
	Open as: Not addressed.	Opens another view of the object in another window.
	Print: Allows a window for more information	**Print:** Allows a window for more information, and allows a cascaded menu for printer selection
	Exit (optional)	Not used; performed by close action of system menu in associated primary window.
Folder	Not addressed.	System-provided container used to group objects.
Group box	Capitalization rules not addressed.	Capitalize first letter only (some exceptions described).
	Not addressed.	Recommend using only when white space or group headings would be insufficient.

Section	CUA Guidelines — 1989	CUA Guidelines — 1991
Help menu	**Help** menu choices displayed with ellipses.	**Help** menu choices are not displayed with ellipses.
	Help for help choice	Terminology change — **Using help.** Position change in the **Help** menu.
	Extended help choice	
	Keys help	Terminology change — **General help**
	Not addressed.	Removed from **Help** menu, now accessed from the help index.
		Recommend describing settings for buttons on pointing device in keys help.
	Help index choice	
	About choice — leads to a logo window.	Position change in **Help** menu.
		Terminology change — **Product information** choice leads to a product-information window.
Hide	Not addressed.	A choice that removes a window and all associated windows from the workplace.
Hourglass pointer	Hourglass pointer term used.	Recommend displaying wait pointer over parts of a window.
		Terminology change — called a wait pointer.
		Two wait pointer visuals are available.
Information area	Not addressed.	Information area defined as part of a window where information appears about the object or choice that the cursor is on. Information about the normal completion of a process can also appear in the information area.

Section	CUA Guidelines — 1989	CUA Guidelines — 1991
Information message	Used for normal processing situations when there are no additional actions available.	Used when additional information about a completed process is available and no progress indicator is displayed, or when a process cannot complete and there are no additional actions available.
In-use emphasis	Not addressed.	In-use emphasis defined for opened objects.
Keyboard	Accelerator keys	Terminology change — Shortcut keys
	No guidance given about user changes.	If changed by users, changes reflected in menus and help.
	Case sensitivity not addressed.	Allow either upper or lowercase characters.
	Use of preferred modifiers not addressed.	Recommend using the Alt key element of shortcut key assignments to only provide access to mnemonics and to provide access to operating-environment-provided shortcut keys.
Message box	Special type of dialog box used for messages (modal and sizable)	Secondary windows used for messages. Recommend they are modeless and sizable.
		Terminology change — message box term no longer used.

Section	CUA Guidelines — 1989	CUA Guidelines — 1991
Messages	Application name used for window title.	*Object name — action* used in window title.
	Messages are application modal and nonsizable.	Recommend to allow a user to continue interacting with parts of an object while message displayed and size messages.
	Controls in messages not addressed.	Recommend providing interactive controls in messages.
	Not addressed.	Describes displaying message symbol on icon if window is not open.
Modal and modeless	Modeless dialogs used only for repeat actions.	Modeless windows encouraged for all windows.
Mouse	Using mouse to create a reflection not addressed.	Ctrl+Shift+Manipulation button assigned to create reflection operation.
	Effect of move and copy operations on pointer visuals not addressed.	Move and copy operations effect on pointer visuals defined.
Multiple document interface	Used to view many objects or multiple views of same object. All windows contained within one window and share a menu bar.	Multiple windows used to view many objects or multiple views of the same object. Multiple document interface only addressed in the context of migration. Also see the **Windows** menu.
Notebook	Not addressed.	New control. Recommended for displaying settings and some types of objects.
Options menu	Contains product-specific choices related to the application.	Used primarily in application-oriented windows. Encourages using a notebook control for these types of choices.
Pop-up menu	Not defined	Pop-up menus defined to display actions for indicated object. Shift+F10 and chording selection and manipulation buttons display pop-up menu of indicated object.

Section	CUA Guidelines — 1989	CUA Guidelines — 1991
Progress indicator	Display a progress indicator for complex tasks.	Display a progress indicator for tasks that take more than 5 seconds.
	Not addressed.	
		Display a progress indicator in action window where process is requested.
	Only a **Stop** push button is defined for controlling the process.	**Stop, Pause,** and **Resume** push buttons defined for controlling the process. **Close** push button not allowed for stopping the process.
	Title not addressed.	
		Use the word "progress" in the window title.
	Help not addressed.	
		Recommend providing **Help.**
	Removing the progress indicator not addressed.	Product removes the progress indicator if no special completion information needed; otherwise the user removes the progress indicator.
Pull-down menu	Recommended at least two choices in a pull-down menu.	Not addressed.

Section	CUA Guidelines — 1989	CUA Guidelines — 1991
Push button	Changing contents of a push button not addressed.	Use two push buttons, do not change content of same push button.
	Normal position is in lower area of window.	Place push buttons that affect an entire window horizontally at the bottom of the window, justified from the left edge. If a push button is associated with a component, place it near the component.
	Push buttons not allowed in windows with menu bars.	Push buttons allowed in windows with menu bars.
	Position of push buttons when sizing or scrolling not addressed.	Push buttons remain in same relative position when sizing or scrolling.
	Default push button required for each window containing push buttons.	Default push button recommended for each window containing push buttons.
	Pause, Resume, Close, and **Continue:** not addressed.	Recommended usage described for **Pause, Resume, Close,** and **Continue.**
Radio button	**None** choice not addressed.	Recommend **None** choice if a user can choose not to select any of a set of choices.
Reflection	Not addressed.	An object represented by more than one icon.
Restore of minimized windows	**Restore** returns to middle size.	**Restore** returns to previous size and position.
Scroll bar	Slider box — part of the scroll bar used to scroll.	Terminology change — scroll box.
Scroll increment	General descriptions given, text examples provided.	Recommendations included for icons, graphics, and text.

Section	CUA Guidelines — 1989	CUA Guidelines — 1991
Secondary window	Term used only to refer to movable, sizable windows dependent on another primary window.	Terminology change—definition expanded to include all windows dependent on another primary window (independent of whether they are movable or sizable).
	May not be minimized	May be minimized when used to display views of objects.
Selected emphasis	Referred to as selected emphasis	Terminology change — selected-state emphasis.
	Use inverse color for selected emphasis on text.	For all objects show by changing the foreground and background colors.
Selected menu	Functions were available in the **File** menu for list handlers.	New menu-bar choice used for actions on selected objects within the window.
	Open as choice — Not addressed.	Choice used to display another view of an object in a window.
Separators	Not addressed.	White space recommended except in menus.
Single-line entry field	Specific rules for visible length not addressed.	When the length of data is predictable, such as time or date, the field should be entirely visible.
Slider	Not addressed.	New control to represent a quantity and its relationship to a range of possible values.
	Usage of scroll bar for numeric values not addressed.	Slider control used.
Source emphasis and target emphasis	Not defined	Defines source emphasis and target emphasis for direct-manipulation operations.
Spin button	Not defined.	Order of choices is based on type of data.
Split window	Allows only one vertical and one horizontal split.	Allows multiple vertical and horizontal splits.

Section	CUA Guidelines — 1989	CUA Guidelines — 1991
Status area	Not addressed.	Status area defined as part of a window where information appears about the state of an object or the state of a particular view of an object.
System menu	**Close** choice does not address saving window status information. **Close** choice only addressed for dialog boxes.	**Close** choice recommends saving window state, such as its position, size, and associated messages. Result of **Close** choice defined depending on window content.
Title bar mini-icon	Introduced in the workplace environment and referred to as the Title bar mini-icon. Not addressed.	Referred to as the small icon in the title bar. Defines use of target emphasis during direct-manipulation operations.
Tool palette	Briefly described	Content and usage described.
Value set control	When to use value set as opposed to a radio button was not addressed. Type of choices to allow not addressed Minimum number of choices not addressed How to display shared setting not addressed Providing a default choice not addressed.	Use a value set for graphical and short textual choices. Use a radio button for textual choices. Display only setting choices in a value set. Use at least two choices when a value set is used. Use the same sharing emphasis that is used for radio buttons. Provide one of the choices as a default choice.

Section	CUA Guidelines — 1989	CUA Guidelines — 1991
View menu	Names of views addressed in the **View** menu.	Names of views are listed at the top of the **View** menu.
	All: Used to see the entire contents.	**Include:** Used to see the entire contents or part of the contents.
	Some: Used to see part of the contents.	**Include:** Used to see the entire contents or part of the contents.
	By: Used to sort the contents.	
		Terminology change — **Sort.**
	Refresh: Not addressed.	**Refresh** → **On/Off** used to allow a user to control updates to the window contents.
	Refresh now: Not addressed.	**Refresh now:** Used to update the window contents immediately.
Warning message	**Yes** and **No** push buttons allowed.	Recommend using **Continue** push buttons and action push buttons.
Window menu	Used for MDI windows.	Terminology change — **Windows** menu used to access and manage related windows.
Window title	"Application name — OS/2 file name"	Added window title rules for object-oriented windows
Work area	Not addressed.	A container used to group objects by task.

Appendix D. Common User Access and National Language Support

The purpose of the Common User Access (CUA) guidelines of the Systems Application Architecture (SAA) is to facilitate the design of products that are easy to learn, easy to use, productive and consistent. While consistency is well understood, "ease of learning" and "ease of use" is very much dependent on a user's cultural environment, particularly their language.

The CUA guidelines are given in the main body of this publication. This appendix assumes you are familiar with those guidelines and only describes features of the interface that may require different guidelines or need clarification when applied in different users' cultural environments.

General Considerations for National Language and the CUA Guidelines

The following clarifies some of the CUA guidelines when applied to a National Language environment.

Capitalization	The guidelines stated for capitalization in this manual are for the English language developer. When a product is developed in another language or translated to another language, the rules of that language must be followed. For example, in the German language all nouns are capitalized, no matter what their position in a phrase or sentence.
Column Headings	The space needed for a column heading after translation may increase. For usability purposes, the additional space may be achieved by increasing the number of rows in the heading.
Descriptive Text	Descriptive text will sometimes reflect a localized or culturally sensitive format. Allow the user to edit the descriptive text in place.
Field Prompts	The translation of field prompts may cause a field to be moved. Fields must be realigned after translation.
First-Letter Cursor Navigation	Allow a user to press the unaccented, uppercase, or lowercase character to access accented first letters.

Icon	An icon designed for the international market place should follow these additional design criteria. • Avoid body parts • Use international symbols where possible • Do not include text • If alphabetic characters are included, use uppercase • Avoid symbolic written material that is oriented for left-to-right text • Avoid stars and crosses • Do not use humor • Do not use regional metaphors.
Length of Text	When a product will be translated to another language, developers should consider translation space when evaluating length of text in entry fields. For example, CUA guidelines recommend 60 or fewer characters in a single-line entry field. If the product will be translated, 40 or fewer characters are recommended.
Shortcut Keys	The use of Alt+(A-Z) for shortcut keys can be very awkward on non-US keyboards since only either the left hand Alt key or the right hand Alt key may be available for this function.
Sort	Each country has a different way of sorting, and may have several ways of sorting within the country, such as in a telephone book or a dictionary. The sort menu should be defined by each country or application. The sort menu may have to allow selection of these criteria based on the requirements of the country or application. In addition, when lists are ordered alphabetically, as in spin buttons, the list must be reordered after translation.

Double-Byte Character Sets

The following are some of the special considerations when applying the CUA guidelines to Double-Byte Character Sets.

• Mnemonic Selection: A *mnemonic* is a single character that provides a fast interaction technique for selecting choices from the keyboard. When users type a valid mnemonic, the selection cursor moves to the choice that the mnemonic is assigned to and the choice is automatically selected or deselected as appropriate. This saves keystrokes for choices that are usually selected explicitly.

All the guidelines for mnemonics in a single-byte-character-set (SBCS) language apply to a double-byte-character-set (DBCS) language except for how the mnemonics are shown. If all the letters in a choice are already assigned, or the choice consists of DBCS characters, you may choose another letter or a keyboard character, such as the comma (,). Choices that appear many times in an application should be assigned the same mnemonic throughout.

Applications translated from SBCS languages to DBCS languages can keep the SBCS mnemonics.

- DBCS Keyboard Shift Status: In the DBCS environment, the Presentation Manager has the capability to display the keyboard shift status in the information area. This technique should be used in primary and secondary windows that accept keyboard data entry for DBCS applications.

- Sort: For components, such as the combination box control, that specify choices should be shown in a specific sort order such as alphabetic order, the sort order may actually depend on the application. For example, for Japanese Kanji it may be better to sort by Japanese phonetic order or some other appropriate order depending on the information in the field.

Bidirectional Languages

The main factor affecting CUA guidelines for users of bidirectional languages (Arabic and Hebrew) is the right-to-left (RTL) orientation of these languages; Hebrew or Arabic text is written from right to left and from top to bottom. However, English words and numbers are written from left to right (LTR). This makes bidirectionality a must in any system intended for Arabic or Hebrew users.

This is the basic rule of bidirectional applications.

In CUA-interface-conforming applications, all pieces of data must be displayed in the orientation that is correct for the application user. Data input must be supported in the orientation that is natural for users.

General information concerning the Arabic language can be found in *National Language Information and Design Guide, Volume 3: Arabic Script Languages, (SE09-8003)*. This publication describes the Arabic language, and the main keyboard functions implemented on terminals and programmable workstations with Arabic support.

General information concerning the Hebrew language may be found in *National Language Information and Design Guide, Volume 4: Hebrew* (SE09-8004). This publication describes the Hebrew language, and the main keyboard functions implemented on terminals and programmable workstations with Hebrew support.

In most cases, Arabic and Hebrew can be handled in the same way. We will use "Arabic and Hebrew" as a generic designator for the national language used by a bidirectional application. Whenever special considerations apply to Arabic only or to Hebrew only, they will be mentioned explicitly.

In all examples, Arabic and Hebrew text is represented by lowercase Latin, written from right to left. English text is represented by uppercase, although in reality it would be written in mixed case, if appropriate.

Language Usage

Arabic and Hebrew applications must generally use the national language for titles, instructions, headings, prompts, and other window components, with the following exceptions:

- English acronyms or terms commonly used untranslated, for example, DOS, EXE, CICS.

- Key names must be identical to the key top engraving, for example, F1, Alt, Ctrl, Enter.

- Key combinations must be displayed as English phrases, for example, "Alt+F2."

Application Language Specification

An application may allow dynamic language selection. When a new language is chosen by a user, headings, messages, and commands should adhere to the new language. For RTL languages, the application interface reflects CUA guidelines with this bidirectional language addendum. When the application contains a mixture of RTL and LTR language elements, the LTR elements follow the unmodified CUA guidelines while the RTL elements follow CUA guidelines with this bidirectional Languages addendum.

The application language must be mentioned in the product information window, if the application is not unilingual. If the application allows dynamic language selection, the initial language must be mentioned in the product information window.

Mnemonics

In a RTL window, choices appear in Arabic and Hebrew and their mnemonics are in Arabic and Hebrew. However, if a choice is in English, its corresponding mnemonic must also be English.

In Arabic, any shape of a letter can be used for mnemonic.

Character Presentation Shapes in Arabic

Arabic characters take various presentation shapes according to the writing context and the writer's intention:

- For continuous text, traditional characters' presentation shapes may be automatically selected for each character according to its linkage capabilities and to the linkage capabilities of its neighbors.

- In some cases (like acronyms, abbreviations, paragraph numbering, or stock item part numbers), character presentation shapes are usually selected by the writer without following the traditional contextual writing rules.

- Applications, and users within the limits defined by the application, must be allowed to decide on characters' presentation shapes and on their relevance in the various contexts.

Data Entry: Arabic keyboards provide one single representative (one shape) for each Arabic character, using one of its shapes selected for the best balanced readability of the whole keyboard. Specific function keys allow the user to either activate automatic contextual selection of Arabic characters' presentation shapes, or to specify which is the desired presentation shape for a given occurrence of a character.

Data Handling: According to the type of data and to the processing required, various cases may occur:

- Actual character shape is significant: exact match on shapes where another shape of the same letter will result in a no-match. For example: text formatting for final presentation.

- Actual shape is indifferent: any can be used and all should be permitted. This is the case where a shape has been selected as a mnemonic for a choice in an menu bar, and any shape for this character must be allowed as a correct match to the mnemonic.

Numeric Shape Selection in Arabic
In any given Arabic-language environment:

- Digits appearing in a Latin context will be presented in their usual Arabic shapes.

- Digits appearing in an Arabic context will be presented in either their Hindi shapes or their Arabic shapes, according to the prevailing local tradition.

- Applications, and users within the limits defined by the application, must be allowed to select digit presentation shapes and to decide on their relevance in the various contexts.

Data entry: Hindi and Arabic shapes for the same digit are on the same key on the keyboard. Depending on the customization done for digit-shape selection and on the currently selected keyboard language, the corresponding digit codes and shapes are generated and presented.

Data handling: The possible cases are very similar to those for Arabic characters: digit shapes may be indifferent (for arithmetic processing) or mandatory (for presentation preparation).

Orientation

Arabic and Hebrew applications, since written for the Arabic and Hebrew language, use the screen space in RTL orientation. Thus the right side of a window becomes the "begin" side, and its left side is the "end" side. Most references to "right" and "left" in the CUA guidelines for LTR languages remain true in Arabic and Hebrew, providing that "right" and "left" are exchanged (in some cases, "right" and "left" must be conserved as-is for Arabic and Hebrew. They are mentioned in the following paragraph).

The appearance of an Arabic and Hebrew window is mostly the mirror symmetric of a corresponding English window ("mostly" because the position of system and maximize and minimize push buttons in the title bar does not change. A discussion about vertical scroll bars appears in the following paragraphs).

For instance, a window with some choices could look like Figure 211.

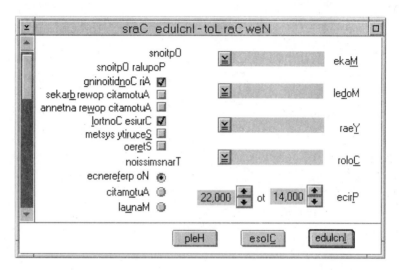

Figure 211. Window with Choices

It must be understood that orientation applies at multiple levels:

- In a bidirectional environment, the end user selects the orientation of the workplace (for example, screen orientation). Selection is done according to the user's main usage, standards, or preferences and controls the way the screen and windows are organized. If this orientation is RTL:

  - Windows are tiled, cascaded, or superimposed with the older primary window on the right and the newer secondary on the left

  - Application icons are ordered from right-to-left beginning from the right side of the screen.

  - In a workplace environment, icons should be originally ordered from right-to-left and top-to-bottom if there is a meaningful sequence among them.

- An application has a general orientation for its windows, which is LTR for English applications and generally RTL for Arabic and Hebrew applications.

- A window has an orientation. If the window orientation is RTL, its elements are logically ordered from right-to-left and from top-to-bottom.

  For a RTL window, the priority for positioning associated secondary windows (like help windows) is: to the left of, to the right of, above, or below the application window.

  Note that an Arabic or Hebrew application can include some LTR windows.

  Note also that a LTR window can be used on a RTL screen and vice-versa. This means that English services and applications can be used while the screen is oriented RTL and Arabic and Hebrew (RTL) applications can be used on a LTR screen.

- Within the same window, text and graphics may have differing orientations. This may be the case, for instance, for a geographic map where the graphics will be left-to-right (as for an English application), but the Arabic and Hebrew captions will be right-to-left.

- Entry fields are a special case: for each field, an orientation is defined, which by default is RTL within RTL windows. However, fields which are to receive numeric data or English text should be defined as LTR oriented.

  Within an entry field, the keying (or cursor) direction may be RTL or LTR, according to the data entered (Arabic or Hebrew text, or English and numbers).

  More explanations on entry fields will be found in the following paragraphs.

Note: While the "right" and "left" have exchanged their meaning, the physical right and left are still the same, thus the following have the same effect for Arabic and Hebrew as for English:

- Cursor movement keys (left and right arrows) must still move the cursor according to the direction of the arrow engraved on the key top (this is also true for combinations of the left and right arrow keys with Shift, Ctrl or Alt).

  Likewise, Ctrl+PgUp must always scroll to the left, and Ctrl+PgDn scroll to the right.

- Right and left buttons of a pointing device.

- Right and left movement of a pointing device.

- Graphics may be unaffected by the window orientation: for instance, a map must still have the East on the right side and the West on the left side.

RTL Flavor of CUA-Interface Components

The following topics address the various aspects of the CUA guidelines as applied in the bidirectional Language environment.

Title Bar

Title bars have the same general layout in right-to-left windows as in left-to-right windows:

- Window-menu icon on the left
- Window title in the middle
- Window-sizing buttons on the right.

When the window title itself has a right-to-left orientation (written in Arabic or Hebrew), it must truncate on the left whenever it would truncate on the right if written in English. This is true both for right-to-left and left-to-right windows.

Scroll Bars

- Vertical scroll bars are on the right side for left-to-right windows, on the left side for right-to-left windows.

- Horizontal scroll bars never extend under the vertical scroll bar of the same window. If the vertical scroll bar is on the left (right-to-left window), the horizontal scroll bar may extend from the right window border to the right side of the vertical bar.

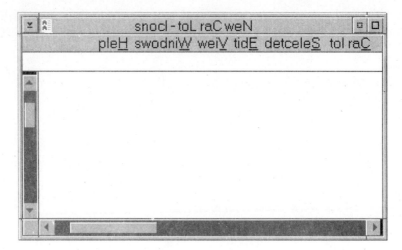
Figure 212. Scroll Bars in a Right-to-Left Window

Menu Bar
- The text of the menu bar choices is aligned on the right.

- If the list of actions is too long to be contained in one line, it is its "end" part that wraps to an additional line: left part for a right-to-left window, right part for a left-to-right window.

Menu Bar Pull-Down Menus in a RTL Window
- The right border of a pull-down menu is aligned with the right side of its corresponding menu bar choice.

- Text of pull-down choices is aligned on the right.

- Ellipses (...) appear on the left of the corresponding choice.

- Shortcut keys appear on the left of the corresponding choice.

- For cascaded menus, a left-pointing arrow appears at the left of the pull-down choice text as a visual cue that this choice has an associated, hidden pull-down. The cascaded pull-down will be displayed on the left of its first-level choice.

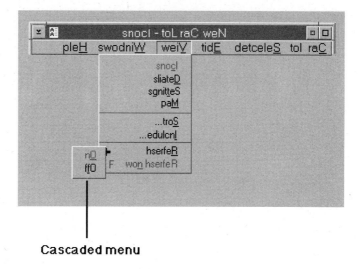

Cascaded menu

Figure 213. Cascaded Menu

RTL Radio Button
- The circle appears to the right of the choice.
- The text of the choice is aligned on the right.

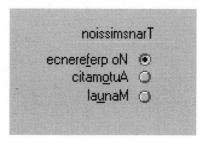

Figure 214. Radio Buttons

RTL Check Box
- The square box appears to the right of the choice.
- The text of the choice is aligned on the right.

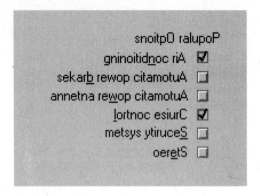

Figure 215. Check Boxes

RTL List Box
- The text of the choice is aligned on the right.
- The vertical scroll bar is on the left side.

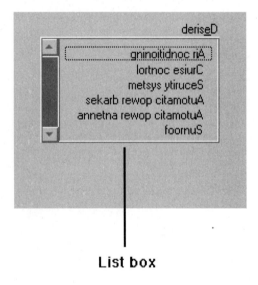

Figure 216. List Box

Push buttons in a RTL Window
- Push buttons are ordered from right to left.

- The label in a push button is centered.

- If there is not enough room to place push buttons horizontally in the lower part of a window, they may be placed vertically at the left side of a window.

Progress Indicator in a RTL Window
- The progress indicator in a right-to-left window advances from right to left.

RTL Message Window
- The text must appear on the left side of the icon.

- In information messages and action messages, the label in the icon must be the national equivalent of "i" and "STOP," respectively.

RTL Combination Box
- A combination box in a right-to-left window combines the bidirectional characteristics of an entry field in a right-to-left window and a list box in a right-to-left window.

- The list box appears beneath and to the left of an entry field.

- The vertical scroll bar of the list box appears on its left side.

- The left side of the list box is aligned with the left side of the entry field.

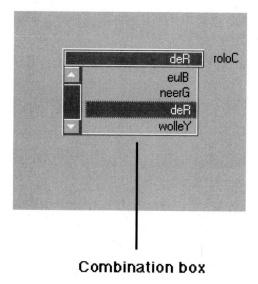

Combination box

Figure 217. Combination Box

RTL Drop-Down Combination Box

- The list button containing a downward-pointing arrow is at the left side of the entry field.

- The left side of the list box is aligned with the left side of the list button.

- The vertical scroll bar is on the left side.

Drop down combination boxes

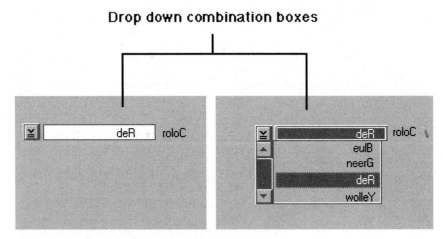

Figure 218. Drop-Down Combination Box

RTL Drop-Down List

- The list button containing a downward-pointing arrow is at the left side of the selection field.

- The vertical scroll bar is on the left side.

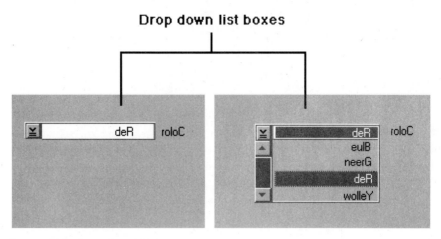

Figure 219. Drop-Down List

RTL Value Set
- Values are ordered from right-to-left (and from top-to-bottom).

RTL Spin Button
- The up and down arrow buttons are at the left side of the entry field.

- The prompt text, next to the arrow, is right aligned.

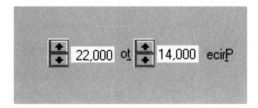

Figure 220. Spin Button

Field Prompt in a RTL Window
- The field prompt is located above or to the right of the affected field. Its text is aligned on the right.

- If it is located above the field, it is right-aligned with the right side of the field.

- If it is located to the right of a field, it must be right-aligned with other field prompts.

- If descriptive text supplements the field prompt, it must be placed to the left of the affected entry field.

```
99 ot pu  [          ]  :seipoc
```

Figure 221. Descriptive Text. "99 ot pu" is descriptive text

Column and Group Headings in a RTL Window
- All alignments are to the right.

Group Box in a RTL Window
- The title appears at the top-right side of a group box (see the examples for radio button and check box).

Notebook
- A RTL notebook has back pages painted on the left side by default.

- If the tabs are on the top or bottom edge, they are ordered logically from right to left.

- If the notebook has arrows to turn the pages forward or backward, they should be on the left side of the page.

Slider
- Place slider buttons to the left of the slider shaft.

- Horizontal slider shafts should be filled from the right to the slider arm.

Entry Fields

In a bidirectional application, each field has an orientation that is defined by the application (by default, entry fields assume the same orientation as the encompassing window). According to the expected contents of the field, the application must define it as RTL (Arabic and Hebrew textual data) or LTR (numeric data, or English textual data).

RTL Entry Fields
RTL fields differ from LTR fields in the following ways:

- Data are right-aligned in the field.

- At initial entry, the cursor is located at the rightmost position.

- The cursor movement is initiated as right-to-left: in **Replace** mode, with each entry the text cursor moves left to the next entry position; in **Insert** mode, the cursor and all characters to the left of the cursor are shifted one position to the left with each entry.

- If the field is scrollable, the rightmost field positions are initially visible. When the cursor moves to the left, the information scrolls so as to show more characters on the left side. In summary, the beginning of the information is on the right side, its end on the left side.

The following example illustrates initial cursor placement and cursor movement when typing RTL data in a RTL entry field (in **Insert** mode).

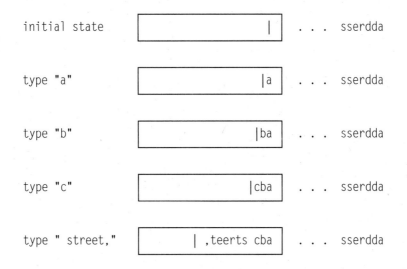

Figure 222. Typing in a RTL field

When text must be typed in an orientation opposite to the field orientation (like numbers within a RTL field), the special bidirectional functions "Push" and "EndPush" are used.

In the following example, the house number (LTR) is added to the address (RTL field).

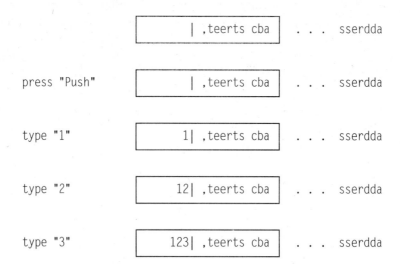

Figure 223. Typing a Push Segment

Note that during a Push operation, the cursor does not move (calculator effect). The cursor stands on the character at the boundary between the surrounding RTL text (the street name in our example) and the Push segment (the house number).

When "EndPush" is pressed to end the operation, the cursor skips beyond the Push segment. This allows to continue the RTL text if necessary.

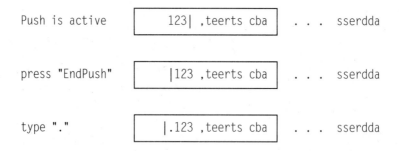

Figure 224. Ending a Push Segment

Text Cursor Appearance

It must be apparent whether the cursor stands at a "Push boundary" or not. The Push boundary is where the latest character typed in a Push operation appears (assuming that arrow keys were not used to move the cursor away). Typing data at the Push boundary does not always have the same effect ("calculator" effect) as typing elsewhere, thus some visual feedback must help the user differentiate between the two.

Text Cursor Position in Insert Mode

In general, the cursor has the same appearance as described for LTR text. However, in Insert mode the vertical bar representing the cursor must be on the proper side of the position of the cursor.

```
    FMPLOYEE'S NUMBER . . .    ┌──────────┐          (Insert  mode)
                               │  12|345  │
                               └──────────┘
```

Figure 225. Cursor Placement in LTR Text (Insert Mode). "3" is the cursored character; new text is inserted between "2" and "3."

```
    ┌──────────┐
    │  edc|ba  │    . . .    eman s'eeyolpme          (Insert  mode)
    └──────────┘
```

Figure 226. Cursor Placement in RTL Text (Insert Mode). "c" is the cursored character; new text is inserted between "b" and "c."

Bidirectional Keyboard Functions in Entry Fields

Note: The descriptions given in this section are only an overview. For more details, product-specific documentation must be consulted.

SAA-conforming and CUA-interface-conforming applications must support the Arabic or Hebrew keyboard functions:

Language selection (Arabic or Hebrew/English): This function manually selects the active keyboard layer.

Shape selection (for Arabic only): These functions allow the user to enable automatic shape determination (ASD) or to select the requested letter shapes manually.

Shape (for Arabic only): These functions lets the user reshape the whole content of an entry field using the ASD mechanism.

DeShape (for Arabic only): These functions let the user convert the content of an entry field to base shapes.

Field Reverse: This function swaps the field orientation. It overrides the application-defined field orientation for the current entry operation. For instance, a "customer name" field, defined as having RTL orientation, is overridden to LTR orientation in order to type the name of an English customer.

Push/EndPush: These functions allow the typing of a piece of text with an orientation opposite to the general orientation of the field. This may be used to type numbers or English words within a RTL field, or Arabic and Hebrew words within a LTR field.

AutoPush: This feature (which can be enabled or disabled by the user) automatically exercises the Push and EndPush functions when certain characters are typed. For instance, typing digits or English letters within a RTL field automatically begins a Push operation; typing Arabic or Hebrew afterwards begins an EndPush operation.

Bidirectional Status Window: This function puts a window on the screen that displays the status of all bidirectional indicators.

How Various Keys Work in RTL Entry Fields

Left-Arrow Key: The Left-Arrow key moves the text cursor one character position to the left until it reaches the last visible position. If the field scrolls, the Left-Arrow key moves the cursor until it reaches the next available character space after the end of the information in the field, at the same time information scrolls to the right.

Right-Arrow Key: The Right-Arrow key moves the text cursor one character position to the right until it reaches the entry field boundary; that is, until the cursor is under the first character for **Replace** mode, or until it is to the right of the first character for **Insert** mode. If the field scrolls, the Right-Arrow key moves the cursor to the beginning of the field, while information scrolls left.

Word-Left Key: The Word-Left key moves the cursor to the first logical position of the word on the left of the nearest blank to the left on the line.

Word-Right Key: The Word-Right key moves the cursor to the first logical position of the word on the right of the nearest blank to the right on the line.

Delete Key in RTL Text: If something is selected, this key deletes the selection. If no selection exists (for example, in **Insert** mode), it deletes the character to the left of the text cursor. Characters to the left of the deleted character move right to fill the vacated position. The cursor remains stationary at the point where the character was deleted.

Backspace Key in RTL Text: If something is selected, this key deletes the selection. If no selection exists (for example, in **Insert** mode), it deletes the character to the right of the cursor and moves the cursor one space to the right. The characters to the left of the cursor move right one position to fill the vacated space. The Backspace key has no effect when the cursor is at the beginning of an entry field.

Note: The descriptions given in this section are only an overview. For more details, product-specific documentation must be consulted.

Note: Some keys mentioned in this section may cause a change in the shape of Arabic characters at the cursor position and adjacent to it.

Multiple-Line Entry Field

For RTL multiple-line entry fields, the following additional consideration applies. If the cursor is in a multiple-line entry field, pressing the Enter key moves the cursor to the next line. Any text that was to the left of the cursor prior to pressing the Enter key is repositioned on the next line. The cursor is positioned at the beginning of the line.

Navigation in a RTL Window

Tab

This key moves the cursor to the next field, either the next entry field or the first choice of a selection field if no choice is selected, The cursor moves from right to left and top to bottom. At the bottom-leftmost field, the cursor moves to the top-rightmost field.

Backtab

This key moves the cursor to the previous field, either the previous entry field or the first choice of a selection field if no choice is selected, The cursor moves from left to right and bottom to top. At the top-rightmost field, the cursor moves to the bottom-leftmost field.

Beginning of Data

This key moves the cursor to the first logical position in the current field: top-rightmost for a RTL field, top-leftmost for a LTR field.

End of Data

This key moves the cursor to the last logical position in the current field: bottom-leftmost for a RTL field, bottom-rightmost for a LTR field.

Beginning of Line

This key moves the cursor to the rightmost choice.

End of Line

This key moves the cursor to the leftmost choice.

Up Arrow

This key moves the cursor to the next choice above the current choice in the field. At the topmost choice, the cursor wraps to the bottom of the next choice to the right. At the top-rightmost choice, the cursor wraps to the bottom-leftmost choice in the field. Scrolling should be performed as required to ensure that the selection cursor remains visible.

Down Arrow

This key moves the cursor to the next choice below the current choice in the field. At the bottommost choice, the cursor wraps to the top of the next choice to the left. At the bottom-leftmost choice, the cursor wraps to the top-rightmost choice in the field. Scrolling should be performed as required to ensure that the selection cursor remains visible.

Left Arrow key

This key moves the cursor to the next choice to the left of the current choice in the field. At the leftmost choice, the cursor wraps to the rightmost choice below the current position in the field. At the bottom-leftmost choice, the cursor wraps to the top-rightmost choice in the field. Scrolling should be performed as required to ensure that the selection cursor remains visible.

Right Arrow

This key moves the cursor to the next choice to the right of the current choice in the field. At the rightmost choice, the cursor wraps to the leftmost choice above the current position in the field. At the top-rightmost choice, the cursor wraps to the bottom-leftmost choice in the field. Scrolling should be performed as required to ensure that the selection cursor remains visible.

Next Key

The Next key moves the cursor one position forward according to the logical sequence. On the boundary between segments of different orientations, this key steps through the transition states from one segment to the logically following one.

Previous Key

The Previous key moves the cursor one position backward according to the logical sequence. On the boundary between segments of different orientations, this key steps through the transition states from one segment to the logically preceding one.

Key Assignments

The following notes apply to the table below:

1. The key combinations in the table are used for Arabic and Hebrew keyboard functions and therefore must not be used in any way for any other purpose.

2. The entries for "Personal Computer" apply equally to native Personal Computer operation and to terminal emulation.

3. Current Arabic and Hebrew products implement subsets or variants of the functions appearing in the table. The table reflects the SAA and CUA interface guidelines for Arabic and Hebrew functions from now on.

Function	Key Combinations	Key Numbers
National Language		
Personal Computer	Alt+(right shift)	60,62 + 57
System/3X and AS/400	Alt+(right shift)	60,62 + 57
System/370	Alt+(right shift)	60,62 + 57
English Language		
Personal Computer	Alt+(left shift)	60,62 + 44
System/3X and AS/400	Alt+(left shift)	60,62 + 44
System/370	Alt+(left shift)	60,62 + 44
Push		
Personal Computer	Shift+NumLock	44,57 + 90
System/3X and AS/400	Push	90
System/370	Push	90
EndPush		
Personal Computer	Shift+(Pad /)	44,57 + 95
System/3X and AS/400	EndPush	95
System/370	EndPush	95

Function	Key Combinations	Key Numbers
Field Reverse		
Personal Computer	Alt+NumLock	60,62 + 90
System/3X and AS/400	Alt+Push	60,62 + 90
System/370	Alt+Push	60,62 + 90
AutoPush		
Personal Computer	Alt+(Pad /)	60,62 + 95
System/3X and AS/400	Alt+EndPush	60,62 + 95
System/370	Alt+EndPush	60,62 + 95
Next		
Personal Computer	Alt+(Pad 0)	60,62 + 99
System/3X and AS/400	Alt+(Pad 0)	60,62 + 99
System/370	Alt+(Pad 0)	60,62 + 99
Previous		
Personal Computer	Alt+(Pad .)	60,62 + 104
System/3X and AS/400	Alt+(Pad .)	60,62 + 104
System/370	Alt+(Pad .)	60,62 + 104
Screen Reverse		
Personal Computer	Alt+Enter (Hebrew)	60,62 + 43
	Alt+Newline (Arabic)	60,62 + 43
System/3X and AS/400	Alt+(Field Exit)	60,62 + 43
System/370	Alt+NewLine	60,62 + 43
AutoReverse		
Personal Computer	Alt+(Pad 5)	60,62 + 97
System/3X and AS/400	--	
System/370	Alt+(Pad 5)	60,62 + 97
Indicator Window		
Personal Computer	Alt+ScrollLock	60,62 + 125
System/3X and AS/400	--	
System/370	--	
ASD Active (Arabic)		
Personal Computer	Alt+(Pad 4)	60,62 + 92
System/3X and AS/400	Alt+(Pad 4)	60,62 + 92
System/370	Alt+(Pad 4)	60,62 + 92
Isolated Shape (Arabic)		
Personal Computer	Alt+(Pad 2)	60,62 + 98
System/3X and AS/400	Alt+(Pad 2)	60,62 + 98
System/370	Alt+(Pad 2)	60,62 + 98
Initial Shape (Arabic)		
Personal Computer	Alt+(Pad 1)	60,62 + 93
System/3X and AS/400	Alt+(Pad 1)	60,62 + 93
System/370	Alt+(Pad 1)	60,62 + 93

Function	Key Combinations	Key Numbers
Middle Shape (Arabic)		
Personal Computer	Alt+(Pad 7)	60,62 + 91
System/3X and AS/400	Alt+(Pad 7)	60,62 + 91
System/370	Alt+(Pad 7)	60,62 + 91
Final Shape (Arabic)		
Personal Computer	Alt+(Pad 8)	60,62 + 96
System/3X and AS/400	Alt+(Pad 8)	60,62 + 96
System/370	Alt+(Pad 8)	60,62 + 96
Passthrough Shape (Arabic)		
Personal Computer	Alt+(Pad 3)	60,62 + 103
System/3X and AS/400	Alt+(Pad 3)	60,62 + 103
System/370	Alt+(Pad 3)	60,62 + 103
FLD/X Shape (Arabic)		
Personal Computer	Alt+(Pad 9)	60,62 + 101
System/3X and AS/400	Alt+(Pad 9)	60,62 + 101
System/370	Alt+(Pad 9)	60,62 + 101
FLD/B Deshape (Arabic)		
Personal Computer	Alt+(Pad 6)	60,62 + 102
System/3X and AS/400	Alt+(Pad 6)	60,62 + 102
System/370	Alt+(Pad 6)	60,62 + 102

Appendix E. Translated Terms

This section contains a list of user terms that are part of the Common User Access architecture and that non-English speaking application developers use in their native languages. These terms, shown in English and translated, are presented to users in windows and in information about windows, such as messages, help, and documentation. Use only the designated translations for these terms.

In this appendix, the terms are translated into the following languages:

- Arabic
- Brazilian Portuguese
- Chinese
- Danish
- Dutch
- Finnish
- French and French (Canadian)
- German
- Hebrew
- Italian
- Japanese
- Korean
- Norwegian
- Portuguese
- Spanish
- Swedish.

Arabic

Arabic

Two terms have been added for the bidirectional CUA guidelines.

direction   The order of a sequence of objects which can be LTR or RTL. For instance, the typing direction (order of the generated characters) may be RTL or LTR.

orientation   Attribute of an object which can be LTR or RTL as defined by the order of its subordinate elements. For instance, a field has RTL orientation if its characters are ordered from right to left.

English Term	Arabic Term
action	تصرّف
active window	نافذة فعّالة
Apply	يطبّق
border	حد
button	زر
Cancel	الغاء
cascaded menu	قائمة متتابعة
cascading choice	اختيار متتابع
check box	صندوق اختيار
check mark	علامة اختيار
choice	اختيار
chord	ضغط مزدوج
Clear	اخلاء
click	ضغط
clipboard	مسودة
Close	انهاء
container	حاوية
contextual help	مساعدة سياقيّة
Continue	استمرار
Copy	نسخ
Create	تكوين
cursor	مؤشر
Cut	قطع
Delete	حذف
Delete folder	حذف حافظة
Deselect all	الغاء كل الاختيارات
dialog	حوار
Direction	اتجاه
direct manipulation	تحكّم مباشر
directory	دليل
do-not pointer	شبر الخطأ
double-click	ضغط ثنائي
drag	جر
drag and drop	جر ووضع
Edit	تحرير
emphasis	اظهار
entry field	مجال ادخال
field	مجال
field prompt	حث المجال
File	ملف
Find	ايجاد

Arabic

English Term	Arabic Term
folder	حافظة
Full menus	قوائم كاملة
General help	مساعدة عامة
group heading	عنوان مجموعة
Help	مساعدة
Help index	فهرس مساعدة
Hide	اخفاء
I-beam pointer	مشير الادخال
icon	شارة
inactive window	نافذة غير فعّالة
Include	تضمّن
information area	مساحة المعلومات
Keys help	مساعدة على المفاتيح
list button	زر كشف
manipulation button	زر تحكّم
Maximize	تكبير
maximize button	زر تكبير
menu	قائمة
menu bar	خط القائمة
menu-bar choice	اختيار خط القائمة
menu button	زر قائمة
menu choice	اختيار القائمة
message	رسالة
Minimize	تصغير
minimize button	زر تصغير
mouse	فأرة
mouse button	زر الفأرة
Move	تحريك
New	جديد
notebook	مفكرة
object	عنصر
Off	ايقاف
OK	حسنا
On	تشغيل
Open	فتح
Open as	فتح باسم
Options	اختيارات
Orientation	وجهة
palette	مجموعة
pane	جزء
Paste	لصق
Pause	توقّف موءقّت
pointer	مشير
pointing device	جهاز اشارة
pop-up menu	قائمة اظهار
Print	طباعة
Product information	معلومات المنتج
progress indicator	موشّر التقدّم
push button	زر ضاغط
radio button	زر دائري
Redo	اعادة
Reflection	انعكاس

English Term	Arabic Term
Refresh	تجديد
Refresh now	تجديد فوري
Rename	اعادة تسمية
Reset	ارجاع
Restore	استعادة
restore button	زر استعادة
Resume	استئناف
Retry	اعادة المحاولة
Save	حفظ
Save as	حفظ باسم
screen	شاشة
scroll bar	خط التصفّح
scroll box	صندوق التصفّح
select	اختيار
Select all	اختيار كل
Selected	مختار
selection button	زر اختيار
selection cursor	مؤشّر الاختيار
Settings	محدّدات
shortcut key	مفتاح مسار مختصر
Short menus	قوائم قصيرة
Size	حجم
slider	المنزلق
slider arm	ذراع الانزلاق
slider button	زر الانزلاق
Sort	فرز
spin button	زر الدوران
Split	انقسام
split box	صندوق منقسم
status area	مساحة الحالة
Stop	توقّف
system menu	قائمة النظام
system-menu symbol	رمز قائمة النظام
tabbed-divider page	فاصل الصفحات
text cursor	مؤشّر النص
title bar	خط العنوان
tool palette	مجموعة الأدوات
Tutorial	تعليمي
Undo	فك
Using help	استخدام المساعدة
View	مشاهدة
windows	نافذة
Windows	نافذة
Window list	كشف النافذه
Window title	عنوان النافذة
work area	مساحة العمل
workplace	منطقة العمل

Brazilian Portuguese

English Term	Brazilian Portuguese Term
action	ação
active window	janela ativa
Apply	Aplicar
border	margem
button	botão
Cancel	Cancelar
cascaded menu	menu em cascata
cascading choice	escolha em cascata
check box	caixa de verificação
check mark	visto
choice	escolha
chord	acorde
Clear	Limpar
click	clique
clipboard	memória temporária
Close	Fechar
container	contêiner
contextual help	auxílio contextual
Continue	Continuar
Copy	Copiar
Create	Criar
cursor	cursor
Cut	Remover
Delete	Eliminar
Delete folder	Pasta de eliminação
Deselect all	Cancelar seleções
dialog	diálogo
direct manipulation	manipulação direta
directory	diretório
do-not pointer	Indicador não-fazer
double-click	clique duplo
drag	arrastar
drag and drop	arrastar e fixar
Edit	Editar
emphasis	destaque
entry field	campo de entrada
field	campo
field prompt	orientador de campo
File	Arquivo
Find	Pesquisar
folder	pasta

English Term	Brazilian Portuguese Term
Full menus	Menus completos
General help	Auxílio geral
group heading	cabeçalho de grupo
Help	Auxílio
Help index	Índice remissivo de auxílio
Hide	Esconder
I-beam pointer	Indicador-I
icon	ícone
inactive window	janela inativa
Include	Incluir
information area	área de informação
Keys help	Auxílio para teclas
list button	botão de lista
manipulation button	botão de manipulação
Maximize	Maximizar
maximize button	botão de maximizar
menu	menu
menu bar	barra de opções
menu-bar choice	escolha da barra de opções
menu button	botão de menu
menu choice	opção de menu
message	mensagem
Minimize	Minimizar
minimize button	botão de minimizar
mouse	rato
mouse button	botão do rato
Move	Mover
New	Novo
notebook	arquivo de notas
object	objeto
Off	Desativar
OK	OK
On	Ativar
Open	Abrir
Open as	Abrir como
Options	Opções
palette	paleta
pane	painel
Paste	Anexar
Pause	Pausa
pointer	indicador
pointing device	dispositivo de indicação

Brazilian Portuguese

English Term	Brazilian Portuguese Term
pop-up menu	menu sobreposto
Print	Imprimir
Product information	Informações do produto
progress indicator	indicador de processamento
push button	botão de comando
radio button	botão de opção
Redo	Refazer
Reflection	Reflexo
Refresh	Atualizar
Refresh now	Atualizar imediatamente
Rename	Redenominar
Reset	Restabelecer
Restore	Restaurar
restore button	botão de restaurar
Resume	Prosseguir
Retry	Tentar novamente
Save	Salvar
Save as	Salvar como
screen	tela
scroll bar	barra de deslocamento
scroll box	caixa de deslocamento
select	selecionar
Select all	Selecionar todos
Selected	Selecionado
selection button	botão de seleção
selection cursor	cursor de seleção
Settings	Configuração
shortcut key	tecla de atalho
Short menus	Menus reduzidos
Size	Tamanho
slider	barra de rolagem
slider arm	caixa de rolagem
slider button	botão de rolagem
Sort	Classificar
spin button	botão giratório
Split	Dividir
split box	caixa de dividir
status area	área de status
Stop	Interromper
system menu	menu do sistema
system-menu symbol	símbolo de menu do sistema

tabbed-divider page	página divisória
text cursor	cursor de texto
title bar	barra de título
tool palette	paleta de ferramenta
Tutorial	Guia
Undo	Desfazer
Using help	Usando o auxílio
View	Ver
window	janela
Windows	Janelas
Window list	Lista de janelas
window title	título de janela
work area	área de trabalho
workplace	local de trabalho

Chinese

Chinese

English Term	Chinese Term
action	动作
active window	现用窗口
Apply	应用
border	边沿
button	按钮
Cancel	取消
cascaded menu	串接项目单
cascading choice	串接选择
check box	选择框
check mark	选择标记
choice	选择
chord	和弦
Clear	清除
click	咔嚓
clipboard	夹板
Close	关闭
container	容器
contextual help	原文求助
Continue	继续
Copy	复制
Create	建立
cursor	光标
Cut	切开
Delete	删除
Delete folder	删除文件夹
Deselect all	删除所有选择
dialog	对话
direct manipulation	直接操纵
directory	目录
do-not pointer	不准指示符
double-click	双重咔嚓
drag	牵引
drag and drop	牵引及放下
Edit	编辑
emphasis	强调
entry field	输入字段
field	字段
field prompt	字段提示
File	存入文件
Find	找寻
folder	文件夹
Full menus	完整项目单
General help	一般求助
group heading	组标题
Help	求助

English Term	Chinese Term
Help index	求助索引
Hide	隐藏
I-beam pointer	I型指示符
icon	图象
inactive window	待用窗口
Include	包括
information area	资料区
Keys help	各键求助
list button	列表按钮
manipulation button	操纵按钮
Maximize	尽量放大
maximize button	放大按钮
menu	项目单
menu bar	项目单杆
menu-bar choice	项目单杆选择
menu button	项目单按钮
menu choice	项目单选择
message	信息
Minimize	尽量缩小
minimize button	缩小按钮
mouse	鼠标器
mouse button	鼠标器按钮
Move	移动
New	新的
notebook	笔记簿
object	目标
Off	关闭
OK	完成
On	开启
Open	打开
Open as	打开为
Options	任选项
palette	颜色板
pane	窗格
Paste	粘贴
Pause	暂停
pointer	指示符
pointing device	指示设备
pop-up menu	上托项目单
Print	打印
Product information	产品资料
progress indicator	进度指示符
push button	按钮
radio button	选择按钮
Redo	重做
Reflection	反射
Refresh	刷新

Chinese

English Term	Chinese Term
Refresh now	即时刷新
Rename	重新命名
Reset	重置
Restore	复原
restore button	复原按钮
Resume	接续
Retry	重试
Save	保存
Save as	保存为
screen	屏幕
scroll bar	卷动杆
scroll box	卷动框
select	选择
Select all	选择全部
Selected	已选择
selection button	选择按钮
selection cursor	选择光标
Settings	设置
shortcut key	简捷键
Short menus	短项目单
Size	大小
slider	标尺
slider arm	标尺臂
slider button	标尺按钮
Sort	排序
spin button	旋转钮
Split	分割
split box	分割框
status area	状态区
Stop	停止
system menu	系统项目单
system-menu symbol	系统项目单符号
tabbed-divider page	标号区分页
text cursor	文本光标
title bar	标题杆
tool palette	工具颜色板
Tutorial	指导资料
Undo	取消
Using help	使用求助
View	视图
window	窗口
Windows	窗口
Window list	窗口列表
window title	窗口标题
work area	工作区
workplace	工作间

Danish

English Term	Danish Term
action	funktion
active window	aktivt vindue
Apply	Aktivér
border	ramme
button	knap
Cancel	Annullér
cascaded menu	undermenu
cascading choice	punkt med undermenu
check box	afkrydsningsfelt
check mark	hak
choice	valgmulighed
chord	trykke samtidigt
Clear	Ryd
click	klikke
clipboard	udklipsholder
Close	Luk
container	opbevaringssted
contextual help	specifik hjælp
Continue	Fortsæt
Copy	Kopiér
Create	Opret
cursor	markør
Cut	Klip
Delete	Slet
Delete folder	Makuleringsfolder
Deselect all	Ophæv markering af alle
dialog	dialog
direct manipulation	direkte manipulering
directory	bibliotek
do-not pointer	forbudsmarkør
double-click	dobbeltklikke
drag	trække
drag and drop	trække og placere
Edit	Redigér
emphasis	fremhævning
entry field	indtastningsfelt
field	felt
field prompt	ledetekst
File	Fil
Find	Søg
folder	folder

Danish

English Term	Danish Term
Full menus	Hele menuer
General help	Generel hjælp
group heading	gruppeoverskrift
Help	Hjælp
Help index	Stikord
Hide	Skjul
I-beam pointer	I-markør
icon	ikon
inactive window	ikke-aktivt vindue
Include	Inkludér
information area	informationsområde
Keys help	Taster
list button	oversigtsknap
manipulation button	manipuleringsknap
Maximize	Maksimér
maximize button	maksimérknap
menu	menu
menu bar	menulinie
menu-bar choice	punkt på menulinien
menu button	menuknap
menu choice	menupunkt
message	meddelelse
Minimize	Minimér
minimize button	minimérknap
mouse	mus
mouse button	museknap
Move	Flyt
New	Ny
notebook	notesbog
object	objekt
Off	Deaktiveret
OK	OK
On	Aktiveret
Open	Åbn
Open as	Åbn som
Options	Tilpasning
palette	palet
pane	delvindue
Paste	Klistre
Pause	Pause
pointer	pilmarkør
pointing device	pegeudstyr

pop-up menu	pop-op-menu
Print	Udskriv
Product information	Produktinformation
progress indicator	statusindikator
push button	trykknap
radio button	valgknap
Redo	Fortryd igen
Reflection	Afspejling
Refresh	Opfrisk
Refresh now	Opfrisk nu
Rename	Nyt navn
Reset	Reset
Restore	Gendan
restore button	gendanknap
Resume	Genoptag
Retry	Prøv igen
Save	Gem
Save as	Gem som
screen	skærm
scroll bar	bladringsfelt
scroll box	bladringsboks
select	vælge, markere
Select all	Markér alle
Selected	Markerede objekter
selection button	valgknap
selection cursor	valgmarkør
Settings	Indstillinger
shortcut key	genvejstast
Short menus	Korte menuer
Size	Tilpas størrelse
slider	skala
slider arm	skyder
slider button	finindstillingsknap
Sort	Sortér
spin button	bladringsknap
Split	Opdel
split box	opdelingsboks
status area	statusområde
Stop	Stop
system menu	systemmenu
system-menu symbol	symbol for systemmenu
tabbed-divider page	skilleblad
text cursor	tekstmarkør

Danish

English Term	Danish Term
title bar	overskriftslinie
tool palette	redskabspalet
Tutorial	Øveprogram
Undo	Fortryd
Using help	Brug af hjælp
View	Vis
window	vindue
Windows	Vinduer
Window list	Vinduesoversigt
window title	vinduesnavn
work area	arbejdsområde
workplace	arbejdsplads

Dutch

English Term	Dutch Term
action	actie
active window	werkvenster
Apply	Aanbrengen
border	kader
button	knop (1); knop (2); symbool (3)
Cancel	Annuleren
cascaded menu	vervolgmenu
cascading choice	optie met vervolgmenu
check box	aankruisvakje
check mark	vinkje
choice	optie
chord	combinatieklik
Clear	Verwijderen
click	klikken
clipboard	klembord
Close	Sluiten
container	opbergplaats
contextual help	specifieke Help
Continue	Doorgaan
Copy	Kopiëren
Create	Maken
cursor	cursor
Cut	Knippen
Delete	Wissen
Delete Folder	Wismap
Deselect all	Alle selecties opheffen
dialog	dialoog
direct manipulation	rechtstreekse actie
directory	directory
do-not pointer	verbodsaanwijzer
double-click	dubbelklikken
drag	slepen
drag and drop	slepen en neerzetten
Edit	Bewerken
emphasis	accentuering
entry field	invoerveld
field	veld
field prompt	aanwijzing
File	Bestand
Find	Zoeken

Dutch

English Term	Dutch Term
folder	map
Full menus	Volledige menu´s
General help	Algemene Help
group heading	groepskop
Help	Help
Help index	Help-index
Hide	Verbergen
I-beam pointer	invoegsymbool
icon	pictogram
inactive window	achtergrondvenster
Include	Opnemen
information area	informatiegebied
Keys help	Help bij toetsen
list button	lijstsymbool
manipulation button	actieknop
Maximize	Maximumvenster
maximize button	symbool Maximumvenster
menu	menu
menu bar	menubalk
menu-bar choice	menubalk-optie
menu button	menuknop
menu choice	menu-optie
message	bericht
Minimize	Pictogram
minimize button	symbool Pictogram
mouse	muis
mouse button	muisknop
Move	Verplaatsen
New	Nieuw
notebook	notitieboek
object	object
Off	Uit
OK	OK
On	Aan
Open	Openen
Open as	Openen als
Options	Opties
palette	palet
pane	deelvenster
Paste	Plakken
Pause	Onderbreken
pointer	aanwijzer

English Term	Dutch Term
pointing device	aanwijsapparaat
pop-up menu	voorgrondmenu
Print	Afdrukken
Product information	Info
progress indicator	voortgangsindicatie
push button	opdrachtknop
radio button	keuzerondje
Redo	Herstellen
reflection	reflectie
Refresh	Vernieuwen
Refresh now	Nu vernieuwen
Rename	Naam wijzigen
Reset	Beginwaarde; Beginwaarden
Restore	Vorig formaat
restore button	symbool Vorig formaat
Resume	Doorgaan
Retry	Herhalen
Save	Opslaan
Save as	Opslaan als
screen	beeldscherm
scroll bar	schuifbalk
scroll box	schuifblokje
select	selecteren
Select all	Alles selecteren
Selected	Geselecteerd
selection button	selectieknop
selection cursor	selectiecursor
Settings	Instellingen
shortcut key	sneltoets
Short menus	Beknopte menu´s
Size	Formaat wijzigen
slider	schuifregelaar
slider arm	schuifarm
slider button	regelknop
Sort	Sorteren
spin button	ringveldknop
Split	Splitsen
split box	splitsblokje
status area	statusgebied
Stop	Stoppen
system menu	systeemmenu
system-menu symbol	symbool Systeemmenu

Dutch

tabbed-divider page	tabblad
text cursor	tekstcursor
title bar	titelbalk
tool palette	werkpalet
Tutorial	Zelfstudie
Undo	Ongedaan maken
Using help	Help gebruiken
View	Beeld
window	venster
Windows	Vensters
Window list	Taakoverzicht
window title	venstertitel
work area	werkgebied
workplace	werkplek

Finnish

English Term	Finnish Term
action	toiminto
active window	actiivinen ikkuna
Apply	Aktivointi
border	kehys,reuna
button	painike, nappi
Cancel	Peruutus
cascaded menu	limittyvä valikko
cascading choice	limitysvalinta
check box	valintaruutu
check mark	valintamerkki
choice	valinta, vaihtoehto
chord	yhdistelmänapsautus
Clear	Tyhjennys
click	napsauttaa, napsautus
clipboard	leikepöytä
Close	Sulkeminen
container	säilö
contextual help	kohdeohje
Continue	Jatko
Copy	Kopiointi
Create	Luonti
cursor	kohdistin
Cut	Leikkaus
Delete	Poisto
Delete Folder	Kansion poisto
Deselect all	Valintojen peruutus
dialog	keskustelu, valintaikkuna
direct manipulation	suorakäsittely
directory	hakemisto
do-not pointer	kielto-osoitin
double-click	napsauttaa kahdesti, kaksoisnapsautus
drag	vetäminen, veto
drag and drop	veto ja pudotus
Edit	Muokkaus
emphasis	korostus
entry field	syöttökenttä
field	kenttä
field prompt	kentän selite
File	Tiedosto
Find	Etsintä

Finnish

English Term	Finnish Term
folder	kansio
Full menus	Pitkät valikot
General help	Yleisohje
group heading	ryhmäotsikko
Help	Ohje
Help index	Ohjehakemisto
Hide	Piilotus
I-beam pointer	I-osoitin
icon	kuvake
inactive window	passiivinen ikkuna
Include	Sisältö, sisällytys
information area	ilmoitusalue
Keys help	Näppäinohje
list button	luettelopainike
manipulation button	käsittelypainike
Maximize	Suurennus
maximize button	suurennuspainike
menu	valikko
menu bar	valikkorivi
menu-bar choice	valikkorivin vaihtoehto
menu button	valikkopainike
menu choice	valikon vaihtoehto
message	sanoma
Minimize	Pienennys
minimize button	pienennyspainike
mouse	hiiri
mouse button	hiiren painike
Move	Siirto
New	Uusi
notebook	muistikirja
object	objekti
Off	Ei käytössä
OK	OK
On	Käytössä
Open	Avaus
Open as	Avauksen valinta
Options	Muut valinnat, asetukset
palette	valikoima
pane	ruutu
Paste	Littäminen
Pause	Keskeytys
pointer	osoitin

English Term	Finnish Term
pointing device	paikannuslaite
pop-up menu	kohovalikko
Print	Tulostus (kirjoittimella)
Product information	Tietoja ohjelmasta
progress indicator	tilanneilmaisin
push button	painike
radio button	valintanappi
Redo	Uusinta
reflection	heijastus, heijaste
Refresh	Verestys
Refresh now	Verestys nyt
Rename	Nimeäminen
Reset	Palautus
Restore	Palautus
restore button	palautuspainike
Resume	Jatko
Retry	Uusinta
Save	Tallennus
Save as	Tallennus nimellä
screen	kuvaruutu
scroll bar	vierityspalkki
scroll box	vieritysruutu
select	valita, valinta
Select all	Kaikkien valinta
Selected	Valitut
selection button	valintapainike
selection cursor	valintakohdistin
Settings	Asetukset
shortcut key	pikanäppäin
Short menus	Lyhyet valikot
Size	Koon muutto
slider	liukusäädin
slider arm	liukuruutu
slider button	liukupainike
Sort	Lajittelu
spin button	selauspainike
Split	Jaettu ikkuna
split box	jakoruutu
status area	tilakenttä
Stop	Lopetus
system menu	ohjausvalikko
system-menu symbol	ohjausvalikon symboli

Finnish

tabbed-divider page	välilehti
text cursor	tekstikohdistin
title bar	otsikkorivi
tool palette	työkaluvalikoima
Tutorial	Opetusohjelma
Undo	Kumous
Using help	Ohjeiden käyttö
View	Näyttö, esitystapa
window	ikkuna
Window list	Ikkunaluettelo
Windows	Ikkunat
window title	ikkunan otsikko
work area	työalue
workplace	työpöytä

French and French (Canadian)

English Term	French Term
action	action
active window	fenêtre active
Apply	Validation
border	cadre
button	bouton
Cancel	Annulation
cascaded menu	menu en cascade
cascading choice	option en cascade
check box	case à cocher
check mark	marque
choice	option
chord	clic simultané
Clear	Effacement
click	clic
clipboard	presse-papiers
Close	Fermeture
container	contenant
contextual help	aide contextuelle
Continue	Continuer
Copy	Copie
Create	Création
cursor	curseur
Cut	Couper
Delete	Suppression
Delete folder	Dossier suppression
Deselect all	Désélecter tout
dialog	dialogue
direct manipulation	manipulation directe
directory	répertoire
do-not pointer	panneau d'interdiction
double-click	cliquer deux fois
drag	faire glisser
drag and drop	amener
Edit	Édition
emphasis	mise en évidence
entry field	zone d'entrée
field	zone
field prompt	indicatif de zone
File	Fichier
Find	Recherche
folder	dossier

French and French Canadian

English Term	French Term
Full menus	Menus complets
General help	Aide générale
group heading	en-tête de groupe
Help	Aide
Help index	Index d'aide
Hide	Cacher
I-beam pointer	pointeur en I
icon	icône
inactive window	fenêtre inactive
Include	Inclusion
information area	zone d'information
Keys help	Aide sur les touches
list button	bouton de listage
manipulation button	bouton de manipulation
Maximize	Agrandissement
maximize button	bouton d'agrandissement
menu	menu
menu bar	barre de menus
menu-bar choice	option de barre de menus
menu button	bouton de menu
menu choice	option de menu
message	message
Minimize	Réduction
minimize button	bouton de réduction
mouse	souris
mouse button	bouton de la souris
Move	Déplacement
New	Nouveau
notebook	bloc-notes
object	objet
Off	Hors fonction
OK	OK
On	En fonction
Open	Ouvrir
Open as	Ouvrir et présenter
Options	Options
palette	palette
pane	sous-fenêtre
Paste	Coller
Pause	Pause
pointer	pointeur
pointing device	périphérique de pointage

English Term	French Term
pop-up menu	incrustation
Print	Impression
Product information	Infos produit
progress indicator	indicateur de déroulement
push button	plaquette
radio button	pastille
Redo	Refaire
reflection	double
Refresh	Régénération
Refresh now	Régénération immédiate
Rename	Renommer
Reset	Réinitialisation
Restore	Restauration
restore button	bouton de restauration
Resume	Reprendre
Retry	Reprise
Save	Sauvegarde
Save as	Sauvegarde en
screen	écran
scroll bar	barre de défilement
scroll box	case de défilement
select	sélection
Select all	Sélecter tout
Selected	Objets sélectés
selection button	bouton de sélection
selection cursor	curseur de sélection
Settings	Paramètres
Short menus	Menus courts
shortcut key	raccourci-clavier
Size	Dimensionnement
slider	règle
slider arm	index de la règle
slider button	bouton de la règle
Sort	Tri
spin button	sélecteur rotatif
Split	Partager
split box	marque de partage
status area	zone d'état
Stop	Stop
system menu	menu système
system-menu symbol	symbole de menu système
tabbed-divider page	intercalaire

French and French Canadian

text cursor	curseur texte
title bar	barre de titre
tool palette	palette d'outils
Tutorial	Tutoriel
Undo	Défaire
Using help	Utiliser l'aide
View	Visualisation
window	fenêtre
Windows	Fenêtres
Window list	Liste de fenêtres
window title	titre de fenêtre
work area	zone de travail
workplace	bureau électronique

German

The German translations may change in order to be kept up to date.

English Term	German Term
action	Aktion
active window	aktives Fenster
Apply	Anwenden
border	Rahmen
button	Taste, Knopf
Cancel	Abbrechen
cascaded menu	Untermenüfenster
cascading choice	weiterführende Auswahl
check box	Markierungsfeld
check mark	Haken
choice	Auswahl
chord	gleichzeitiges Klicken
Clear	Löschen
click	klicken
clipboard	Zwischenablage
Close	Schließen
container	Behälter
contextual help	Kontexthilfe
Continue	Weiter
Copy	Kopieren
Create	Erstellen
cursor	Cursor
Cut	Trennen
Delete	Löschen
Delete Folder	Ordner löschen
Deselect all	Auswahl zurücknehmen
dialog	Dialog
direct manipulation	direkte Manipulation
directory	Verzeichnis
do-not pointer	Verbotssymbol
double-click	doppelt klicken
drag	ziehen
drag and drop	ziehen und übergeben
Edit	Editieren
emphasis	Hervorhebung
entry field	Eingabefeld
field	Feld
field prompt	Feldbezeichnung
File	Datei
Find	Suchen

German

English Term	German Term
folder	Ordner
Full menus	Gesamtmenüs
General help	Allgemeine Hilfe
group heading	Gruppenüberschrift
Help	Hilfe
Help index	Hilfeindex
Hide	Verdecken
I-beam pointer	Textcursor
icon	Symbol
inactive window	inaktives Fenster
Include	Anzeigeoptionen
information area	Informationsbereich
Keys help	Hilfe für Tasten
list button	Listenknopf
manipulation button	Manipulationstaste
Maximize	maximale Größe
maximize button	Knopf für maximale Größe
menu	Menü
menu bar	Menüauswahl
menu-bar choice	Menüleistenauswahl
menu button	Menüknopf
menu choice	Menüauswahl
message	Nachricht
Minimize	Symbolgröße
minimize button	Knopf für Symbolgröße
mouse	Maus
mouse button	Maustaste
Move	Verschieben
New	Neu
notebook	Notizbuch
object	Objekt
Off	Aus
OK	OK
On	Ein
Open	Öffnen
Open as	Öffnen als
Options	Optionen
palette	Palette
pane	Teilfenster
Paste	Einfügen
pointer	Zeiger
pointing device	Zeigereinheit

English Term	German Term
pop-up menu	Dialogmenü
Print	Drucken
Product information	Produktinformation
progress indicator	Statusanzeigefeld
push button	Druckknopf
radio button	Radioknopf
Redo	Widerruf zurücknehmen
reflection	Gespiegeltes Symbol
Refresh	Neuanzeige
Refresh now	Neuanzeige sofort
Rename	Umbenennen
Reset	Zurücksetzen
Restore	Wiederherstellen
restore button	Knopf für Wiederherstellung
Resume	Wiederaufnehmen
Retry	Wiederholen
Save	Sichern
Save as	Sichern als
screen	Bildschirm
scroll bar	Schiebeleiste
scroll box	Schiebefeld
select	auswählen
Select all	Alles auswählen
Selected	Ausgewählt
selection button	Auswahltaste
selection cursor	Auswahlcursor
Settings	Einstellungen
shortcut key	Direktaufruf
Short menus	Kurzmenüs
Size	Größe ändern
slider	Schiebeleiste
slider arm	Schiebefeld
slider button	Schiebepfeil
Sort	Sortieren
spin button	Drehknopf
Split	Geteiltes Fenster
split box	Trennmarke
status area	Statusbereich
Stop	Stoppen
system menu	Systemmenü
system-menu symbol	Systemmenüsymbol
tabbed-divider page	Registerblatt

German

text cursor	Textcursor
title bar	Titelleiste
tool palette	Funktionspalette
Tutorial	Lerntext
Undo	Widerrufen
Using help	Hilfe für Hilfe
View	Anzeige
window	Fenster
Windows	Fenster
Window list	Fensterliste
window title	Fenstertitel
work area	Arbeitsbereich
workplace	Arbeitsoberfläche

Hebrew

Two terms have been added for the bidirectional CUA guidelines.

direction   the order of a sequence of objects which can be LTR or RTL. For instance, the typing direction (order of the generated characters) may be RTL or LTR.

orientation   attribute of an object which can be LTR or RTL as defined by the order of its subordinate elements. For instance, a field has RTL orientation if its characters are ordered from right to left.

Hebrew

English Term	Hebrew Term
action	פעולה
active window	חלון פעיל
Apply	יישם
border	גבול
button	כפתור
Cancel	בטל
cascaded menu	תפריט מדורג
cascading choice	בחירה מדורגת
check box	תא תיוג
check mark	תג
choice	ברירה
chord	אקורד
Clear	נקה
click	קליק
clipboard	משטח עזר
Close	סגור
container	מיכל
contextual help	עזרה בהקשר
Continue	המשך
Copy	העתק
Create	יצר
cursor	סמן
Cut	גזור
Delete	מחק
Delete Folder	אוגדן למחיקה
Deselect all	בטל כל הבחירות
dialog	דו-שיח
direct manipulation	תפעול ישיר
direction	כיוון
directory	מדריך
do-not pointer	מחוון לא-כאן
double-click	קליק כפול
drag	גרור
drag and drop	גרור והנח
Edit	ערוך
emphasis	הדגשה
entry field	שדה קלט
field	שדה
field prompt	הנחיה לשדה
File	תייק
Find	מצא
folder	אוגדן
Full menus	תפריטים מלאים

English Term	Hebrew Term
General help	עזרה כללית
group heading	כותרת קבוצה
Help	עזרה
Help index	מפתח עזרה
Hide	החבא
I-beam pointer	מחוון I
icon	ציור
inactive window	חלון לא-פעיל
Include	הכלל
information area	אזור מידע
Keys help	עזרה למקשים
list button	לחצן רשימה
manipulation button	לחצן תפעול
Maximize	הגדל מירבית
maximize button	לחצן הגדלה
menu	תפריט
menu bar	פס תפריט
menu-bar choice	בחירה מפס תפריט
menu button	לחצן תפריט
menu choice	בחירה מתפריט
message	הודעה
Minimize	מזער
minimize button	לחצן מיזעור
mouse	עכבר
mouse button	לחצן עכבר
Move	העבר
New	חדש
notebook	דפדפת
object	רכיב
Off	השבת
OK	OK
On	הפעל
Open	פתח
Open as	פתח כ...
Options	אופציות
Orientation	כיווניות
palette	מגוון צבעים
pane	שמשה
Paste	הדבק
pointer	מחוון
pointing device	אביזר הצבעה
pop-up menu	תפריט צץ
Print	הדפס
Product information	מידע על המוצר
progress indicator	מחוון התקדמות
push button	לחצן
radio button	לחיץ רדיו
Redo	עשה שוב

Hebrew

English Term	Hebrew Term
Reflection	השתקפות
Refresh	רענון
Refresh now	רענן עכשיו
Rename	שינוי שם
Reset	איפוס
Restore	שחזר
restore button	לחצן שחזור
Resume	שוב
Retry	נסה שוב
Save	שמור
Save as	שמור כ...
screen	מרקע
scroll bar	פס גלילה
scroll box	תיבת גלילה
select	בחר
Select all	בחר הכל
Selected	נבחרים
selection button	לחצן בחירה
selection cursor	סמן בחירה
Settings	הצבות
Short menus	תפריטים מקוצרים
shortcut key	מקש מהיר
Size	גודל
slider	מחלק
slider arm	ידית מחלק
slider button	לחצן מחלק
Sort	מיין
spin button	כפתור מחזורי
Split	פצל
split box	תיבת פיצול
status area	איזור מצב
Stop	עצור
system menu	תפריט מערכת
system-menu symbol	סמל תפריט-מערכת
tabbed-divider page	דף חוצץ
text cursor	סמן לתמליל
title bar	פס כותרת
tool palette	מגש כלים
Tutorial	הדרכה
Undo	חזור בך
Using help	שימוש בעזרה
View	עיין
Window	חלון
Window list	רשימת חלונות
window title	כותרת חלון
work area	איזור עבודה
workplace	שטח עבודה

Italian

English Term	Italian Term
action	azione
active window	finestra attiva
Apply	Applicare
border	bordo
button	tastino
Cancel	Annullare
cascaded menu	menu a cascata
cascading choice	scelta a cascata
check box	casella di spunta
check mark	segno di spunta
choice	scelta
chord	accordo
Clear	Pulire
click	fare click
clipboard	notes
Close	Chiudere
container	contenitore
contextual help	aiuto specifico
Continue	Continuare
Copy	Copiare
Create	Creare
cursor	cursore
Cut	Ritagliare
Delete	Cancellare
Delete Folder	Cancellare cartella
Deselect all	Annullare selezioni
dialog	dialogo
direct manipulation	manipolazione diretta
directory	indirizzario
do-not pointer	puntatore di divieto
double-click	fare doppio click
drag	trascinare
drag and drop	trascinare e rilasciare
Edit	Editare
emphasis	enfasi
entry field	campo di immissione
field	campo
field prompt	richiesta per il campo
File	File
Find	Cercare
folder	cartella

Italian

English Term	Italian Term
Full menus	Menu completi
General help	Aiuto generale
group heading	intestazione del gruppo
Help	Aiuto
Help index	Indice analitico dell´aiuto
Hide	Nascondere
I-beam pointer	puntatore a I
icon	icona
inactive window	finestra non attiva
Include	Includere
information area	area di informazione
Keys help	Aiuto per tasti funzione
list button	pulsante per lista
manipulation button	tasto per manipolazione
Maximize	Ingrandire al massimo
maximize button	pulsante per ingrandimento al massimo
menu	menu
menu bar	barra menu
menu-bar choice	scelta della barra menu
menu button	tasto di menu
menu choice	scelta del menu
message	messaggio
Minimize	ridurre al minimo
minimize button	pulsante per riduzione al minimo
mouse	mouse
mouse button	tastino del mouse
Move	Spostare
New	Nuovo
notebook	taccuino
object	oggetto
Off	Spento
OK	OK
On	Acceso
Open	Aprire
Open as	Aprire come
Options	Opzioni
palette	tavolozza
pane	riquadro di finestra
Paste	Attaccare
Pause	Pausa

pointer	puntatore
pointing device	dispositivo di puntamento
pop-up menu	menu concatenato
Print	Stampare
Product information	Informazioni sul prodotto
progress indicator	indicatore di avanzamento
push button	pulsante
radio button	pallino
Redo	Rifare
reflection	riflessione
Refresh	Aggiornamento
Refresh now	Aggiornare ora
Rename	Rinominare
Reset	Reimpostare
Restore	Ripristinare
restore button	pulsante di ripristino
Resume	Riprendere
Retry	Riprovare
Save	Salvare
Save as	Salvare con nome
screen	schermo
scroll bar	barra di scorrimento
scroll box	indicatore di posizione
select	selezionare
Select all	Selezionare tutto
Selected	Selezionato
selection button	pulsante di selezione
selection cursor	cursore di selezione
Settings	Impostazioni
shortcut key	tasto di accesso rapido
Short menus	Menu sintetici
Size	Dimensione
slider	slitta
slider arm	indicatore della slitta
slider button	pulsante della slitta
Sort	Ordinare
spin button	pulsante per rotazione
Split	Dividere
split box	cassella di divisione
status area	area di stato
Stop	Arrestare
system menu	menu di sistema

Italian

English Term	Italian Term
system-menu symbol	simbolo del menu di sistema
tabbed-divider page	separatore pagine
text cursor	cursore del testo
title bar	barra del titolo
tool palette	tavola degli strumenti
Tutorial	Supporto didattico
Undo	Regressione
Using help	Utilizzo dell´aiuto
View	Visualizzare
window	finestra
Window list	Elenco finestre
Windows	Finestre
window title	titolo di finestra
work area	area di lavoro
workplace	postazione di lavoro

Japanese

English Term	Japanese Term
action	アクション
active window	活動ウィンドウ
Apply	適用
border	ボーダー
button	ボタン
Cancel	取消
cascaded menu	二次メニュー
cascading choice	二次メニュー選択項目
check box	チェック・ボックス
check mark	チェック・マーク
choice	選択項目，項目
chord	ボタン組合せ
Clear	消去
click	クリック
clipboard	クリップボード
Close	クローズ
container	コンテナ
contextual help	項目ヘルプ
Continue	継続
Copy	複写
Create	作成
cursor	カーソル
Cut	切抜き
Delete	削除
Delete Folder	フォルダー削除
Deselect all	全選択解除
dialog	対話，ダイアログ
direct manipulation	ダイレクト・マニピュレーション（直接操作）
directory	ディレクトリー
do-not pointer	禁止ポインター
double-click	ダブルクリック
drag	ドラッグ
drag and drop	ドラッグ・ドロップ
Edit	編集
emphasis	強調
entry field	入力フィールド
field	フィールド
field prompt	フィールド・プロンプト
File	ファイル
Find	検索
folder	フォルダー
Full menus	全メニュー
General help	一般ヘルプ
group heading	グループ見出し
Help	ヘルプ

English Term	Japanese Term
Help index	ヘルプ索引
Hide	隠す
I-beam pointer	I形ポインター
icon	アイコン
inactive window	非活動ウィンドウ
Include	選択表示
information area	情報域
Keys help	キー・ヘルプ
list button	リスト・ボタン
manipulation button	操作ボタン
Maximize	最大化
maximize button	最大化ボタン
menu	メニュー
menu bar	メニュー・バー
menu-bar choice	メニューバー選択
menu button	メニュー・ボタン
menu choice	メニュー選択
message	メッセージ
Minimize	最小化
minimize button	最小化ボタン
mouse	マウス
mouse button	マウス・ボタン
Move	移動
New	新規
notebook	ノート
object	オブジェクト
Off	オフ
OK	了解
On	オン
Open	オープン
Open as	オープン
Options	オプション
palette	パレット
pane	区画
Paste	貼付け
Pause	保留
pointer	ポインター
pointing device	指示装置
pop-up menu	ポップアップ・メニュー
Print	印刷
Product information	製品情報
progress indicator	進行標識
push button	押しボタン
radio button	ラジオ・ボタン
Redo	再実行
Reflection	反映
Refresh	最新表示
Refresh now	即時最新表示

Japanese

English Term	Japanese Term
Rename	名前変更
Reset	リセット
Restore	復元
restore button	復元ボタン
Resume	レジューム
Retry	再実行
Save	保管
Save as	別名保管
screen	画面
scroll bar	スクロール・バー
scroll box	スクロール・ボックス
select	選択
Select all	全選択
Selected	選択
selection button	選択ボタン
selection cursor	選択カーソル
Settings	設定
Short menus	簡略メニュー
shortcut key	簡略キー
Size	サイズ
slider	スライダー
slider arm	スライダー標識
slider button	スライダー・ボタン
Sort	分類
spin button	スピン・ボタン
Split	分割
split box	分割ボックス
Split window	分割ウィンドウ
status area	状況域
Stop	停止
system menu	システム・メニュー
system-menu symbol	システムメニュー・シンボル
tabbed-divider page	タブ区分ページ
text cursor	テキスト・カーソル
title bar	タイトル・バー
tool palette	ツール・パレット
Tutorial	学習
Undo	取消
Using help	ヘルプ使用法
View	表示
wait pointer	お待たせポインター
window	ウィンドウ
Window	ウィンドウ
Window list	ウィンドウ・リスト
window title	ウィンドウ・タイトル
work area	作業域
workplace	ワークプレース

Korean

English Term	Korean Term
action	조치
active window	활동 창
Apply	적용
border	경계
button	단추
Cancel	취소
cascaded menu	중첩 메뉴
cascading choice	연속 선택
check box	선택란
check mark	체크 표시
choice	선택, 선택사항
chord	조합
Clear	지움
click	누름, 눌렀다 뗌
clipboard	클립보드
Close	닫기
container	용기
contextual help	문맥 도움말
Continue	계속
Copy	복사
Create	작성
cursor	커서
Cut	자름
Delete	삭제
Delete Folder	폴더 삭제
Deselect all	모든 선택 취소
dialog	대화
direct manipulation	직접 조작
directory	등록부
do-not pointer	사용 불가능 지시기
double-click	두번 누름, 두번 눌렀다 뗌
drag	끌기
drag and drop	끌어서 놓기
Edit	편집
emphasis	강조
entry field	입력 필드
field	필드
field prompt	필드 프롬프트
File	파일
Find	찾기
folder	폴더
Full menus	전체 메뉴
General help	일반 도움말
group heading	그룹 표제
Help	도움말
Help index	도움말 색인

Korean

English Term	Korean Term
Hide	숨겨짐
I-beam pointer	I-모양
icon	아이콘
inactive window	비활동 창
Include	포함
information area	참조 영역
Keys help	키 도움말
list button	일람 단추
manipulation button	조작 단추
Maximize	최대화
maximize button	최대화 단추
menu	메뉴
menu bar	메뉴 막대
menu-bar choice	메뉴 막대 선택사항
menu button	메뉴 단추
menu choice	메뉴 선택사항
message	메세지
Minimize	최소화
minimize button	최소화 단추
mouse	마우스
mouse button	마우스 단추
Move	이동
New	신규
notebook	공책
object	오브젝트
Off	오프
OK	OK
On	온
Open	열기
Open as	표시 방법 지정 열기
Options	선택, 선택 항목
palette	파레트
pane	분할 창
Paste	붙임
Pause	정지
pointer	지시기
pointing device	지시 장치
pop-up menu	팝업 메뉴
Print	인쇄
Product information	제품 소개
progress indicator	진행 표시기
push button	누름 단추
radio button	라디오 단추
Redo	재변경
Reflection	영상
Refresh	재표시
Refresh now	즉시 재표시

English Term	Korean Term
Rename	재명명
Reset	재설정
Restore	복원
restore button	복원 단추
Resume	재개
Retry	재시도
Save	보관
Save as	파일명 지정 보관
screen	화면
scroll bar	화면이동 막대
scroll box	화면이동 표시란
select	선택
Select all	모두 선택
Selected	선택된 사항
selection button	선택 단추
selection cursor	선택 커서
Settings	설정
Short menus	단축 메뉴
shortcut key	지름길 키
Size	크기
slider	슬라이더
slider arm	슬라이더 암
slider button	슬라이더 단추
Sort	분류
spin button	스핀 단추
Split	분할
split box	분할 박스
Split window	분할 창
status area	상태 영역
Stop	종료
system menu	시스템 메뉴
system-menu symbol	시스템 메뉴 기호
tabbed-divider page	간지
text cursor	원문 커서
title bar	제목 막대
tool palette	도구 빠레뜨
Tutorial	학습
Undo	복원
Using help	도움말 사용법
View	열람
window	창
Windows	창
Window list	창 일람표
window title	창 제목
work area	작업 영역
workplace	작업 구역

Norwegian

Norwegian

English Term	Norwegian Term
action	handling
active window	aktivt vindu
Apply	Prøve
border	ramme
button	knapp
Cancel	Avbryt
cascaded menu	undermeny
cascading choice	valg med undermeny
check box	valgrute
check mark	hake
choice	valg
chord	klikke samtidig
Clear	Fjerne
click	klikke
clipboard	utklippstavle
Close	Lukke
container	container
contextual help	spesifikk hjelp
Continue	Fortsett
Copy	Kopiere
Create	Opprette
cursor	markør
Cut	Klippe ut
Delete	Slette
Delete folder	Sletting
Deselect all	Oppheve valg av alle
dialog	dialog
direct manipulation	direkte manipulering
directory	katalog
do-not pointer	forbudsskilt
double-click	dobbeltklikke
drag	dra
drag and drop	dra og slippe
Edit	Redigere
emphasis	utheving
entry field	inndatafelt
field	felt
field prompt	ledetekst
File	Fil
Find	Søke
folder	mappe

English Term	Norwegian Term
Full menus	Fullstendige menyer
General help	Generell hjelp
group heading	gruppeoverskrift
Help	Hjelp
Help index	Stikkord
Hide	Skjule
I-beam pointer	skrivepeker
icon	ikon
inactive window	passivt vindu
Include	Ta med
information area	informasjonsområde
Keys help	Tasthjelp
list button	listeknapp
manipulation button	manipuleringsknapp
Maximize	Maksimere
maximize button	maksimeringsknapp
menu	meny
menu bar	handlingslinje
menu-bar choice	valg på handlingslinjen
menu button	menyknapp
menu choice	menyvalg
message	melding
Minimize	Minimere
minimize button	minimeringsknapp
mouse	mus
mouse button	museknapp
Move	Flytte
New	Ny / Nytt
notebook	notisbok
object	objekt
Off	Av
OK	Enter
On	På
Open	Åpne
Open as	Åpne som
Options	Alternativer
palette	palett
pane	vindussegment
Paste	Lime inn
Pause	Pause
pointer	peker
pointing device	pekeenhet

Norwegian

English Term	Norwegian Term
pop-up menu	tilleggsmeny
Print	Skrive ut
Product information	Om programmet...
progress indicator	statusindikator
push button	skjermtast
radio button	valgknapp
Redo	Gjøre om
reflection	speilbilde
Refresh	Fornye
Refresh now	Fornye nå
Rename	Endre navn
Reset	Tilbakestill
Restore	Gjenopprette
restore button	gjenopprettingsknapp
Resume	Gjenoppta
Retry	Prøv igjen
Save	Lagre
Save as	Lagre som
screen	skjerm
scroll bar	blafelt
scroll box	posisjonsviser
select	velge
Select all	Velge alle
Selected	Valgte
selection button	valgknapp
selection cursor	valgmarkør
Settings	Innstillinger
shortcut key	direktetast
Short menus	Korte menyer
Size	Endre størrelse
slider	skala
slider arm	skalaindikator
slider button	skalaknapp
Sort	Sortere
spin button	blaknapp
Split	Dele
split box	delemerke
status area	statusområde
Stop	Stopp
system menu	systemmeny
system-menu symbol	systemmeny-symbol
tabbed-divider page	skilleark

text cursor	tekstmarkør
title bar	tittellinje
tool palette	verktøypalett
Tutorial	Opplæring
Undo	Oppheve
Using help	Bruke hjelp
View	Se på
window	vindu
Window list	Vindusoversikt
Windows	Vinduer
window title	vindustittel
work area	arbeidsområde
workplace	arbeidsvindu

Portuguese

English Term	Portuguese Term
action	acção
active window	janela ativa
Apply	Aplicar
border	contorno
button	botão; selector
Cancel	Cancelar
cascaded menu	submenu
cascading choice	opção com submenu
check box	selector de confirmação
check mark	marca de confirmação
choice	opção
chord	premir simultaneamente
Clear	Limpar
click	fazer clique
clipboard	área de transição
Close	Fechar
container	contentor
contextual help	ajuda contextual
Continue	Continuar
Copy	Copiar
Create	Criar
cursor	cursor
Cut	Cortar
Delete	Eliminar
Delete Folder	Eliminar Arquivador
Deselect all	Desmarcar tudo
dialog	diálogo
direct manipulation	manipulação directa
directory	directório
do-not pointer	indicador de proibição
double-click	fazer duplo clique
drag	arrastar
drag and drop	arrastar e largar
Edit	Editar
emphasis	realce
entry field	campo de entrada
field	campo
field prompt	identificação do campo
File	Ficheiro
Find	Encontrar
folder	arquivador

English Term	Portuguese Term
Full menus	Menus completos
General help	Ajuda geral
group heading	título do grupo
Help	Ajuda
Help index	Índice da Ajuda
Hide	Ocultar
I-beam pointer	indicador em I
icon	ícone
inactive window	janela inativa
Include	Incluir
information area	área de informações
Keys help	Ajuda para teclas
list button	botão de lista
manipulation button	botão de manipulação
Maximize	Maximizar
maximize button	botão de maximização
menu	menu
menu bar	barra de acções
menu-bar choice	opção da barra de acções
menu button	botão de menu
menu choice	opção de menu
message	mensagem
Minimize	Minimizar
minimize button	botão de minimização
mouse button	botão do rato
mouse	rato
Move	Mover
New	Novo
notebook	bloco de notas
object	objecto
Off	Inactivo
OK	OK
On	Activo
Open	Abrir
Open as	Abrir como
Options	Opções
palette	paleta
pane	área da janela
Paste	Colar
Pause	Pausa
pointer	indicador
pointing device	dispositivo indicador

Portuguese

English Term	Portuguese Term
pop-up menu	menu emergente
Print	Imprimir
Product information	Informação sobre o produto
progress indicator	indicador de progressão
push button	selector de acção
radio button	selector de opção
Redo	Refazer
reflection	duplicação
Refresh	Actualizar
Refresh now	Atualizar agora
Rename	Mudar o nome
Reset	Repor
Restore	Restaurar
restore button	botão de restauro
Resume	Retomar
Retry	Repetir
Save	Guardar
Save as	Guardar como
screen	écran
scroll bar	barra de deslocamento
scroll box	selector de deslocamento
select	seleccionar
Select all	Seleccionar tudo
Selected	Seleccionados
selection button	botão de selecção
selection cursor	cursor de selecção
Settings	Definições
shortcut key	tecla de acção directa
Short menus	Menus resumidos
Size	Dimensionar
slider	escala
slider arm	selector de escala
slider button	botão de escala
Sort	Ordenar
spin button	selector rotativo
Split	Dividir
split box	selector de divisão
status area	área de estado
Stop	Parar
system menu	menu do sistema
system-menu symbol	símbolo do menu do sistema

tabbed-divider page	página do bloco
text cursor	cursor de texto
title bar	barra do título
tool palette	paleta de funções
Tutorial	Inciação
Undo	Desfazer
Using help	Utilizar a Ajuda
View	Ver
window	janela
Window list	Lista
Windows	Janelas
window title	título da janela
work area	área de trabalho
workplace	interface de trabalho

Spanish

Spanish

English Term	Spanish Term
action	acción
active window	ventana activa
Apply	Aplicar
border	marco
button	botón
Cancel	Cancelar
cascaded menu	menú en cascada
cascading choice	elección de cascada
check box	recuadro de selección
check mark	marca de selección
choice	elección
chord	acorde
Clear	Limpiar
click	pulsar el botón
clipboard	área común
Close	Cerrar
container	contenedor
contextual help	ayuda según contexto
Continue	Continuar
Copy	Copiar
Create	Crear
cursor	cursor
Cut	Cortar
Delete	Suprimir
Delete Folder	Suprimir Carpeta
Deselect all	Anular selecciones
dialog	diálogo
direct manipulation	manipulación directa
directory	directorio
do-not pointer	puntero de prohibición
double-click	doble pulsación
drag	arrastrar
drag and drop	arrastrar y soltar
Edit	Editar
emphasis	énfasis
entry field	campo de entrada
field	campo
field prompt	indicador de campo
File	Archivo
Find	Encontrar
folder	carpeta

English Term	Spanish Term
Full menus	Menús completos
General help	Ayuda general
group heading	cabecera de grupo
Help	Ayuda
Help index	Indice de la ayuda
Hide	Ocultar
I-beam pointer	indicador en I
icon	icono
inactive window	ventana inactiva
Include	Incluir
information area	área de información
Keys help	Ayuda para teclas
list button	botón de lista
manipulation button	botón de manipulación
Maximize	Maximizar
maximize button	botón de maximizar
menu	menú
menu bar	barra de menús
menu-bar choice	elección de barra de menús
menu button	botón de menú
menu choice	elección de menú
message	mensaje
Minimize	Minimizar
minimize button	botón de minimizar
mouse	ratón
mouse button	botón de ratón
Move	Mover
New	Nuevo
notebook	cuaderno
object	objeto
Off	Desactivar
OK	Bien
On	Activar
Open	Abrir
Open as	Abrir como
Options	Opciones
palette	paleta
pane	panel
Paste	Pegar
Pause	Pausa
pointer	puntero
pointing device	dispositivo de puntero

Spanish

English Term	Spanish Term
pop-up menu	menú emergente
Print	Imprimir
Product information	Información sobre el producto
progress indicator	indicador de progreso
push button	pulsador
radio button	botón de selección
Redo	Rehacer
Reflection	Reflejo
Refresh	Renovar
Refresh now	Renovar ahora
Rename	Renombrar
Reset	Restablecer
Restore	Restaurar
restore button	botón de restaurar
Resume	Reanudar
Retry	Reintentar
Save	Guardar
Save as	Guardar como
screen	pantalla
scroll bar	área de desplazamiento
scroll box	recuadro de desplazamiento
select	seleccionar
Select all	Seleccionar todo
Selected	Seleccionado
selection button	botón de selección
selection cursor	cursor de selección
Settings	Valores
shortcut key	tecla de atajo
Short menus	Menús abreviados
Size	Tama]o
slider	graduador
slider arm	nivel del graduador
slider button	botón del graduador
Sort	Ordenar
spin button	selector cíclico
Split	Partir
split box	recuadro de partición
status area	área de estado
Stop	Parar
system menu	menú del sistema

system-menu symbol	símbolo del menú del sistema
tabbed-divider page	página separadora
text cursor	cursor de texto
title bar	área de título
tool palette	paleta de utensilios
Tutorial	Guía de Aprendizaje
Undo	Deshacer
Using help	Utilizar ayuda
View	Ver
window	ventana
Windows	Ventanas
Window list	Lista de ventanas
window title	Título de la ventana
work area	ärea de trabajo
workplace	lugar de trabajo

Swedish

Swedish

English Term	Swedish Term
action	åtgärd
active window	aktivt fönster
Apply	Prova
border	ram
button	knapp
Cancel	Avbryt
cascaded menu	undermeny
cascading choice	alternativ med undermeny
check box	kryssruta
check mark	bock
choice	alternativ
chord	kombinationsklicka
Clear	Ta bort
click	klicka
clipboard	urklipp
Close	Stäng
container	behållare
contextual help	relaterad hjälp
Continue	Fortsätt
Copy	Kopiera
Create	Skapa
cursor	markör
Cut	Klipp ut
Delete	Ta bort
Delete folder	Borttagsmapp
Deselect all	Avmarkera alla
dialog	dialog
direct manipulation	direkthantering
directory	katalog
do-not pointer	stopptecken
double-click	dubbelklicka
drag	dra
drag and drop	dra och släpp
Edit	Redigera
emphasis	framhävning
entry field	indatafält
field	fält
field prompt	ledtext
File	Arkiv
Find	Sök
folder	mapp

English Term	Swedish Term
Full menus	Långa menyer
General help	Allmän hjälp
group heading	grupprubrik
Help	Hjälp
Help index	Hjälpindex
Hide	Göm
I-beam pointer	textmarkör
icon	ikon
inactive window	inaktivt fönster
Include	Inkludera
information area	informationsfält
Keys help	Tangentfunktioner
list button	listknapp
manipulation button	direkthanteringsknapp
Maximize	Maximera
maximize button	maximeringsknapp
menu	meny
menu bar	menyrad
menu-bar choice	alternativ på menyraden
menu button	menyknapp
menu choice	menyalternativ
message	meddelande
Minimize	Minimera
minimize button	minimeringsknapp
mouse	mus
mouse button	musknapp
Move	Flytta
New	Ny, Nytt
notebook	anteckningar
object	objekt
Off	Av
OK	OK
On	På
Open	Öppna
Open as	Öppna som
Options	Inställningar
palette	palett
pane	ruta
Paste	Klistra in
Pause	Paus
pointer	pekare
pointing device	pekdon

Swedish

English Term	Swedish Term
pop-up menu	tilläggsmeny
Print	Skriv ut
Product information	Produktinformation
progress indicator	statusindikator
push button	(kommando)knapp
radio button	radioknapp
Redo	Upphäv ångra
reflection	reflex
Refresh	Förnya
Refresh now	Förnya nu
Rename	Döp om
Reset	Återställ
Restore	Återställ
restore button	återställningsknapp
Resume	Fortsätt
Retry	Försök igen
Save	Lagra
Save as	Lagra som
screen	skärm
scroll bar	bläddringsstapel
scroll box	bläddringsruta
select	markera
Select all	Markera alla
Selected	Markerade objekt
selection button	(val)knapp
selection cursor	(val)markör
Settings	Inställningar
shortcut key	kortkommando
Short menus	Korta menyer
Size	Ändra storlek
slider	skjutreglage
slider arm	skjutreglage
slider button	(inställnings)knapp
Sort	Sortera
spin button	(bläddrings)knapp
Split	Dela
split box	delningsruta
status area	statusfält
Stop	Stopp
system menu	systemmeny
system-menu symbol	systemmenysymbol
tabbed-divider page	registerblad

text cursor	textmarkör
title bar	rubrikrad
tool palette	verktygspalett
Tutorial	Självstudiekurs
Undo	Ångra
Using help	Om hjälpfunktionen
View	Vy, Visa
window	fönster
Window list	Lista
Windows	Fönster
window title	fönsterrubrik
work area	arbetsfält
workplace	arbetsplats

Appendix F. Documenting the CUA User Interface in Products

The following information is provided to help you document your product's user interface and associated information. The following table contains both technical and user terms. The user terms are defined and suggestions are given on how to explain the technical concepts to users.

General Terminology Guidelines

The terminology used in your product should be suited to the task domain of the product's users. For example, if the primary users of a product are programmers, use terms programmers are familiar with and understand; similarly, if the primary users are members of the medical community or the insurance community, use terms those users will expect and understand.

If your product has a particular implementation of a concept that you want to include in the definition, you may append that information to the end of the definition. Precede the appended information with a phrase such as: In `myproduct`, ...

Predefined user-interface terminology (terms that appear in the table in **bold** text) must be used for all users. Synonyms for these terms are not allowed.

How to Use This Table

Use the terms and their definitions in your product documentation just as they appear in the following table. Some of the terms that appear as choices on the user interface can either be action or routing choices. If they are used by your product as routing choices, append either an ellipsis or a right-pointing arrow to the term as appropriate.

Some of the technical terms in this table do not have equivalent user terms. To help you explain to users the concepts represented by these technical terms, suggestions are given in the right-hand column of the table. The documentation suggestions appear in *italic* text to distinguish them from term definitions.

Other technical terms in the table have equivalent user terms; for example, look at the term "action message" in the table. In the right-hand column, you are referred to "message" for the definition; "message" is the user equivalent of "action message."

Note: Predefined capitalization rules have been applied to the user-interface terminology in the following table. Terms in **bold** text appear in CUA-conforming user interfaces as choices in menus, labels on push buttons, and labels associated with icons.

Figure 227 (Page 1 of 23). Technical Terms with Equivalent User Terms and User Definitions

Technical Term	User Term	User Definition or Documentation Suggestion
action	action	An action performs a task on an object. A user requests actions by selecting a choice from a menu, interacting with buttons in a window, or by manipulating objects directly.
action message		See *message*.
active window	active window	The window that can receive input from the keyboard. It is distinguishable by the unique color of its title bar and window border.
Apply	**Apply**	A push button that carries out the selected choices in a window without closing the window.
audible feedback		*Use "beep" or describe the sound.*
automatic selection		*A selection technique in which moving the keyboard cursor automatically changes the current selection. A user does not have to identify a choice or object to select it, selection occurs automatically as the cursor moves among the choices or objects.*
border	border	A visual indication of the boundaries of a window.

Technical Term	User Term	User Definition or Documentation Suggestion
button	button	(1) A mechanism on a pointing device, such as a mouse, used to request or initiate an action or a process. (2) A graphical device that identifies a choice. (3) A graphical mechanism that, when selected, performs a visible action. For example, when a user clicks on a list button, a list of choices appears.
Cancel	**Cancel**	A push button that removes a window without applying any changes made in that window.
cascaded menu	cascaded menu	A menu that appears from, and contains choices related to, a cascading choice in another menu.
cascading choice	cascading choice	A choice on a menu that, when selected, presents another menu with additional related choices.
check box	check box	A square box with associated text that represents a choice. When a user selects the choice, the check box is filled to indicate that the choice is selected. The user can clear the check box by selecting the choice again, thereby deselecting the choice.
check mark	check mark	A character ($\sqrt{}$) that indicates that a choice is active.
choice	choice	Graphics or text that a user can select to modify or manipulate an object. Choices appear in menus, on push buttons, and in fields as in, for example, a field of radio buttons.

Technical Term	User Term	User Definition or Documentation Suggestion
chord	chord	To press more than one button on a pointing device while the pointer is within the limits that the user has specified for the operating environment.
Clear	**Clear**	A choice that removes a selected object and leaves the visible space that it occupied.
click	click	To press and release a button on a pointing device without moving the pointer off of the object or choice.
clipboard	clipboard	An area of storage provided by the system to hold data temporarily.
Close	**Close**	A choice that removes a window and all of the windows associated with it from the workplace. For example, if a user is performing a task in a window and a message appears, or the user asks for help, both the message and the help windows disappear when the user closes the original window.
combination box		*Refer to the list of objects or choices that a user can access by selecting the list button, and the entry field into which a user can type directly.*
container	container	A visual user-interface component whose specific purpose is to hold objects.

Technical Term	User Term	User Definition or Documentation Suggestion
contextual help	contextual help	Help information about the specific choice or object that the cursor is on. The help is contextual because it provides information about the item in its current context.
control		*Name the control if it is a user term; otherwise describe it, its various parts, or tell the user how to interact with it.*
Copy	**Copy**	A choice that places a copy of a selected object onto the clipboard.
Create	**Create**	An action choice that produces a new object, similar to a selected object, and places it on the clipboard.
current-setting indicator		*A mark, such as a checkmark, an "X" in a check box, or a filled circle in a radio button, that indicates that a choice is currently selected.*
current state		*The state of an object or choice, active or inactive, that allows it to be selected or directly manipulated.*
cursor	cursor	A visible indication of the position where user interaction with the keyboard will appear. The keyboard cursors are the selection cursor and the text cursor.
Cut	**Cut**	A choice that moves a selected object and places it onto the clipboard. The space it occupied is usually filled by the remaining object or objects in the window.

Technical Term	User Term	User Definition or Documentation Suggestion
data transfer		*The movement of data from one object to another by way of the clipboard or by direct manipulation*
Delete	**Delete**	A choice that removes a selected object. The space it occupied is usually filled by the remaining object or objects in the window.
delete folder	delete folder	A folder that holds objects and that will remove the objects it holds from a user's system. A delete folder could delete objects immediately, or it could allow the user to specify when the objects are to be deleted.
Deselect all	**Deselect all**	A choice that cancels the selection of all of the objects that have been selected in that window.
default action		*Explain to the user that when some action is taken, such as pressing the Enter key, the default action (describe the emphasis that identifies it) will be performed.*
descriptive text		*Text used in addition to a field prompt to give more information about a field.*
detent		*A point on a slider that represents an exact value to which a user can move the slider arm.*
dialog	dialog	The interaction between a user and a computer.

Technical Term	User Term	User Definition or Documentation Suggestion
dimmed		*Reduced contrast that indicates that a choice or object cannot be selected or directly manipulated.*
direct manipulation	direct manipulation	Techniques that a user employs to work with objects directly, through a pointing device, or through the objects' context menus.
directory	directory	A container of files and other directories.
double-click	double-click	To press and release a button on a pointing device twice while a pointer is within the limits that the user has specified for the operating environment.
drag	drag	To use a pointing device to move an object. For example, a user can drag a window border to make it larger.
drag and drop	drag and drop	To directly manipulate an object by moving it and placing it somewhere else using a pointing device.
drop-down combination box		*Tell the user how to interact with it; refer to the entry field and the list button.*
drop-down list		*Tell the user how to interact with it; refer to the list of items that are shown when the user clicks on the list button.*
Edit	**Edit**	A choice on a menu bar that provides access to other choices that enable a user to modify data.

Technical Term	User Term	User Definition or Documentation Suggestion
emphasis	emphasis	Highlighting, color change, or other visible indication of the condition of an object or choice and the effect of that condition on a user's ability to interact with that object or choice. Emphasis can also give a user additional information about the state of an object or choice.
		Note: Describe to the user what the emphasis indicates. For example, that selected-state emphasis shows that a choice or object is selected.
entry field	entry field	An area into which a user types or places text. Its boundaries are usually indicated.
extended selection		*A type of selection usually used for the selection of a single object. A user can extend selection to more than one object, if required.*
field	field	An identifiable area in a window. Examples of fields are: an entry field, into which a user can type or place text, and a field of radio button choices, from which a user can select one choice.
field prompt	field prompt	Text that identifies a field, such as an entry field or a field of check boxes.
File	**File**	A choice on a menu bar that provides access to other choices that enable a user to work with the object in the window as a whole.

Technical Term	User Term	User Definition or Documentation Suggestion
Find	**Find**	A choice or push button that initiates a search for an object or within an object displayed in that window. A user can specify the criteria to be used for the search.
first-letter navigation		*A navigation and selection technique in which users select a choice in a list by typing the first character of the choice they want to select*
folder	folder	A container used to organize objects.
Full menus	**Full menus**	A choice that a user selects to see all of the choices available in menus.
General help	**General help**	A choice that gives a user a brief overview of each action or task, or both, that a user can perform within a window.
group heading	group heading	A heading that identifies a set of related fields.
Help	**Help**	A choice that gives a user access to helpful information about objects, choices, tasks, and products. A **Help** choice can appear on a menu bar or as a push button.
Help index	**Help index**	A choice on the **Help** menu that presents an alphabetic listing of help topics for an object or a product.
Hide	**Hide**	A choice that removes a window and all associated windows from the workplace.

Technical Term	User Term	User Definition or Documentation Suggestion
I-beam pointer	I-beam pointer	A pointer that indicates that the pointer is over an area that can be edited, for example, an entry field.
icon	icon	A graphical representation of an object, consisting of an image, image background, and a label.
inactive window	inactive window	A window that is not receiving keyboard input. It can be distinguished from an active window by the difference in its title bar and border colors.
Include	**Include**	A choice that presents a window in which a user can specify a reduced or expanded set of objects, so that only the objects included in the reduced or expanded set are displayed.
information area	information area	A specific part of a window in which information about the object or choice that the cursor is on is displayed. The information area can also contain a message about the completion of a process.
information message		See *message*.
initial value		*Information that appears in an entry field when that entry field is first displayed*
input focus		*The position, indicated on the screen, where a user's interaction with the keyboard will appear.*
in-use emphasis		See *emphasis*.

Technical Term	User Term	User Definition or Documentation Suggestion
Keys help	**Keys help**	A choice that presents a listing of all the key assignments for an object or a product.
list box		*A control that contains a list of objects or settings choices that a user can select from.*
list button	list button	A button labeled with an underlined down-arrow that presents a list of valid objects or choices that can be selected for that field.
manipulation button	manipulation button	The button on a pointing device a user presses to directly manipulate an object, for example mouse button 2 is the default manipulation button on a two-button mouse.
marquee box		*The rectangle that appears during a selection technique in which a user selects objects by drawing a box around them with a pointing device.*
marquee selection		*A technique that a user employs to select objects by using a pointing device to draw a box around them.*
Maximize	**Maximize**	A choice that enlarges a window to its largest possible size.
maximize button	maximize button	A button in the rightmost part of a title bar that a user clicks on to enlarge the window to its largest possible size.
menu	menu	A list of choices that can be applied to an object. A menu can contain choices that are not available for selection in certain contexts. Those choices are indicated by reduced contrast.

Technical Term	User Term	User Definition or Documentation Suggestion
menu bar	menu bar	The area near the top of a window, below the title bar and above the rest of the window, that contains choices that provide access to other menus.
menu-bar choice	menu-bar choice	A graphical or textual item on a menu bar, which provides access to menus that contain choices that can be applied to an object.
menu button	menu button	The button on a pointing device that a user presses to view a pop-up menu associated with an object, for example mouse button 3 is the default menu button on a three-button mouse.
menu choice	menu choice	A graphical or textual item on a menu. A user selects a menu choice to work with an object in some way.
message	message	Information not requested by a user but displayed by a product in response to an unexpected event or when something undesirable could occur.
Minimize	**Minimize**	A choice that reduces a window to its smallest possible size and removes all of the windows associated with that window from the screen.
minimize button	minimize button	A button, located next to the rightmost button in a title bar, that reduces the window to its smallest possible size and removes all the windows associated with that window from the screen.

Technical Term	User Term	User Definition or Documentation Suggestion
mnemonic		*A selection technique; refer to the "underlined character" or the "character in parentheses" that a user can type to move the cursor to a choice or to select the choice that the cursor is on.*
mouse	mouse	A commonly used pointing device, containing one or more buttons, with which a user can interact with a product or the operating environment.
mouse button	mouse button	A mechanism on a mouse pointing device used to select objects or choices, initiate actions, or directly manipulate objects. that a user presses to interact with a computer system. The button makes a "clicking" sound when pressed and released.
Move	**Move**	A choice that moves a window to a different location on the work area.
multiple-line entry field	entry field	See *entry field.*
New	**New**	A choice that creates another object from an existing object. The new object will appear in the existing window.
notebook	notebook	A graphical representation that resembles a spiral-bound notebook that contains pages separated into sections by tabbed divider-pages. A user can turn the pages of a notebook to move from one section to another.

Technical Term	User Term	User Definition or Documentation Suggestion
object	object	An item that a user can manipulate as a single unit to perform a task. An object can appear as text, an icon, or both.
Off	**Off**	A choice that appears in the cascaded menu from the **Refresh** choice. It sets the refresh function to off.
OK	**OK**	A push button that accepts the information in a window and closes it. If the window contains changed information, those changes are applied before the window is closed.
On	**On**	A choice that appears in a cascaded menu from the **Refresh** choice. It immediately refreshes the view in a window.
Open	**Open**	A choice that leads to a window in which users can select the object they want to open.
Open as	**Open as**	A cascading choice that leads to a cascaded menu which contains choices that a user can select to determine how an object is presented.
Options	**Options**	A choice on a menu bar that provides access to other choices that enable a user to customize a product or application.
palette	palette	A set of mutually exclusive, typically graphical, choices.
pane	pane	One of the separate areas in a split window.

Figure 227 (Page 14 of 23). Technical Terms with Equivalent User Terms and User Definitions

Technical Term	User Term	User Definition or Documentation Suggestion
Paste	**Paste**	A choice that places the contents of the clipboard at the current cursor position.
pointer	pointer	A symbol, usually in the shape of an arrow, that a user can move with a pointing device. Users place the pointer over objects they want to work with.
pointing device	pointing device	A device, such as a mouse, trackball, or joystick, used to move a pointer on the screen.
point selection	point selection	*A selection technique in which a user selects or deselects an item by clicking the selection button on a mouse while the pointer is positioned over an object or choice.*
pop-up menu	pop-up menu	A menu that, when requested, appears next to the object it is associated with.
primary window		See *window*.
Print	**Print**	A choice that prepares and schedules an object to be printed on a designated printer.
Product information	**Product information**	A choice that displays a window that contains information about an application or product, such as its copyright notice, a logo, or both.
progress indicator	progress indicator	Visual user-interface components that inform a user about the status of a computer process.
pull-down menu		See *menu*.

Technical Term	User Term	User Definition or Documentation Suggestion
push button	push button	A button, labeled with text, graphics, or both, that represents an action that will be initiated when a user selects it.
radio button	radio button	A circle with text beside it. Radio buttons are combined to show a user a fixed set of choices from which the user can select one. The circle becomes partially filled when a choice is selected.
random-point selection		*A selection technique in which a user presses a mouse button and holds it down while moving the pointer so that the pointer travels to a different location on the screen. Everything the pointer touches while the button is held down is selected. Random-point selection ends when the mouse button is released.*
range selection		*A technique in which a user selects multiple objects in a range by identifying a beginning and end corner. When the second corner is identified, all objects within the specified range are selected.*
range-swipe selection		*A selection technique in which a user moves a pointer across a range of objects. Each object becomes selected as the pointer touches it.*

Technical Term	User Term	User Definition or Documentation Suggestion
Redo	**Redo**	A choice that reverses the effect of the most recently performed undo operation on an object, returning the object to the state it was in before the undo operation was performed.
reflection		*An object that is represented by more than one icon.*
Refresh	**Refresh**	A cascading choice that gives a user access to other choices (**On** and **Off**) that control whether changes made to underlying data in a window are displayed immediately, not displayed at all, or displayed at a later time.
Refresh now	**Refresh now**	A choice that shows changes made to underlying data in a window immediately.
Reset	**Reset**	A push button that returns an object to the condition it was in when it was last opened, or to the condition it was in before the most recent changes were applied to it.
Restore	**Restore**	A choice that returns a window to the size it was and the position it was in before the user minimized or maximized the window.
restore button	restore button	A button that appears in the rightmost corner of the title bar after a window has been maximized. When the restore button is selected, the window returns to the size it was before it was maximized.

Technical Term	User Term	User Definition or Documentation Suggestion
Retry	**Retry**	A push button that, when selected, attempts to complete an interrupted process.
Save	**Save**	A choice that stores an object onto a storage device, such as a disk or diskette.
Save as	**Save as**	A choice that creates a new object from an existing object and leaves the existing object as it was.
screen	screen	The physical surface of a display device upon which information is shown to users.
scrollable entry field		*An entry field that can be scrolled.*
scroll bar	scroll bar	A window component that shows a user that more information is available in a particular direction and can be scrolled into view. Scroll bars can be either horizontal or vertical.
scroll box	scroll box	The part of a scroll bar that indicates the position of the visible information relative to the total amount of information available in a window. A user clicks on a scroll box with a pointing device and manipulates it to see information that is not currently visible.
scrolling increment		*A fixed amount of information that can be scrolled with a single scrolling action.*
secondary window		See *window.*

Technical Term	User Term	User Definition or Documentation Suggestion
select	select	To explicitly identify one or more objects to which a subsequent choice will apply.
Select all	**Select all**	A choice that causes all of the objects in a window to be selected.
Selected	**Selected**	A choice in the menu bar that provides access to choices that apply to the selected objects in the current view. Products can change the name of the choice to match the types of objects that appear in the current view, for example if a view contains only document objects, a product might name this choice **Documents.**
selected-state emphasis		See *emphasis.*
selection	selection	The process of explicitly identifying one or more objects to which a subsequent choice will apply.
selection button	selection button	The button on a pointing device that a user presses to select an object, for example mouse button 1 is the select button on a two-button mouse.
selection cursor	selection cursor	A keyboard cursor, in the shape of a dotted outline box, that moves as users indicate the choice they want to interact with.
Settings	**Settings**	A choice that sets characteristics of objects or displays identifying characteristics of objects.

Technical Term	User Term	User Definition or Documentation Suggestion
shortcut key	shortcut key	A key or combination of keys assigned to a menu choice that initiates that choice, even if the associated menu is not currently displayed.
Short menus	**Short menus**	A choice that reduces the number of choices that appear in menus.
single-line entry field		See *entry field*.
Size	**Size**	An action choice that allows a user to change the size of a window.
slider	slider	A visual component of a user interface that represents a quantity and its relationship to the range of possible values for that quantity. A user can also change the value of the quantity.
slider arm	slider arm	The visual indicator in the slider that a user can move to change the numerical value.
slider button	slider button	A button on a slider that a user clicks on to move the slider arm one increment in a particular direction, as indicated by the directional arrow on the button.
slider shaft		*The part of the slider on which the slider arm moves.*
Sort	**Sort**	A choice that arranges the objects in a view into a specified order.
source emphasis		See *emphasis*.

Technical Term	User Term	User Definition or Documentation Suggestion
spin button	spin button	A component used to display, in sequence, a ring of related but mutually exclusive choices. A user can accept the value displayed in the entry field or can type a valid choice into the entry field.
split box	split box	A box in the scroll bar of a window that a user can interact with to split a window into separate panes.
Split	**Split**	A choice that divides a window into more than one pane. Also, a choice used to change the size of each pane.
status area	status area	A part of a window where information appears that shows the state of an object or the state of a particular view of an object.
system menu	system menu	A menu that appears from the system menu symbol in the leftmost part of a title bar. It contains choices that affect the window or the view it contains.
system-menu symbol	system-menu symbol	A symbol (shaped like a Spacebar) in the leftmost corner of a title bar that gives a user access to choices that affect the window or the view it contains.
tabbed divider-page	tabbed divider-page	A graphical representation of a tabbed page in a notebook. Tabbed divider-pages separate sections of the notebook.

Figure 227 (Page 21 of 23). Technical Terms with Equivalent User Terms and User Definitions

Technical Term	User Term	User Definition or Documentation Suggestion
table	table	An object, such as a spreadsheet, that is organized in a grid of rows and columns. Each intersection is called a cell and can contain objects, such as text or graphics, or both.
target emphasis		See *emphasis*.
text cursor	text cursor	A symbol displayed in text that shows a user where typed input will appear.
title bar	title bar	The area at the top of each window that contains the system menu symbol, a small icon, a window title, and the maximize, minimize, and restore buttons.
tool palette	tool palette	A palette whose choices represent tools. When a user selects a choice from the tool palette and moves the pointer into the window, the pointer changes to the shape of the selected choice and the pointing device performs the operation indicated by the pointer. For example, a user might select a "pencil" choice from the tool palette to make a drawing in the window.
Tutorial	**Tutorial**	A choice that gives a user access to online educational information.
unavailable-state emphasis		See *emphasis*.

Technical Term	User Term	User Definition or Documentation Suggestion
Undo	**Undo**	A choice that reverses the effect of the most recently performed operation on an object, returning the object to the state it was in before the operation was performed.
Using help	**Using help**	A choice on the **Help** menu that gives a user information about how the help function works.
value set		*A set of mutually exclusive, graphical or textual choices.*
View	**View**	A choice on a menu bar that provides access to other choices that enable a user to choose how an object is presented, how much information is presented, what order it is presented in, and other choices related to the way an object is presented.
visible cue		*Describe the visual cue and tell the user what it indicates.*
wait pointer		*A pointer that indicates that the computer is performing a process and that the user cannot interact with the part of the underlying window that the wait pointer is positioned over.*
window	window	An area with visible boundaries that presents a view of an object or with which a user conducts a dialog with a computer system.
Windows	**Windows**	A choice on a menu bar that provides access to other choices with which users can manage all of the open windows on their system that are associated with the product.

Technical Term	User Term	User Definition or Documentation Suggestion
Window list	**Window list**	A choice that presents a list of all of the open windows associated with the window from which the **Window list** choice was selected.
window title	window title	The area on a title bar that contains a short description of the contents of the window.
work area	work area	A container used to group windows and objects to perform a task. Users can modify sample work areas to suit their own needs.
workplace	workplace	A container that fills the entire screen and holds all of the objects that make up the user interface.

Glossary

This glossary is intended to be used by the reader of this book as a reference to the terminology contained herein. For CUA terms and definitions that can be used in product glossaries, refer to the *CUA Reference.*

action choice. A choice that immediately begins to process a request made by a user or immediately applies settings to an object.

application. A collection of related components with which a user performs a task.

audible cue. A sound generated by the computer to draw a user's attention to, or provide feedback about, an event or state of the computer. Audible cues enhance and reinforce visible cues.

automatic selection. A selection technique in which moving the keyboard cursor automatically changes the current selection. Automatic selection is provided as a convenience so that a user does not have to select an object explicitly.

border. A visual indication of the boundaries of a window.

button. (1) A mechanism on a pointing device, such as a mouse, used to request or initiate an action or a process. (2) A graphical device that identifies a choice. (3) A graphical mechanism that, when selected, performs a visible action. For example, when a user clicks on a list button, a list of choices appears.

cascaded menu. A menu that appears from, and contains choices related to, a cascading choice in another menu. Cascaded menus are used to reduce the length of a pull-down menu or a pop-up menu.

cascading choice. A choice on a menu that leads to a cascaded menu containing related choices. A cascading choice is indicated by a rightward-pointing arrow ($\rightarrow$) to the right of the choice.

check box. A square box with associated text that represents a choice. When a user selects the choice, an "X" appears in the check box to indicate that the choice is selected. The user can clear the check box by selecting the choice again, thereby canceling the selection.

check mark. A character ($\sqrt{}$) that indicates that a settings choice is active.

choice. Text or graphics that a user can select. Examples of choices are: push buttons, radio buttons, and menu items. There are three kinds of choices: action, routing, and settings. Choices appear in menus, on push buttons, and in fields, for example a field of radio buttons.

chord. To press more than one button on a pointing device while the pointer is within the limits that the user has specified for the operating environment.

class. See *object class.*

class hierarchy. A collection of object classes organized to indicate the other classes from which they have inherited various attributes.

click. To press and release a button on a pointing device without moving the pointer off of the object or choice.

clipboard. An area of storage provided by the system to hold data temporarily.

combination box. A control that combines the functions of an entry field and a list box. A combination box contains a list of objects that a user can scroll through and select from to complete the entry field. Alternatively, a user can type text directly into the entry field.

composite object. An object that contains other objects, usually of a different type. For example, a document object that contains not only text, but graphics or image objects that may each be separate objects.

composed view. A view of an object in which relationships of the parts contribute to the overall meaning. Composed views are provided primarily for data objects.

container object. An object whose specific purpose is to hold other objects. A folder is an example of a container object.

containment. The principle that objects hold other objects and can be held by other objects.

contents view. A view of an object that shows the contents of the object in list form. Contents views are provided for container objects and for any object that has container behavior, for example, a device object such as a printer. The two types of contents views are the icons view and the details view.

controls. Visual user-interface components that allow a user to interact with data. Controls are usually identified by text, for example, headings, labels in push buttons, field prompts, and titles in windows.

current-setting indicator. A visible indication that a choice is active or inactive, for example the "X" that appears in a check box when it is selected.

cursor. A visible indication of the position where user interaction with the keyboard will appear. The keyboard cursor can be either the selection cursor or the text cursor.

data object. An object whose primary purpose is to convey information, such as text, graphics, audio, or video. A newsletter is an example of a data object.

deselection. The process of removing selection from a previously selected object.

details view. A standard contents view in which a small icon is combined with text to provide descriptive information about an object. The text is arranged in rows and columns so that there is one row for each object and one column for each type of descriptive information displayed.

device object. An object that provides a means for communication between a computer and another piece of equipment. A printer and an electronic mail out-basket are examples of device objects.

dialog. The interaction between a user and a computer.

direct manipulation. A set of techniques that allow a user to work with an object by dragging it with a pointing device or interacting with its pop-up menu.

double-click. To press and release a button on a pointing device twice while a pointer is within the limits that the user has specified for the operating environment.

drag. To use a pointing device to move or copy an object. For example, a user can drag a window border to make it larger. To drag something, a user presses and holds a button on the pointing device while moving the pointing device.

drag and drop. To directly manipulate an object by moving it and placing it somewhere else using a pointing device.

drop-down combination box. A combination box in which the list is hidden until a user takes an action to make it visible.

drop-down list. A control that is a variation of a list box. A drop-down list only displays one item until the user takes an action to display the other objects or choices.

emphasis. Highlighting, color change, or other visible indication of the condition of an object or choice and the effect of that condition on a user's ability to interact with that object or choice. Emphasis can also give a user additional information about the state of an object or choice.

entry field. A control into which a user places text. Its boundaries are usually indicated. Entry fields can scroll if more information is available than is currently visible.

exception. An event or situation that prevents, or could prevent, an action requested by a user from being completed in a manner that the user would expect. Exceptions occur when a product is unable to interpret a user's input.

explicit selection. A type of selection in which users expressly identify the item or items that they want to select.

extended selection. A type of selection optimized for the selection of a single object. A user can extend selection to more than one object, if required.

field. An identifiable area in a window, for example an entry field into which a user can type text, or a field of radio buttons from which a user can select one choice in the field.

field prompt. Text that identifies a field, such as an entry field or a field of check boxes.

folder. A container used to organize objects.

graphical user interface. A type of user interface that takes advantage of high-resolution graphics. In common usage, a graphical user interface includes a combination of graphics, the object-action paradigm, the use of pointing devices, menu bars and other menus, overlapping windows, and icons.

group heading. A heading that identifies a set of related fields.

help view. A view of an object that provides information to assist users in working with that object.

hide button. A button on a title bar that a user clicks on to remove a window from the workplace without closing the window. When the window is hidden, the state of window, as represented in the window list, changes.

I-beam pointer. A pointer, shaped like a steel girder, that indicates that the pointer is over an area where text can be typed.

icon. A graphical representation of an object, consisting of an image, image background, and a label.

icons view. A standard contents view in which each object contained in a container object is displayed as an icon.

implicit selection. A type of selection in which a user does not expressly select the item on which an action will be taken, but still has access to the actions available for the item.

inactive window. A window that cannot receive keyboard input at a given moment.

information area. A specific part of a window in which information about the object or choice that the cursor is on is displayed. The information area can also contain a message about the completion of a process.

inheritance. The principle that objects acquire attributes from other classes of objects.

keys help. A type of help information that lists all the key assignments for an object or a product.

list box. A control that contains a list of objects or settings choices that a user can select.

manipulation button. The button on a pointing device a user presses to directly manipulate an object. For example mouse button 2 is the default manipulation button on a two-button mouse.

maximize button. A button on the rightmost part of a title bar that a user clicks on to enlarge the window to its largest possible size.

menu. A list of choices that can be applied to an object. A menu can contain choices that are not available for selection in certain contexts. Those choices are indicated by reduced contrast.

menu bar. The area near the top of a window, below the title bar and above the rest of the window, that contains routing choices that provide access to pull-down menus.

menu-bar choice. A graphical or textual item on a menu bar that provides access to pull-down menus which contain choices that can be applied to an object.

menu choice. A graphical or textual item on a menu. A user selects a menu choice to work with an object in some way.

message. Information not requested by a user but displayed by a product or application in response to an unexpected event, or when something undesirable could occur.

metaphor. A word, phrase, or visual representation that denotes or depicts one object or idea but suggests a likeness or analogy with another object or idea.

minimize button. A button, located next to the rightmost button in a title bar, that reduces the window to its smallest possible size and removes all the windows associated with that window from the screen.

mode. A method of operation in which the actions that are available to a user are determined by the state of the system.

model. The conceptual and operational understanding that a person has about something.

mouse. A commonly used pointing device that has one or more buttons that a user presses to interact with a computer system.

mouse button.   A mechanism on a mouse pointing device used to select choices, initiate actions, or manipulate objects with the pointer. The button makes a "clicking" sound when pressed and released.

multiple selection. A selection technique in which a user can select any number of objects, or not select any.

notebook. A graphical representation that resembles a bound notebook that contains pages separated into sections by tabbed divider pages. A user can turn the pages of a notebook to move from one section to another.

object. A visual component of a user interface that a user can work with to perform a task. An object can appear as text or an icon.

object-action paradigm. A pattern for interaction in which a user selects an object and then selects an action to apply to that object.

object class. A categorization or grouping of objects that share similar behaviors and characteristics.

object decomposition. The process of breaking an object into its component parts.

object hierarchy. A way of illustrating relationships among objects. Each object that appears in a level below another object is an example of the upper object.

object inheritance. *See* inheritance.

object orientation. An orientation in a user interface in which a user's attention is directed toward the objects the user works with to perform a task.

object-oriented programming. A type of programming in which code is divided into modules called "objects" that communicate with each other by passing messages.

object-oriented user interface. A type of user interface that implements the object-action paradigm.

object subclass. An object created from another object and from which the properties of the original object are inherited.

object superclass. The object from which subclass objects are created. The properties of the superclass object are inherited by the subclass object.

one-based selection. A scope of selection in which one item within the scope must always be selected.

pane. One of the separate areas in a split window.

paradigm. An example, pattern, or model.

pointer. A visible cue, usually in the shape of an arrow, that a user can move with a pointing device. Users place the pointer over objects they want to work with.

pointing device. A device, such as a mouse, trackball, or joystick, used to move a pointer on the screen.

pop-up menu. A menu that, when requested, is displayed next to the object it is associated with. It contains choices appropriate for a given object or set of objects in their current context.

primary window. A window in which the main interaction between a user and an object takes place.

progress indicator. One or more controls used to inform a user about the progress of a process.

properties. The particular characteristics and attributes of an object.

pull-down menu. A menu that extends from a selected choice on a menu bar or from the system-menu symbol. The choices in a pull-down menu are related to one another in some manner.

push button. A button, labeled with text, graphics, or both, that represents an action that will be initiated when a user selects it.

radio button. A circle with text beside it. Radio buttons are combined to show a user a fixed set of choices from which the user can select one. The circle becomes partially filled when a choice is selected.

read-only field. A variation of an entry field into which a user cannot type or otherwise place text to replace the existing information. The information displayed in a read-only field can be static or can be automatically calculated by the product containing the read-only field.

reflection. An object that is represented by more than one icon. If a user changes an object that is a reflection, all other reflections of the object are changed. If a user deletes a reflection, other reflections of the object are not necessarily deleted.

routing choice. A choice that displays a pull-down menu, a cascaded menu, or a window containing additional choices.

scope of selection. Any area in which the selection of one item can affect the selection of another item.

screen. The physical surface of a display device upon which information is shown to users.

scroll bar. A window component that shows a user that more information is available in a particular direction and can be scrolled into view. Scroll bars can be either horizontal or vertical.

scroll box. The part of a scroll bar that indicates the position of the visible information relative to the total amount of information available in a window. A user clicks on a scroll box with a pointing device and manipulates it to see information that is not currently visible.

secondary window. A window that contains information that is dependent on information in a primary window and is used to supplement the interaction in the primary window.

selection. The act of explicitly identifying one or more objects to which a subsequent choice will apply.

selection button. The button on a pointing device that a user presses to select an object. For example, mouse button 1 is the default selection button on a two-button mouse.

selection cursor. A keyboard cursor, in the shape of a dotted outline box, that moves as users indicate the choice they want to interact with.

selection technique. The method by which users indicate items on the interface that they want to work with.

settings choice. A type of choice that sets characteristics of objects or displays identifying characteristics of objects.

settings view. A view of an object that provides a way to display the parameters and options associated with the object.

single selection. A selection technique in which a user selects one, and only one, item at a time.

shortcut key. A key or combination of keys assigned to a menu choice that initiates that choice, even if the associated menu is not currently displayed.

slider. A visual component of a user interface that represents a quantity and its relationship to the range of possible values for that quantity. A user can also change the value of the quantity.

slider arm. The visual indicator in the slider that a user can move to change the numerical value.

slider button. A button on a slider that a user clicks on to move the slider arm one increment in a particular direction, as indicated by the directional arrow on the button.

Sort. A choice that arranges the objects in a view into a specified order.

source object. An object that is the source of a direct-manipulation operation; for example, if a user drags a document to a printer to print it, the document is the source object.

spin button. A control used to display, in sequence, a ring of related but mutually exclusive choices. It contains a field that can accept user input, which allows a user to make a selection by typing a valid choice, or a field that can display a value that the user can merely accept. The user can change the value by spinning through the ring of choices.

split box. A box in the scroll bar of a window that a user can interact with to split a window into separate panes.

status area. A part of a window where information appears that shows the state of an object or the state of a particular view of an object.

system menu. A menu that appears from the system-menu symbol in the leftmost part of a title bar. It contains choices that affect the window.

system-menu symbol. A symbol (shaped like a Spacebar) in the leftmost corner of a title bar that gives a user access to choices that affect the window or the view it contains.

tabbed divider page. A graphical representation of a tabbed page in a notebook. Tabbed divider pages separate sections of the notebook.

target object. The object that is the target of a direct-manipulation operation; for example, if a user drags a document to a printer to print it, the printer is the target object.

text cursor. A keyboard cursor used in text that shows a user where typed input will appear.

title bar. The area at the top of each window that contains the system menu symbol from which the system menu appears, a small icon, a window title, and the window sizing buttons.

tool palette. A palette containing choices that represent tools. When a user selects a choice from the tool palette and moves the pointer into the window, the pointer changes to the shape of the selected choice and the pointing device performs the operation indicated by the pointer. For example, a user might select a "pencil" choice from the tool palette to draw a line in the window.

touch input. An input technique in which the pointing device is a user's finger.

touch pointer. A kind of pointer that can be provided for touch-input environments. A

touch pointer indicates to a user which items will be affected by the user's input.

user interface. The area at which a user and an object come together to interact. As applied to computers, the ensemble of hardware and software that allows a user to interact with a computer.

user's conceptual model. The concepts and expectations a person develops through experience.

value set. A control that allows a user to select one choice from a group of mutually exclusive choices. A value set is used primarily for graphical choices.

view. The form in which an object is presented. There are four basic types of views: composed, contents, settings, and help.

window. An area with visible boundaries that presents a view of an object or with which a user conducts a dialog with a computer system.

window title. The area on a title bar that contains the name of the object or a short description of the contents of the window.

work area. A container used to organize objects according to a user's tasks. When a user closes a work area, all windows opened from objects contained in the work area are removed from the workplace.

workplace. A container that fills the entire screen and holds all of the objects that make up the user interface.

zero-based selection. A selection technique that does not require that any items within the scope of selection be selected.

Recommended Readings

This bibliography lists selected publications that provide technical information on key principles, examples of user-centered design, and behaviorally oriented discussions of user interface technology and techniques. The first set of references will help you get started with user interface design. The second set, organized by topics, provides more in-depth technical coverage for specialists or those who want to learn more.

Getting Started

Baecker, R. and Buxton, W. (Eds.) *Readings in human-computer interaction: A multi-disciplinary approach.* Los Altos, CA: Morgan Kaufmann Publishers, Inc., 1987.
(This is a good source for learning how to become a part of the growing, interdisciplinary community of people interested in human-computer interaction. The appendixes describe key books, journals, and conferences. The body of the collection consists of reprints of key papers covering pre-1980s through 1986, including papers on input devices and output devices, user-centered design, and socio-technical perspectives.)

Heckel, P. *The elements of friendly software design.* New York: Warner Books, 1984.
(Discussion of general principles and guidelines.)

Kelly, George. "Man as scientist—Developing models." *A theory of personality.* New York: Wm. Norton & Co., Inc., 1963.

Norman, D. *The psychology of everyday things.* Hillsdale, NJ: L. Frlbaum, 1988.
(Very good, useful discussion of cognitive psychology in the context of understanding human-artifact interaction at large.)

Rubenstein, R. and Hersch, H. *The human factor: Designing computer systems for people.* Massachusetts: Digital Press, 1984.
(Highly recommended, very readable discussion of user-centered design in its full scope: task analysis, prototyping, empirical evaluating, interface techniques, and guidelines.)

Shneiderman, B. *Designing the user interface.* Massachusetts: Addison-Wesley Publishing Company, 1987.

Tufte, Edward R. *Envisioning information.* Connecticut: Graphics Press, 1990.

Tufte, Edward R. *The visual display of quantitative information.* Connecticut: Graphics Press, 1983.

User Interface Technology and Techniques

The references cited in the "Getting Started" section survey many user interface technologies and techniques. The references in this section cover key technologies and techniques in more depth.

Carroll, J., Smith-Kerker, P., Ford, J., and Mazur, S. "The minimal manual." *Human-computer interaction.* 3(2), 1987-1988. 123-154.

Doheny-Farina, S. (Ed.) *Effective documentation: What we have learned from research.* Cambridge, MA: The MIT Press, 1988.

Foley, J. D., Wallace, V. L., and Chan, P. "The human factors of computer graphics interaction techniques." *IEEE computer graphics and applications,* November 1984: 13-48.

Helander, M. (Ed.) *Handbook of human-computer interaction.* North-Holland: Elsevier Science Publishers, 1988.
(Very comprehensive and useful collection covering nearly all major areas of human-computer interaction, including many chapters on specific user interface technology and techniques, aspects of task analysis, organizational impact of computer technology, software engineering tools, cognitive psychology, user-centered design and evaluation methods. The following list summarizes some chapters dealing with interface techniques:

Billingsley, P. "Taking panes: Issues in the design of windowing systems." (Chapter 19)
Elkerton, J. "On-line aiding for human-computer interfaces." (Chapter 16)
Greenstein, J. and Arnaut, L. "Input devices." (Chapter 22)
Ogden, W. "Using natural language interfaces." (Chapter 13)
Smith, S. "Standards versus guidelines for designing user interface software." (Chapter 40)
Tullis, T. "Screen design." (Chapter 18)
Verplank. W. "Graphic challenges in designing object-oriented user interfaces." (Chapter 17)
Wright, P. "Issues of content and presentation in document design." (Chapter 28)
Ziegler, J. and Fahnrich, K. "Direct manipulation." (Chapter 6))

Hutchins, E. L., Hollan, J. D., and Norman, D. A. "Direct manipulation interfaces." In *User-centered system design: New perspectives on human-computer interaction.* Ed. D. A. Norman and S. W. Draper. New York: Lawrence Erlbaum Associates, 1986. 87-124.

International Business Machines Corporation. *Icon reference book.* SC34-4348-00.

Smith, D., Irby, C., Kimball, R., and Verplank, W. "Designing the Star user interface." *Byte.* 7(4), April 1983. 242-282.

Thorell, L. G. and Smith, W. J. *Using computer color effectively: An illustrated reference.* Englewood Cliffs, NJ: Prentice Hall, 1990.

User-Centered Design: General Principles

The following references provide an overview of key principles of user-centered design and usability engineering.

Gould, J. and Lewis, C. "Designing for usability: Key principles and what designers think." *Communications of the ACM.* 28(3), March 1985. 300-311.

Helander, M. (Ed.) *Handbook of human-computer interaction.*
North-Holland: Elsevier Science Publishers, 1988.
(Cited earlier; in this context see especially:

Gould, J. "How to design usable systems." (Chapter 35)
Whiteside, J., Bennett, J., and Holtzblatt, K. "Usability engineering: Our experience and evolution." (Chapter 36))

Rubenstein, R. and Hersch, H. *The human factor: Designing computer systems for people.* Massachusetts: Digital Press, 1984.
(Cited earlier; in this context see especially chapters 2, 3, 4, and 11)

User-Centered Design: Case Studies

A sampling of case studies in user-centered design, discussed in more depth.

Good, M., Whiteside, J., Wixon, D., and Jones, S. "Building a user-derived interface." *Communications of the ACM.* 27(10), October 1984. 1032-1043.

Gould, J., Boies, S., Levy, S., Richards, J., and Schoonard, J. "The 1984 Olympic message system: A test of the behavioral principles of system design." *Communications of the ACM.* 30(9), September 1987. 758-769.

Percival, L. and Johnson, S. "Network management software usability test design and implementation." *IBM systems journal.* 25(1), 1986.

Understanding Users and Their Tasks

The following highly selective group of publications discusses users and task analysis at many levels, from computer interaction tasks to broad analyses of organizational change resulting from the introduction of technology. See also the discussions in references cited in "User-Centered Design: General Principles," such as Helander or Rubenstein and Hersh.

Blackler, F. and Oborne, D. (Eds.) *Information technology and people: Designing for the future.* Leicester, UK: The British Psychological Society, 1987.
(This collection is wide-ranging, but it can point you to a large volume of literature outside the USA on task and work analysis.)

Brady, L. "User system analysis." In *Human factors in organizational design and management.* Eds. H. Hendrick and O. Brown. North-Holland: Elsevier Science Publishers, Inc., 1984.
(An example of a paper in a collection of short papers from a conference on the analysis of work and information technology.)

Bullen, C., Bennett, J., and Carlson, E. "A case study of office workstation use." *IBM systems journal.* 21(3), 1982.

Carroll, J., Mack, R., and Kellogg, W. "Interface metaphors and user interface design." In *Handbook of human-computer interaction.* Ed. M. Helander. Chapter 3, 67-86.

Carroll, J. and Reitman Olson, J. "Mental models in human-computer interaction." In *Handbook of human-computer interaction.* Ed. M. Helander. Chapter 2, 45-61.

Carroll, J. and Rosson, M. B. "Usability specifications as a tool in iterative development." In *Advances in human-computer interaction.* Ed. H. Hartson. Norwood, NJ: Ablex Publishing, 1985.
(Task analysis from the perspective of setting product objectives that can be tested.)

Carroll, J. and Rosson, M. B. "The paradox of the active user." In *Interfacing thought: Cognitive aspects of human-computer interaction.* Ed. J. Carroll. Cambridge, MA: MIT Press, 1986.

Egan, D. "Individual differences in human-computer interaction." In *Handbook of human-computer interaction.* Ed. M. Helander North-Holland: Elsevier Science Publishers, 1988. 543-568.

Gould, J., Boies, S., Levy, S., Richards, J., and Schoonard, J. "The 1984 Olympic message system: A test of the behavioral principles of system design." *Communications of the ACM.* 30(9), September 1987. 758-769.
(Cited above; relevant here for discussion of initial field work to understand users and their requirements.)

Lewis, C. and Norman, D. "Designing for error." In *User centered system design: New perspectives on human-computer interaction.* Eds. D. Norman and S. Draper. 411-432.

Norman, D. "Cognitive engineering." In *User centered system design: New perspectives on human-computer interaction.* Eds. D. Norman and S. Draper. Hillsdale, NJ: L. Erlbaum Associates, 1986. 31-61.

Percival, L. and Johnson, S. "Network management software usability test design and implementation." *IBM systems journal.* 25(1), 1986.
(Cited above; relevant here for references to initial field work to understand users and their requirements.)

Potosnak, K. (Panel chair), Hayes, P., Rosson, M. B., Schneider, M., and Whiteside, J. "Classifying users: A hard look at some controversial issues." *Proceedings CHI '86 human factors in computing systems.* (Boston, April 13-17, 1986), ACM, New York. 84-88.
(Brief panel discussion of issues; reference section useful.)

Regan, E. and O'Conner, B. *Automating the office: Office systems and end-user computing.* Chicago, IL: Science Research Associates, Inc., 1989.
(Textbook treatment, with focus on office automation; see especially chapters 17-22 on developing requirements, evaluating technology in the field.)

Reitman Olson, J. "Cognitive analysis of people's use of software." In *Interfacing thought: Cognitive aspects of human-computer interaction.* Ed. J. Carroll. Cambridge, MA: MIT Press, 1986.
(Theoretical discussion of similarities and differences between analysis schemes for low-level computer-implemented tasks, and schemes for broader analysis of tasks in the workplace. References to academic literature on task and work analysis.)

Rockart, J. and Bullen, C. (Eds.) *The rise of managerial computing: The best of the Center for Information Systems Research.* Homewood, IL: Dow Jones-Irwin, 1986.
(Wide-ranging collection of papers on decision support tasks, users and requirements, including executive support. Lots of pointers into academic literature.)

The following publications provide comprehensive, technical overviews of psychological principles of human-computer and human-machine interaction, from traditional human performance perspectives to more cognitive interpretations.

Bailey, R. W. *Human performance engineering: A guide for system designers.* New Jersey: Prentice Hall, 1982.

Boff, K., Kaufman, L., and Thomas, J. *Handbook of perception and human-performance. Vol. 1, 2* New York: Wiley Publications, 1986.

Card, S. K., Moran, T. P., and Newell, A. *The psychology of human-computer interaction.* New York: Lawrence Erlbaum Associates, 1983.

Carroll, J. (Ed.) *Interfacing thought: Cognitive aspects of human-computer interaction.* Cambridge, MA: MIT Press, 1986.

Kantowitz, B. H. and Sorkin, R. D. *Human factors: Understanding people-system relationships.* New York: John Wiley & Sons, 1983.

Nickerson, R.S. *Using computers: Human factors in information systems.* Cambridge, MA: MIT Press, 1986.

Norman, D. and Draper, S. (Eds.) *User centered system design: New perspectives on human-computer interaction.* Hillsdale, NJ: L. Erlbaum Associates, 1986.

Object-Oriented Programming and Design

Coad, Peter and Yourdan, Edward. *Object-oriented analysis.* West Nyack, NY: Prentice Hall, 1991.

Coad, Peter and Yourdan, Edward. *Object-oriented design.* West Nyack, NY: Prentice Hall, 1991.

Cox, Brad J. *Object-oriented programming: An evolutionary approach.* Reading, MA: Addison-Wesley Publishing Company, 1987.

National Language Support

You can find the IBM rules and guidelines for supporting translation in the following books:

Designing enabled products, rules and guidelines, SE09-8001

National language support reference manual, SE09-8002.

Index

A

About choice
   See Product information choice
accelerator
   See shortcut key
access, restricting 117, 145
accommodating differences
   in experience 35
   in skill 28
   in system configurations 525
   in users 30
action
   choice 204
   default 250
   keyboard function 316
   user definition 632
action bar
   See menu bar
action bar pull-down
   See pull-down menu
action choice
   applying to selected object, and selection
    state 440
   definition 655
   description 59, 204
   displaying unavailable-state emphasis
    on 331
   illustration 59
   on a push button 65
   overview of 185
   push button 400
   recommendations 220
   using menus 331
action message
   audible cue in 207
   default action 252
   message symbol
    question mark 207
    stop sign 207
   message text 207

action message *(continued)*
   overview of 183
   providing controls 206
   providing push buttons 206
   removing 206
   technical definition 206
   using audible feedback in 212
   when to use 206
   withdrawing request 207
action push button, labeling 401
action window, technical definition 208
actions
   immediate 27
   naming 35
   reversible 27
active pane, switching 472
active window 155
   controls not visible in 500
   designing the initial size and layout of 500
   displaying cursor in 210
   displaying in secondary window 433
   interacting with a partially covered 211
   Open 373
   overview of 181
   pane, displaying cursor in 472
   Save as 425
   Sort 463
   technical definition 210
   user definition 632
   window list 503
   window title 511
adding objects, in car dealership product 117
address book, represented in different
  models 14
Advanced Interface Design Guide (AIDG)
aesthetic appeal
   and color 527
   in visual representations 18
   influencing user attitudes 36
   techniques for creating 36

capitalization
  choice
    in a menu bar   335
    name   219
  column heading   227
  combination box   230
  drop-down combination box   267
  drop-down list   269
  field prompt   279
  group box   290
  group heading   292
  list box   326
  of check box choices   217
  of choice names in a menu   332
  of radio-button choice   410
  push button label   401
  value set   491
car dealership product
  composed view   115
  container object   108, 109
  contents view   113, 116, 117
  data object   108, 109
  data transfer   111
  default results of direct manipulation   111
  defining objects   107
  designing windows for   136
  details view
    of car lot object   113, 138
    of customer list   116, 117
  device object   109
  direct manipulation   111
  electronic mail   111
  filtering feature, window for   139
  filtering views in   114
  general information view of car object   137
  help, windows for
  how to use   150
  icons   138
  icons view
    of car lot object   113, 137
    of customer list   116
    of worksheet list   117
  indirect manipulation in   111
  map view   115

car dealership product *(continued)*
  message   148
  objects   108
  relationships among objects in,
    illustration   110
  settings view   115
  source objects   111
  target objects   111
  views   112
  windows
    for car lot object   137
    for car object   137
    for customer object   145
    for worksheet object   149
car lot object
  description   108
  menus   120
  views
    details view   113, 138
    icons view   113, 137
    map view   115, 144
  windows   137
car object
  description   108
  general information view   112, 155
  menus   118
  views   112
  windows   137
car sale scenario   150
cascaded menu
  definition   655
  description   62, 214
  displaying   214, 331
  providing mnemonics in   345
  using   238
  when to use   214, 333
cascading choice
  and displaying pop-up menu   389
  identifying   214
cascading choice, definition   655
cascading menu
  See cascaded menu
casual user, support for   29

choice *(continued)*
    Product information 395
    product-specific, in Help menu 296
    providing contextual help for 233
    providing mnemonic 344
    providing mnemonics for 507
    push button 400
    Redo 487
    Refresh 415
    Refresh and Refresh now 415
    Refresh now 415
    removing from a menu 331
    Restore 418
    routing
        See also routing choice
        description 421
        in a menu bar 334
        menu from 421
        overview of 185
    Save 423
    Save as 427
    Select all 435
    Selected menu 437
    settings
        See also settings choice
        and radio button 409
        check box 216
        description 220
        in a menu 332
        in a notebook 332
        overview of 185
    Short menus 454
    size of 519
    Sort 463
    Split 469
    Switch to 505
    technical definition 218
    Tutorial 484
    type
        action 204
        routing 421
        settings 448
    types of 59
    unavailable
        and audible cues 212

choice *(continued)*
    unavailable *(continued)*
        and information area 485
    Undo 487
    user definition 633
    using graphics for 335
    Using help 489
    when to use 459
    Window list 506
choice names, capitalizing 219
chord
    action performed by 350
    user definition 633
chord, definition 655
    See also click, double-click
class hierarchy
    definition 655
    description 8
    illustration 8, 94
class name, label of object-oriented File
  menu 282
class, object
    definition 658
    description 31
Clear
    description 223
    in Edit menu 222, 271
    keyboard function 316
    user definition 634
click
    description 350
    user definition 634
click, definition 655
    See also double-click, chord
client area
    See window
client subarea
    See split window
clipboard
    and Copy choice 240
    and Create choice 243
    and object state 240, 243
    data transfer of text using 479
    definition 655

clipboard *(continued)*
  description   83, 224
  Paste choice   224
  supporting multiple formats   224
  user definition   634
  when to use   224
clipping
  controls   235
  guidelines for   500
  window title   511
Close
  choice, closing window   496
  description   225
  displaying, in warning message   225
  in progress indicator   397
  in system menu   476
  keyboard function   316
  push button
    closing window   405, 496
  user definition   634
Close push button, in car dealership
  product   141
closing
  a primary window, and behavior of
    associated secondary window   433
  a window, saving while   497
  window   496
    input focus   312
closing a window   154, 164
color
  as a visible cue   527
  customizing   30, 31
  design considerations   527
  reverting to default   31
  used for exceptions   91, 148
  used in car dealership product   151
color blindness   527
column
  adjusting size in window   501
  direct manipulation of   501
  width in window   501
column heading   139
  and field prompt   278
  description   227

combination box
  combination box, displaying default choice
    in entry field of   230
  definition   655
  description   63, 229
  documenting for users   634
  drop-down
    See drop-down combination box
  drop-down, using   238
  using   238
  wrapping cursor in   229
combining multimedia objects   520
command-line user interface, characteristics
  of   3
Common User Access (CUA) user interface   3
  See also CUA
communicating with a user   84
completion message, in information area   307
components of the CUA user interface   37
composed view
  definition   656
  description   47
  distinguished from contents view   53
  of car lot object   115
composite object, definition   655
conceptual model, user's   11, 13
consecutive choices, how to display   467
consistency
  and prediction   33
  compromising   34
  design principles   33
  in product responses   35
  limitations   34
  of interaction   19
  purpose of   34
  used for transferring knowledge   33
  used to shape user's conceptual model   20
  visual   18
container
  and data transfer   248
  delete folder   256
  description   231
  icon
    augmenting   232
    displaying count on   301

controls *(continued)*
    used in car dealership product 140
    used in message window 91
Copy 240
    and the clipboard 224
    data transfer override key assignment 264
    description 240
    in Edit menu 240, 271
    keyboard function 316
    user definition 635
Copy arrow pointer 380
copying an object 82
Create 242
    and direct manipulation 263
    and reflections 243
    and the clipboard 224
    description 242
    in Edit menu 271
    user definition 635
create-on-drag
    in folder 288
    setting 263
creating aesthetic appeal 36
creating an object 82, 156
cross-hair pointer 25
Ctrl
    extended selection 275, 440
    using 315
    using for shortcut keys 451
Ctrl+manipulation button, copy data transfer
  key assignment 264
Ctrl+Tab, in entry field 273
CUA (Common User Access)
    books xxiii
    designer's model 93
    guidelines 3
    user interface
        components 37
        description 3
        designing a product with 99
        goals 23
        limitations 4
cue
    audible
        See audible cue

cue *(continued)*
    audible, and unavailable choices 212
    description 199, 200
    textual
        See textual cue
    used to sustain context 34
    visible
        See visible cue
current state 635
current-setting indicator
    check mark 332
    documenting for users 635
    unavailable-state emphasis 333
current-setting indicator, definition 656
current-state indicator
    See current-setting indicator
cursor
    and automatic selection 213
    and default action 252
    and mnemonics 344
    and push button 401
    definition 656
    description 39, 40, 244
    displaying in active window 210
    first-letter cursor navigation 286
    in split window 472
    key 41
    movement 41, 147
    movement of, in a split window 472
    not wrapping
        in combination box 229
        in drop-down combination box 266
        in drop-down list 268
        in list box 325
        in non-scrollable component 245
    overview of 198
    placement 389, 507
    selection
        See selection cursor
    text
        See text cursor
    types of 40
    used to indicate a mode 25
    user definition 635

Edit menu *(continued)*
    Copy choice 240, 271
    Create choice 242, 271
    Cut choice 246, 270
    Delete choice 254, 271
    description 270
    Deselect all choice 271
    Find choice 271, 284
    on menu bar 334
    overview of 190
    Paste choice 271, 376
    user definition 637
Edit, choice, in car dealership product 156
editing
    column heading 228
    icon label 302
    window title 511
editing text 33, 41
electronic mail
    and user's conceptual model 20
    in car dealership product 109, 111, 163
ellipsis in choice name, meaning of 59
ellipsis, for routing choice, on push
  button 402
emphasis
    See also highlighting
    definition 657
    description 87
    displaying in inactive window 303
    displaying on icon 301
    displaying, and cursor 245
    during direct manipulation 262
    in-use
        and small icon in title bar 301
        displaying 314
    overview of 199
    selected-state
        displaying on icons in marquee
          box 328, 386
        displaying on objects in marquee
          box 328, 386
        how and when to display 439
    source 465
    target 477

emphasis *(continued)*
    unavailable-state
        description 485
        displaying choices with 218
        displaying on Deselect all choice 435
        displaying on Maximize choice 329
        displaying on Minimize choice 342
        displaying on Select all choice 435
        in a menu 331
        on a scroll button 429
        providing contextual help for choice
          with 233
    user definition 637, 650
end of data, keyboard function 316
end of line, keyboard function 316
Enter key, default action 252
entry field 220, 272, 638
    changing color of to indicate an
      exception 91
    definition 657
    description 62, 272
    in a combination box 63
    in a drop-down combination box 64
    in Open window 373
    pre-filling 146
    providing for Save as window 425
    providing mnemonics 345
    used in car dealership product 146
    user definition 638
    using 238
environment, operating, overview of 169
error
    See also exception
    handling 88
    message 26, 89
    reduction 23
error-checking 148
error, in entry field, indicating 273
Esc key, used to switch window 211
exception
    definition 657
    description 88
    examples 90
    handling 88

exception *(continued)*
    message 89
    reducing 100
exclamation mark warning message
  symbol 495
expert user 28
explicit selection
    definition 657
    description 71
exploring, learning by 28
Extended help choice
    See General help choice
extended selection
    and automatic selection 213
    and marquee selection 327
    and point-to-endpoint selection 385
    and random-point selection 411
    Ctrl key 440
    definition 657
    description 74, 75, 275
    documenting for users 638
    illustration 76
    in window list window 504
    keyboard technique 318
    Shift+F8 440
extending user's conceptual model 20

F

F1, Help key 234
F10, and Shift, function of 388
feedback 27, 97, 100
feedback, audible 212
feel, in designer's model 15
field prompt 278, 638
    aligning in window 501
    definition 657
    description 278
    for control 235
    providing mnemonics 345
    used in car dealership product 147
    user definition 638
    using descriptive text with 258
field, definition 657
    See also entry field, read-only field

field, unavailable, interacting with 508
File menu
    application-oriented 280
      mnemonic key assignment 281
      New choice 281, 361
      Open choice 281, 369
      order of choices in 281
      Print choice 281, 282, 393
      providing product-specific choices 281
      Save as choice 281, 427
      Save choice 281, 282, 423
      when to use 280
    object-oriented 282
      labeling with class name 282
      mnemonic key assignment 283
      Open as choice 282
      order of choices in 282
      Print choice 282
      providing product-specific choices 282
      Save choice 282
    overview of 190
    user definition 638
filtering views, in car dealership product
    illustration 154
    mechanisms for 114, 116, 139
finance manager object 109
Find
    description 284
    in Edit menu 271, 284
    user definition 638
finger, used for input 515
Finnish, translated terms 587
first-letter cursor navigation 286
    description 286
    user definition 639
focus
    input 312
      pointer 312
folder
    changing to work area 287, 512
    containing sample objects 368
    definition 657
    description 37, 287
    icon, changing 301

icon *(continued)*
    small, in title bar   496
    types of   38
    used for an object   366
    user definition   640
    using on workplace   514
    view of an object   38
icons view
    content of, in car dealership product   137
    definition   657
    description   49
    illustration   50, 138
    of car lot object   113
    of customer list object   116
    of worksheet list object   117
    window for, in car dealership product   137
identifier, message   339
images, multimedia   519
immediate action   27
implicit selection
    definition   657
    description   72
in-use emphasis
    and icons   301, 314
    description   314
    user definition   640
inactive window
    description   303
    user definition   640
inactive window, definition   657
Include   305
    choice, in car dealership product   153
    description   305
    in View menu   305, 492
    providing for containers   231
    push button, in car dealership product   141,
        154
    user definition   640
Include Cars window
    description   139
    illustration   140, 142, 153
Include Customers window   116
Include Worksheets window   117

Include, choice, in car dealership product   139
increasing user satisfaction, aesthetics
    and   36
increment, scrolling
    See scrolling increment
index, help   294
indicator
    current-setting, definition   656
    mode   25
    progress
        definition   659
        description   85
indirect manipulation
    and controls   61
    description   54
    in car dealership product   111
    mechanisms for   54, 58
information area
    and unavailable choices   485
    definition   657
    description   86, 307
    in car dealership product   141
    placement in a window   501
    purpose of   44, 86
    user definition   640
    when to provide   86
information message
    and progress indicator   396
    default action   252
    description   310
    displaying in progress indicator   337
    overview of   182
    user definition   640
information, layering in user interface   21
informing a user   84
inheritance
    definition   657
    in the CUA designer's model   94
initial value
    displaying for drop-down combination
        box   266
    documenting for users   640
    in entry field   274
    providing for drop-down list   268

J

K

L

menu *(continued)*
  customizing 30
  definition 658
  description 61, 331
  displaying shortcut key assignments 450
  Edit 270
  full 28
  Help 296
  in car dealership product
    car lot object 121
    car object 118
    customer list object 127
    customer object 124
    designing 117
    worksheet list object 133
    worksheet object 130
  overview of 189
  pop-up 388
    Create choice 242
    Cut choice 246
    definition 659
    description 55, 57, 61
    input focus 313
    overview of 192
  providing mnemonics 344
  pull-down
    definition 659
    description 61, 398
    Help 296
    overview of 189
  Selected 437
  separator 332, 446
  settings choice 332
  short 28
  simplified 28
  system
    definition 660
    description 118
  user definition 641
  View 492
  Windows 509
  wrapping cursor 331
menu architecture, overview of 189

menu bar
  Alt+mnemonic 345
  and push buttons 402
  and touch input 516
  choice
    Edit 270
    File (application-oriented) 280
  definition 658
  description 61, 334
  File (object-oriented) 282
    Help 296
    Options 375
    push button equivalents for 335, 402
    Selected 437
    View 492
    Windows 509
  overview of 189
  providing access to tool palette from 483
  providing Help choice 296
  providing mnemonics 345
  purpose 44
  routing choice in 59
  user definition 641
  using 238
  window list, keyboard function 318
menu button, and input focus 351
menu choice, definition 658
menu-bar choice, definition 658
menu-bar choice, user definition 642
menu-driven user interface, characteristics
  of 3
message
  action
    description 206
    overview of 183
    symbol for 207
  augmenting icon 338
  completion, in information area 307
  content of 337
  continued interaction during 339
  definition 658
  description 26, 84, 337
  displayed in a secondary window 433
  error 89

object *(continued)*
  device
      See also device object
      and data transfer   260
      and direct manipulation   264
  direct manipulation   261, 367
  displaying in list box   325
  displaying in secondary window   433
  dragging   262
  finance manager   109
  folder   287, 368
  help index listing for   294
  hierarchy
      definition   658
      description   8
  inheritance, in the CUA designer's
      model   95
  interacting with   54
  interaction with pop-up menu   388
  labels   32
  multimedia   520
  multiple, displaying pop-up menu for   389
  on workplace, representing with icon   300
  overview of   171
  placement   36
  placing in folder   287
  placing in work area   512
  placing with Paste choice   376
  printer support for   260
  providing a Print choice for   393
  providing contextual help for   233
  providing default action   250
  providing reflections   367
  recognition   32, 33
  relationships
      description   17
      in car dealership product   110
      in designer's model   15
      in the CUA designer's model   94
  representation
      contributing to usability   16
      in different models   14
      on workplace   37
      resembling real-world object   32

object *(continued)*
  representing with icon   300, 366, 514
  sales manager   109
  salesperson   109
  selected   440
  selecting all   435
  selecting none   435
  selecting with keyboard
      keyboard function   318
      using point selection   383
  selecting with mouse, using point
      selection   383
  separated from action   54
  size   519
  source
      See source object
  source, data transfer   248
  state
      and clipboard   240, 243
      and Copy choice   240
      and Create choice   243
      and help   297
  subclass, definition   659
  superclass, definition   659
  target
      See target object
  target emphasis of   477
  used in car dealership product   108
  user definition   643
  viewed in a window pane   472
  visual representation of   96
  window position after opening   497
  window title   511
  work area   512
  worksheet
      See worksheet object
  worksheet list
      See worksheet list object
object orientation
  definition   659
  description   3
object-action continuum   54, 55, 57
object-action matrix   111

push button *(continued)*
  Restore *(continued)*
    when to provide 418
  Retry 405
  Save, providing for Save as window 426
  scrolling 500
    for entry field 273
  Sort, in car dealership product 144
  Stop 405
  that affects notebook 364
  used for changing window size 500
  user definition 642, 645
  using 238
  window, saving its current state 497
  with control, scrolling 500
  Yes, in a message 338

Q

question mark, action message symbol 207

R

radio button
  choice 220
  definition 659
  description 67, 409
  used in car dealership product 142, 143
  user definition 646
  using 238
random-point selection 78, 411, 480
  and extended selection 411
  description 411
range
  description 385
  for text entry 480
  keyboard function 316
  selection technique 386
range of selection 81
range-swipe selection
  describing to users 646
  description 385
  for text entry 480
read-only entry field, indicating 273

read-only field
  description 63
  used in car dealership product 137, 147
read-only spin button field 467
recall 30
recognition 30
redo 28
Redo choice
  description 487
  in Edit menu 270, 487
  user definition 646
reducing steps 100
reflection 50
  and Create choice 243
  description 413
  for objects 367
Refresh
  description 415
  in View menu 416, 492
  user definition 647
Refresh now 415
  description 415
  in View menu 416, 492
  user definition 647
relationships, object
  description 17
  in car dealership product 110
  in designer's model 15
  in the CUA designer's model 94
removing objects, in car dealership
  product 117, 164
repeating push buttons 403
replace mode
  in text entry 479
  text cursor 244
representation, visual 18
  See also visual representation
required entry field, indicating 272
requirements, matching to tasks 106
researching and planning, as part of
  development process 99, 101
Reset push button 405
  user definition 647

Window list choice *(continued)*
    in system menu   476, 505
    in Windows menu   506
    user definition   653
window navigation   507
window pane
    See split window
window position, saving   330, 343
window size, saving   330, 343
window sizing button, description   44, 66
window title   510, 654
    and column heading   227
    and field prompt   278
    description   510
    for control   235
    help window   297
    of a message   339
    of progress-indicator window   397
    user definition   654
window-sizing icon   654
Windows menu
    description   509
    on menu bar   334
    overview of   190
    user definition   653
    Window list choice   506, 509
word left, keyboard function   319
word right, keyboard function   319
work area   512, 654
    and Close choice   226
    changing to folder   287, 512
    definition   661
    description   37, 512
    icon, changing   301
    restoring   419, 512
    saving state when closing   226
workplace
    definition   661
    description   37, 514
    in the CUA designer's model   94, 95
    user definition   654
worksheet list object
    description   109
    details view   117

worksheet list object *(continued)*
    icons view   117
    menus   133
worksheet object
    description   109
    illustration   150, 162
    menus   130
    views   116, 117
    windows   149
wrapping cursor
    in menu   331
    in scrollable component   245
    in spin button   468

Z

zero-based selection
    definition   661
    description   72, 80
zone, detection   519

What do you think?

Object-Oriented Interface Design
IBM Common User Access Guidelines
Publication No. SC34-4399-00

We are in business to satisfy you. If you are satisfied, please tell us; if not, let us know how we can do better. Thank you!

Overall, how satisfied are you with this book?

	Very satisfied	Satisfied	Neither satisfied nor dissatisfied	Dissatisfied	Very dissatisfied	No opinion
Overall satisfaction						

How satisfied are you that this information is:

	Very satisfied	Satisfied	Neither satisfied nor dissatisfied	Dissatisfied	Very dissatisfied	No opinion
Accurate						
Complete						
Easy to find						
Easy to understand						
Well organized						
Applicable to your tasks						

Please tell us how we can improve this book:

_____
_____
_____
_____

Note that IBM may use or distribute the responses to this form without obligation.

May we contact you to discuss your responses? ☐ Yes   ☐ No

_____

Name   Address

Company or Organization

Phone No.

BUSINESS REPLY MAIL

FIRST CLASS MAIL   PERMIT NO. 40   ARMONK, NEW YORK

POSTAGE WILL BE PAID BY ADDRESSEE

International Business Machines Corporation
Information Development
Department T45
PO Box 60000
Cary, NC 27512-9968

What do you think?
SC34-4399-00

What do you think?

Object-Oriented Interface Design
IBM Common User Access Guidelines
Publication No. SC34-4399-00

We are in business to satisfy you. If you are satisfied, please tell us; if not, let us know how we can do better. Thank you!

Overall, how satisfied are you with this book?

	Very satisfied	Satisfied	Neither satisfied nor dissatisfied	Dissatisfied	Very dissatisfied	No opinion
Overall satisfaction						

How satisfied are you that this information is:

	Very satisfied	Satisfied	Neither satisfied nor dissatisfied	Dissatisfied	Very dissatisfied	No opinion
Accurate						
Complete						
Easy to find						
Easy to understand						
Well organized						
Applicable to your tasks						

Please tell us how we can improve this book:

_____

_____

_____

_____

Note that IBM may use or distribute the responses to this form without obligation.

May we contact you to discuss your responses?   □ Yes   □ No

_____

Name _____   Address _____

Company or Organization _____

Phone No. _____

BUSINESS REPLY MAIL

FIRST CLASS MAIL   PERMIT NO. 40   ARMONK, NEW YORK

POSTAGE WILL BE PAID BY ADDRESSEE

International Business Machines Corporation
Information Development
Department T45
PO Box 60000
Cary, NC 27512-9968

Fold and Tape   **Please do not staple**   Fold and Tape

What do you think?
SC34-4399-00